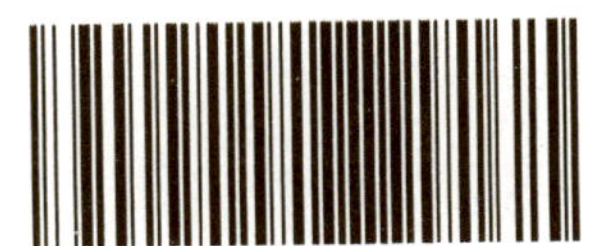
MW01617761

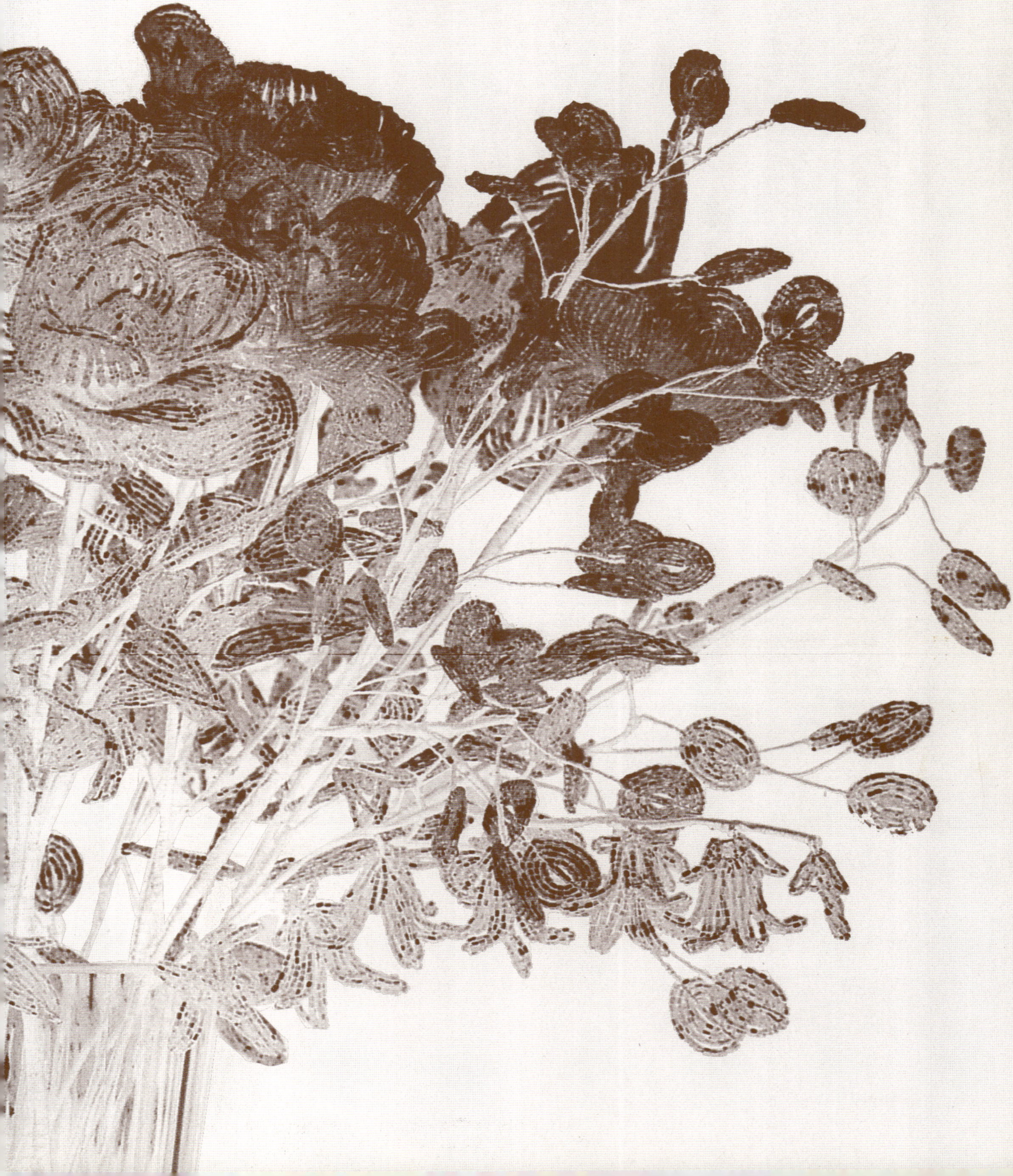

The Flowers of Venice

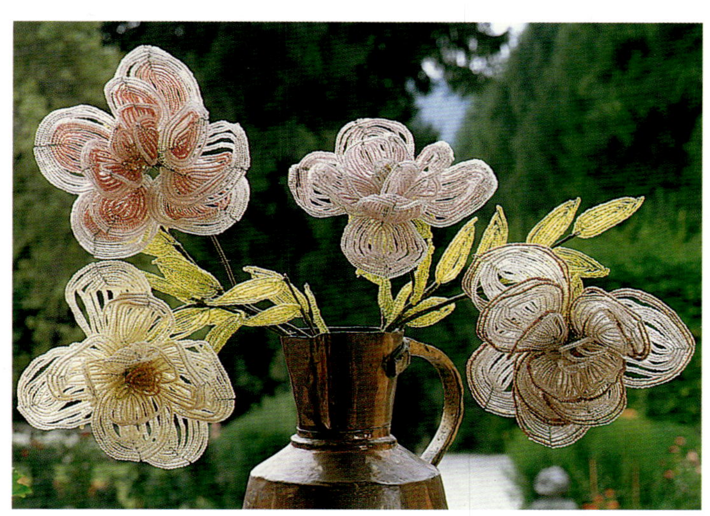

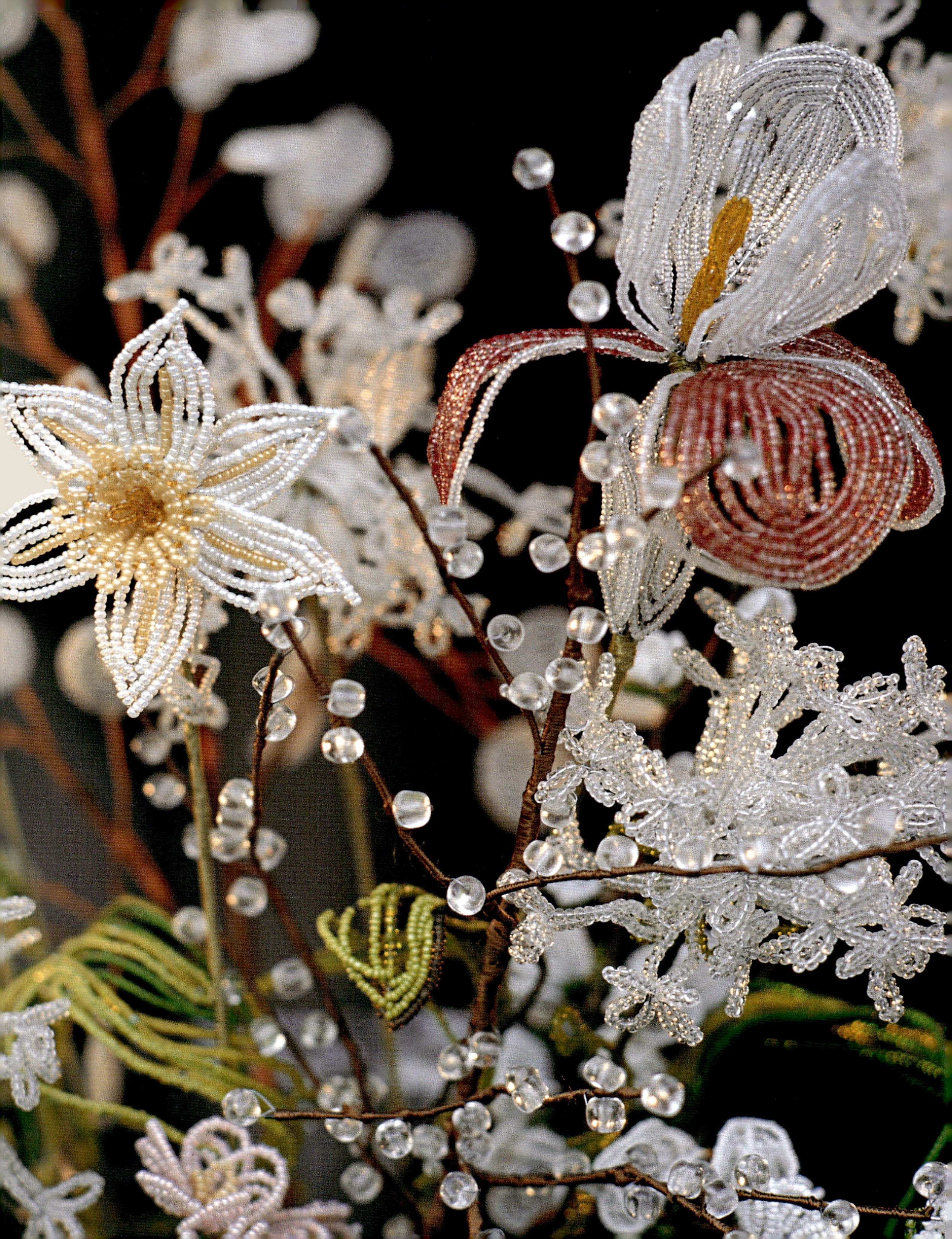

GIOVANNA POGGI MARCHESI

THE FLOWERS OF VENICE

THE ART OF CREATING FLOWERS AND OTHER DECORATIONS WITH VENETIAN GLASS BEADS

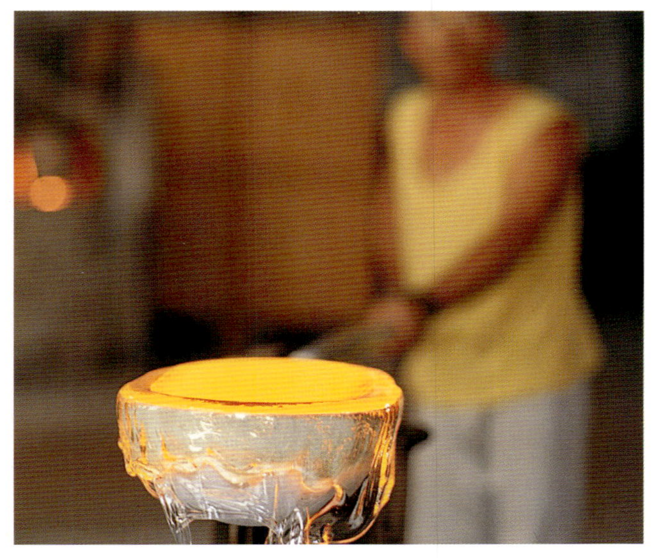

PHOTOGRAPHS BY SERGIO ZANARDI

INTRODUCTION BY ROSA BAROVIER MENTASTI

TRANSLATED BY ROSANNA M. GIAMMANCO FRONGIA, PH.D.

EDITED BY KATHIE SCHROEDER, BOARD OF DIRECTORS
BEAD MUSEUM, GLENDALE ARIZONA

BEADSMITH

ACKNOWLEDGMENTS

The author wishes to thank:
Rosa Barovier Mentasti
Doretta Davanzo Poli
Gianna Costantini and her talented young women
Marina Memo
Irene Gottardi
Federica Wiel
Mariagrazia Gaggia
Emanuela Seguso
Ilaria Ciani Bassetti
Charlotte Sammartini
Francesco Lopez y Royo
Consolata Spanò di San Giuliano
Andriana Marcello del Majno
Antichità Giulia Fabris, Venic

She is also grateful to:
Carlo, Andrea, Uberto, Nadia, Tiziana, Irina, Lodovica, Simonetta, Orsola, Chicca, Chiara, Dodi, Maria and everyone else who assisted in researching and writing this book. Special thanks for the photographs taken at the Murano glassworks of Effetre Industriale S.p.A.

$29.95 US $44.95 Canadian

Published by: Beadsmith/Helby Import Co.
37 Hayward Ave.
Carteret, NJ 07008

WebPages: http://www.beadsmith.com
http://www.helby.com

ISBN# 0-9713690-0-3

Mondadori

Illustrated Books
First edition: May 1999
First English language edition: 2002

http://www.mondadori.com/libri

D.L. TO: 2011-2001

Printed in 2002
by Artes Gràficas Toledo, S.A.
Printed in Spain

Editorial Coordinator:
Mariella De Battisti
Art Director:
Giorgio Seppi
Art Design:
Mirko Milani
Art Work and Editing:
Men at Work - Verona

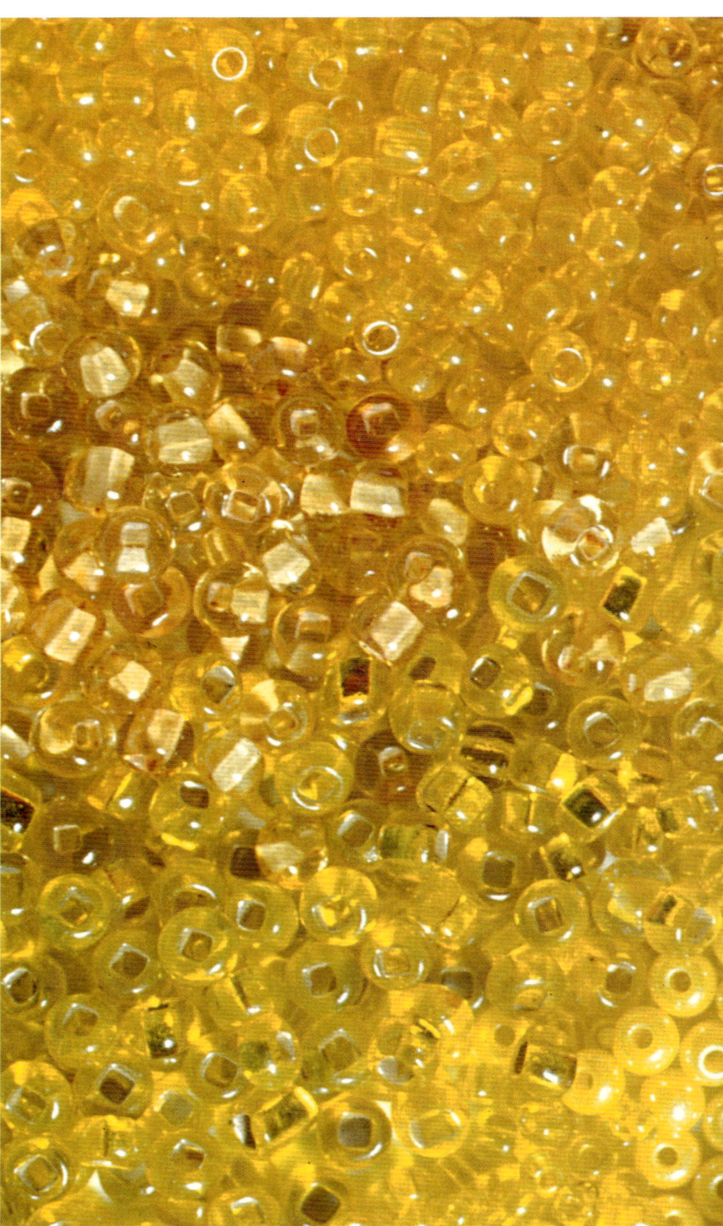

Table of Contents

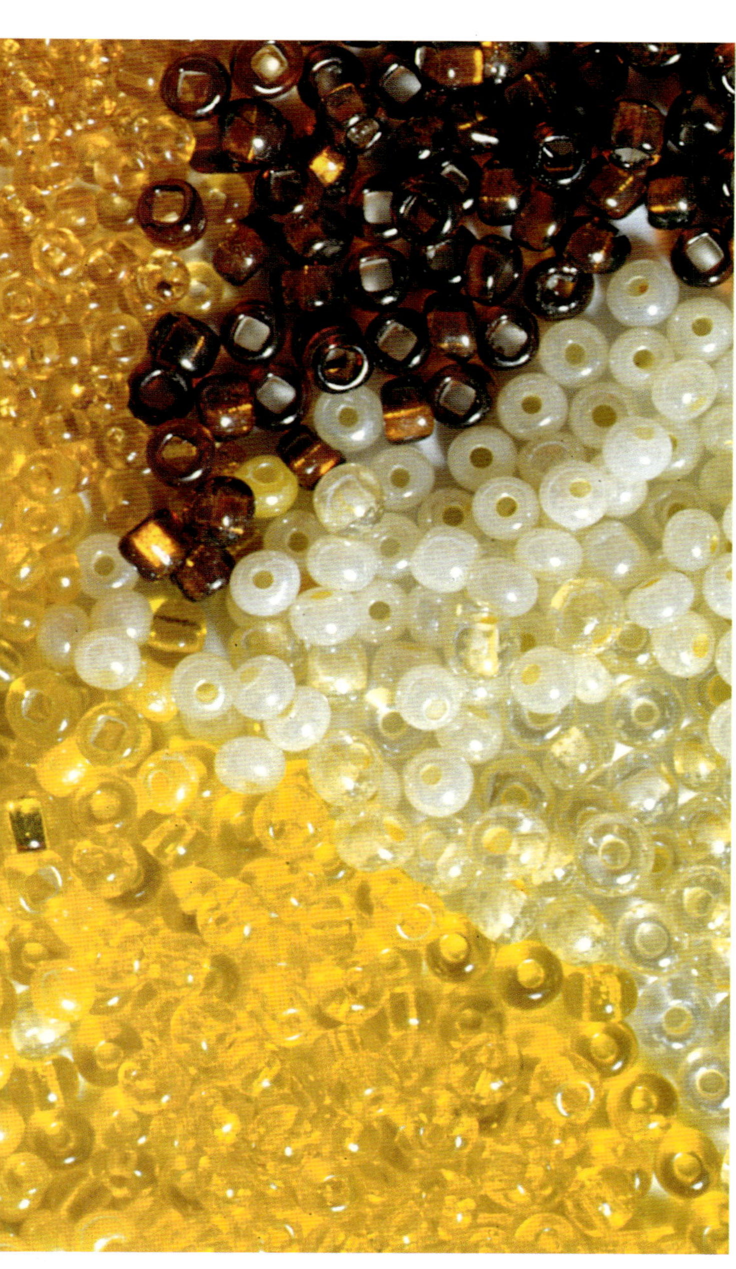

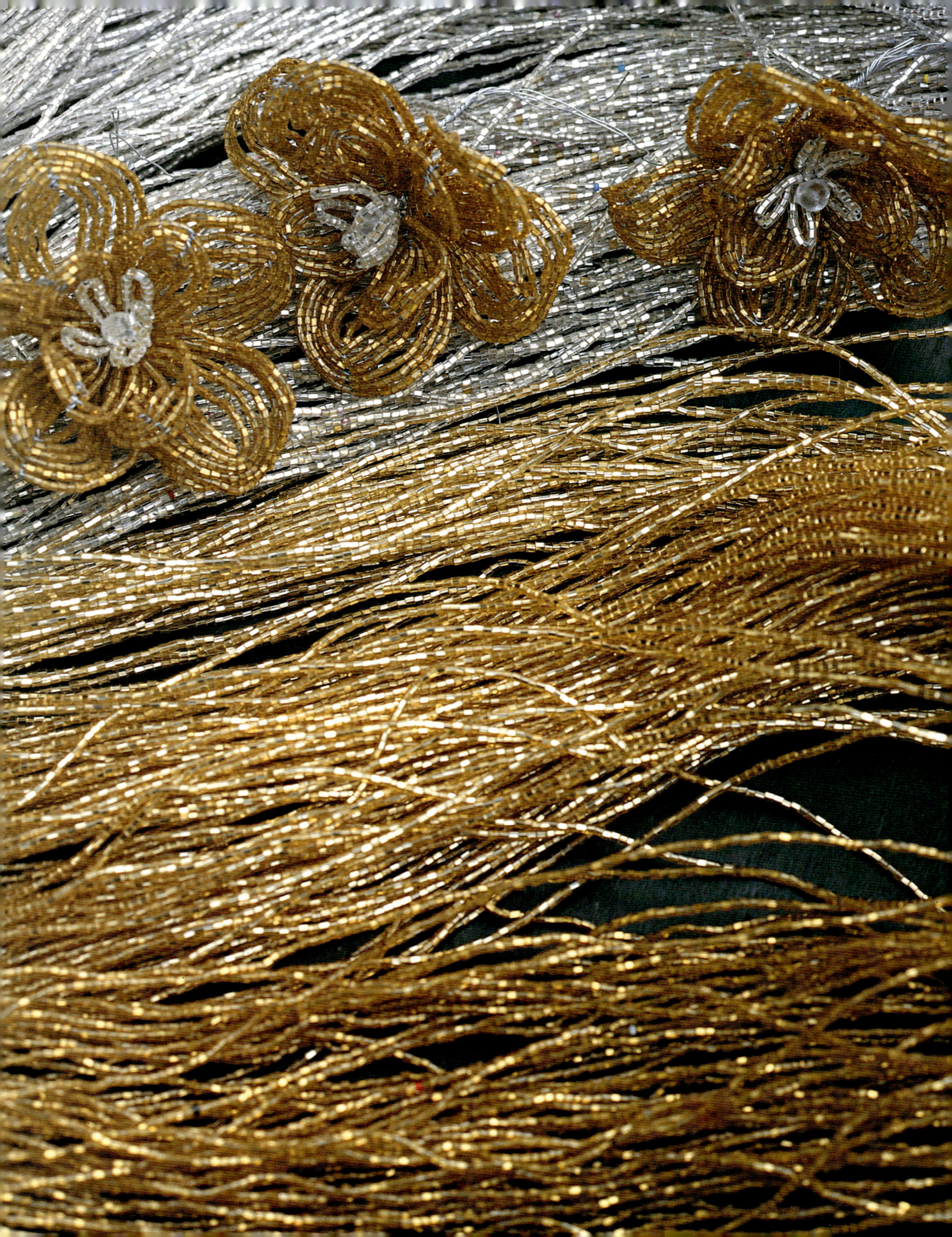

Rediscovering an Ancient Craft

In addition to its vast wealth of art treasures, Venice is a unique city in many ways. Its neighborhoods are not divided into separate working class districts and exclusive residential enclaves. While the most prestigious palaces look onto the Grand Canal—the sea-water channel that winds its way like a serpent through the city—the back entrances of those mansions open on alleys, houses and squares inhabited by a very diverse population. Among the throngs of tourists and residents of all ages and occupations that fill the city, some unusual figures full of charm and elegance stand out. Often no longer in the prime of their youth, their appearance and attitude bespeak an ancient nobility and culture, even as they blend into today's simpler lifestyle. One such personality is Nella Sammartini Lopez y Royo, well known to the Venetians for her grace and discreet manners, and even more so for the unquestionable merits that few other local dowagers can claim. She has brought back to life a forgotten art that requires graceful manual dexterity and good taste, and has taken it upon herself to teach it to her young students; first among them her niece Giovanna, who is now her assistant and the designated heir to the craft. Glass beads, known as conterie, *are a genuine Venetian product, in which the tradition of colored glass and the skill of the Murano glass makers are exquisitely combined. Since the Renaissance, a rich and wide array of objects has been produced. In past centuries,* conterie *were widely exported to colonial lands and were hugely popular, not just in Venice but in all of Europe as well. The craft of creating flowers with them is the most popular and graceful application of the glass beads, for the bright colors of the glass and its fragility*

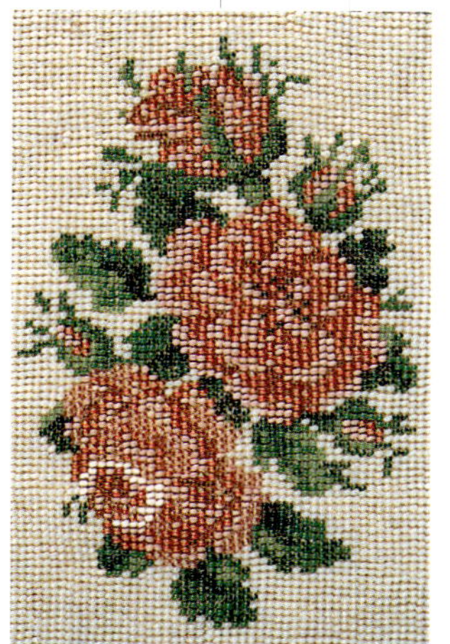

Beaded roses on a cotton fabric, embroidered in the antique fashion.

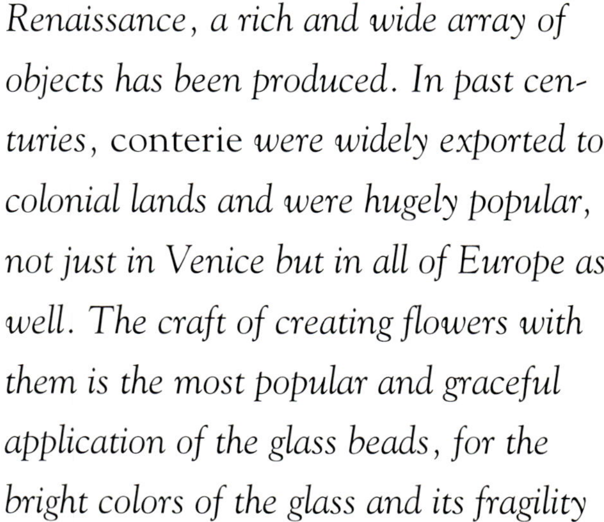

are fitting symbols of the ephemeral beauty of a flower's petals.

While little information about the craft of making Venetian beaded flowers in the eighteenth century survives, we do have ample information about mid-nineteenth century production, when the craft was given new impetus in the context of a general renaissance of the Venetian glass making industry. It was then that flowers of all shapes and for all types of occasions were created with beads of exceptional colors, during one of the periods richest in color in the history of Venetian glass (with the possible exception of the nineteen-fifties). The industry used almost exclusively women workers, the powerful Società Veneziana Conterie in particular. The Dorigo sisters, for example, set up a flourishing business that employed young working-class women from the city and the surrounding islands. Later, the craft entered a period of gradual decline, until it disappeared in the period between the two world wars.
Still today, however, we can find in the islands of the Venetian Lagoon such as Pellestrina, elderly women, now grandmothers, who spent their youth creating beaded flowers with light, deft hands.

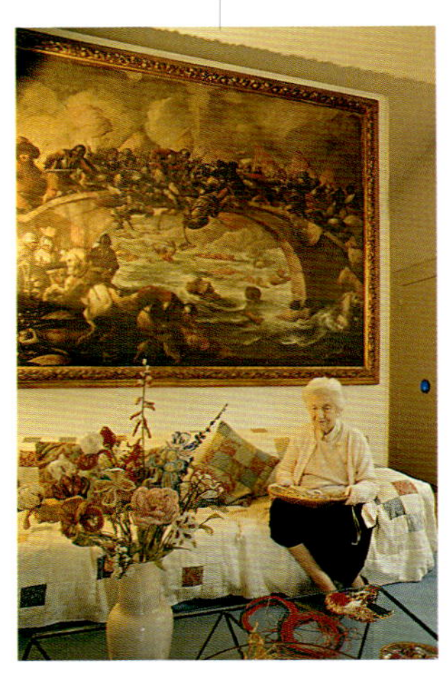

Nella Lopez y Royo in the inviting living room-studio of her Venice home.

Nella Lopez y Royo did not just rescue a technique from oblivion: she did much more. She brought prestige to this craft stamping it with her own personality, her taste, and her rich cultural heritage. Unlike some of the old production, her creations are never stale, but embody fresh and wonderful designs. They are the result of her study of nature, her imagination, and her sensitivity to the art of past centuries.

Gifted with flawless taste and a light, skilled touch, she enters a world where kitsch *is always looming, yet she remains untouched by it. While teaching her craft, she also teaches refinement and exhorts her students to bring all of their sensitivity and cultural background to the making of even one small flower.*

Rosa Barovier Mentasti
Venetian Glass Historian

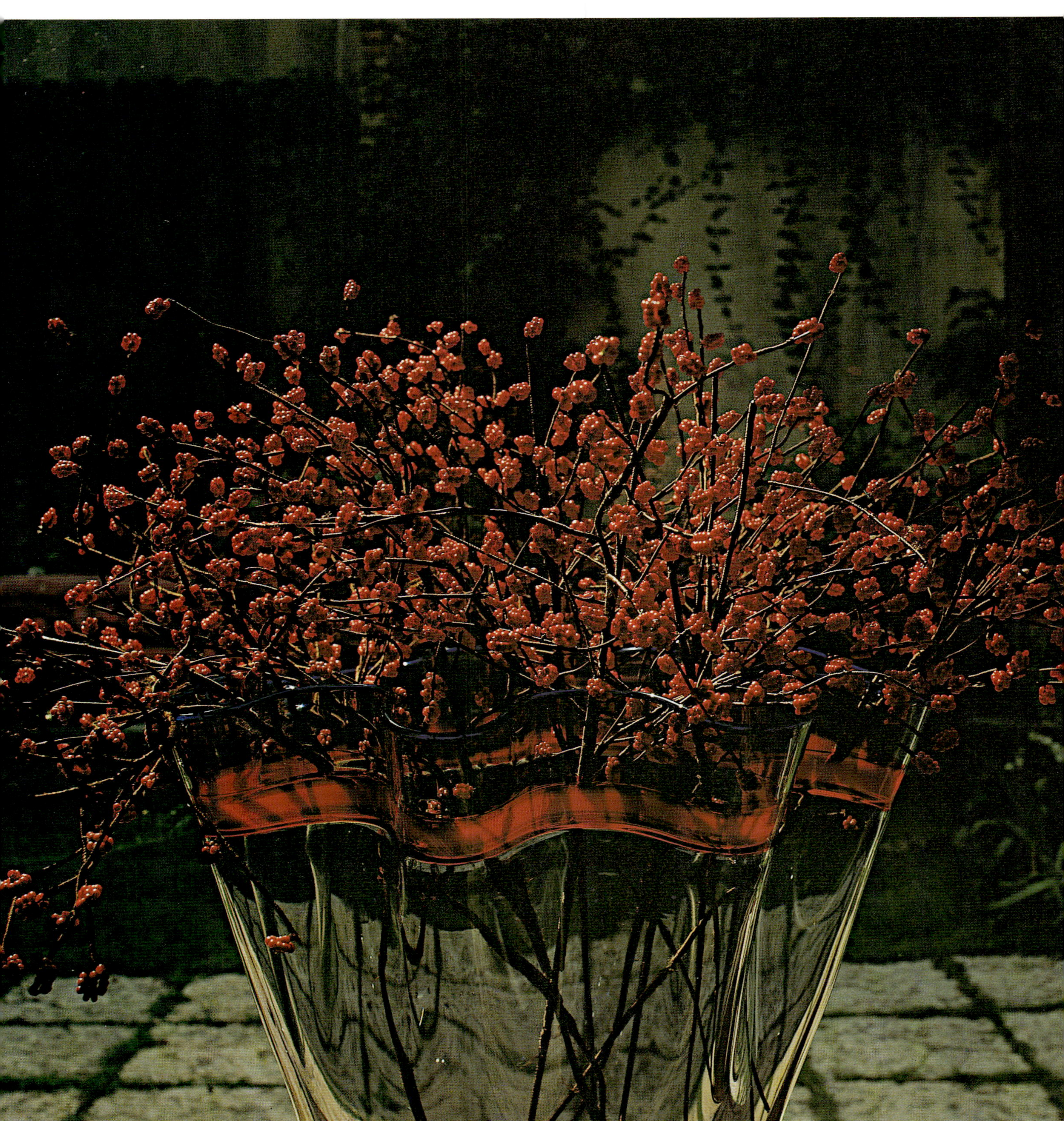

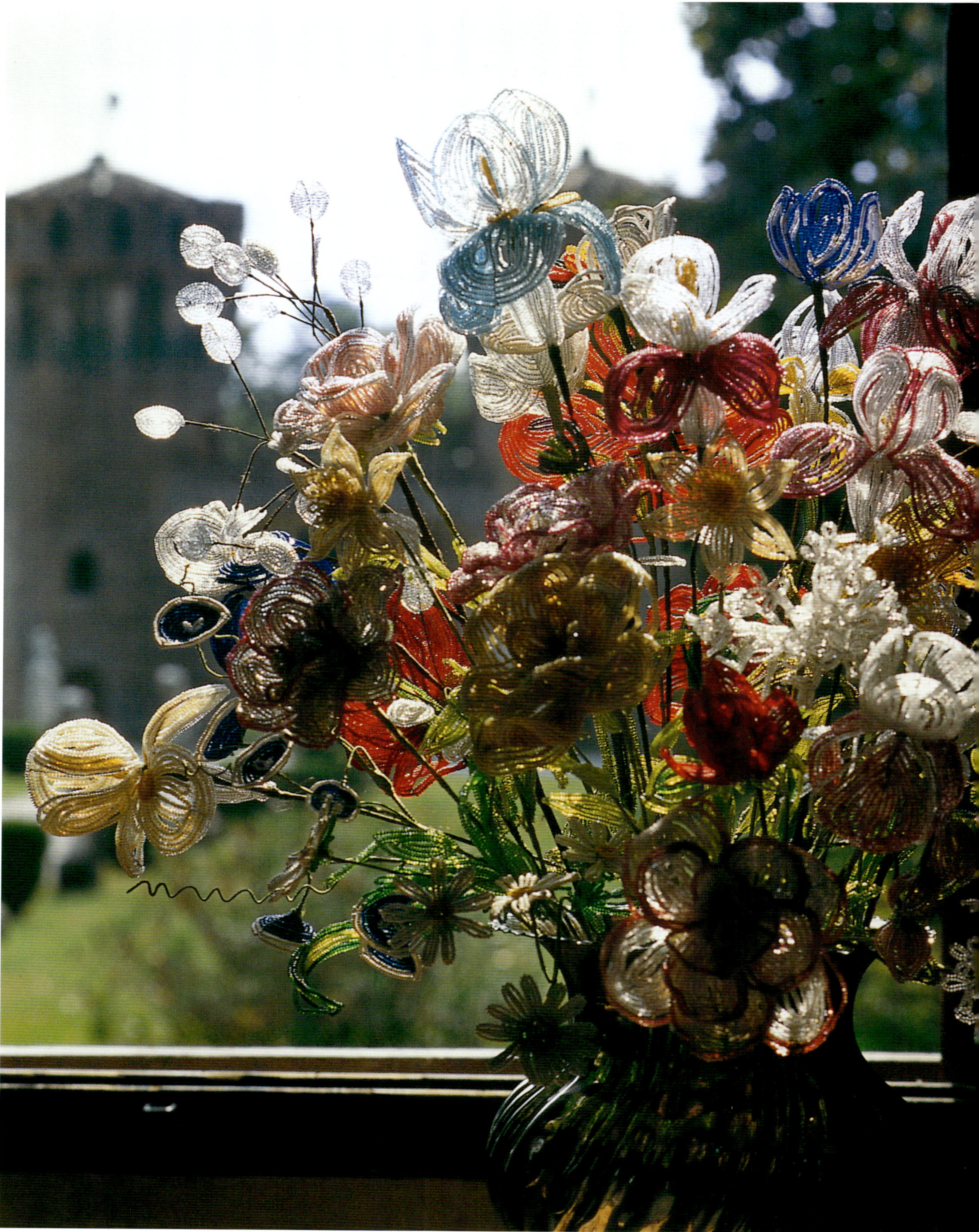

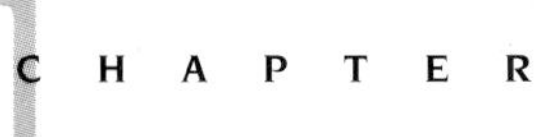

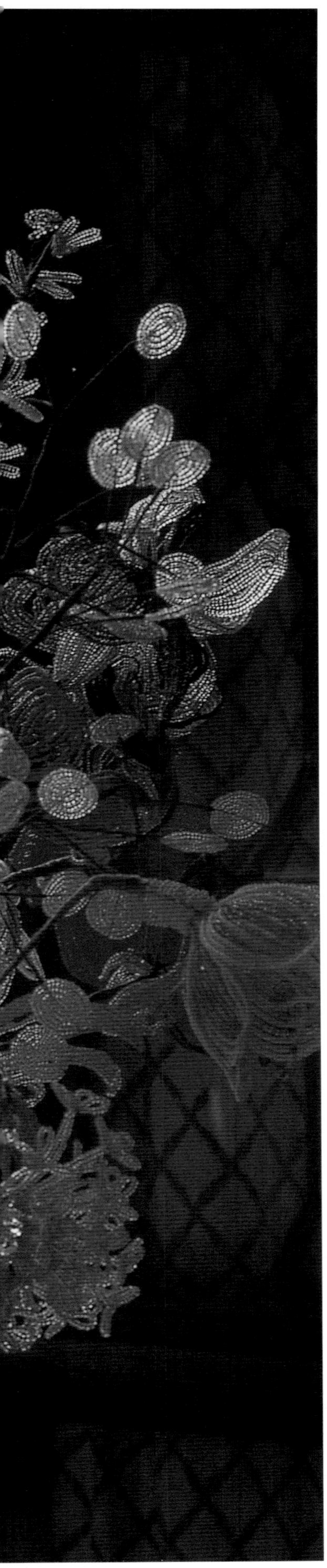

The Flowers of Venice

Flowers are everywhere in Venice: in elegant patterned floors, in stone relief, in the festive, brightly colored chandeliers, in mirrors. We find them etched in glass, woven into lustrous fabrics, reproduced in paintings. We find them in the countless secret gardens scattered all over the city. In times past, the city was the center of the seed market and, not coincidentally, the loveliest botanical gardens of the area were in Venice. For centuries, Venetians have distributed fresh flowers in churches, in theaters, to boats for processions, and for public and private celebrations. To Venetians, flowers are the language of celebration.

A Historical Sketch

The intriguing history of Venetian glass beads touches all the countries of the world and all cultures: it goes hand in hand with the history of man. The term "bead" refers to small, usually spherical objects that in the course of centuries humankind has found or manufactured, smoothed out, polished, then pierced and threaded on either thin metal wire or fabric or leather strings. The simplicity of this definition belies the human ingenuity required to perforate small, fragile objects without breaking them, after manufacturing them in the desired color. Beads are made from a large selection of materials such as deep-sea or fresh-water pearls, amber, rare metals, and precious and semiprecious stones; more common and less expensive materials include seashells, seeds, wood, bone, pebbles, and man-made materials such as terra-cotta, ceramic, glass, and plastic. The invention of glass beads was unique and revolutionary, because it allowed man to manufacture beads in all possible hues and colors from glass, a material transparent to light, with singularly attractive effects. About two thousand years after the discovery of glass, the ancient Romans had found a way to manufacture large quantities of beads in batches, using the glass-cane stretching technique. They had also found the solution to three major problems: how to produce large batches of perforated beads ready for stringing, how to make them all of the same size and color, and how to produce them at a sensible cost.

From that moment on, glass beads became popular throughout the world. Over the centuries, people have attributed healing powers and religious properties to them, including the power to ward off evil spells. Even today they continue to be used for rosaries or worry-bead necklaces, as well as for decoration and personal ornaments of all kinds. For centuries, glass beads were used as currency; they were included in dowries and were even part of war spoils. Collectors today are fascinated by the almost infinite variety of their colors, shades and hues, their small size and durability, and the high prices that some beadwork commands on the market. These small, magical, simple objects were for thousands of years a means of communication. To us, they are evidence of man's ability to utilize different materials and to invent new ones. They document social relations, religious beliefs, commercial routes, and great migrations. Finally, through them we can follow the intriguing history of fashion, for glass beads come in many colors, sizes, and materials, and every corner of the world has its own preferences and traditions.

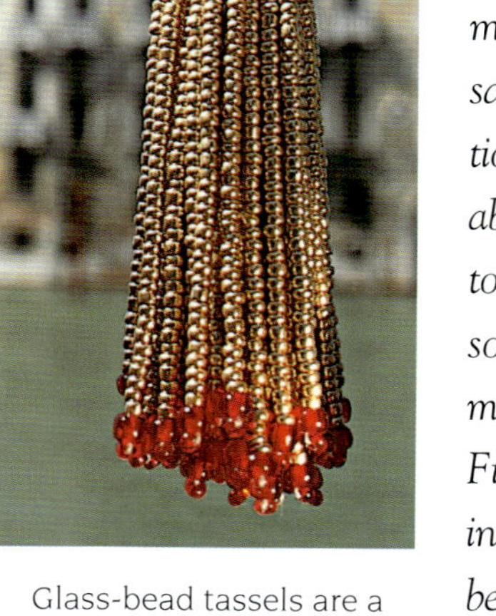

Glass-bead tassels are a typical Venetian product.

Venetian glass beads have been used on and off to trim garments—in some eras more than others, depending on fashion trends—with constantly changing colors and shapes. In all of the nineteenth century, in Europe and the United States glass beads were used especially for braiding and trimming on fabrics. They were also used in women's fashion accessories and for interior decorating, while jewelers preferred to use real pearls and precious stones mounted with traditional designs.

Starting in the twentieth century, a veritable decorating revolution took place. Illustrious representatives of the Art Nouveau style, such as René Jules Lalique in Europe and Louis Comfort Tiffany in the United States, launched a new fashion that included original and wonderful jewelry made with precious metals and stones combined with semiprecious materials such as chrysoprase, opal, ivory, and splendid glass beads.

After World War I, Western European and American society underwent a number of major changes. With the rise of the middle class, women began to work outside the home, and this put an end to the extreme luxury that had characterized the turn of the century. Among other things, this change affected jewelry design, introducing a new preference for simple, moderately priced jewelry that was more in keeping with the new lifestyle. Thus was born costume jewelry, which was manufactured in large quantities starting in the nineteen-twenties to satisfy these new needs and used both new and old materials, with a preference for strong, bold colors and designs.

In this new climate, glass beads found renewed popularity: they were used to imitate precious and semiprecious stones, and also to create new, original objects for interior decoration, fashion accessories, and ornamental designs. Glass beads have been used by European fashion designers since the nineteen-twenties, while they have gradually disappeared from interior decoration. Two important Parisian couturiers, the Maison Lesage for clothing and the Maison Vicaire for theater costumes, still embroider their creations with glass beads. They are important reference points for lovers of the craft, both for the variety of their production and for their elaborate embroidery designs. In Italy, the Tuscan city of Prato is the center of glass-bead embroidery.

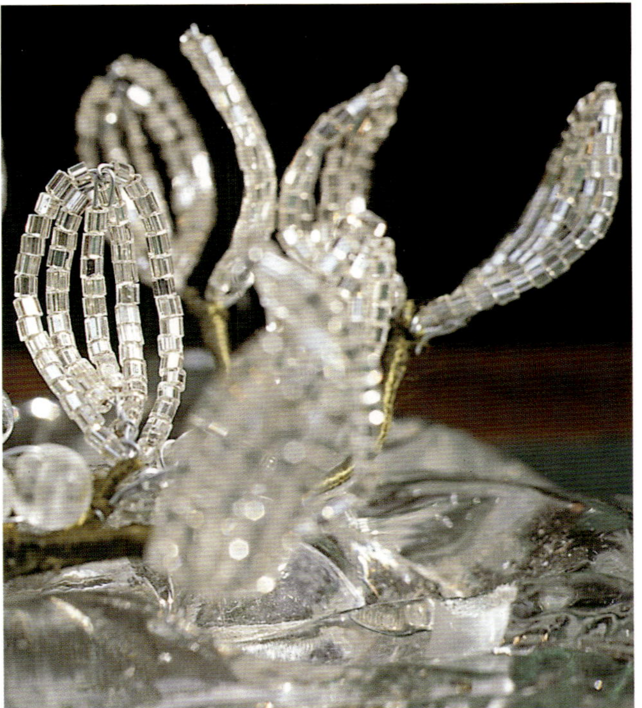

Luminous mistletoe resting on a glass surface.

Glass beads found favor not only with artists and fashion designers, but with the nineteen-sixties generation as well. In those years, the tribal beads of the North American Indians became popular for embroidery and trimming on clothing, shoes and purses, as well as for mounting in necklaces and earrings. Their popularity continued throughout the nineteen-seventies and into today. Beads are also being studied for their anthropological and religious aspects, in addition to their artistic use.

There are over twenty associations and one museum devoted to glass beads in the United States. In Europe, there are various associations and publications, popular with glass bead collectors, stringers, and weavers.

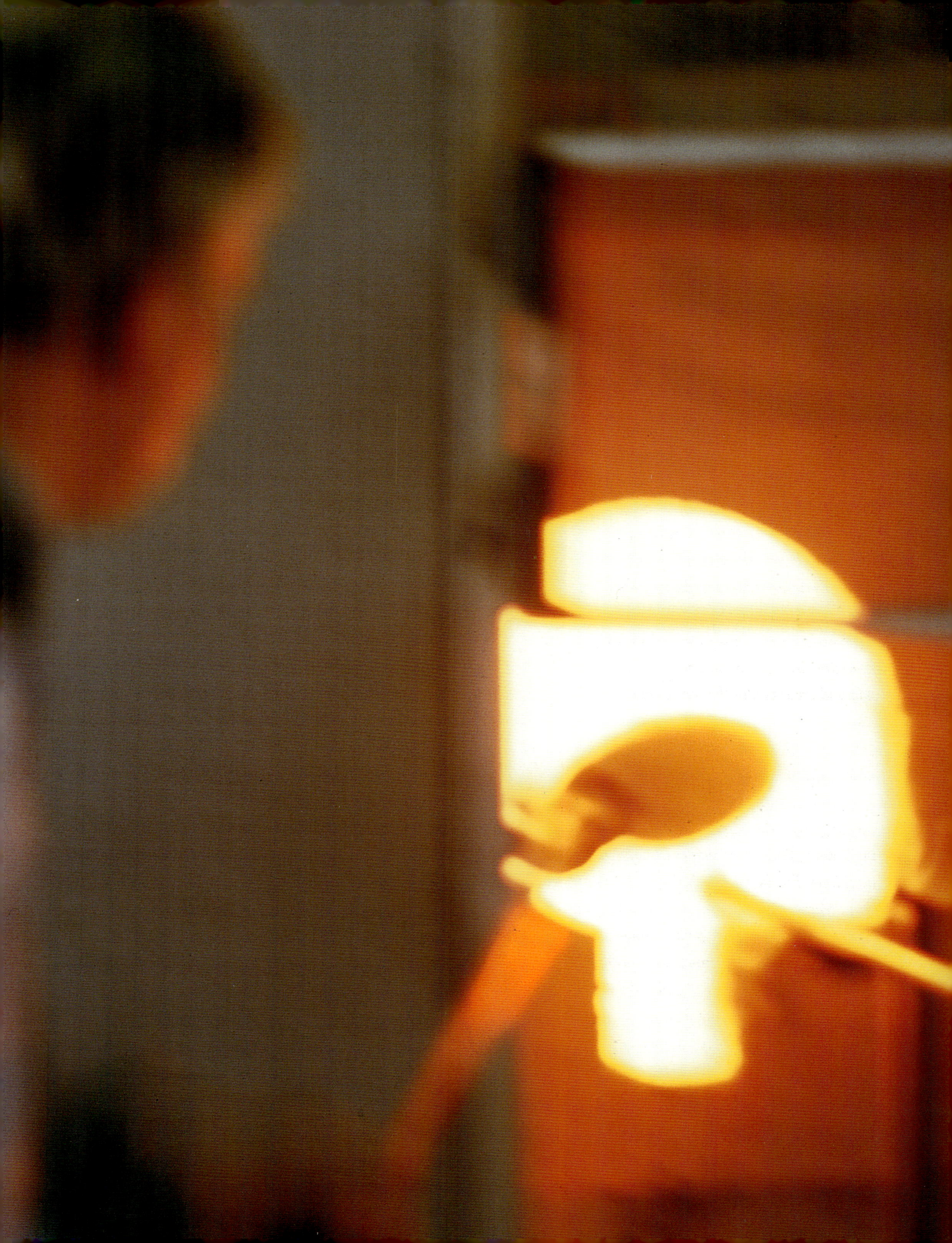

Venice and Murano

Murano, a charming island of the Venetian Lagoon, has been a glass making center since at least the thirteenth century: in the course of its history, it has produced splendid artifacts for the décor of palaces and castles. Some of them are preserved today in museums and collections in many countries, where lovers of glass objects and their enchanting light effects can see them on display.

It was not by mere chance that the magic world of glass making found its home in Venice, an ideal place to develop and grow and to continue to thrive as an industry even today. Thanks to a number of favorable circumstances, even in the alternating fortunes of history, the city was able to preserve traditional processing techniques, even as they were renewed from time to time. In addition to the skill and creativity of the master glass blowers, we owe this circumstance to the importance of Venice and her port, which, starting in the thirteenth century, became an intense center of exchange with the Mediterranean and the Orient, both areas rich in ancient glass making traditions. Furthermore, the Venetian Republic of Saint Mark pursued an economic policy that favored the glass-maker guilds, protecting and safeguarding their craft, so much so that the techniques of many glassworks are still jealously guarded today, and it is not easy to learn about them.

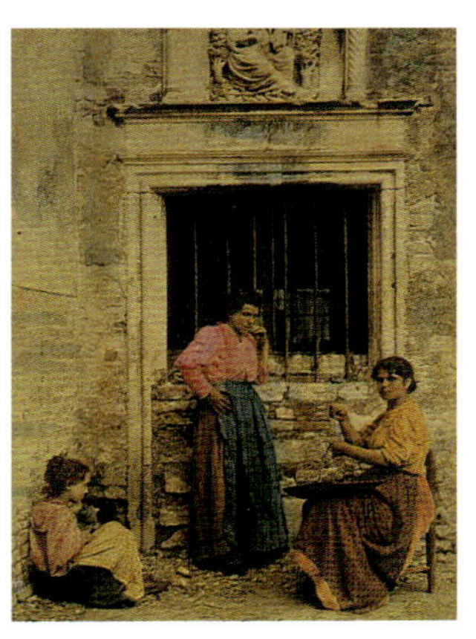

A group of Venetian bead stringers in an 18th century print.
At left, melted glass is placed in the oven.

And yet, in spite of all this activity, the origin of glass making in Venice is still unclear. Archaeological excavations conducted on the island of Torcello in 1961-62 uncovered a four-chamber glass-making furnace near the Church of Santa Maria founded in A.D. 639. Although these excavations have yielded suggestive and fascinating details, they provide no firm data on the Venetian glass industry. The first document on the subject, dated 982, contains a rather vague reference to the activity of one Domenico, a glass maker ("fiolario") in Rialto, a city district. We have more specific data starting in 1271, when the By-laws of the glass-making guilds were approved. This document relates in detail how production was organized in the various furnaces and contains information about equipment, fuel and raw materials, tools, the names of shapes and patterns, together with prices and product marketing information. Other documents from the same period describe in detail the activities of glass makers who actually worked in Murano at the time. In 1291, the Venetian High Council ruled that glass-making furnaces should be limited to the island of Murano, prohibiting them in the city of Venice proper. This decree aimed to protect the city from the danger of fires and to keep manufacturing secrets secure. Such an extensive, strict and detailed body of laws leads us to believe that glass making was already an established industry for some time, especially on the island of Murano, and that it was in fact Venice's leading economic activity.

While this book does not intend to discuss in detail the characteristics of Murano glass, we would like to devote a page or two to describe the glass used to produce the beads, without entering into the details of glass sheets or hollow glass canes.

We are interested in the beads obtained by cutting a long, hollow glass cane; once they have been cut, the beads are given a round shape by heating them in kilns. There are also beads made from filled, non-perforated canes. The glass canes are prepared by master glass makers, known as verieri *in Venetian dialect. The master measures the ingredients in different percentages to produce canes of different degrees of softness and color. Beads made from hollow canes are commonly known as* conterie *in Venice. According to some sources, the term is derived from the Latin noun* comptus *(ornament), though some believe it might be derived from* contare*, to count, and from the ancient use of the beads as barter currency. Another common Venetian name for beads, almost obsolete today, is* margarite *or* margarede*: these are the tiny, monochromatic beads mostly commonly used for trim-*

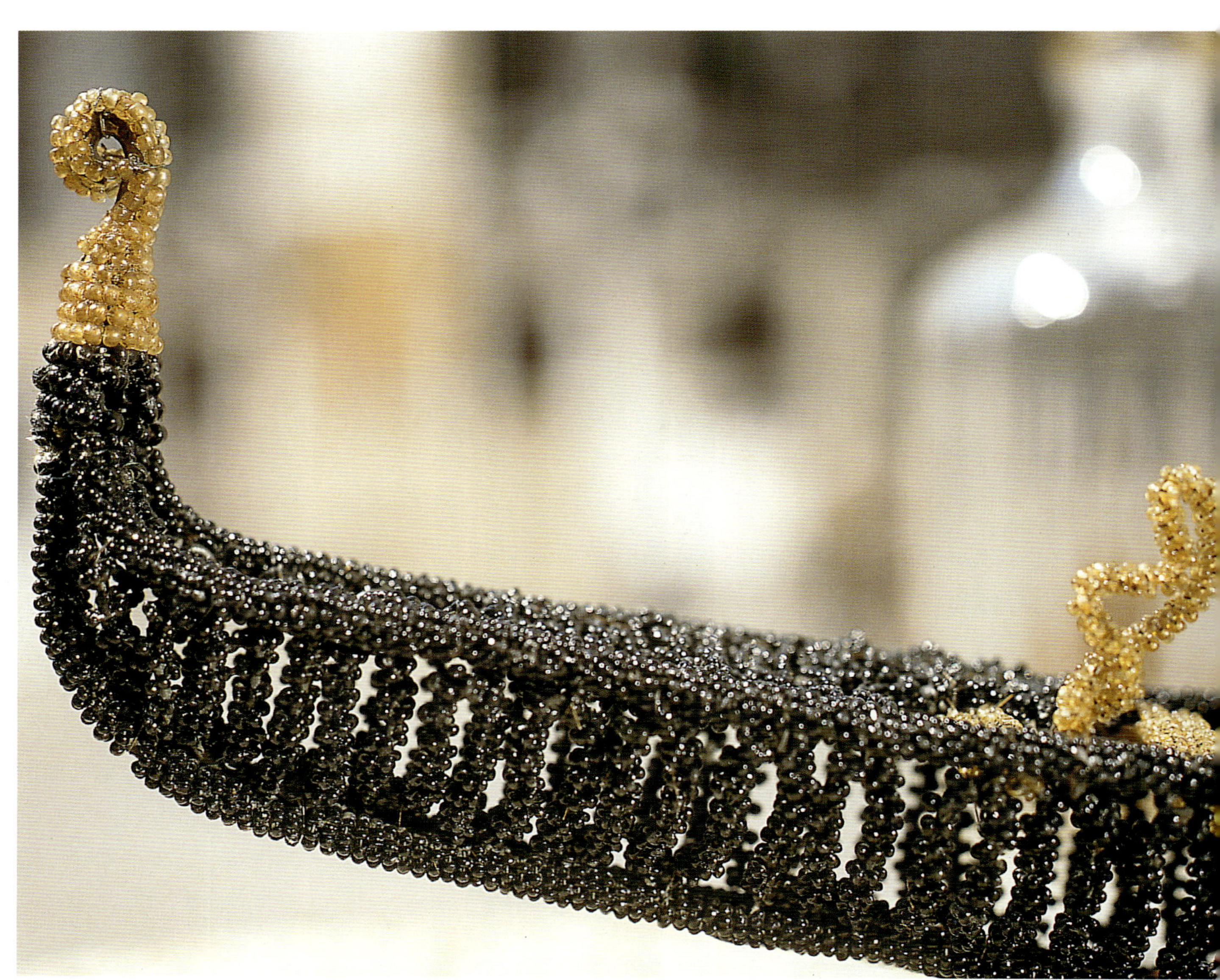

ming. The name has an ancient etymology, common to all Mediterranean cultures: literally, it means "risen from the sea." Margarite beads were especially sensitive to the whim of fashion, with a market that alternated between periods of great popularity and periods when they fell out of favor. These are the beads used for trimming garments, or for embroidery, crochet or knit work; they are used to trim lampshades and reliquaries, boxes and book covers, and to make beaded flowers. They have been forever associated with women's hands, since bead work has always been woman's work.

The manufacture of margarite and conterie is done in several steps, and requires spacious rooms and a large number of workers. First of all, the glass cane must be manufactured. This is done by a team of workers, known as muta, who follow a master's instructions. The team works a mass of vitreous paste into long, hollow canes of different widths, making sure that they are perforated throughout their length. Canes are either crystal-clear or colored; colored, or stained, canes react differently to light depending on whether they are opaque (the so-called enamel or paste cane) or transparent. Different types of glass of

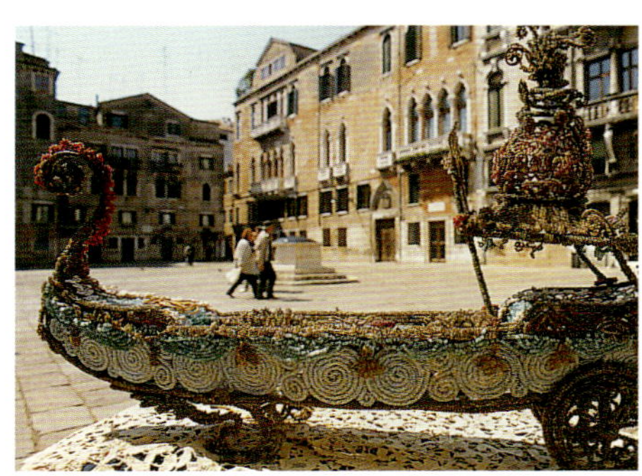

The boat's silver canopy, embroidered with ruby-red bead decorations. In front, a small velvet and bead box, perhaps used to store jewelry.

The Bucintoro

Every year Venice celebrated the wedding of the city to the sea with great pomp and ceremony. For this occasion, the Doge, (the chief magistrates of Venice), sailed in a special, magnificently decorated gondola, the Bucintoro. The miniature reproduced in these photographs, decorated with glass beads, dates to the latter part of the nineteenth century: it faithfully reproduces the opulent and elaborately detailed decorations of the Bucintoro.

Opposite. The bow of an elegant miniature gondola decorated with black and gold beads.

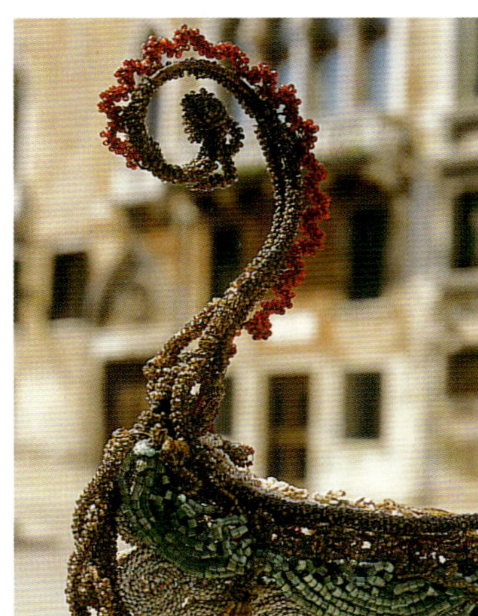

Detail of the decoration on the Bucintoro's bow. A small hold in aquamarine blue decorated with small white flowers is located at the bow's tip

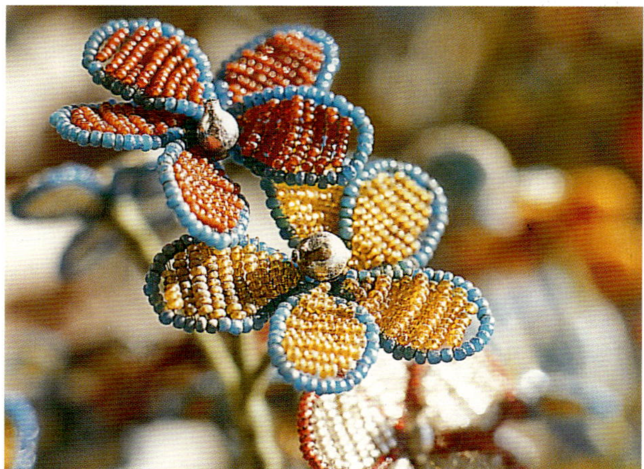

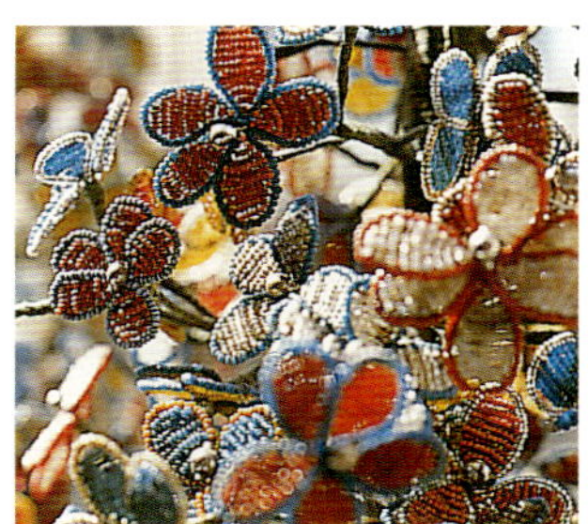

The Palmette

Palmettes made of glass beads were used to decorate altars. They are composed of many small flowers of the same size and shape, but in different colors. Each five-petaled flower was made using a weaving technique, as if woven on a loom. The palmettes in these two photographs are a splendid example of eighteenth century craftsmanship. The central bead, above, is made of silver-washed blown glass.

different colors may be used to make one cane. One such design calls for layering red over white glass, creating the cane from which the celebrated corniola *white heart beads are made; another design creates stripes on the outer surface with strands of different color glass, such as white and blue. The outside of the cane may be given different shapes such as rounded, faceted, or grooved. In turn, the facets can be on the outside or the inside. Each one of these styles requires special molds to shape the vitreous mass before it is stretched into a hollow cane.*

The master is assisted by the serventi, *assistants who help by handing him the tools, and the* tiradori, *the workers who pull the cane by moving in opposite directions from each other for ten yards or more: the faster they stretch the cane, the thinner it will be. Today, this process is for the most part done by machine.*

Now the cane is cut into beads, a process that incorporates several steps. First, the cane is cut into cannelle, *short canes of about one yard, which are inspected by the* cernidrice, *usually a woman worker who classifies them, separating them by sight and touch according to quality and size. The short canes are then passed on to the* tagiador, *a worker who cuts them into small cylinders. Today, the cutting is done by machine, while for most of the nineteenth century it was done exclusively by women workers. After being cut, the beads are inspected by the* schizzador *who sifts them, separating them from glass fragments.*

At this point, two additional steps are possible: the beads may be left as they are, cylindrical, with sharp edges and in the original color of the cane from which they were cut (in this case, they are called pivette*), or they may be rounded, in which case the edges are smoothed out by heating the beads in a kiln. Because in this step the beads could lose their shape, thereby closing the hole, they must first be prepped by the* fregadori, *workers who close the holes by mixing the beads together with a mixture of sand and spent lime that can later be easily removed. The beads are then dropped into a large cask set at constant rotation in the kiln; the friction generated by the tumbling motion bevels the edges,*

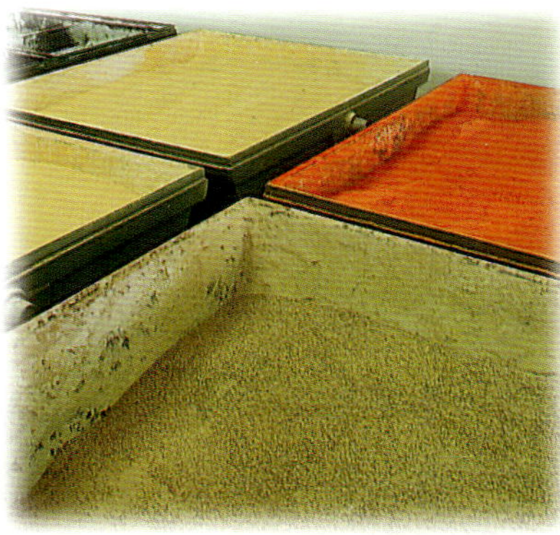

1. *Glass is composed mostly of either sand or silica. Colors are added by mixing in ground metallic oxides, such as the ones we see in the photo at left.*

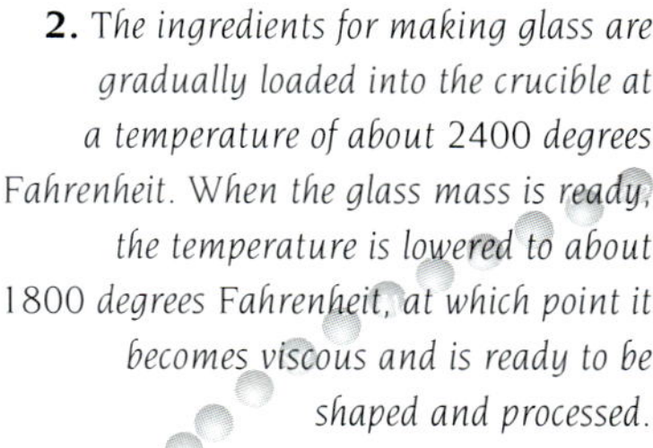

2. *The ingredients for making glass are gradually loaded into the crucible at a temperature of about 2400 degrees Fahrenheit. When the glass mass is ready, the temperature is lowered to about 1800 degrees Fahrenheit, at which point it becomes viscous and is ready to be shaped and processed.*

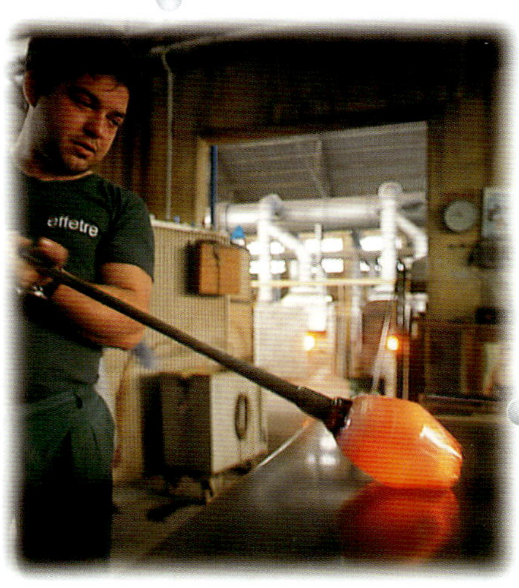

3. *The hollow cane, or tube, of molten glass is handled with specially designed metal rods called* pontelli *and placed on a metal workbench. In the photo at left, the master is cooling the cane before stretching it.*

making the beads smooth and perfectly spherical.

This is the most delicate phase of the bead-making process, because heat could irreversibly change the color or shade but, at the same time, it can create new ones. For example, colors such as pink, ruby red and orange are obtained in this second heating process using crystal-clear glass. Once the beads are cooled, the cavaroba *remove the sand and lime mixture by putting the beads in a sack and shaking them until all the holes are open. Finally, after going through a second round of quality and size selection, the beads are given a final polish.*

This long, costly manual labor has now been partially replaced by machines, though the process has not changed. The names of the tools and the definition of the various jobs have survived.

The Furnace

Glass is a man-made material. Glass-making processes were invented about five thousand years ago; like then, glass is still made by melting together silica, soda and lime, raw materials that are abundantly found in nature. It is shaped when hot and still in liquid form: thanks to its viscosity, it keeps the shape given to it by the master glass maker. At ambient temperature, depending on the ingredients used and their composition, glass can be of different colors and is transparent to light in varying degrees.

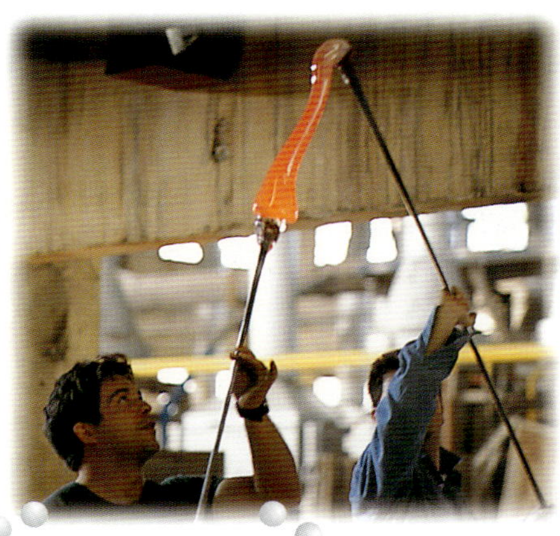

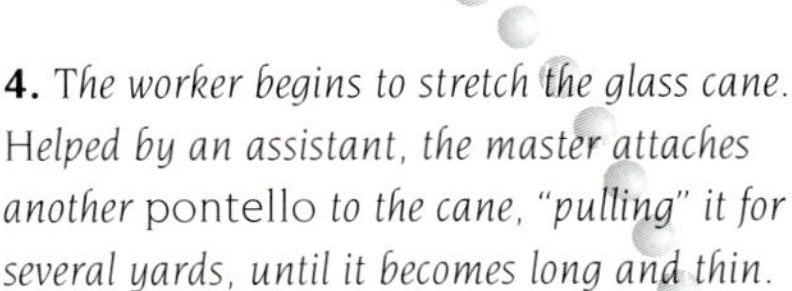

4. *The worker begins to stretch the glass cane. Helped by an assistant, the master attaches another* pontello *to the cane, "pulling" it for several yards, until it becomes long and thin.*

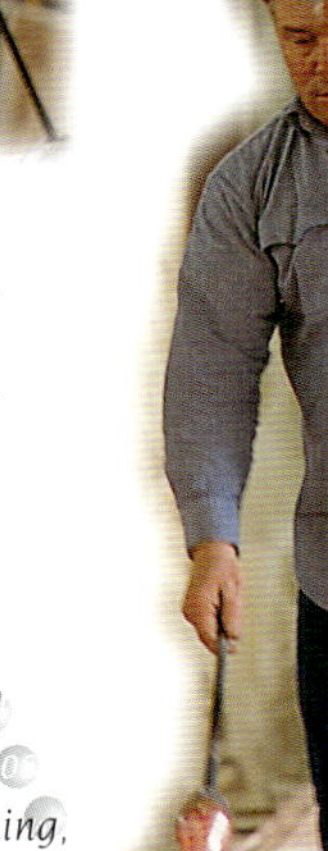

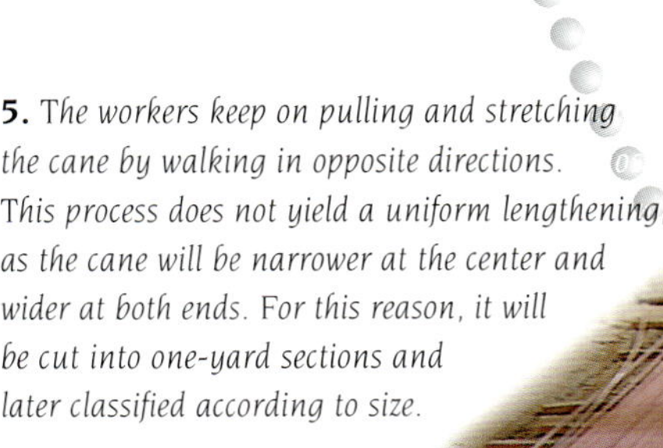

5. *The workers keep on pulling and stretching the cane by walking in opposite directions. This process does not yield a uniform lengthening, as the cane will be narrower at the center and wider at both ends. For this reason, it will be cut into one-yard sections and later classified according to size.*

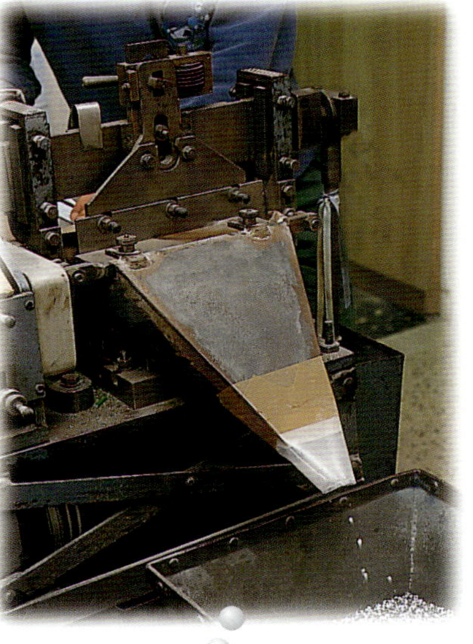

6. *The glass canes are cut by machine to make the beads. The machine has a "guillotine" mechanism invented in 1822.*

Glass-Bead Flowers

The most ancient Venetian documents with detailed descriptions of glass-bead flowers is the Hypnerotomachia Poliphili, *a book printed in 1499 by Aldus Manutius the Elder. This unusual text approaches garden design as if it were an architectural element, worthy of the house it was meant to beautify, and where vegetation was used as if it were a material such as marble or stone. The garden, which contained topiaries as well as statues, was designed according to rigid geometric patterns and could include fountains, arbors, flower beds, and mazes.*

A scale model in silk and Murano conteria *was made of this garden; unfortunately, it has not survived, and all we are left with is its description. Clearly, the book and the model demonstrate that there was a lively dialogue and an exchange of ideas at the time among the various crafts such as garden design, glass making, and weaving. It must have been magic to see and touch a whole garden made of glass!*

The uniquely Venetian art of miniature garden design became popular in European countries such as France, Germany, and England. Unfortunately, very little documentation has survived, especially because these "pocket" gardens were usually created behind castle walls and inside convents. We can still see some significant examples of glass-bead creations at the Victoria and Albert Museum in London, though they are mostly bead-trimmed clothes and precious jewelry boxes.

On the other hand, we have a large number of bibliographical sources that describe sumptuous "triumphs" of artificial flowers, center pieces that decorated the aristocratic halls and the church altars of Venice in the eighteenth and nineteenth century. At the time, the flowers were made of glass beads as well as silk, wax, and paper. Skilled artisans from all schools competed to make objects that

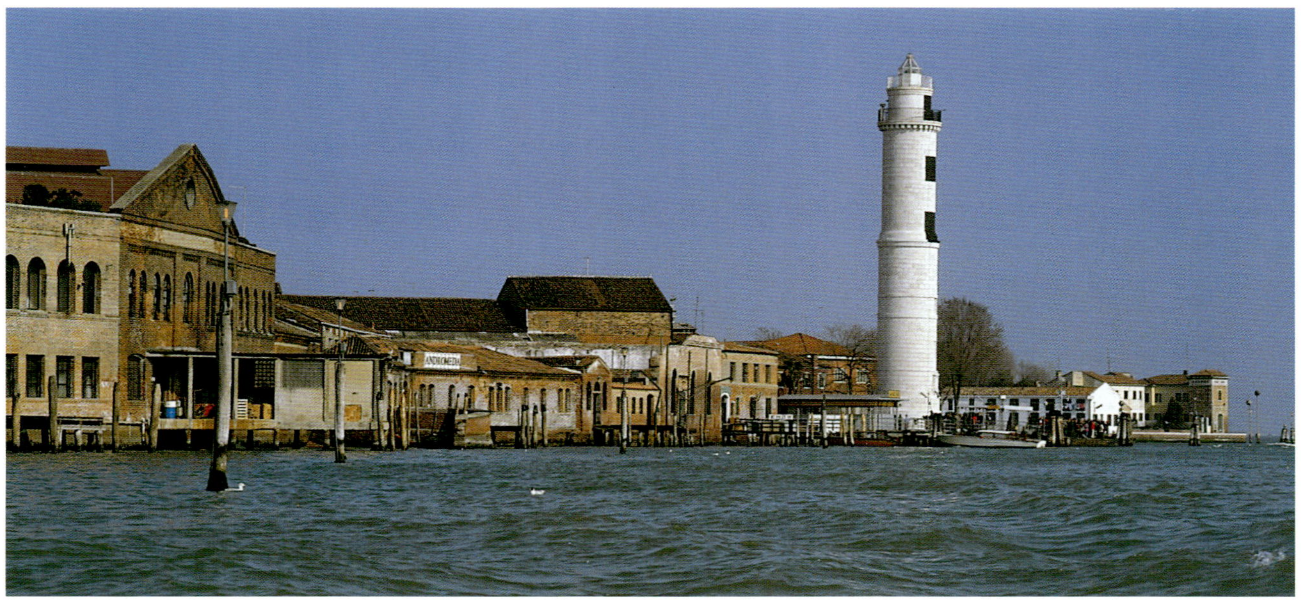

The island of Murano with the lighthouse and some of the glassworks that face the Lagoon, seen from the ferry.

recreated nature. Glass-bead flowers became popular in the nineteenth century as a separate craft from embroidery, and flourished as an independent decorative element of vase compositions. By then, bead making was an important industry in Venice, thanks also to the intense activity of Eulalia and Amalia Dorigo. The Dorigo sisters had refined their taste in Paris and had brought to Venice the secrets of their art, with the dual aim of renovating the glass-making industry as well as supplying jobs and income to a large number of women, as we can read from documentary sources of the time. The creations of the Dorigo sisters became popular almost overnight; France especially became the major market for funeral wreaths made with beaded flowers. In Émile Zola's Carnets d'enquête, *we can read detailed descriptions of graves blanketed with these flowers that had the dual advantage of reflecting light and of never withering.*

By the end of the nineteenth century, Venetian flower compositions were displayed as centerpieces in formal salons, on trays, in vases, around mirrors, and in portrait frames. Begonias, mimosa, wisteria, mignonette, fuchsias, violets, tulips, and lilacs were the most popular flowers. In 1899, Venice began to produce globes for gas lamps, an item that was successful for about twenty years. In later years the production of flowers continued to be high, although the export of conterie *fell as a result of the economic depression. In the nineteen-forties, there were still about 400 women who worked out of their homes making glass-bead flowers, mostly for the foreign market.*

After World War II, the tradition began to die due to changes in fashion and the industrialization of the Venetian district of Marghera: many women left the craft, preferring to work in the new factories. Only a few women today carry on this ancient art and still hand it down to their daughters; for the most part, they live in the Lagoon islands, in Burano, and in the city districts of Cannaregio and Castello. Nella Sammartini Lopez y Royo learned from them the art of flower making, renovating and perfecting it over the years into a unique technique, thus giving new life to this distinguished and time-honored craft.

The "Bocolo"

A favorite present in Venice is the bocolo *(bud, in Venetian dialect), a red rose bud that lovers offer to their beloved on Saint Mark's Day. This present is tied to the legend of Tancredi, the troubadour Crusader, and the lovely Venetian lady Vulcana. Having been mortally wounded in battle, Tancredi falls on a white rose bush that becomes soaked with his blood. He begs his comrade Orlando to bring Vulcana a rose colored with his blood. Orlando arrives in Venice on the eve of Saint Mark's, carrying with him the rose, a present of love and death. When she sees the rose, Vulcana becomes very pale and cannot speak.*

The following day, Vulcana's nurse will find her dead, holding the flower in her hands. In memory of the doomed lovers, on April 25th, Saint Mark's Day, lovers in Venice give their belles a red rose bud. The rose is even more precious if it's made with glass beads.

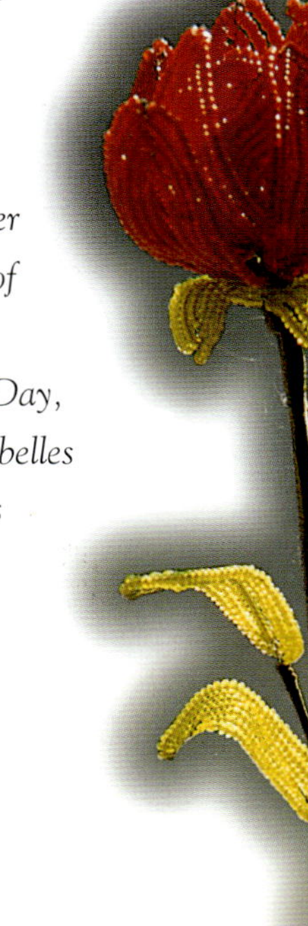

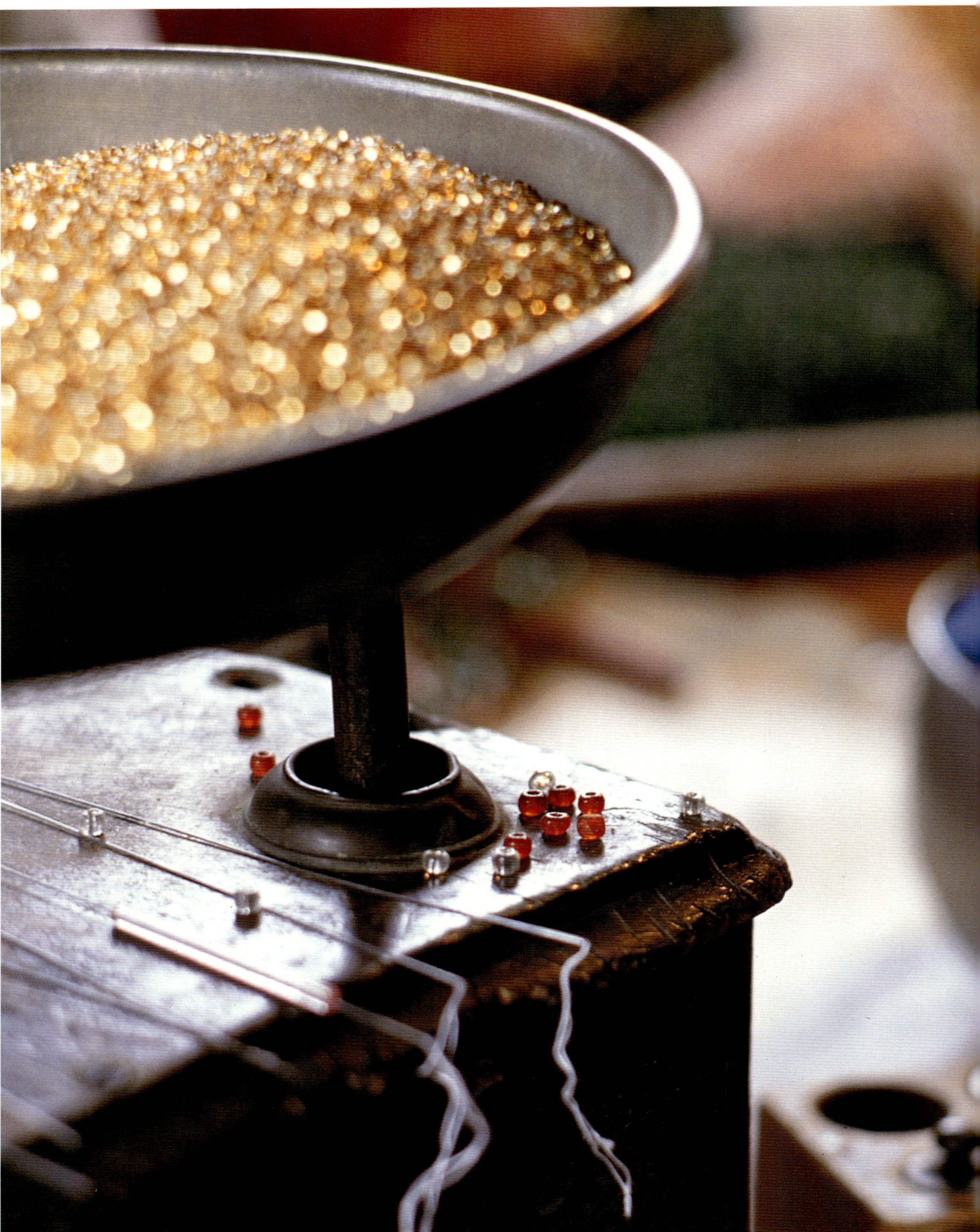

2 CHAPTER

Preparation

To make beaded flowers, we suggest you set up a separate work area or room where you can arrange the tools and materials you will need such as glass beads of all colors, containers of various shapes and sizes, metal wires, silk embroidery yarn or twist, pliers, scissors, etc.

You will need a large, smooth, even work surface, preferably white, so that colors can better stand out. You need to work in full light, therefore close to a large window or a good source of light. If possible and if weather allows, working outdoors is ideal, maybe even close to a flowering garden that can inspire you.

The Materials

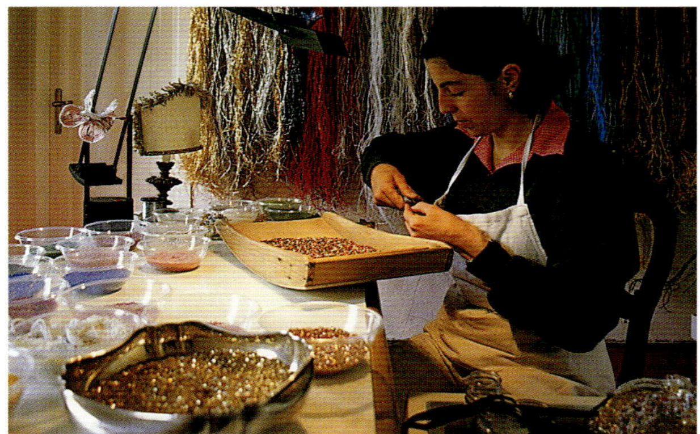

Giovanna Poggi Marchesi in her workshop, in the Treviso countryside, not far from Venice, in a house immersed in green fields and hills.

To work with glass beads, in addition to a good dose of patience and enthusiasm, you need manual dexterity and creativity. Those who have experience working with dry flowers have a clear advantage since they already know how to use the metal wire used by florists. Good cutting tools are important: we suggest costume jewelry pliers, *with sharp blades and elongated, thin tips (long-nose pliers) to hold and cut the wire,* scissors *to cut the silk yarn, and* nippers *to cut the small iron spikes that cannot be cut with the pliers. Each tool should be used only for its specific purpose, so as not to dull the blade.*

Glass beads are strung on iron wire. *Different types of wire are available, those for glass beads are* galvanized florist wires *No. 10, No. 16, and No. 20. Galvanizing is a zinc-coating process that prevents iron from rusting. The number denotes the wire's diameter: the higher the number, the thinner the wire. Wire No. 20 is used for fine* conteria, *while wire No. 16 is used for the more commonly used* conteria. *Wire No. 10 is used to make foliage, and it becomes the leaf's central rib (its "core").*

Other useful types of iron wire are: stiff rods *with a 2/32 of an inch (2 mm) diameter and* pig iron, *used to make flower stems;* wire No. 5,

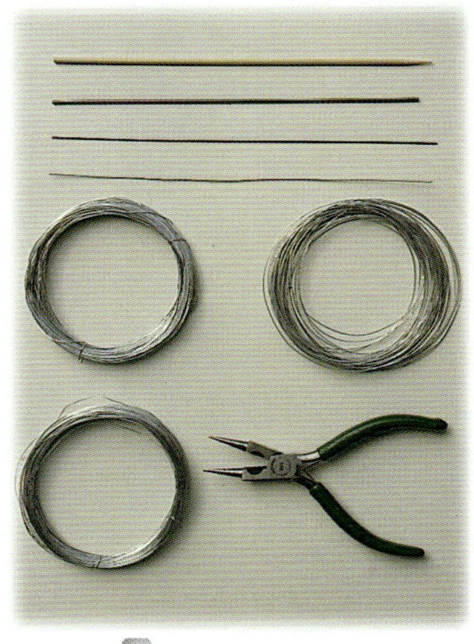

1. *You need a good selection of thin, galvanized iron wire for stringing the beads—it is usually sold rolled up or coiled. For the flower stems you need thicker iron wires or rods sold loose in hardware stores.*

2. *Silk yarn in many colors: dark olive for intensely colored flowers; pale green for delicate spring flowers; gold for summer ears of wheat; brown for rich gold and silver roses and for autumnal red berries. For small white roses, use white wire.*

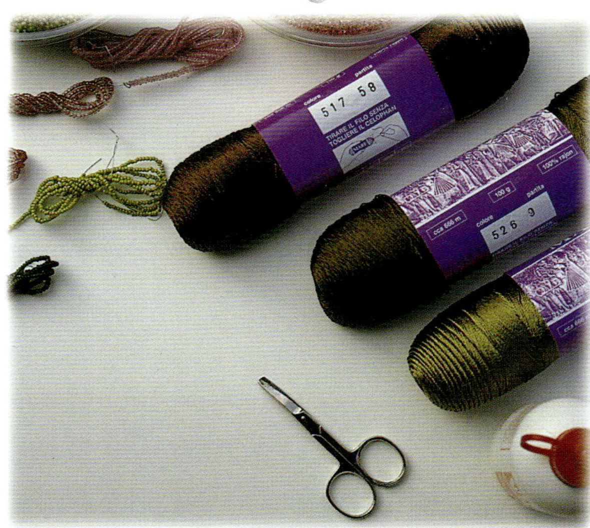

with a 1/32 of an inch (1 mm) diameter, used to make flower peduncles or the smaller stems of the red berry branches; finally, green plastic-coated wire used in flower shops to support fresh flower stems. We will use them for the stems of small flowers and florets. Sometimes, to reproduce the thicker stems of flowers such as the hyacinth, we use 10 inch wooden sticks instead of wire. (See "Craft wire," p.144.)

In addition to wire of varying rigidity and thickness, you also need a good selection of silk yarn or twist; this is an important material you will need in order to cover all the metal parts, thus giving the flower a more natural look.

The silk twist is the same used for embroidery; it is sold in skeins or spools; you need to cut lengths of approximately 16 inches each to cover the wire neatly. (See "Beads," p.144.)

The Tools

The list of tools you need to create glass-bead flowers is short. In fact, the most sensitive and creative tool are your hands. Among the primary materials you will need is a good selection of iron wire of different diameters (gauges) (one good reason for visiting old hardware stores, those that are around), silk yarn or twist in an assortment of colors and, of course, a large selection of colored beads.

3. *Iron rods are sold by weight in hardware stores; because they are not zinc-coated, they will rust easily. For this reason they should be stored in a dry place.*

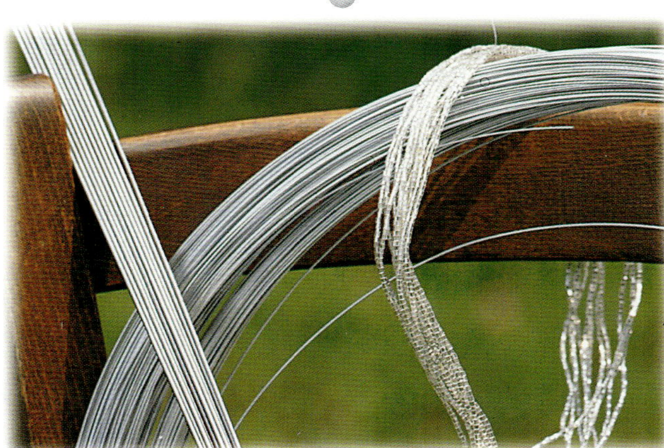

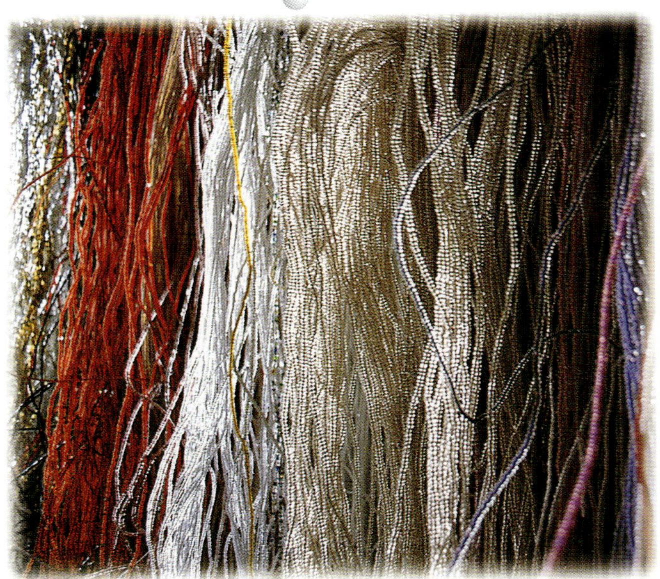

4. *Once the beads are strung on wires, they may be hung, as in the photograph above, or they may be stored rolled up. Hanging them one next to the other creates a magical curtain that comes alive when the light touches it.*

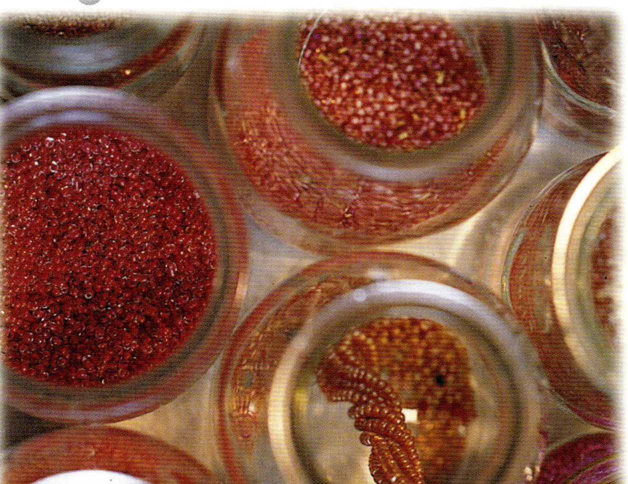

5. *Several clear glass containers to store extra beads are also useful. Sometimes you need to remove some beads from the strings as you create the flower, and small containers such as those in the photo at left are very handy.*

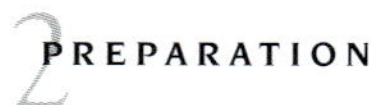

The Work Shop

Are you ready to work together? Let's start, then!

First of all we need a large, smooth, comfortable work surface that is preferably white, so that the colors can stand out in all their glory.

Since full, natural light is important, try to place the work station near a large window or, if the natural light is insufficient, a good lamp. When weather permits, working outdoors is recommended. Try to work in a sitting position, with an erect posture. It is preferable to bring the work up to your eyes with your hands rather than the other way around.

At first, you should work with a tray underneath; in this way, falling beads will fall into the tray and may be used again. Several small containers, one for each color, are also useful. The strings of beads should be hung neatly, so that all you need to do is pull a string when you need it. If this is impractical, then the strings should be rolled up in loose coils.

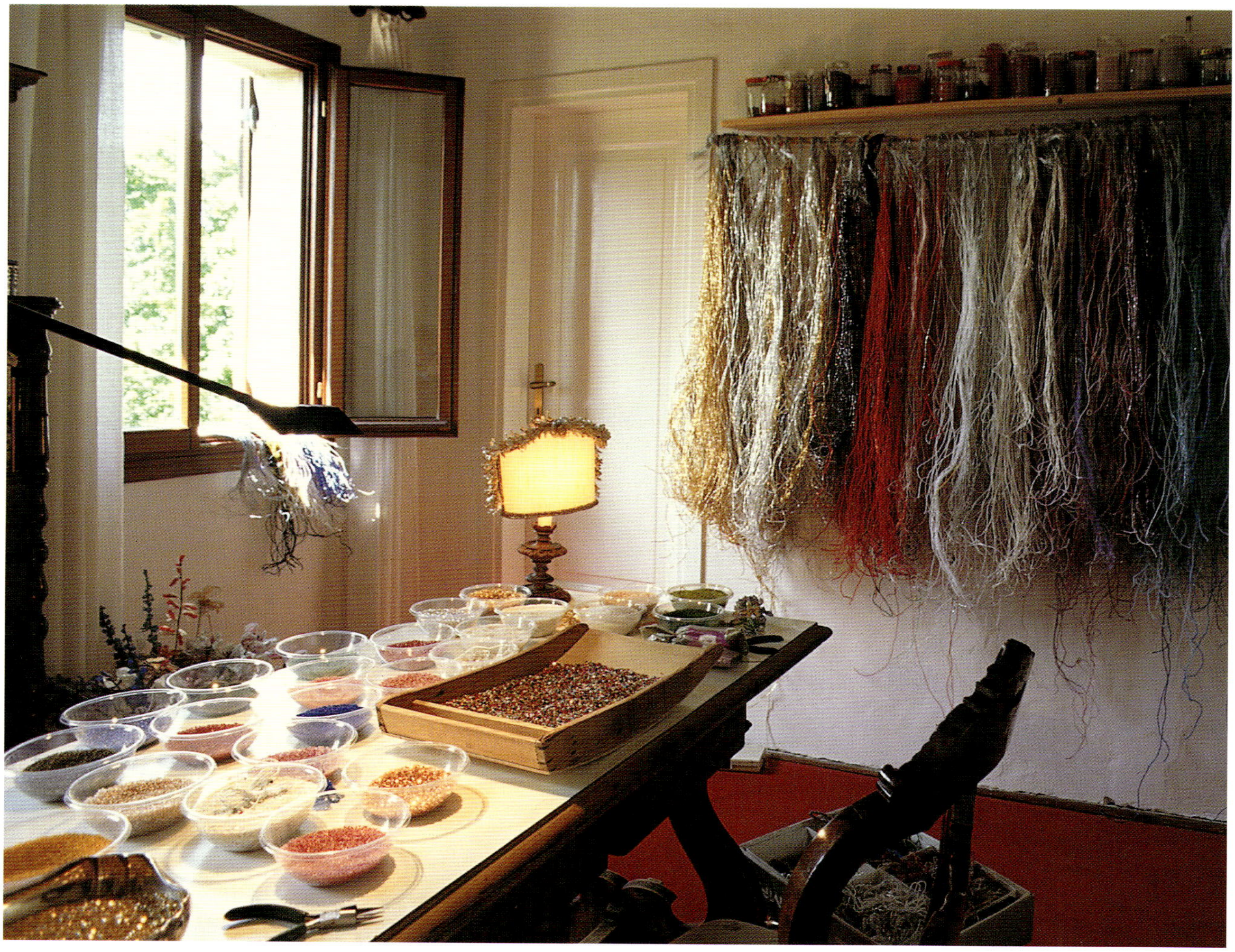

Stringing Beads

To string beads, pour them into a container with raised borders or a tray that is neither too large nor too small.

First, cut wire segments (24–26 gauge craft wire) about 56 inches in length, and cut as many segments as you need to make a flower. Take one end of the wire and secure it with a small twist; take the other end and plunge it in the tray or container full of beads with a regular movement from right to left: the beads will easily string into the wire. If they do not, it is either because their opening is too small for that wire, in which case you should use a thinner wire (for example,

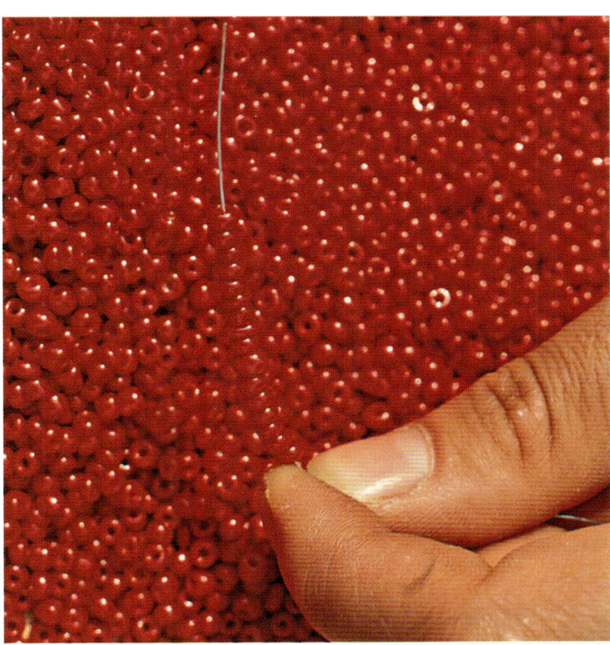

26–28 gauge), or because the openings in the beads are plugged.

String the beads to a length of 40 inches; you will need the remaining 16 inches of wire to shape the various petals. Once they are strung, you may hang the beads by the end that has no beads, separating them by color and shade, or you may roll

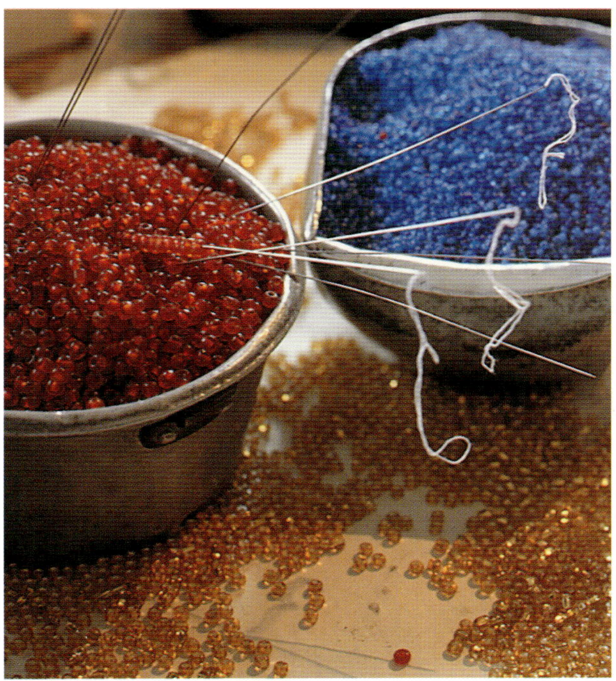

them up into a coil. Beads stored in this manner take up less space. In the following chapters we are going to call the wire segments already strung with beads up to a length of 40 inches strings*, and all the other types of wire we shall call* wire.

. . . When beads fall

One small, incorrect movement and the beads will roll out of your hands, onto the floor and hide in every corner where it will be impossible to find them until you step on them and hear the noise of breaking glass. You will need a good brush and a stiff card to pick up the beads one by one and return them to their container.

The Containers

Each composition should be designed by taking into account the room where it will be displayed and the type of container to be used. For example, rich and stately silver and gold flowers require less light than colored see-through ones; they also require elegant and precious vases to enhance their grave beauty.

To decorate a well-lit corner, place the flowers in a cut or plain crystal vase that will enhance and reflect their natural light. For a marble mantelpiece, an antique porcelain vase decorated with gold profiles will be more appropriate; for a wood-paneled wall, large, monochrome glass vases in warm, soft colors are best.

If you choose to decorate the house with flowers in strong colors, a different approach is required. If the vase is made of colored glass as well, you could place it near a window, maybe against the light. The effect will be stunning because you will enjoy the transparency of the container and of the glass beads. The beads will reflect colored light in every direction. Glass vases come in all sizes and shapes, from small to very

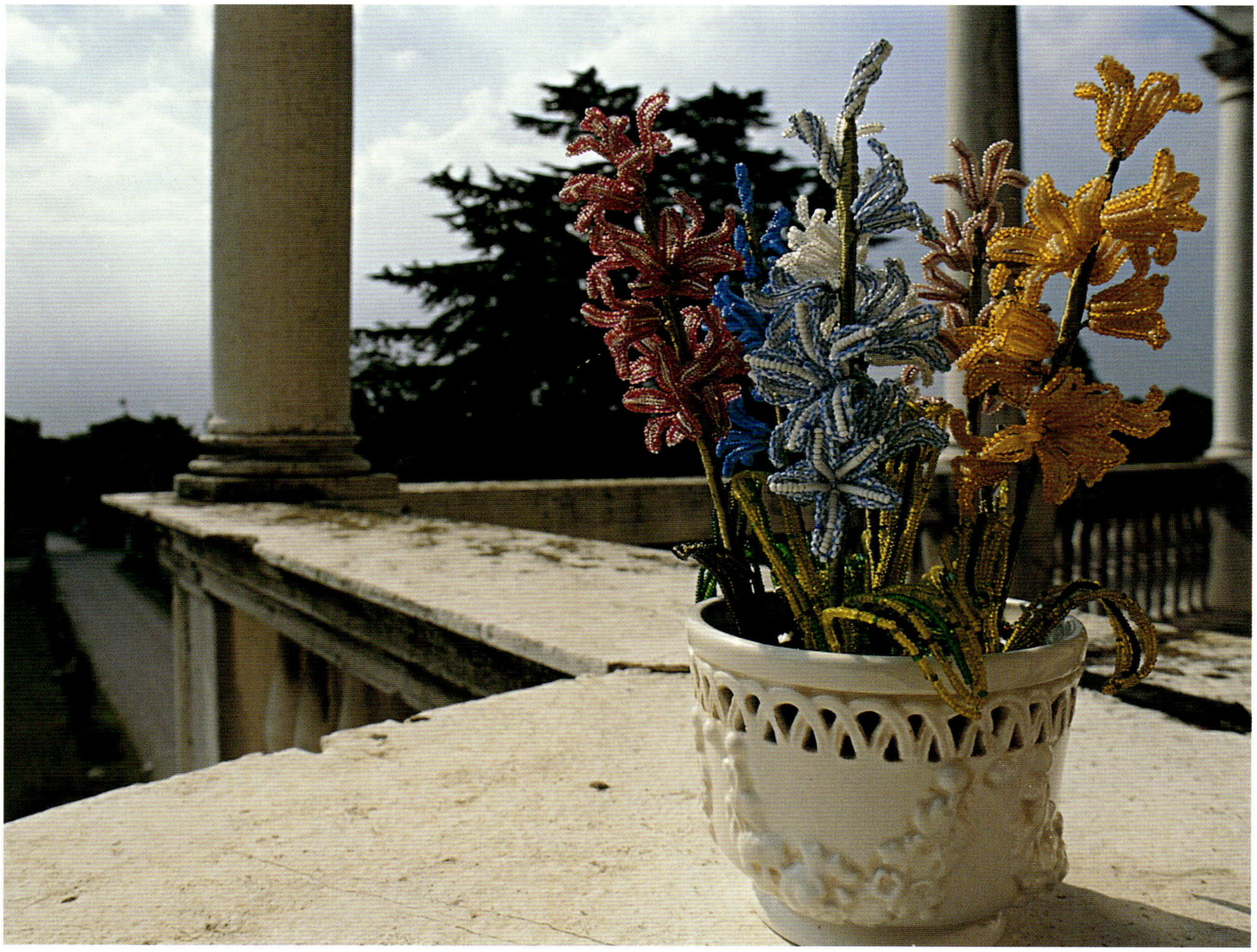

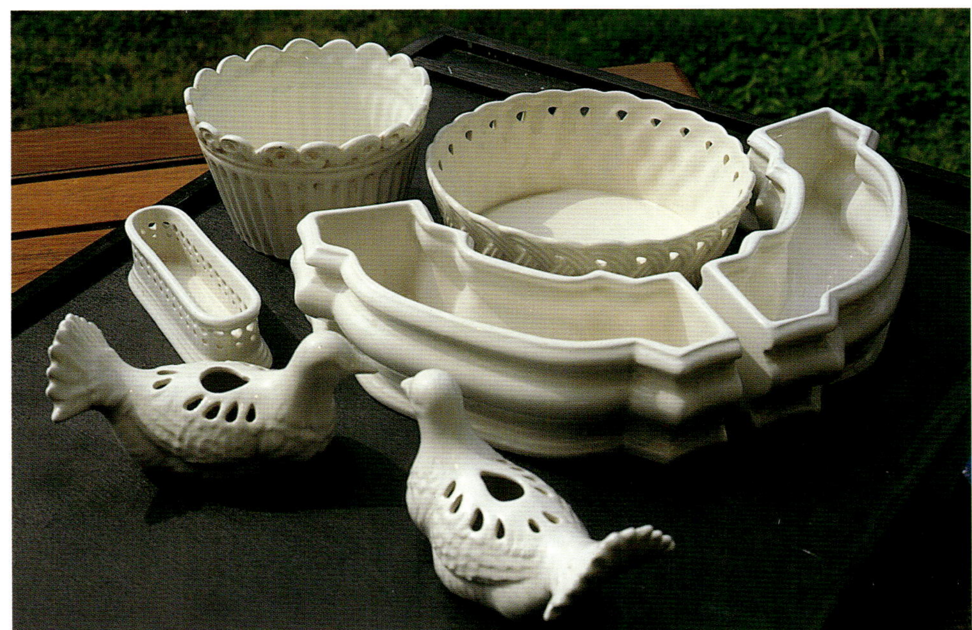

Some examples of ceramic containers in different shapes and sizes. Those reproduced here are recent productions from Bassano del Grappa and Nove.

large, with elongated shapes or short and rounded with a wide opening, shaped like an inverted handkerchief or with harmonious classic lines.

Vases come in all possible colors. Glass makers create an infinite variety of shades, hues and finishes. In fact, the competition in Murano among the different glassworks, over a thousand years old, continues to this day, each offering stunning, splendid creations.

Little by little, with experience and careful reflection, you will be able to choose the proper shape and color for every situation: wide-mouthed vases for red autumnal berries, transparent crystal vases with trapped air bubbles for tulip arrangements; pale opalescent vases for iris or rose bouquets; pale gold-hued vases for large, mixed compositions.

The choice of flowers is yours and depends on your personal taste and the décor of the room where they will be displayed. To avoid monotony, try not to repeat the colors and motifs of the drapes or the wallpaper.

Ceramic vases are especially appropriate as centerpieces, as an alternative to silver bowls. Modern containers with smooth lines, in white or light colors, are quite suitable for small, plain, intensely colored flowers such as forget-me-nots, small daisies, yellow buttercups, morning glories, violets and clover leaves. Traditional, classically shaped ceramic vases with elaborate textures, colors such as ivory, and elongated bases go well with romantic compositions of falling tulips and blushing roses. For a precious, refined dining room table set with gold-rimmed glasses and silverware that reflect the light, a gold and silver flower center piece would be appropriate for all special occasions throughout the year.

In addition to the dining room, other corners of the house can be made brighter by arranging a few glass flowers in an attractive ceramic or porcelain vase and placing them on a windowsill, on a favorite side table or a serious looking desk, in a reading corner, or even in a private space such as the bedroom or the dressing table.

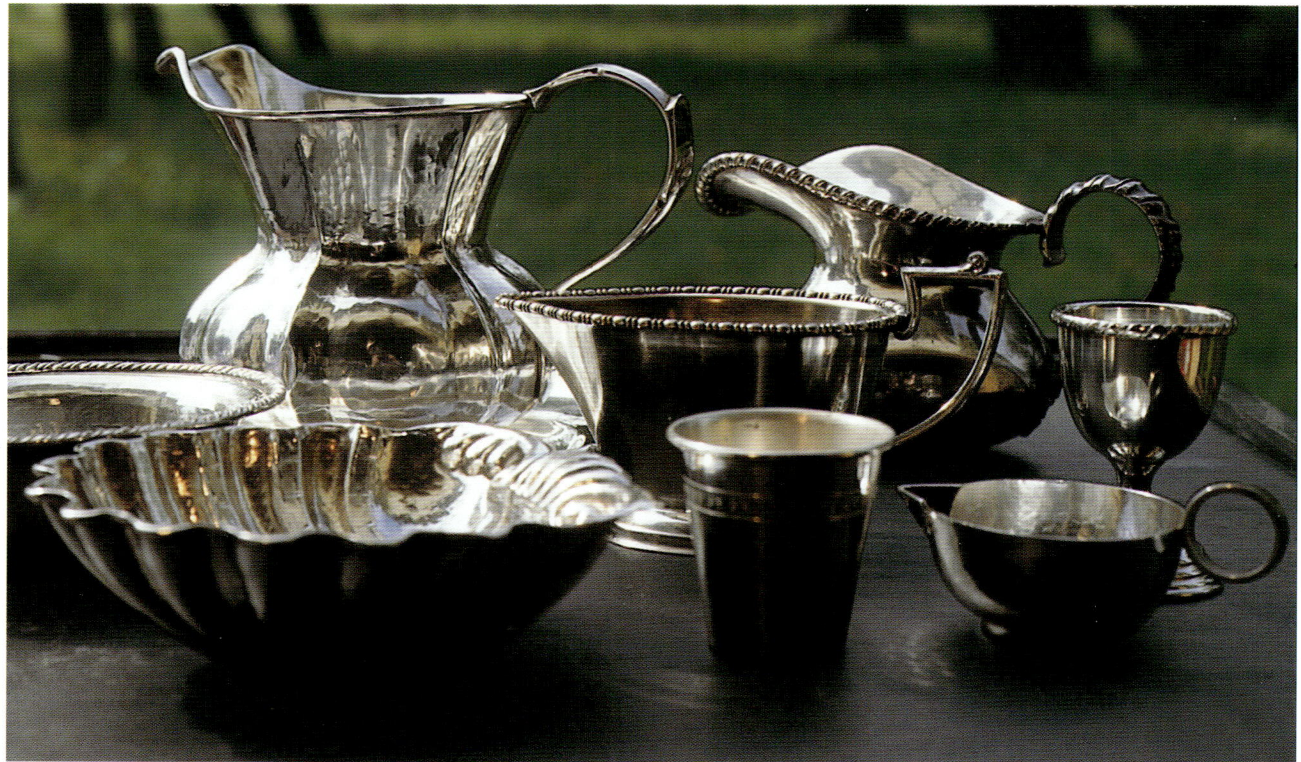

Metal vases are also quite appropriate for flower arrangements, from precious silver goblets to old-fashioned pewter tankards, copper casseroles that recall ancient kitchens, and even imposing bronze braziers. Each container requires its own special ambiance and an accurate choice of flowers and colors. In general, most colored flowers marry well with silver vases; choose colors that harmonize with the décor. Silver containers are an ideal solution because the metal really lights up the flowers, making any type of bead shine and glitter, enhancing the whole composition. Vases in opaque metals such as pewter and bronze will complement intense colors that offer a robust contrast to the dark metal: therefore, brightly colored mountain or woodland flowers are best for pewter tankards, while field flowers such as sunflowers, poppies, ears of golden wheat, and large daisies are perfect for large bronze containers.

For small silver vases two or three small flowers suffice, chosen from among perennial favorites such as small roses, violets, lilies-of-the-valley, narcissus, or hyacinths: two stems are enough to capture a small piece of springtime to always keep by your side.

Above, silver carafes, bowls, and cups in different styles, all recent productions.

Opposite, a piece by Archimede Seguso, one of the most admired master glass makers from Murano.

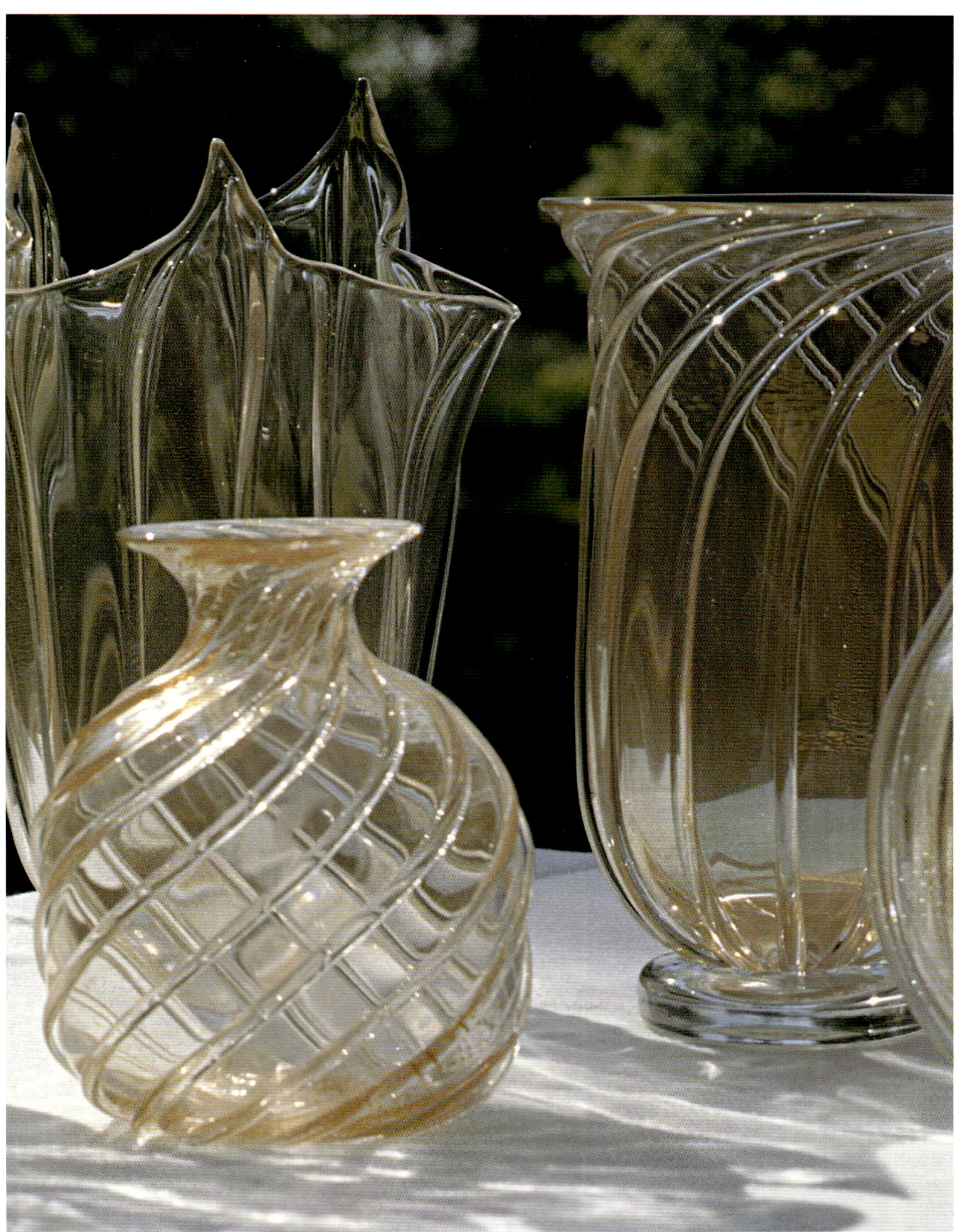

The Colors

Though there are no strict guidelines for combining colors in bouquets, we may use the theory of colors as a guide. There are three so-called primary colors: red, yellow, and blue; mixing them, we obtain green, azure blue (the light blue of clear skies), and magenta. We may vary the tonalities of these colors by mixing them with white, the sum of all colors, or black which is the absence of color. Although colors that are adjacent to each other on the color spectrum might be easier to combine, the end result could be monotonous, since analogous colors do not provide a contrast; contrast is required to give a sense of natural liveliness. Actually, most flowers can be easily harmonized, and the skill of the composer lies in mixing the various colors to achieve results that are pleasing to the eye. Finally, the flowers must fit the surrounding décor, enhancing it without making it monotonous.

For inspiration, all we need to do is look around us: from the brown bark of the tree trunks to the chiaroscuro of clouds sailing through the sky, from the changing green of a spring meadow to the intense color contrasts in a flower bed, from the colors of buildings to the colors of a crowded market . . . the suggestions are infinite. And we can find further inspiration in the worlds of art, of design, of textiles.

What is important is that we dare to experiment; even if we lack a strong creative instinct, experience can be a marvelous teacher.

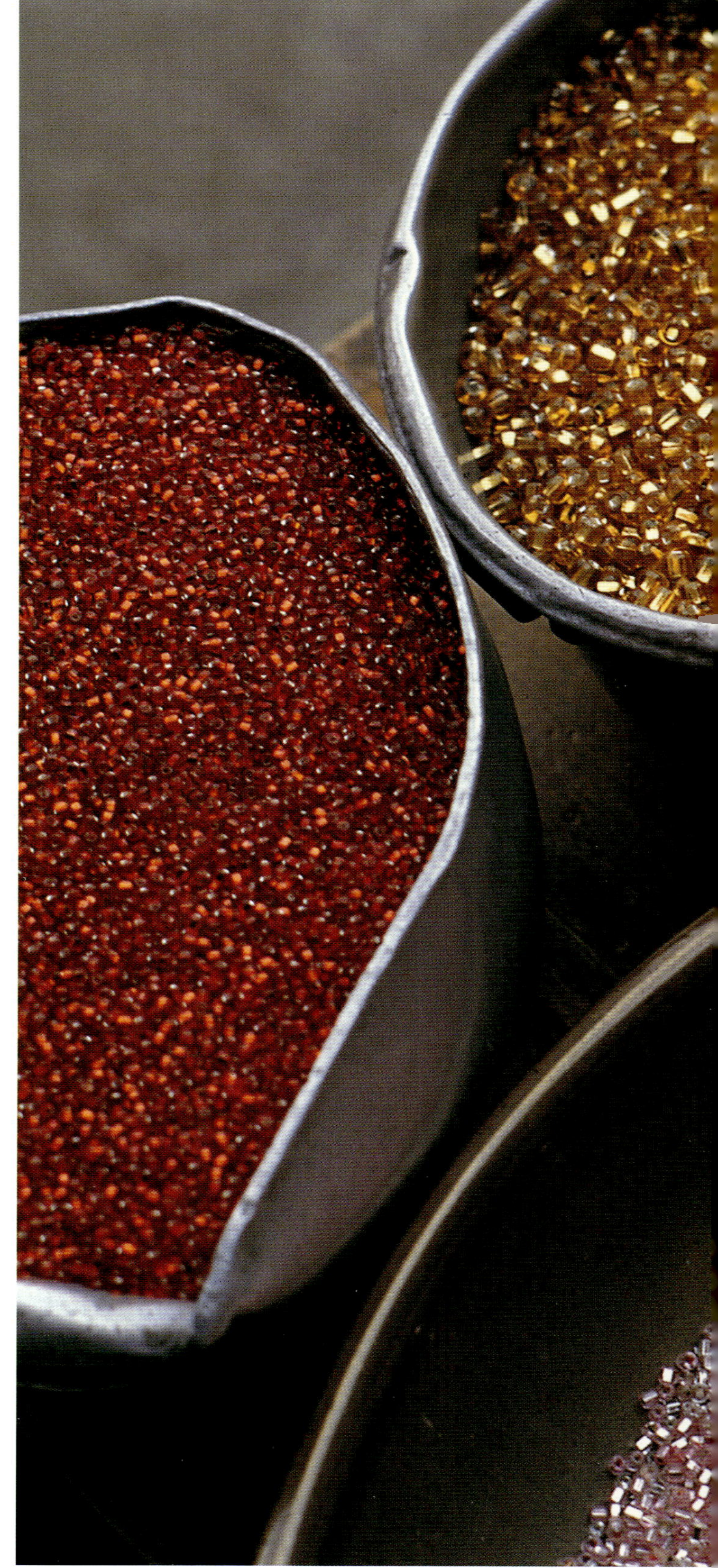

As in nature, splendid results can be achieved by juxtaposing contrasting colors.

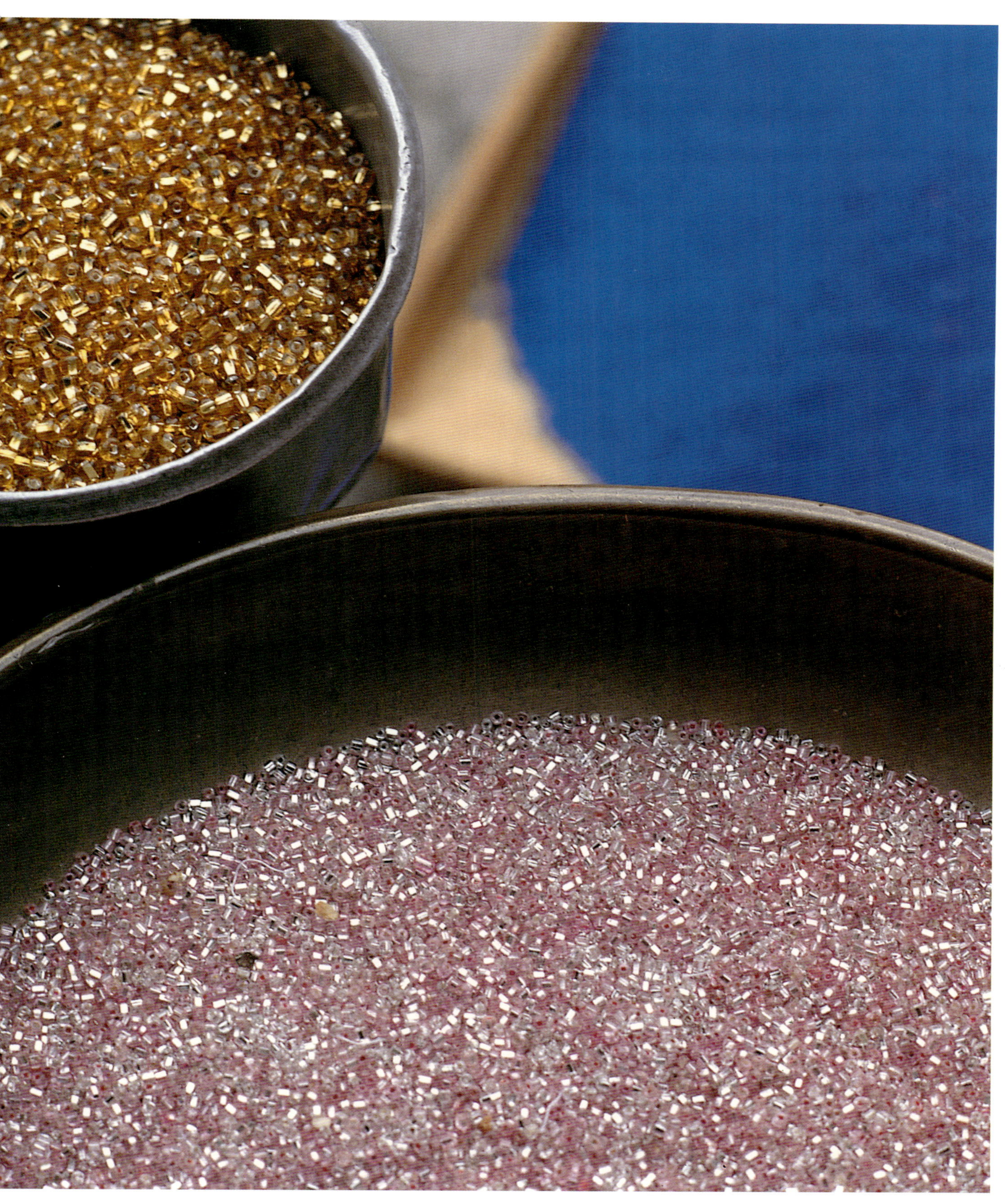

The Glass Beads

There are so many kinds of beads on the market, that some simple instructions might be useful in helping us to choose the most appropriate types for each project, especially with reference to unusual or desirable characteristics.

*Usually, flowers are made with common con-*teria *beads, also known as "seed" beads. Sometimes we might use unusual, novelty beads, displaying them in a special position such as the flower's center.*

Beads are divided into two large categories: light-transparent or clear beads, and opaque beads that still absorb light, also known as enamel beads. This distinction is important when assembling a bouquet, for when touched by the light transparent beads glitter and are incredibly attractive, but when they receive insufficient light, they look sad giving the flowers an old, worn, dusty look. Enamel beads, on the other hand, although opaque and not as glittering as the transparent ones, still maintain their color even under insufficient light conditions and add liveliness to any composition. For a bouquet of different kinds of flowers and colors we suggest you use both types of beads, to take full advantage of their respective characteristics of light and texture.

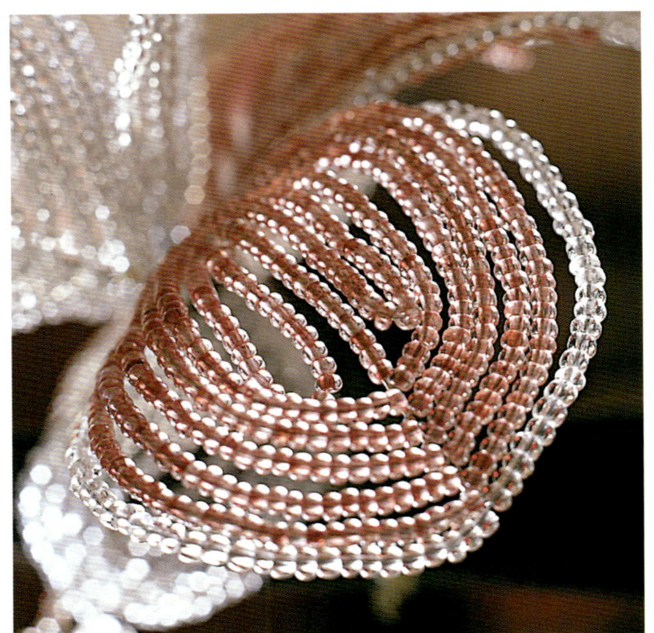

Shimmering highlights created by the sun's rays reflecting on a flower made with transparent beads.

Transparent Beads

Beads may be divided into three major categories:

Beads made of colored, transparent glass

These are the most common beads, they are sold in all shades and colors with the exception of gray. The color pink, expensive to make, is quite rare today: most of the pink beads on the market are painted. Beads with surface finishes are subject to that finish wearing off, even as the beads are manipulated during stringing and construction.

Tosca beads

Color lined beads are vulnerable to the interior color being worn away during manipulation of the wire.

Also called filigrana *beads. These very attractive beads are colored on the inside only and have a transparent outer lining. Because of their transparency, they capture light easily; they are particularly attractive in the center flowers of a bouquet because they add light and focus, in addition to color. They are thus ideal for making irises, African lilies, all types of lilies and flowers with strong, elongated lines. Tosca beads may also be suitably combined in large petals made of opaque beads. For example, if we were to use only opaque beads in a 15-petal rose, the result would be a heavy flower that dominates the bouquet; by alternating enamel beads with* tosca *beads, the result will be luminous, colorful petals.*

Gold and silver beads

Gold beads are made with amber colored glass; silver beads with clear glass; both are then given a wash in either gold or silver, respectively, and polished: this process turns them into a gold or silver color. As a matter of fact, these beads are technically opaque because they are not transparent to the light, although the silver wash gives them mirror-like properties, with the tiny bits of mirror reflecting and multiplying the light in all directions. Gold and silver beads are appropriate for creating stately flowers for important occasions. They are especially suitable for creating attractive satinpods, magical ice flowers, precious irises, and sophisticated, romance-suggestive roses.

All colored glass beads may be washed with silver. As a result, they will appear to be silver inside and colored outside. These beads are usually called silver-washed *beads and are available in a large selection of colors.*

Maccà beads (Charlottes)

Also called "cut crystals." These beads are quite bright thanks to their faceted outer surface that catches the light and glimmers at the slightest movement. Maccà *beads were popular at the time of Queen Victoria who made great use of them during her period of mourning: she loved black* maccà *embroidery on her clothes and accessories. They were also popular at the turn of the century, when they were applied to dresses, necklines, and fringes, or embroidered on handbags in popular colors such as black, white, pale pink, or lilac.* Maccà *beads are becoming fashionable again, especially for evening wear. They are not suitable for vase flowers because of their artificial look, though they are ideal for flower pins or stylized hair pins.*

Enamel Beads (Opaques)

These beads have been popular worldwide. They were exported in incredibly large quantities from the beginning of the European colonial era throughout the nineteenth century, and were used for both interior decoration and costume jewelry. These colorful beads give robustness to a flower's shape, but because they do not reflect light, they tend to weigh down the composition. Therefore, they should be used with care, and their final effect should be carefully measured. They are the best choice for small flowers in dainty bouquets, for a small flower needs well-defined contours and strong colors to stand out among the transparent beads. Use only enamel beads to make red autumn berries, since the bright red will offer a pleasing contrast to the brown of the silk twist that covers the branches, creating airy bouquets that adapt to different types of décor.

Opaque beads, known as "enamel" or "paste" beads, are manufactured in hundreds of colors and are able to capture the light.

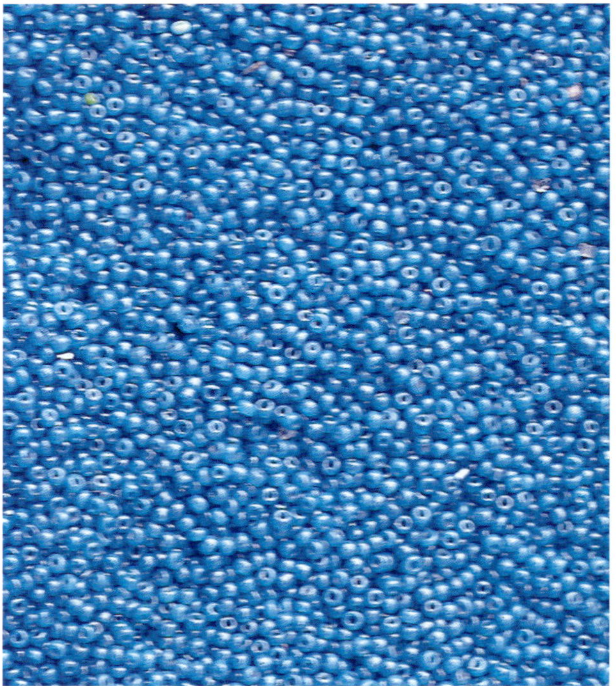

Arranging the Flowers

Since antiquity, flowers have been part of Western art and have been reproduced in frescos, paintings, and sculptures for their decorative value and for their symbolic meanings, which changed through the centuries. Flower decoration proper came into its own much later, starting in England in the nineteenth century when skilled English gardeners began to develop techniques to preserve stems, petals and flowers to embellish dining rooms and salons. Thanks to the popular writings of a few authors, especially from England, in the nineteen-twenties floral composition became a true minor art and precise aesthetic guidelines, rules, and styles were developed. In Italy, floral composition became popular again in the nineteen-sixties, thanks in part to the efforts of a group of amateurs who organized in Sanremo a floral composition school, the Amateur Floral Decoration Association (EDFA). Before we enter into a description of the various types of arrangements, we should note that a bouquet ought first and foremost to reflect the sensitivity of the person creating it, thus avoiding the temptation of creating cold, repetitive, and academic compositions.

Vases and Flower Arrangements

The container we choose and the type of composition that we are looking to achieve will determine the size of the flowers and the intensity of their colors. As a general rule, the height of the container should be approximately one third of the total height of the composition and about half of the total width. The shape of the vase will suggest the actual flower arrangement. In general, floral compositions follow a geometric shape such as a triangle, a sphere, a semicircle, a column, or any variation of these. The triangle shape looks best when displayed frontally, therefore it is ideal for decorating a mantelpiece or a table placed next to a wall or in a corner.

Glass bead flowers are heavy, therefore the base of a narrow vase needs to be stabilized. In the case of transparent vases, glass should be used to fill the vase and hold the flowers in place: use marbles, polished chips or scraps. Crystal beads also work well.

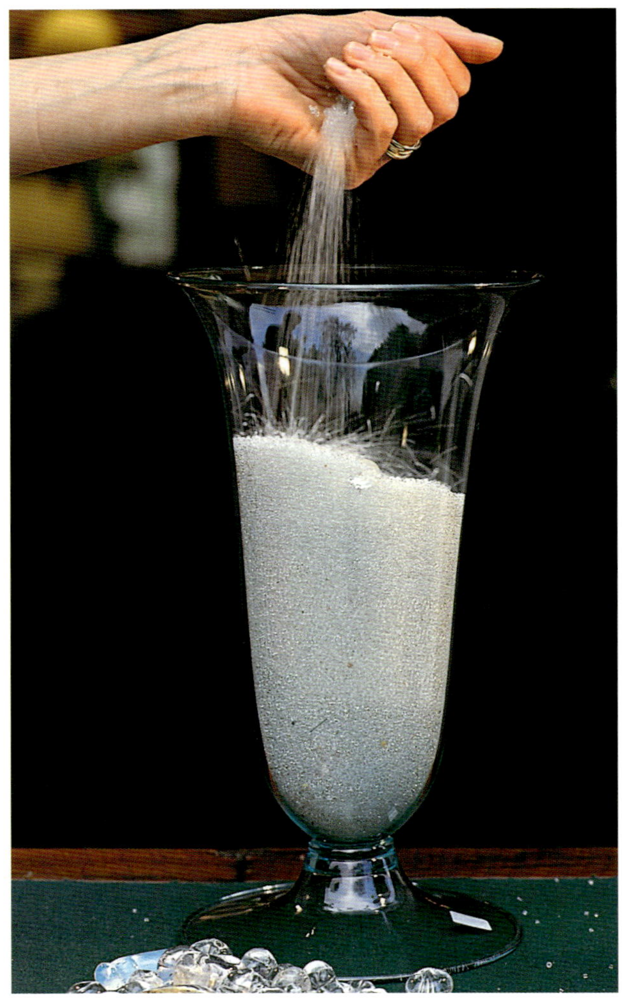

We will achieve even better results if the flowers reflect and multiply in a mirror. Round or cylindrical vases are ideal for round *compositions to be displayed in the center of tables in large rooms. If we want to show only the* front *of the composition, then cylindrical, square, or even rectangular vases, rather than round ones, would be more suitable. A vase with a vertical shape will be ideal for* column-type *compositions that echo the lines of the vase.*

When arranging flowers, position the large flowers first, as they will give a first, general scale to the composition. Often, all you need are one or two centrally placed flowers, with the rest of the flowers arranged along the border of the vase.

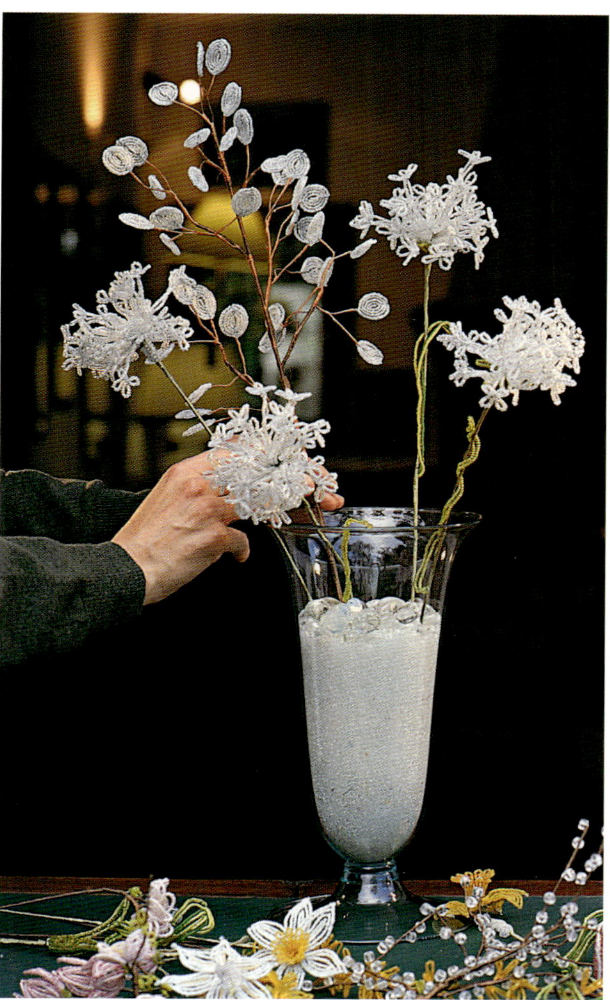

In the photographs on these pages, a clear glass vase is filled to about two thirds of its height with small glass marbles; if the container is opaque and the stems are not visible, sand instead of marbles or pebbles could be used. Synthetic sponges such as those used in flower shops are also a good choice for opaque containers, or even a light metal net resting in the neck of the vase. Lacking these, the stems may be placed criss-cross so that they hold each other up, but this is only a temporary solution.

Add the remaining flowers one by one, filling in the empty spaces, until the arrangement is complete (see following page). A slight asymmetry will add a natural look. The vase is by Archimede Seguso.

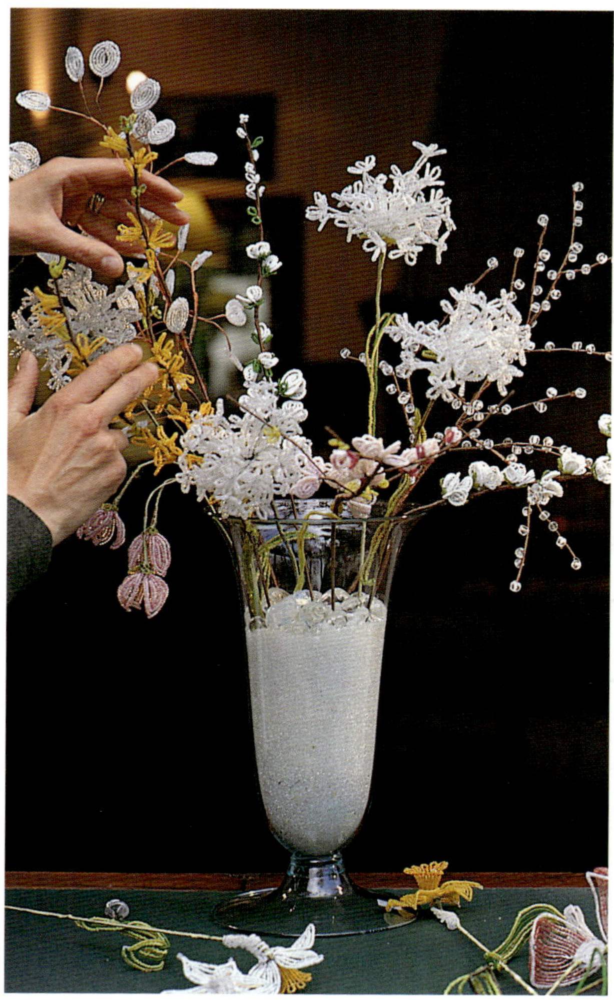

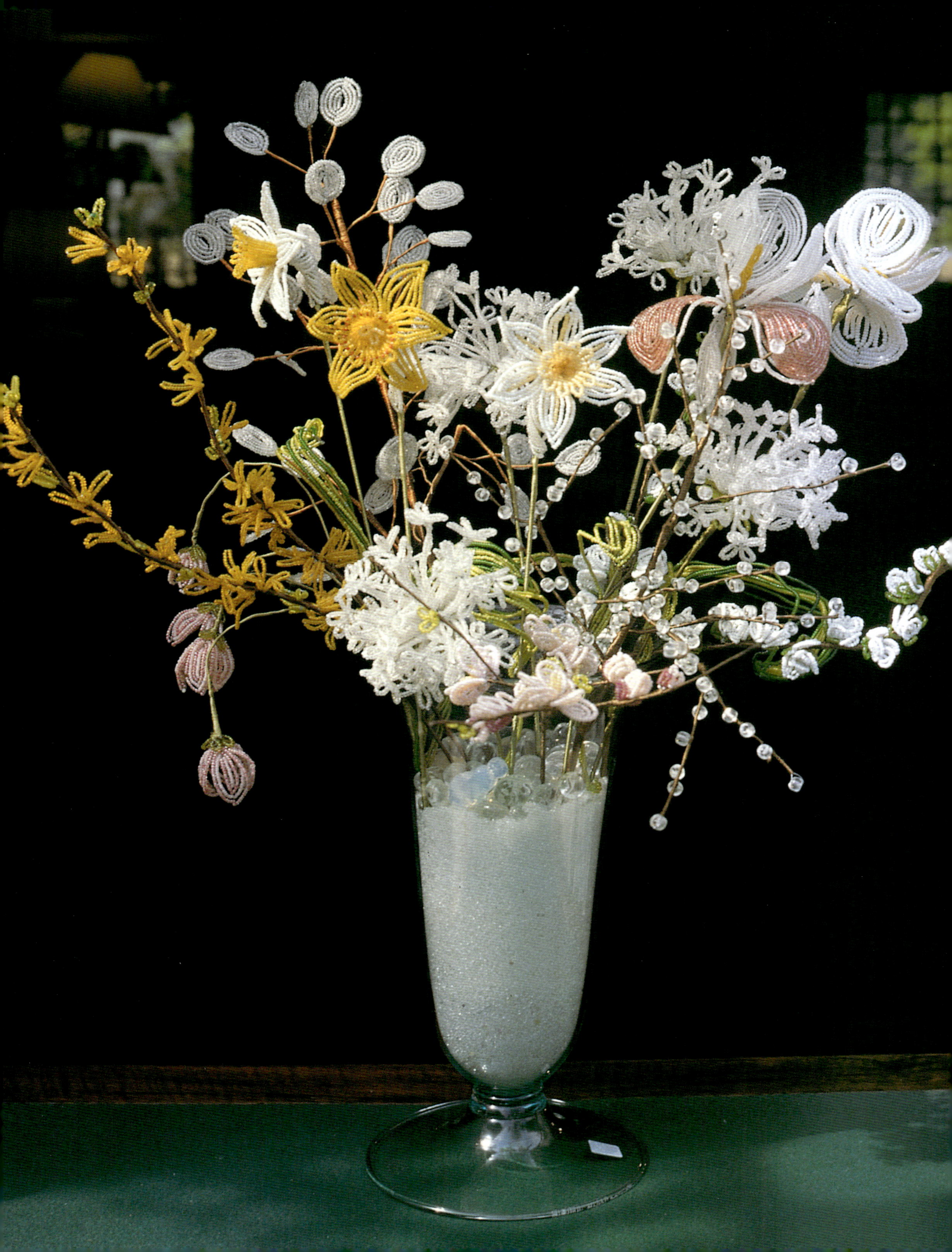

Cleaning the Flowers

Since glass does not deteriorate, glass bead flowers have a long life, but they will become dusty and turn opaque, giving the bouquet an old, tired look.

To prevent this, the flowers should be cleaned regularly, using a soft feather duster to remove all dust particles. If this is not enough, they should be washed.

When you wash them, try to do it outdoors on a sunny day. Wash the flowers one by one using a mild dish detergent and a soft brush, such as a toothbrush, then rinse them carefully in abundant water and dry them in the sun. They will revert to their original brilliance and shine. Try not to wet the stems because wet silk deteriorates easily.

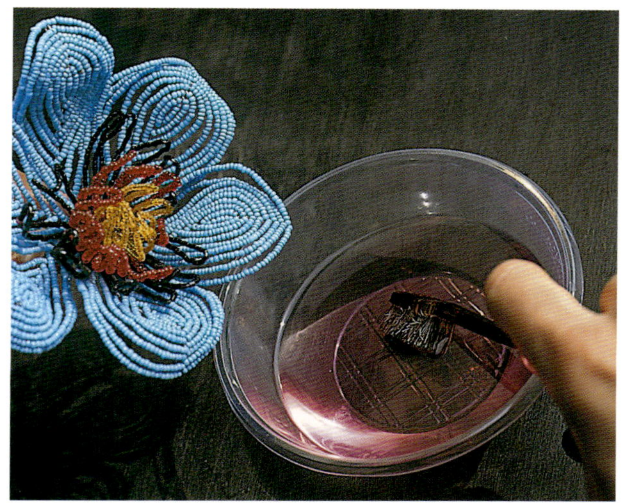

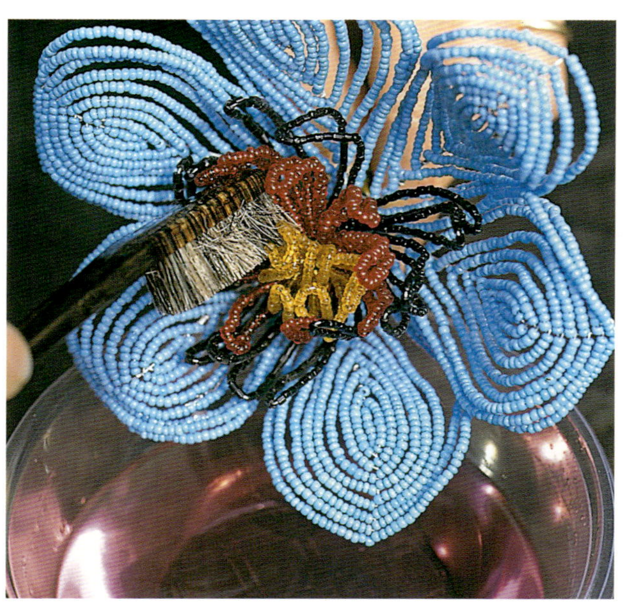

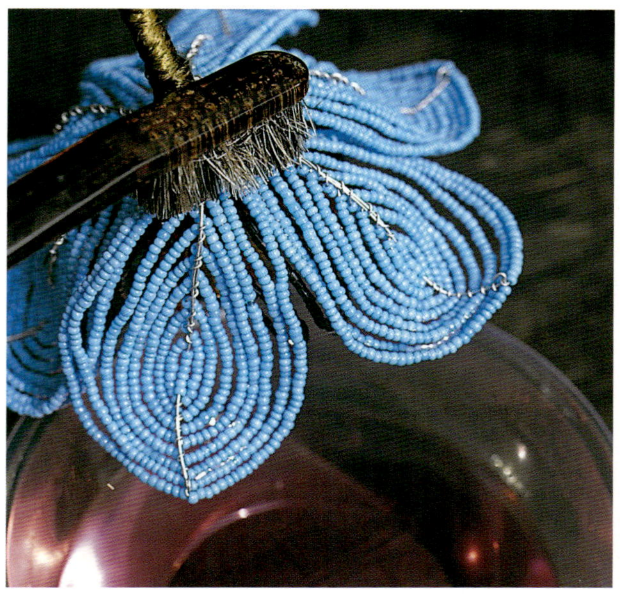

If for some reason you cannot wash the flowers, they may also be dry cleaned. To do this, moisten a soft toothbrush with household alcohol. You may use a little peroxide for very dirty parts, since its foam will lift even deep-seated dirt.

We now turn our attention to the creation of the flowers.

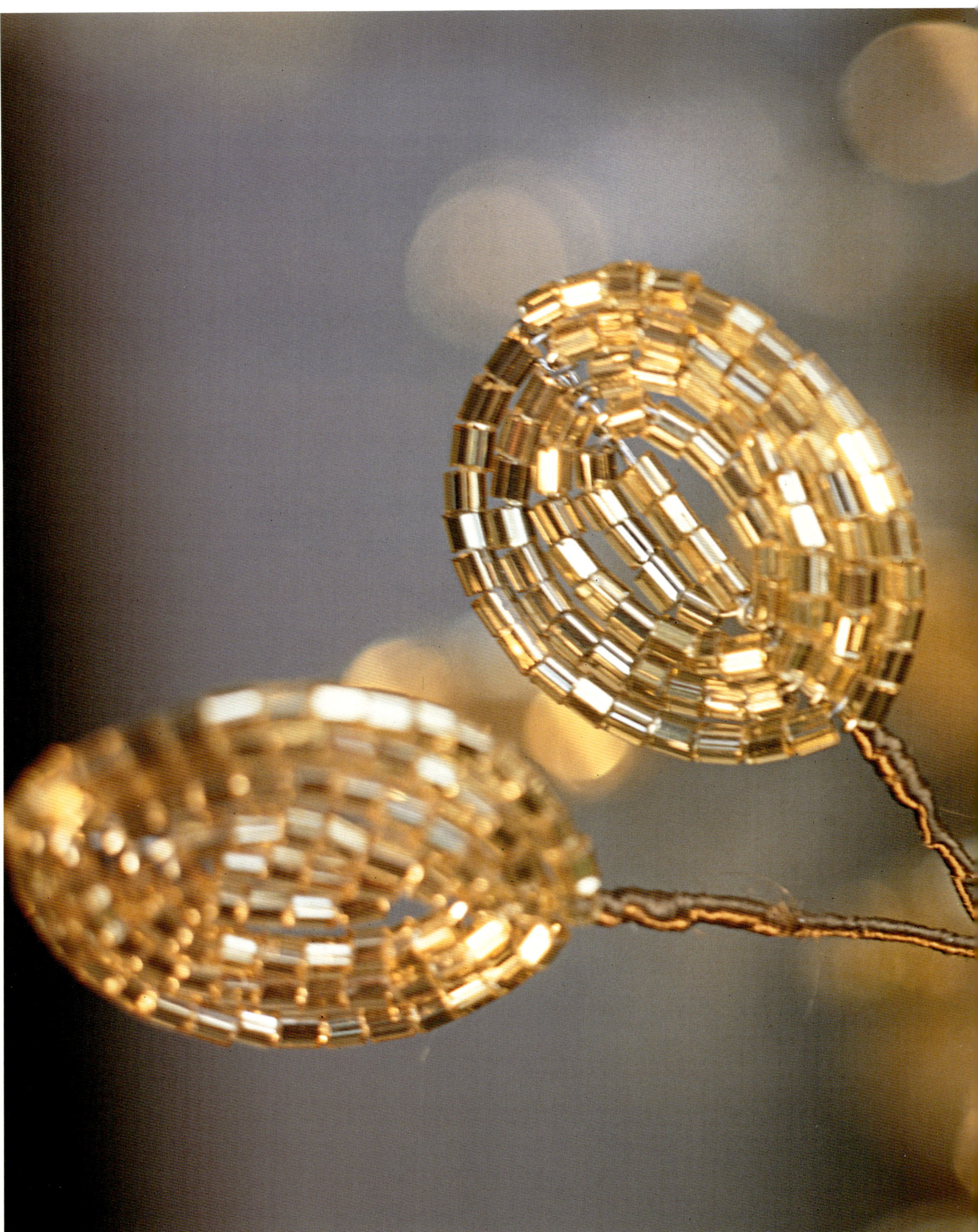

3 CHAPTER

Working Techniques

We are going to begin with the simplest techniques, gradually moving on to more advanced work. Each flower requires a specific technique. Nature offers a different spectacle each month of the year, an incredibly rich kaleidoscope of colors, tones, and scents. From the January calycanthus to the red berries of the December mistletoe, we can reproduce the flowers and foliage of any season, fixing them in time. In the following pages, we will show you the different steps for making each flower. For visual simplicity, we have connected the sequence of steps with a string of beads visible in the background.

1. *Slide ⅓ inch of crystal beads onto a 24 or 26 gauge wire, 6 inches long. This wire will be the leaf's central rib, and is called the "core."*

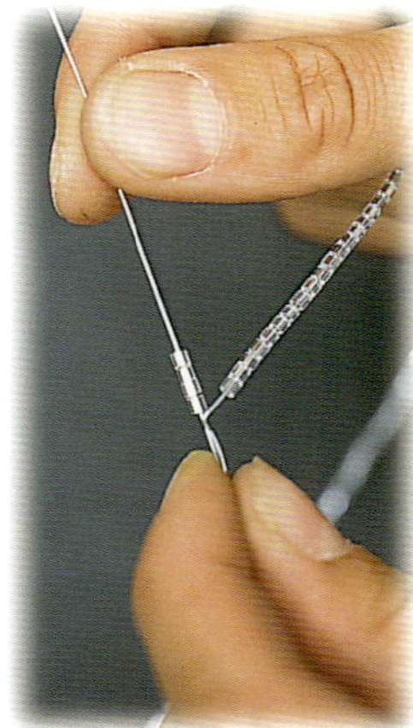

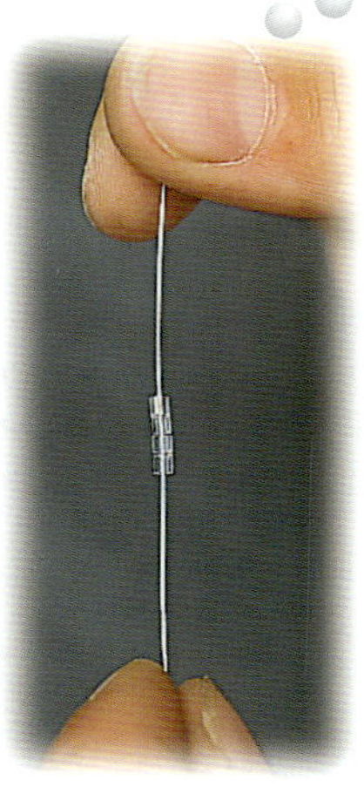

2. *Twist a fully beaded string twice around the core wire, immediately below the beads, to prevent the beads from slipping. As you twist it, hold the core with your left hand and the beaded string with your right.*

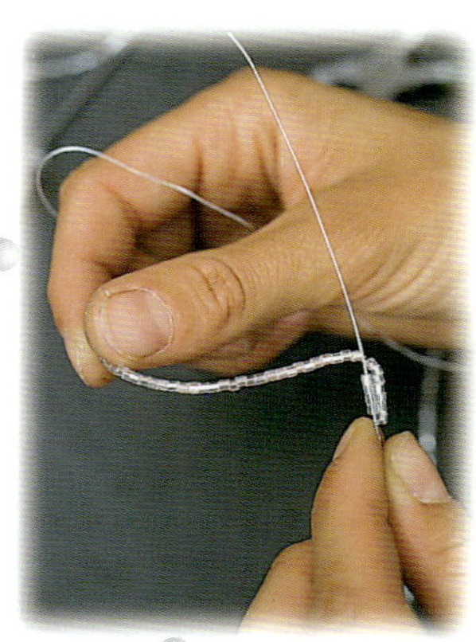

3. *Place the beaded string, (remember this refers to the pre-beaded wire), parallel to the core and twist it again immediately above the beads. It's a difficult movement that will become easier as you gain experience.*

The Satinpod

The satinpod, also known as moonwort or honesty (a plant of the genus Lunaria), is a charming ornamental plant; once it has been dried and cleaned of seeds and integuments (the leaves' thin enveloping layers), its slender white leaves are transparent to the light. To create them, we can use white iridescent beads, clear crystal, or silver or gold beads. Generally, this plant is used for large compositions, since it provides volume without much weight.

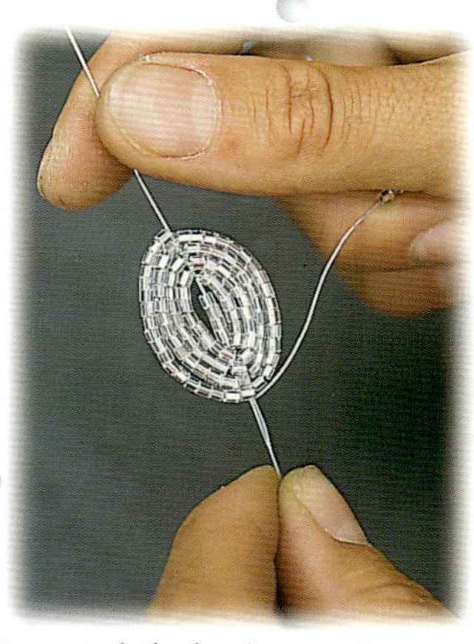

4. *Now wind the bead-covered string four times around the core, shaping the leaf as you go along. Remember to twist the string around the core wire each time they meet.*

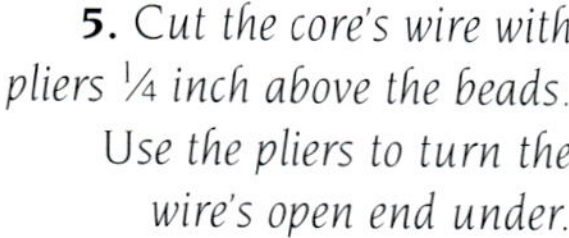

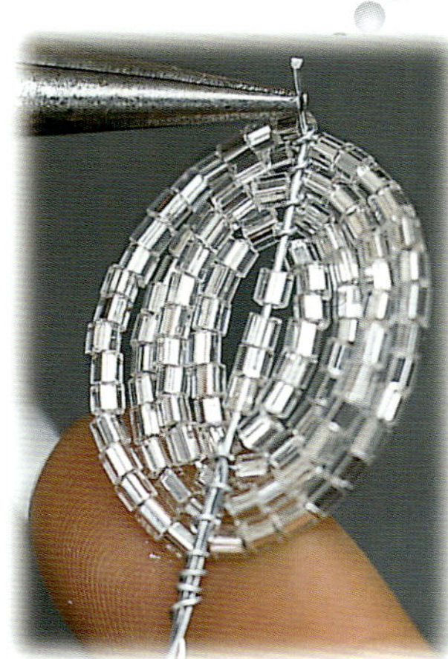

5. *Cut the core's wire with pliers ¼ inch above the beads. Use the pliers to turn the wire's open end under.*

6. *On the back of the leaf, the twists of the beaded string that are wound around the core are clearly visible. The most difficult part is remembering to apply even pressure, because too much pressure might bend the wires.*

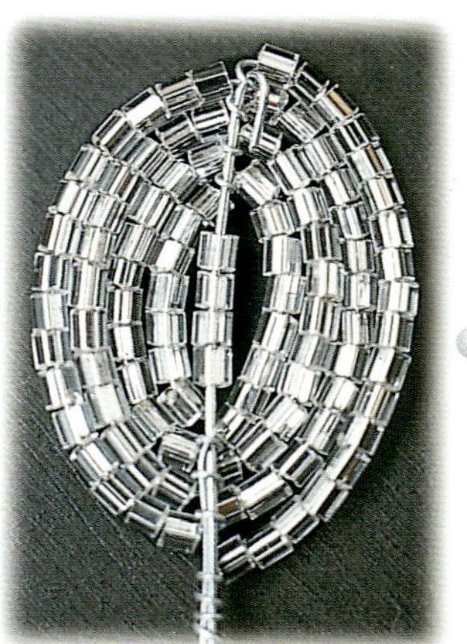

MATERIALS

- 9 strings of crystal beads
- 45 22 gauge wires, 6 inches long
- 6 rolled wires, 20 gauge, 14 inches long
- 1 round rod, 18 gauge, 20 inches long
- Brown silk twist, vinyl glue, pliers.

7. *Using brown silk twist, cover the stems of all 45 leaves. Use a bit of vinyl glue at the beginning to fasten the silk to the wire.*

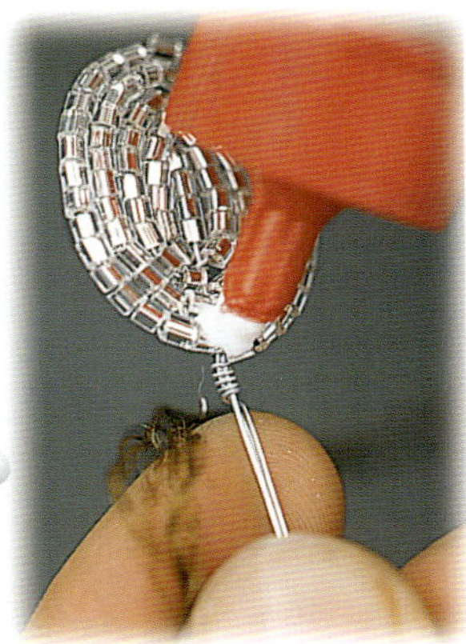

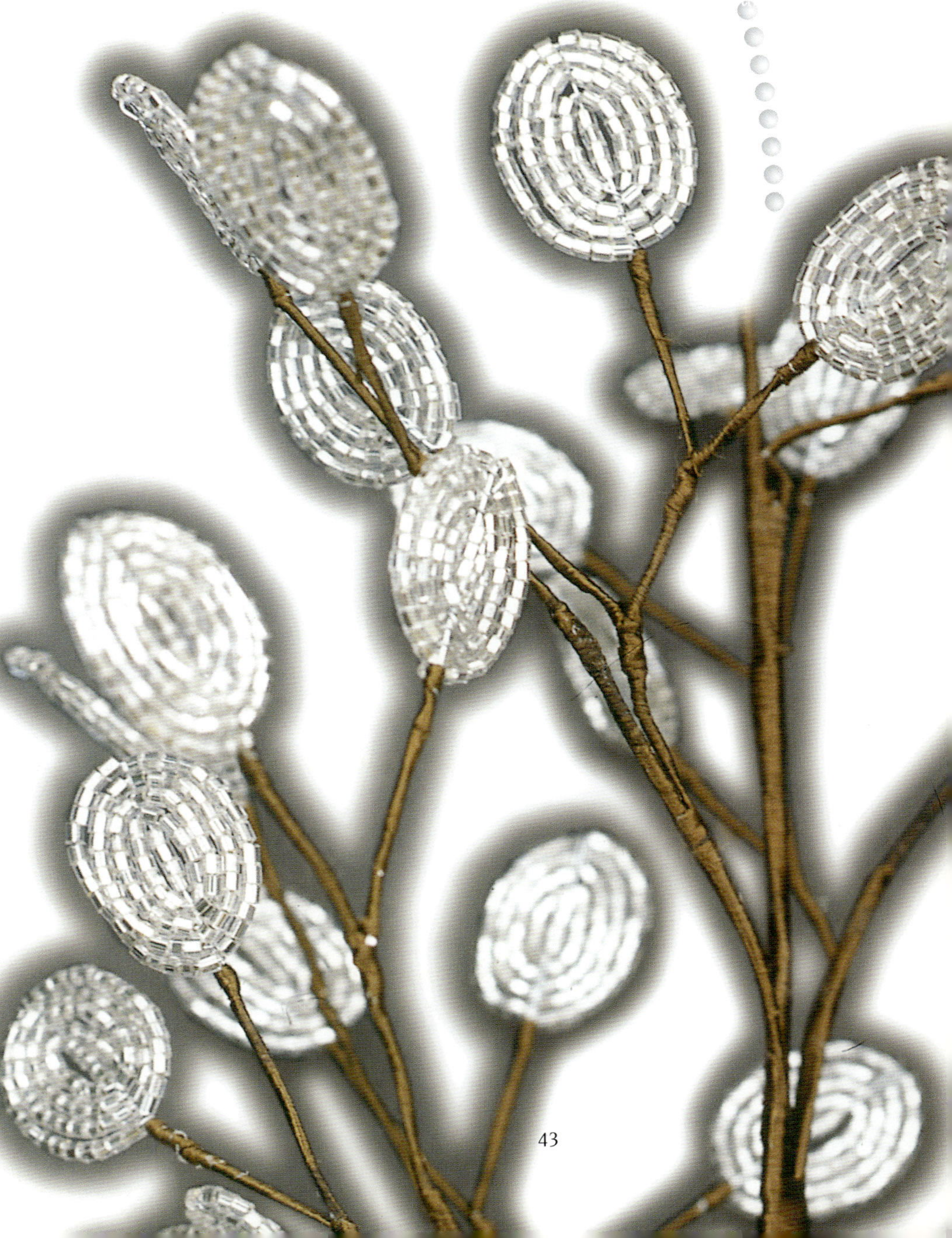

8. *Once all the stems have been wound with silk for about 1½ inches, secure the silk with a bit of vinyl glue.*

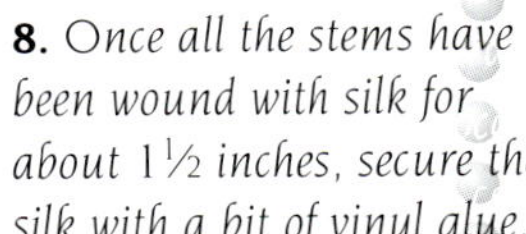

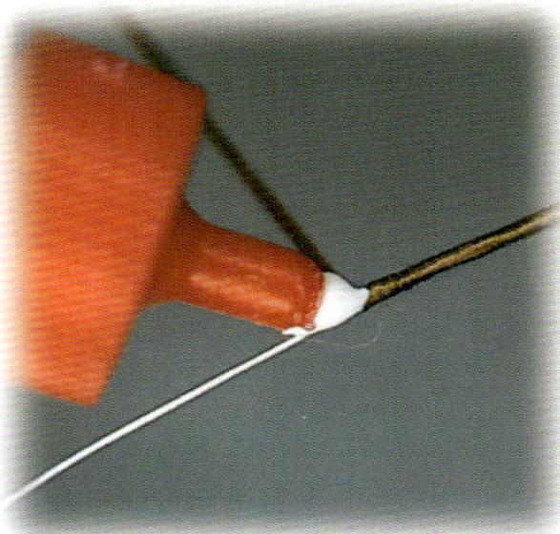

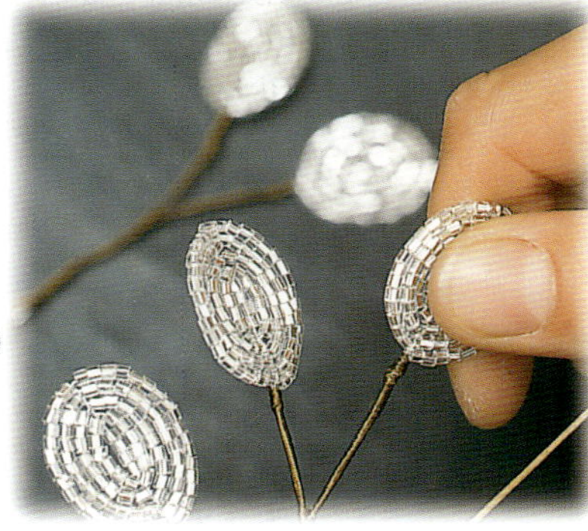

9. *Fasten the leaves to the branches: use two or three leaves for each branch. To make the branches, use 20 gauge wire stems, about 6 inches long. You will need six branches.*

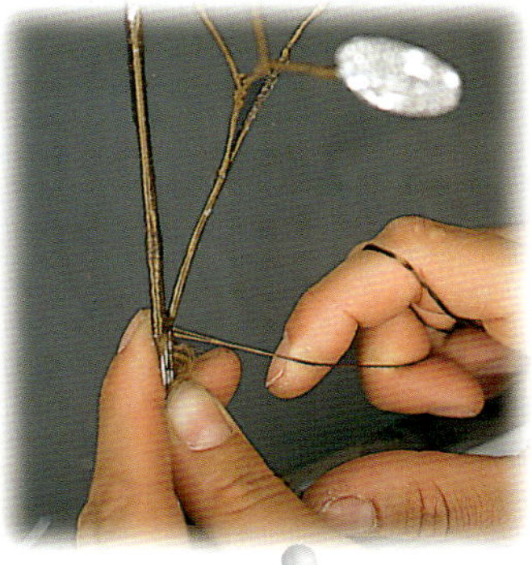

10. *Place the branches on the main stem, which is an 18 gauge, 20 inch long rod. Position the branches by alternating them, starting from the top.*

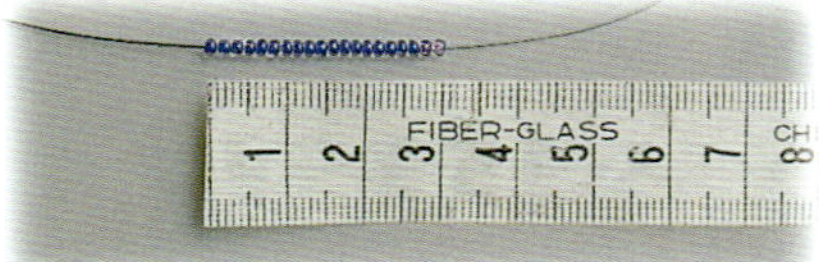

1. Start with the three base petals in a lilac color. String 1 1/4 inches of beads on a 22 gauge, 6 inch long wire. This will be the core of the petal.

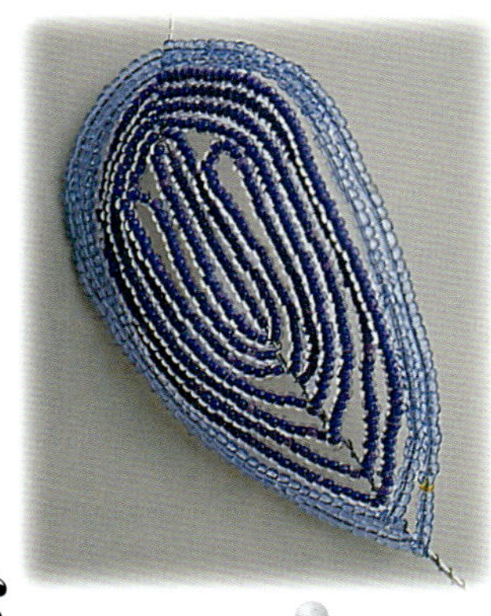

6. The finished petal is 2 inches wide, with a pointed bottom where it joins the stem and a rounded top.

The Iris

Florence was the first city to use the fragrance of this flower in perfumes; in the eighteenth century, the iris was called "flame;" today, it continues to be a symbol of hope. To make an iris you will need nine petals: three for the top part—transparent, light, upward petals; three intensely colored, fleshy base petals that arch toward the floor; three transparent sepals at the base to close the flower on the stem; and finally, a long, green leaf that winds around the stem.

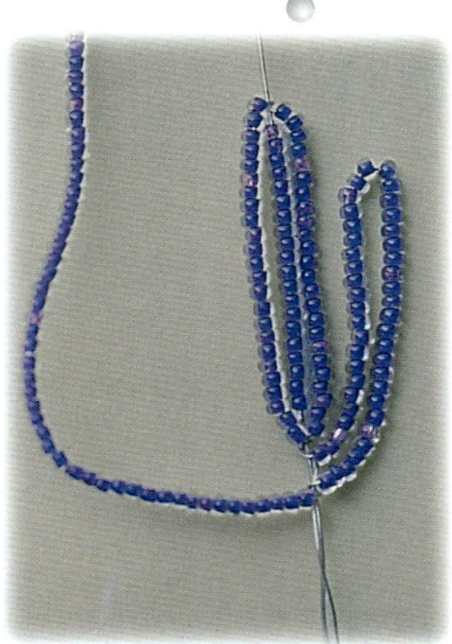

2. Take a 24 or 26 gauge wire that has been fully strung with beads and wind it around the petal core once; now make two loops on each side of the core, parallel to it, to widen the petal in the center.

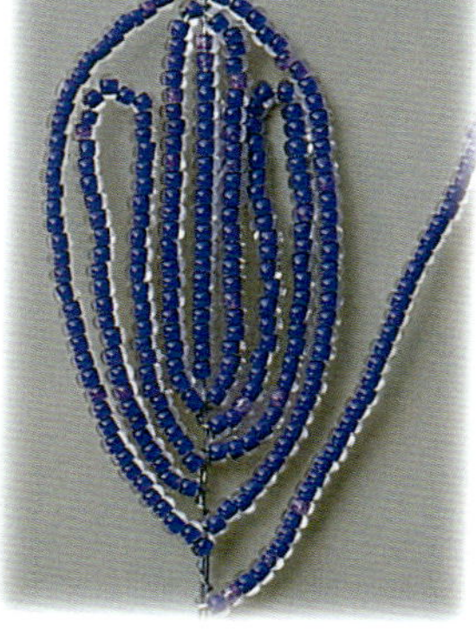

3. Using the same beaded string, continue building the petal winding it five times around the core. Twist the beaded string twice at the bottom of the petal to give it its characteristic pointed shape.

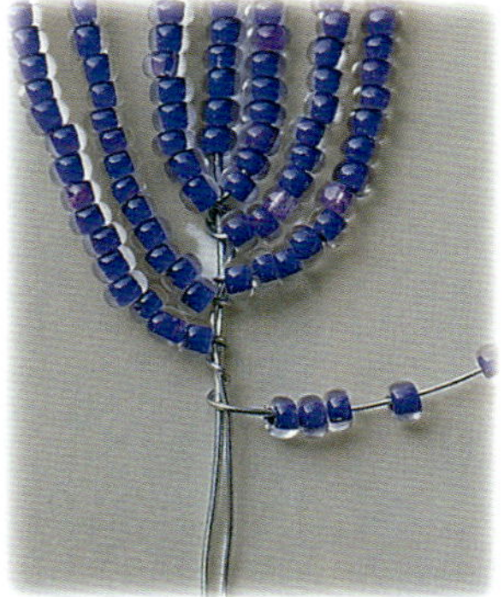

4. From the back, the double twists that form the pointed bottom of the petal are clearly visible. While this operation is somewhat difficult at first, a little patience will produce the desired effect.

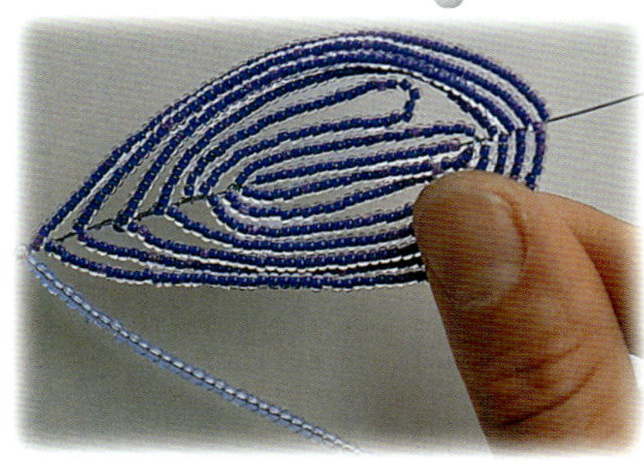

5. To create variety, use beads of a different color for the last two rounds. In this case, we used the same light blue beads as the top petals.

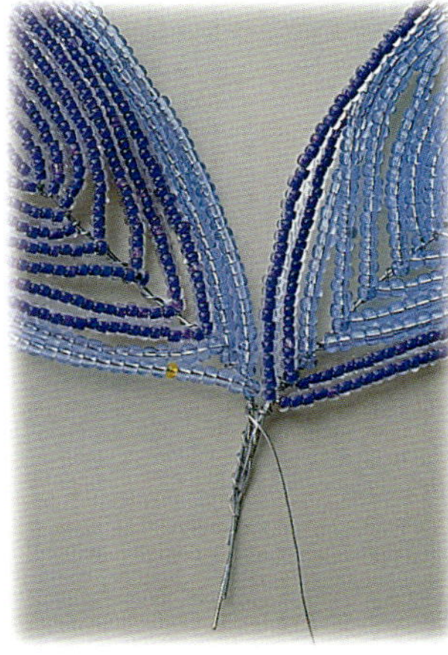

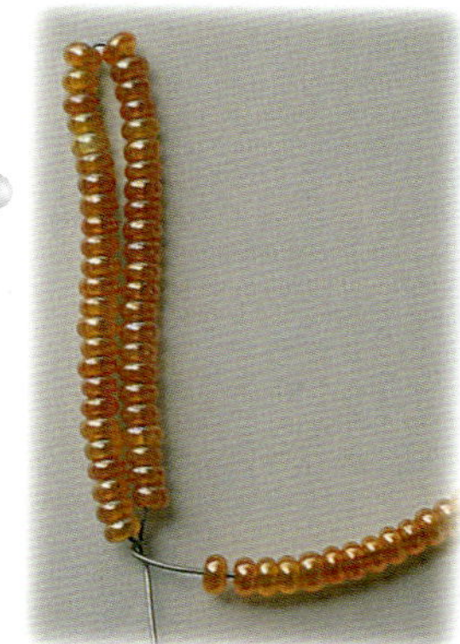

8. *Make an orange flame for the center of the iris. Build a narrow, 1½ inch loop with the orange-beaded string and secure it by twisting the two wires together.*

7. *To make the light blue top petals, use the same procedure as for the lilac petals. Likewise, use beads of a different color (this time, lilac) for the last two rows of the petal.*

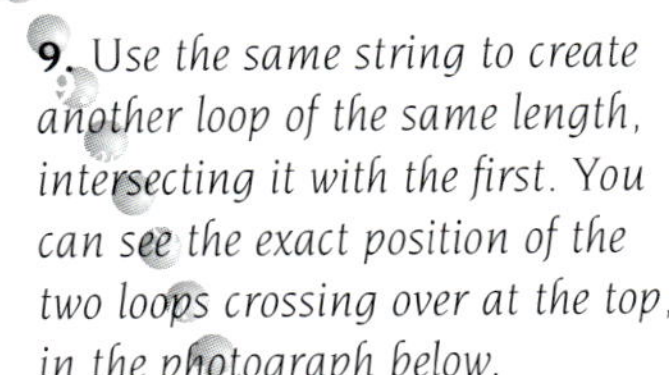

9. *Use the same string to create another loop of the same length, intersecting it with the first. You can see the exact position of the two loops crossing over at the top, in the photograph below.*

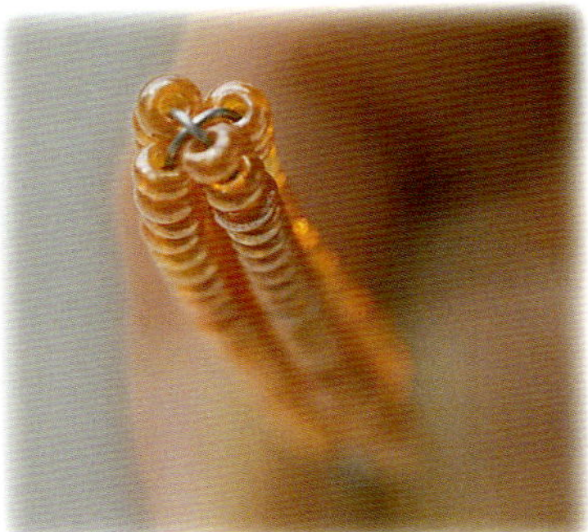

MATERIALS

- 4 strings of lilac beads.
- 4 strings of azure blue beads
- 2 strings of orange beads
- 1 strings of crystal beads
- 2 strings of green beads
- 12 wires: 22 gauge, 6 inches long
- 1 round rod, 18 gauge, 20 inches long
- Pale green silk twist, vinyl glue, pliers.

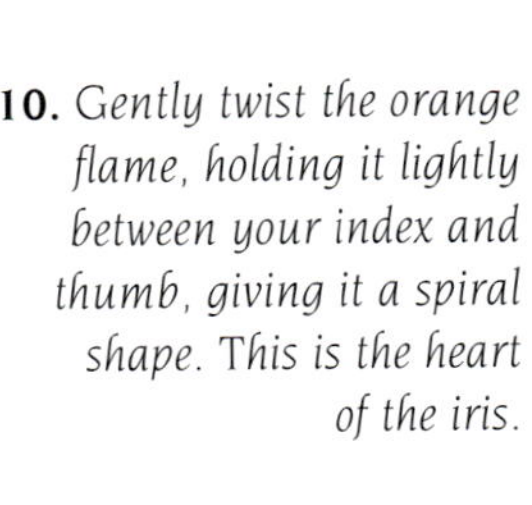

10. *Gently twist the orange flame, holding it lightly between your index and thumb, giving it a spiral shape. This is the heart of the iris.*

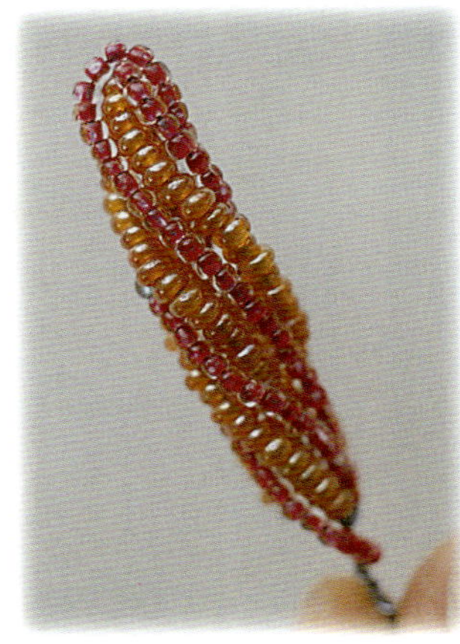

14. *The flower's green leaf that winds around the stem is long and double pointed. The core is 5 inches long and to create the leaf you need to wind three or four rounds of beaded string around the core.*

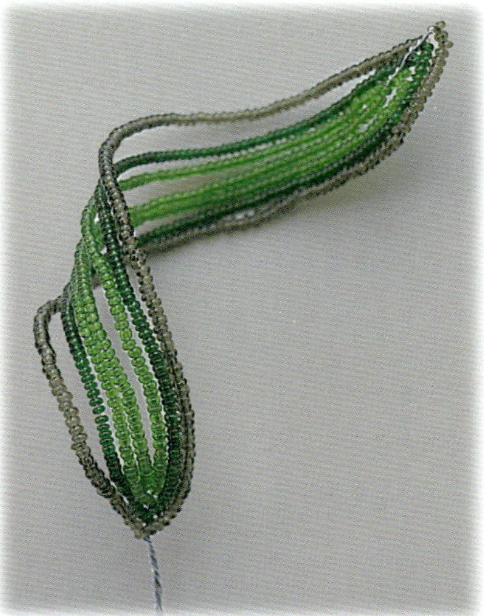

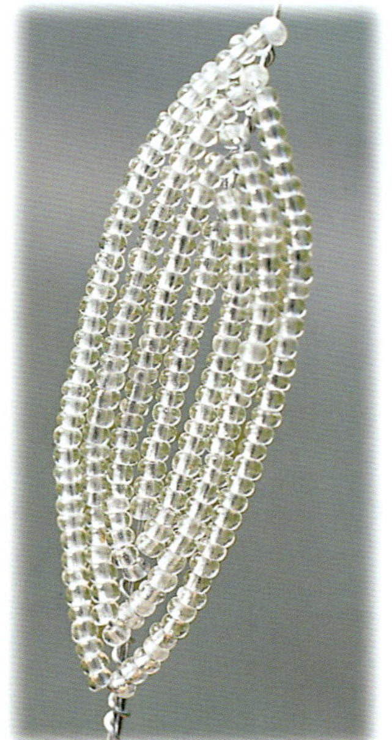

13. *Use three clear crystal sepals to close the flower's corolla. Slide 1¼ inches of crystal beads onto the sepal's core. Now take the crystal-beaded string and wind it three times around the core, shaping the tip as well as the bottom of the leaf as you see in the photograph at left.*

12. *Because of the small size of this flame, wind the orange string around the core only once. Using the pliers, fasten the orange flame to the petal, securing all the end wires.*

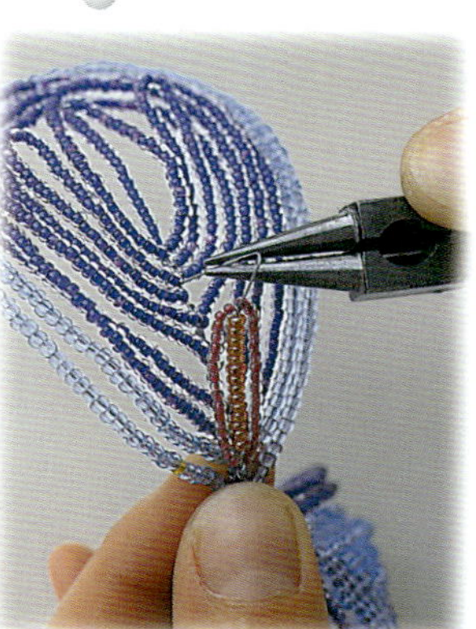

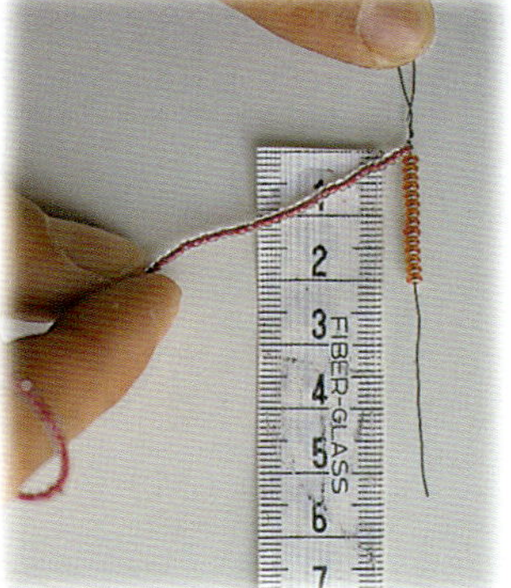

11. *To heighten the color contrast on the petals, add small colored accents to the lilac petals. Make the core by using ¾ of an inch of orange beads strung on a 22 gauge wire.*

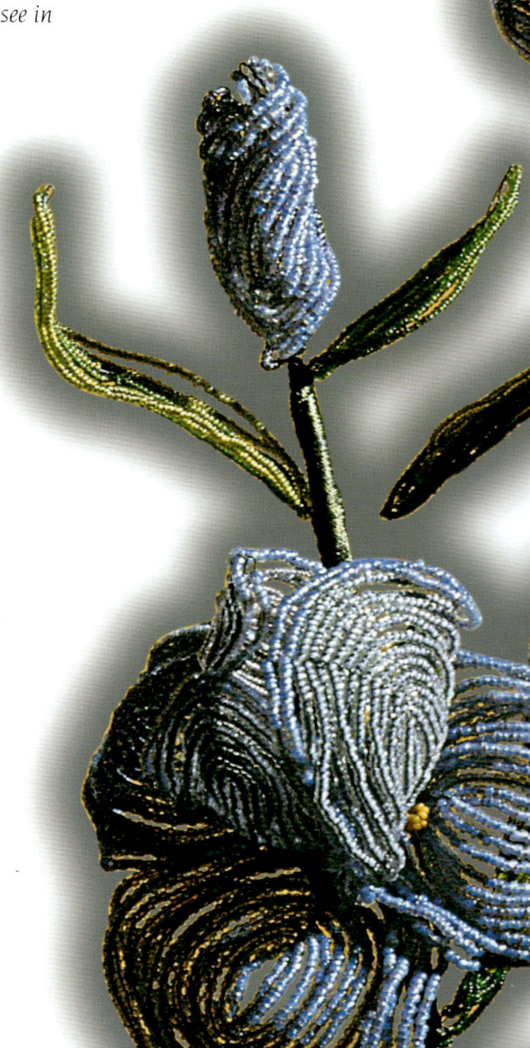

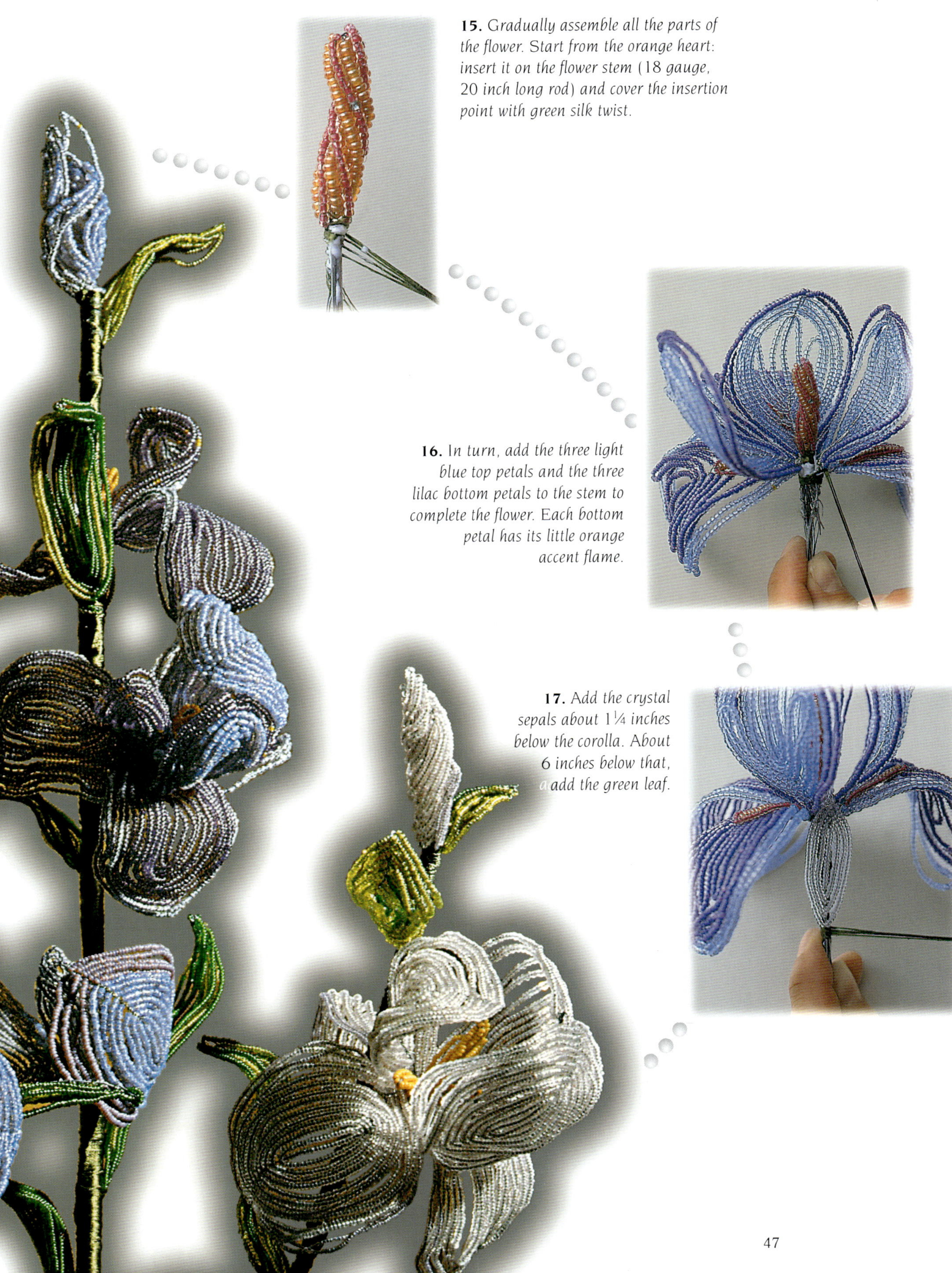

15. *Gradually assemble all the parts of the flower. Start from the orange heart: insert it on the flower stem (18 gauge, 20 inch long rod) and cover the insertion point with green silk twist.*

16. *In turn, add the three light blue top petals and the three lilac bottom petals to the stem to complete the flower. Each bottom petal has its little orange accent flame.*

17. *Add the crystal sepals about $1\frac{1}{4}$ inches below the corolla. About 6 inches below that, add the green leaf.*

The Red Rose

Because of the abundant selection of red and pink beads available, we can use many kinds of colors to create roses with delicate, ethereal shades and roses with strong, fleshy hues. The procedure for making a rose is simple, though somewhat lengthy because of the large number of petals involved. The flower is built starting from the center. We start with the center button whose color contrasts with that of the petals, and gradually build the petals from the inside out. In all, there are three rows of petals in a rose: small, medium, and large, all of the same shape but different size. The flower's corolla is closed by a collar of five pointed sepals, and the stem has two small side branches, each bearing five leaves.

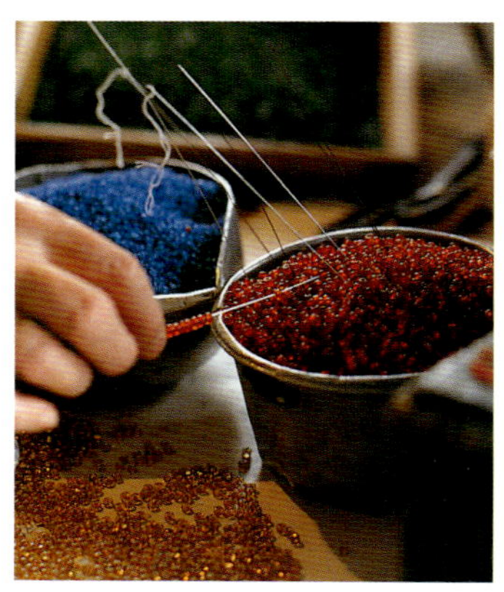

1. *To create rose petals, use the procedure for making round leaves. The four small petals are made by sliding ¾ of an inch of light red beads on a 22 gauge wire (the core), then winding a beaded string of the same color three times around the core, plus a final round using a darker red beaded string to give a sharp outline to the petal.*

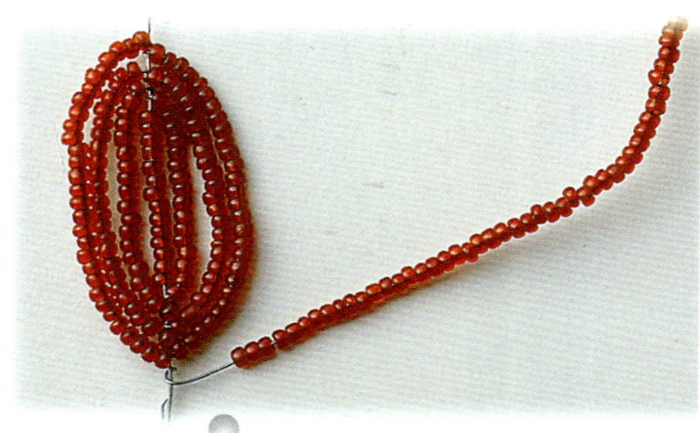

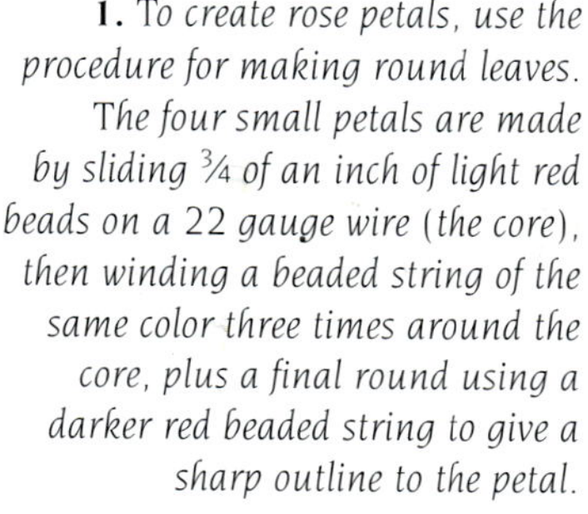

2. *The four medium size petals have a 1¼ inch core. They have four rounds of pale red beads plus two outside rounds of darker red beads. We use two shades of red to give shading and depth to the flower.*

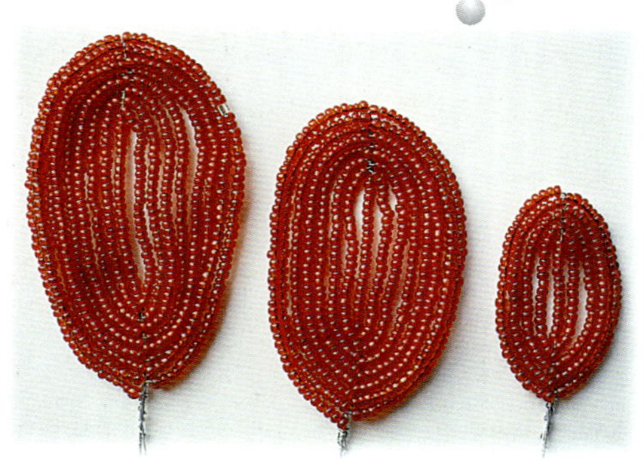

3. *The rose has five large petals. For each petal, slide 1½ inches of pale red beads onto the core wire; around the core wind five rounds of pale red beads plus two rounds of darker red beads to outline the petal.*

4. *To make the collar use pale green beads; you will need five double-pointed leaves made with the usual technique. Slide about ½ inch of green beads onto the core of each leaf and then wind the beaded string around it twice.*

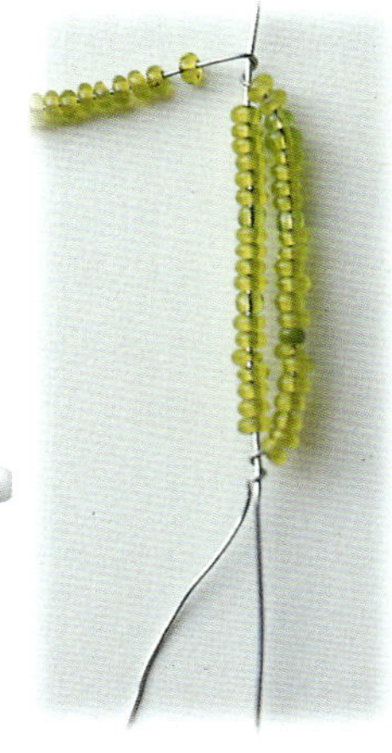

MATERIALS

- 6 strings of light red beads
- 4 strings of dark red beads
- 1 string of yellow beads
- 5 strings of pale green beads
- 28 22 gauge wires, 5 inches long
- 2 wires, 20 gauge, 8 inches long
- 1 round rod, 18 gauge, 20 inches long
- pale green silk twist, vinyl glue, pliers
- 1 crystal bead

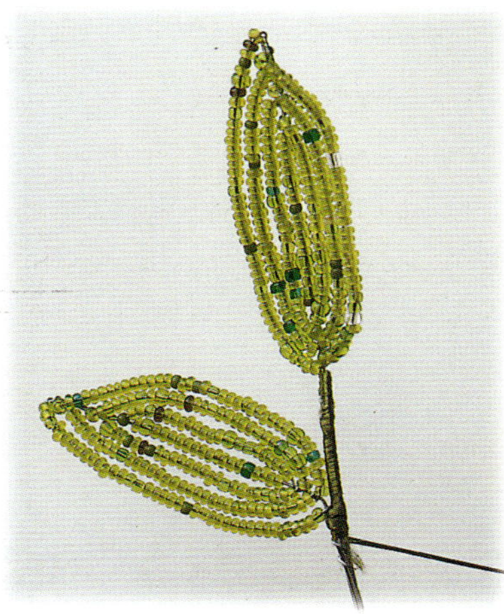

5. *The stem's leaves are made using the same procedure as the collar sepals. You need 10 stem leaves, all double pointed. Slide 1 inch of pale green beads onto the core of each leaf, then take a beaded string and wind it three times around the core.*

6. *To assemble the flower, first prepare the lateral branches. For each branch, take a thick, 20 gauge rod, insert five leaves alternating on each side of the branch, using silk twist to fasten them. Place the first leaf at the top of the branch, and the other leaves at a distance of about 1 to 1½ inches each.*

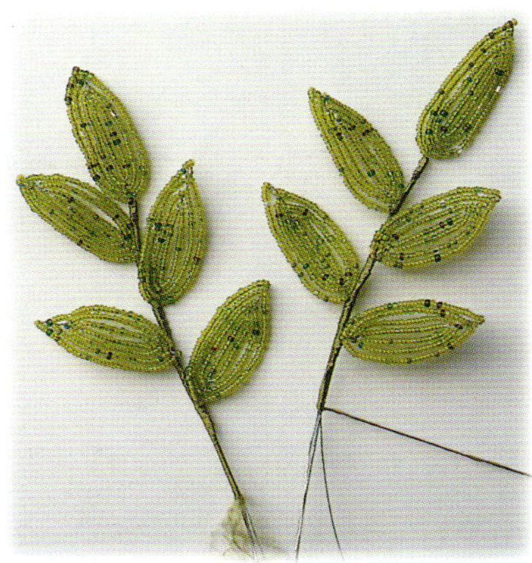

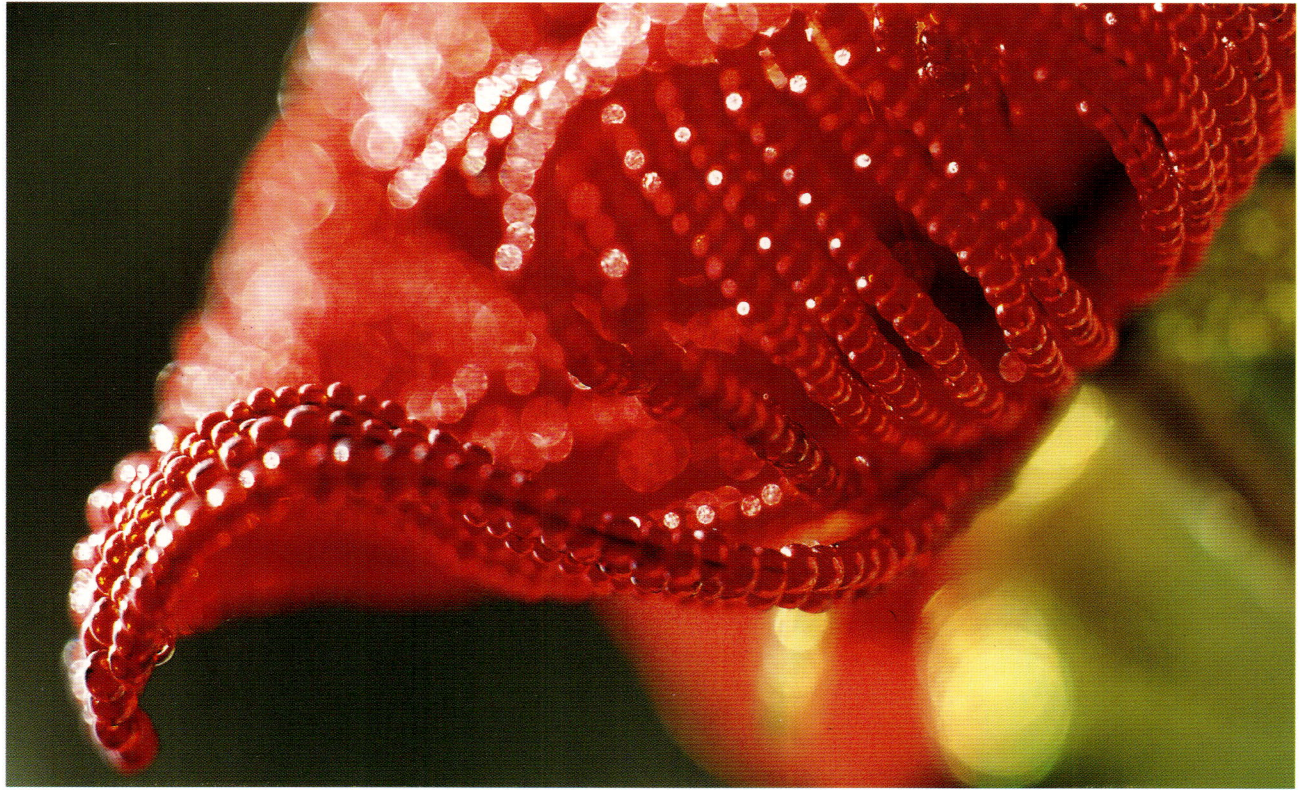

7. *Using the yellow bead string, shape five small loops, each ¾ of an inch in length. Using the pliers, pull the wire of the five loops to give them a curved shape. Twist the ends of the wires together to fasten them, then add a large crystal bead in the center.*

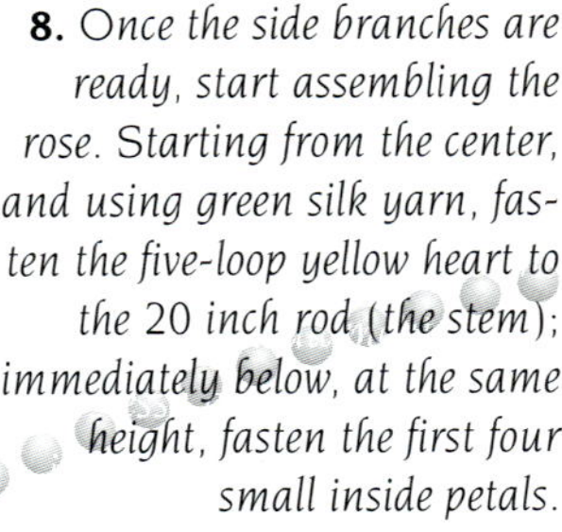

8. *Once the side branches are ready, start assembling the rose. Starting from the center, and using green silk yarn, fasten the five-loop yellow heart to the 20 inch rod (the stem); immediately below, at the same height, fasten the first four small inside petals.*

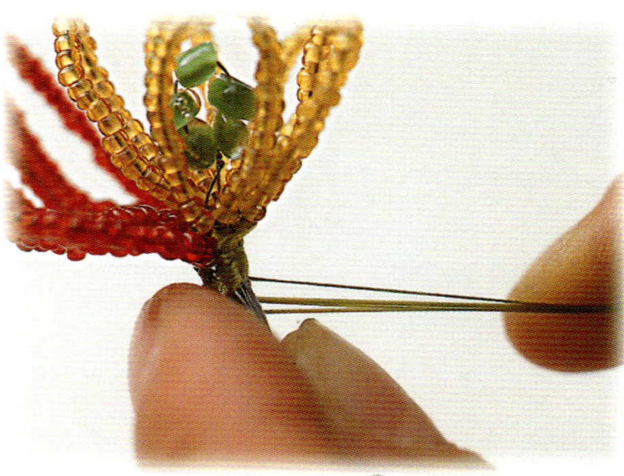

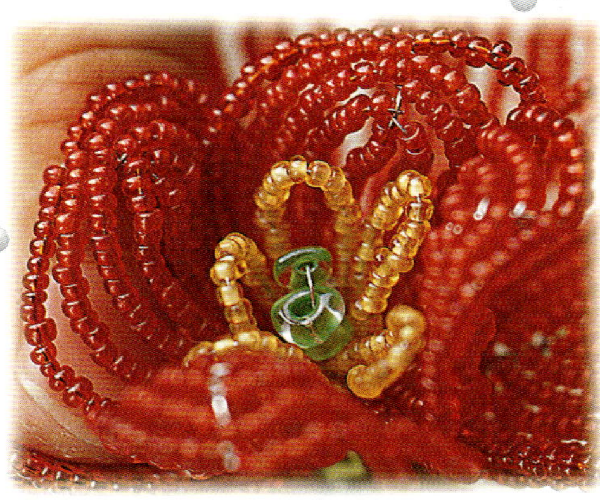

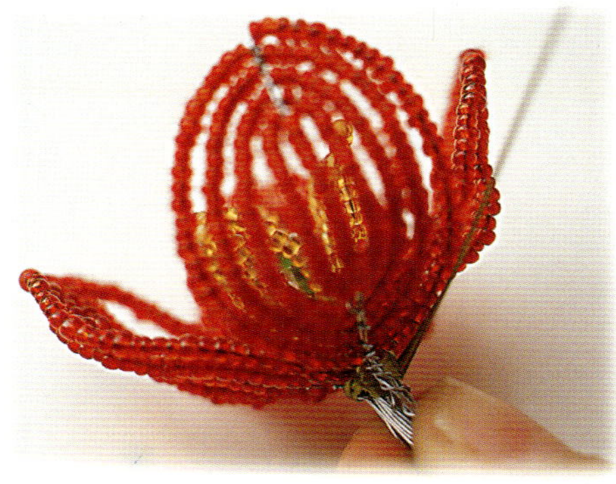

9. *Immediately below the first four petals fasten the four medium sized petals, and below them the five large ones.*

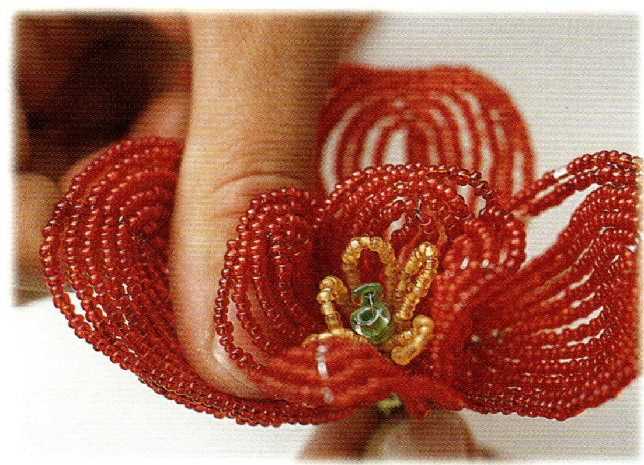

10. *Complete the flower's corolla by adding the green collar underneath consisting of the five double-pointed green sepals. Use your thumbs to shape the petals to the desired shape.*

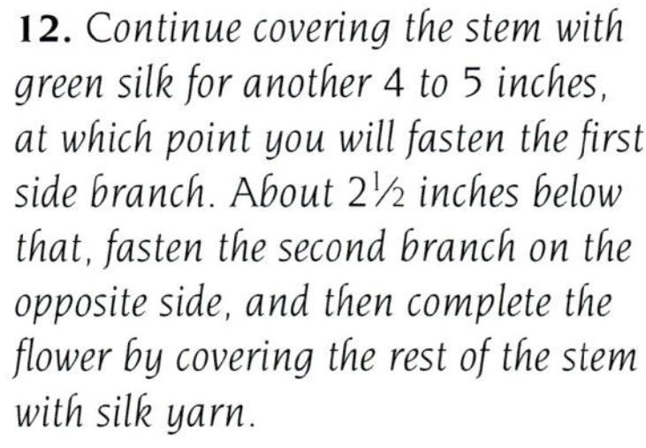

12. *Continue covering the stem with green silk for another 4 to 5 inches, at which point you will fasten the first side branch. About 2½ inches below that, fasten the second branch on the opposite side, and then complete the flower by covering the rest of the stem with silk yarn.*

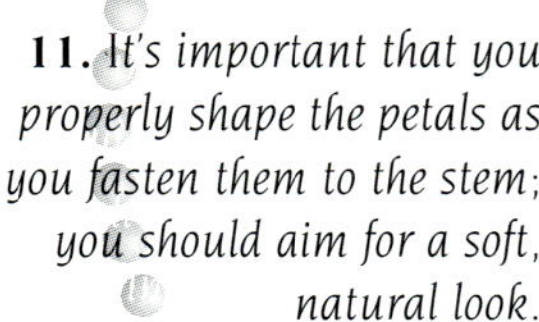

11. *It's important that you properly shape the petals as you fasten them to the stem; you should aim for a soft, natural look.*

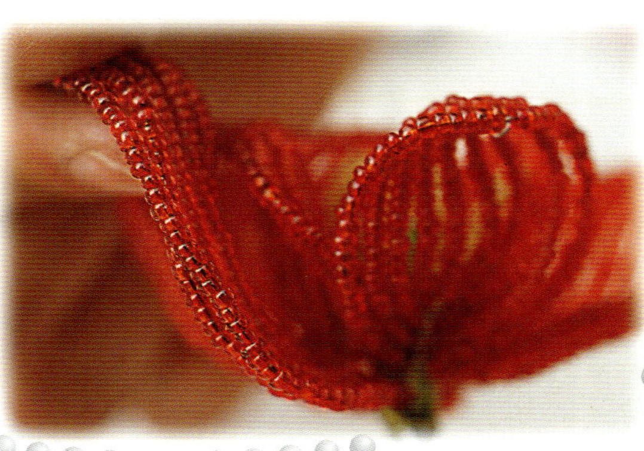

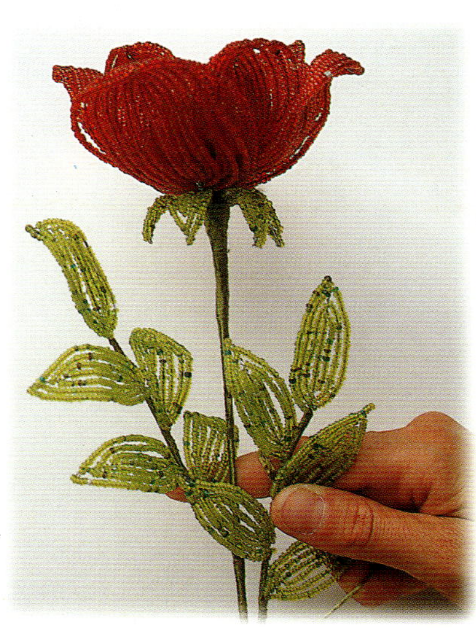

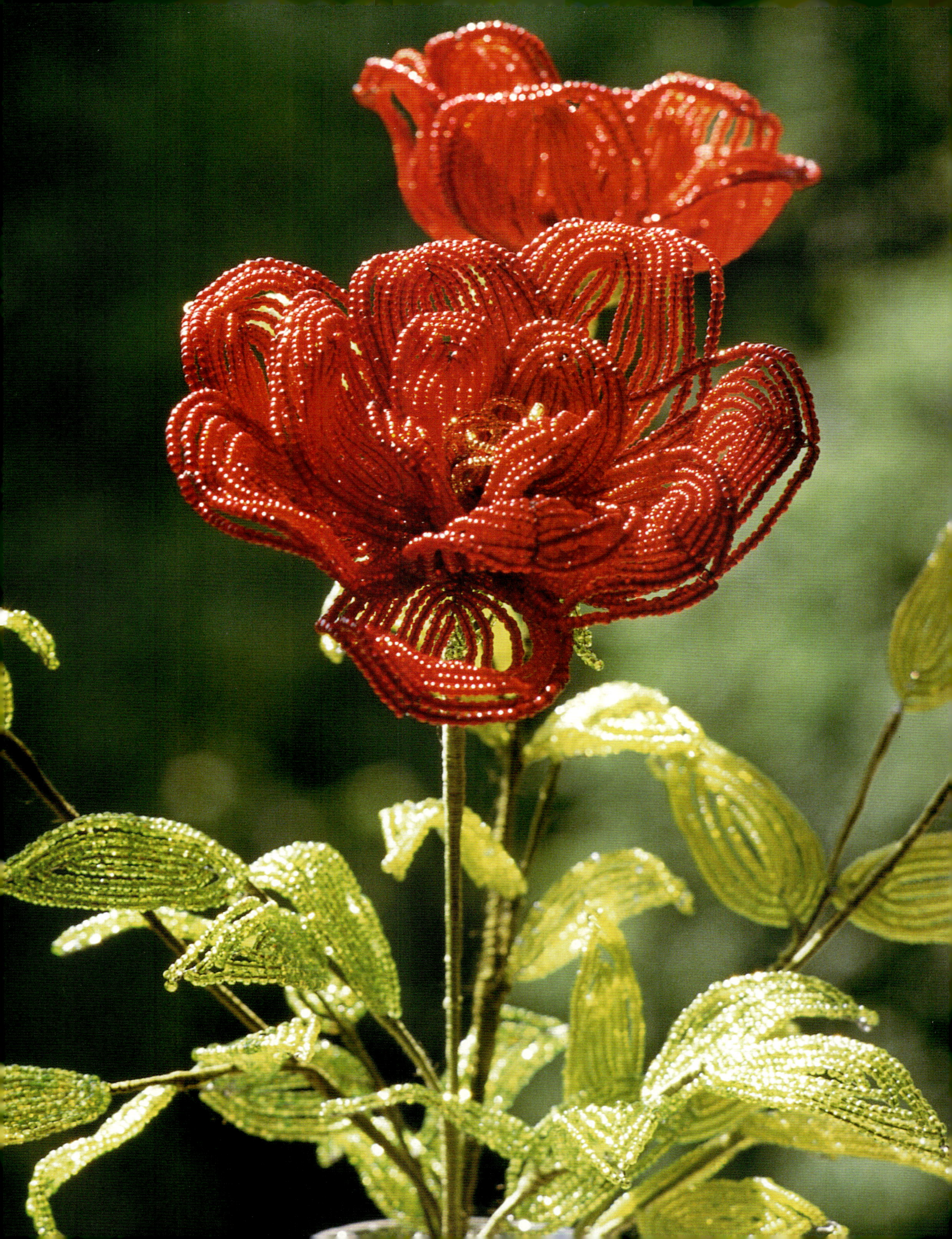

MATERIALS

- 6 strings of white enamel paste beads
- 2 strings of white mother-of-pearl beads
- 1 string of transparent yellow beads
- 2 strings of transparent green beads
- 14 22 gauge wires, 5 inches long
- 3 wires: 24-26 gauge, 6 inches long, each strung with white enamel paste beads for 2 inches and with transparent yellow beads for 1½ inches
- 2 wires, 20 gauge, 6 inches long
- 1 round rod, 18 gauge, 20 inches long
- pale green silk twist, vinyl glue, pliers.

1. *The lily is composed of 6 white double-pointed petals, each with a core 2 inches long and about 1¼ inches wide. For a softer, luminous look, we suggest you use white mother-of-pearl beads for the two outer rows of each petal.*

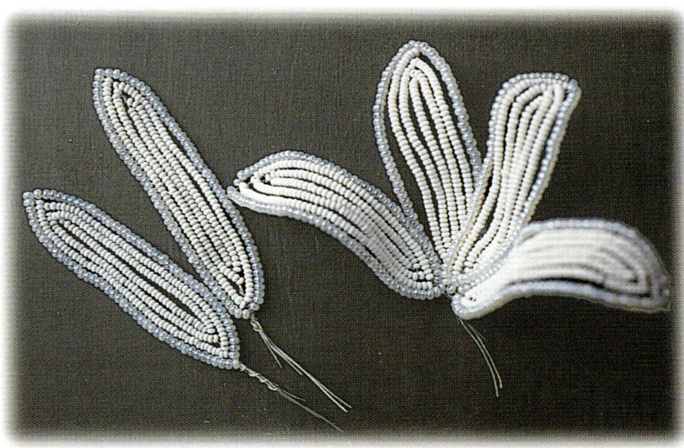

The Lily

Creating a lily with glass beads is satisfying work, for this is a spectacular flower. It has few petals but a harmonious shape. The corolla consists of six large, white, double-pointed petals that protect the flower's central yellow and brown pistils; the calyx consists of green sepals. Two closed buds and several green leaves on the stem add to the overall effect.

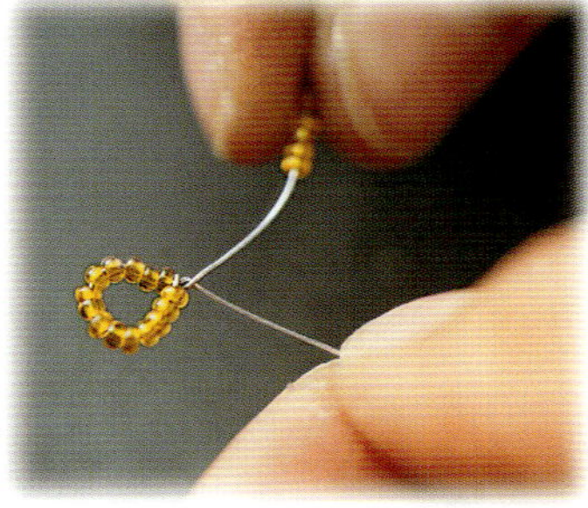

2. *For the pistil, take a 24 or 26 gauge wire, 6 inches long, and string on it 1½ inches of yellow beads followed by 2 inches of white beads. Being careful the beads don't slip, divide the yellow string and twist it, making a small ring, then make a second ring with the rest of the yellow string, creating an "8" shape. Restring the white beads on the open end of the wire, creating the pistil.*

3. *You need at least three pistils per lily. Remember to twist the open end of the wires to prevent the white beads from slipping.*

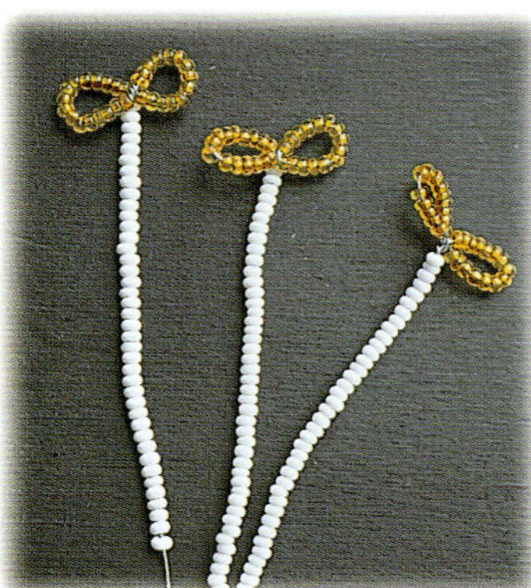

4. *Use green beads to prepare the calyx. Shape the beaded string into loops about ¾ of an inch long. Hold the loop as shown in the photograph below; the beads will slide more easily.*

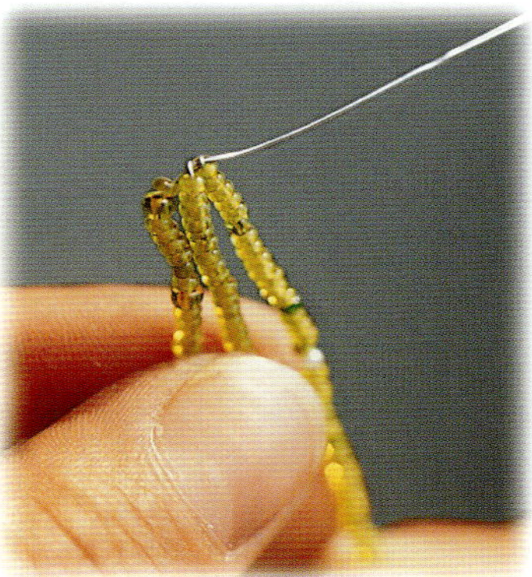

6. *To make the bud, take a 22 gauge wire, 5 inches long, and slide onto it 2½ inches of white enamel beads, forming the core. Take a string of the same white beads and wind it three times around the core, creating a double-pointed petal. Twist the petal, giving it the bud shape that you see in the photo at left.*

5. *You need six loops, all of the same length, to make the calyx. Using the pliers, pull the wire holding the loops, tightening them. You need two of these calyxes or collars: one for the flower, the other one for the bud.*

7. *The four green stem leaves are paired in two different sizes. One pair is 1½ inches long, the other 2 inches long.*

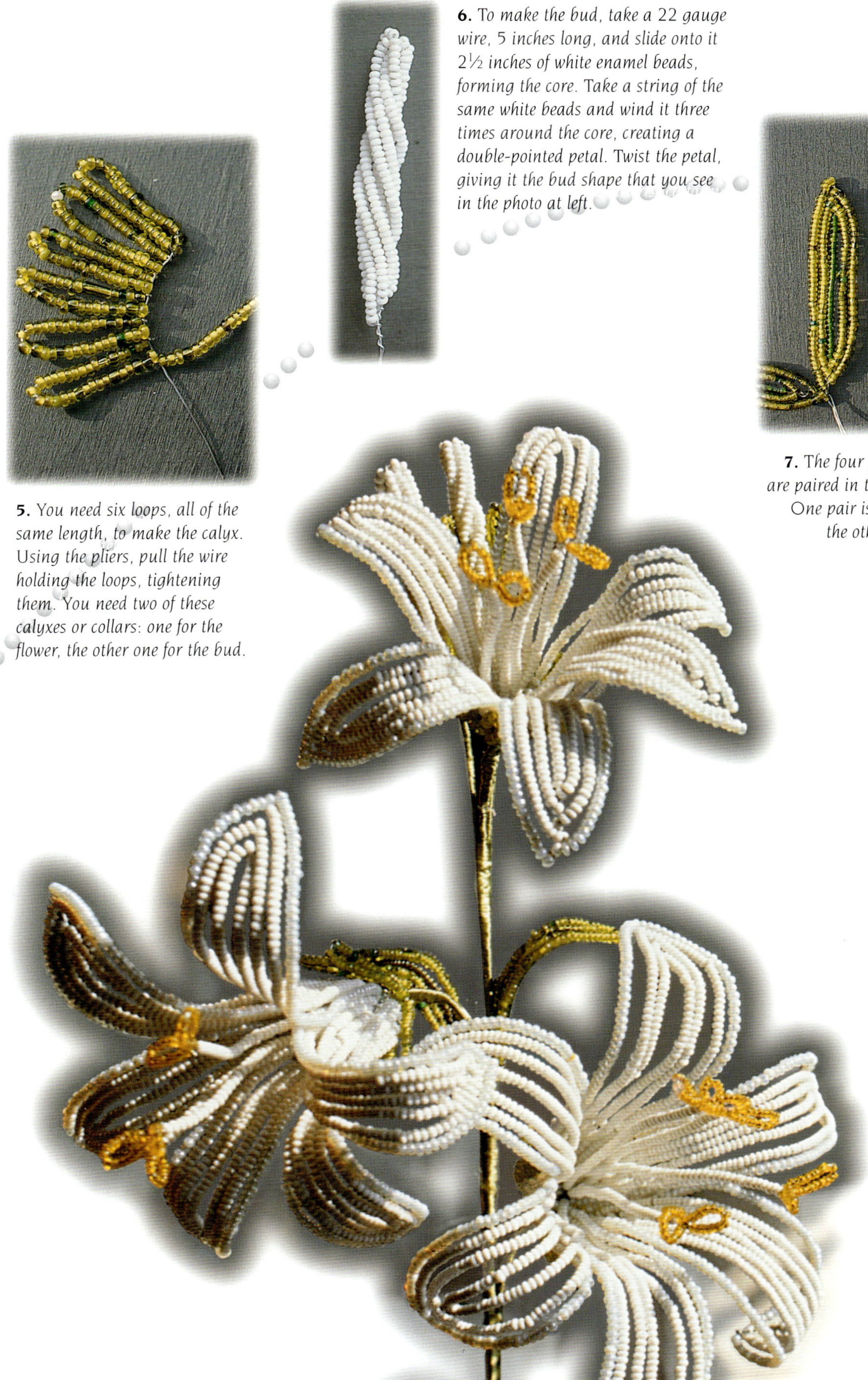

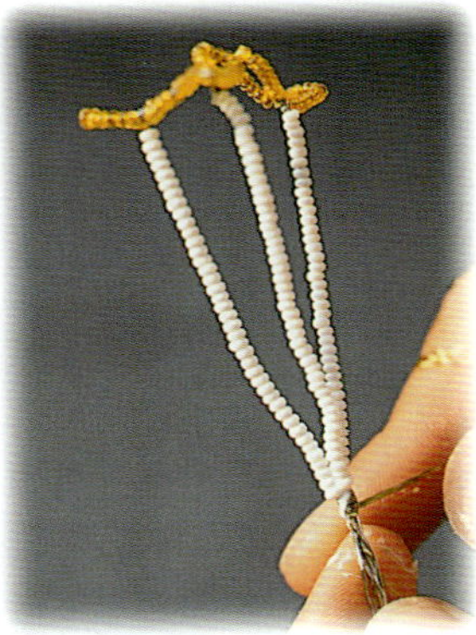

8. To assemble the flower, take a 20 gauge, 6 inches long rod. At the top, fasten the three pistils using silk yarn and a little glue to secure the silk. Then add the six white petals and the collar.

9. Using thumb and index, shape the white petals arching the points downward, to achieve an open flower effect, as shown in the photograph. Continue to cover the stem with the silk twist for another 2 inches , then secure it with a little glue.

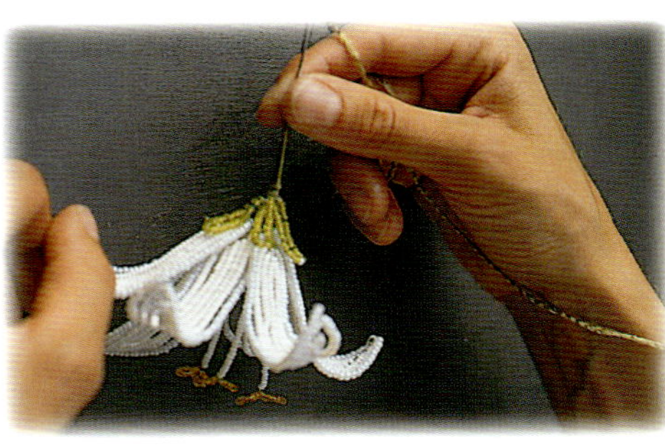

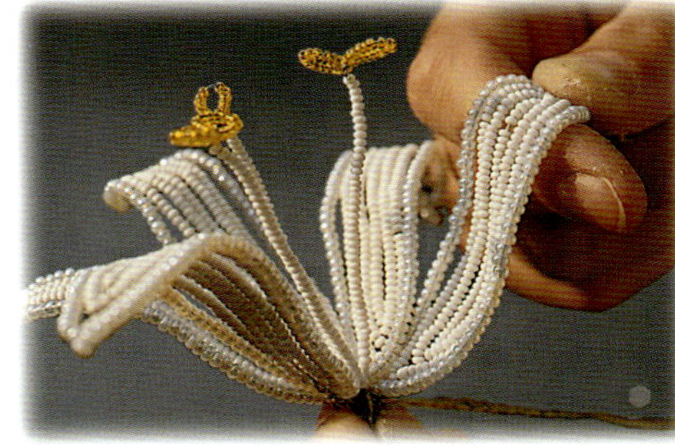

10. Shape the petals gently. Take a round rod, 18 gauge and 20 inches long (the main stalk), at the top fasten the bud and its collar using silk twist. Continue covering the stalk with silk for about 3½ inches , then add the open flower.

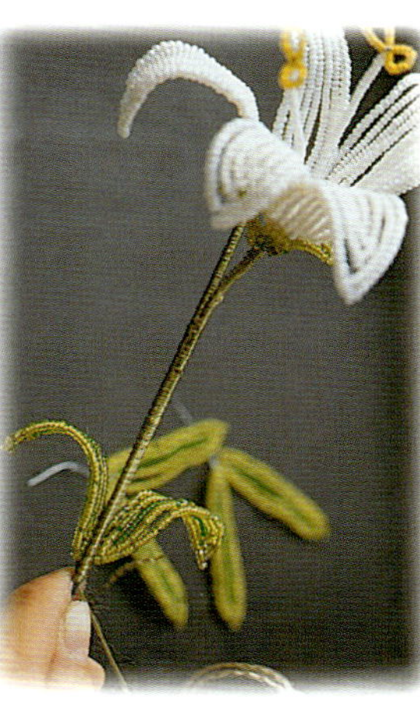

11. Fasten the two pairs of green leaves to the main stalk, about 3 and 6 inches below the point where the open flower is joined to the stalk.

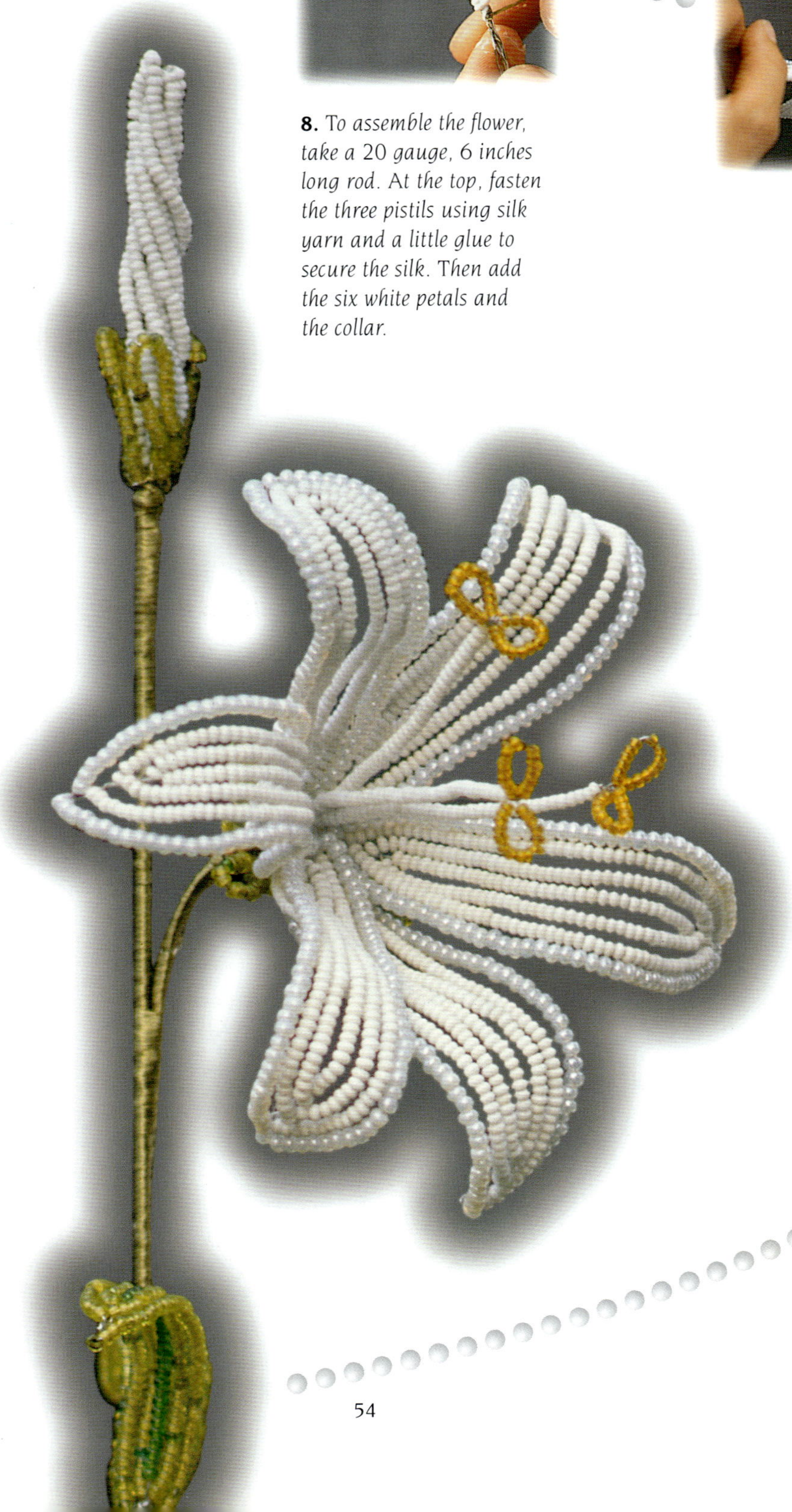

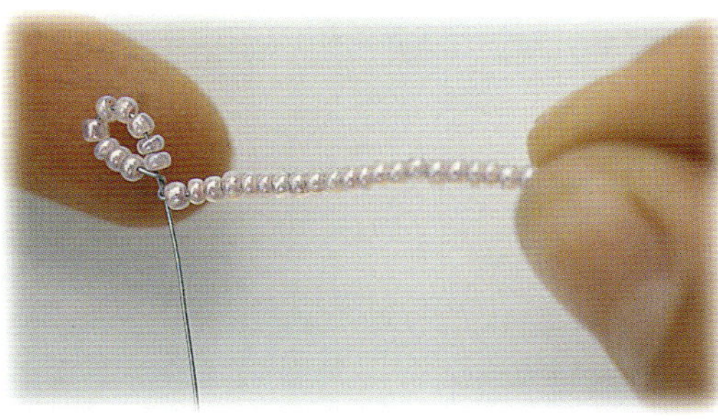

1. *There are many varieties of peach blossoms. Those with a simple shape consist of a small rose with five round petals. Only one beaded string is needed. Begin by making a small loop about ⅓ of an inch long.*

The Peach Blossom

The best beads for creating peach blossoms are pink iridescent ones. The paler pink beads will be used for the petals, while for the pistils you may use either a darker shade of pink or crystal-clear beads. To enliven the branch, place buds in various stages of opening and new, young green foliage next to the open blossoms. Each branch consists of a main stalk and five small, lateral branches that differ in composition and size.

2. *Using the same string, wind it twice around the central loop, securing the wire by twisting it every time you start a new row.*

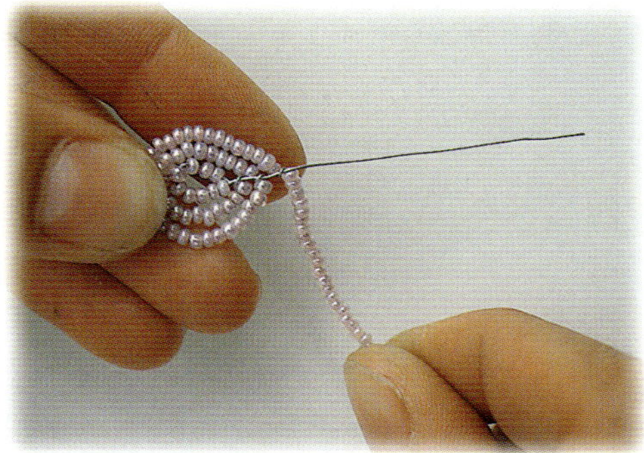

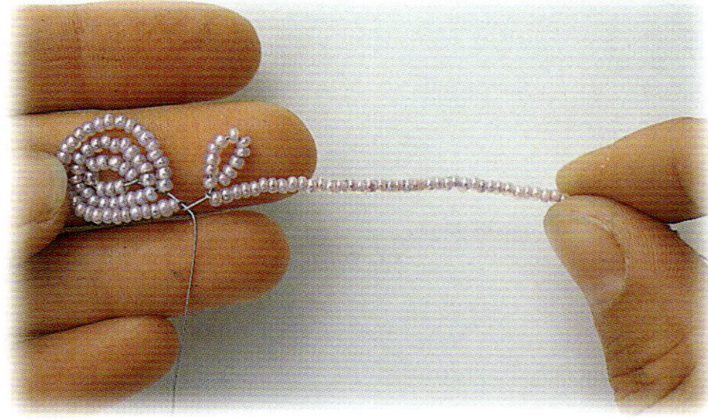

3. *Using the same string, make the other four petals. It's important that you turn the string always in the same direction, so as not to confuse the front and the back of the flower.*

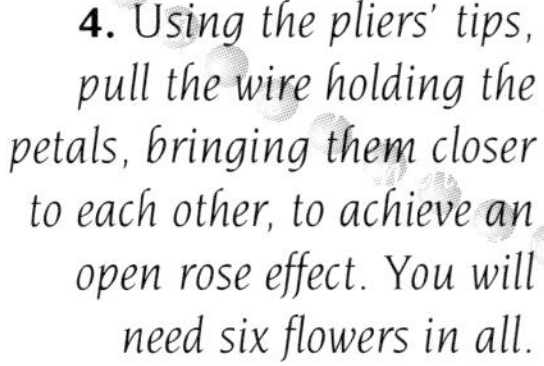

4. *Using the pliers' tips, pull the wire holding the petals, bringing them closer to each other, to achieve an open rose effect. You will need six flowers in all.*

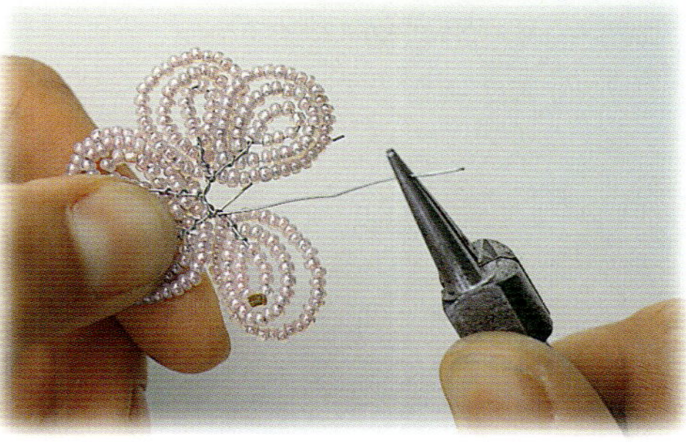

MATERIALS

- For each peach blossom branch you will need:
- 4 strings of pink beads
- 1 string of clear white beads
- 1 string of green beads
- 7 wires, 20 gauge, 8 inches long
- 1 round rod, 18 gauge, 20 inches long
- brown silk twist, vinyl glue, pliers.

5. *To make the pistils, shape the white beaded string into three loops, each 1/4 of an inch long. Pull the wire with the pliers to tighten the loops, following the technique described above.*

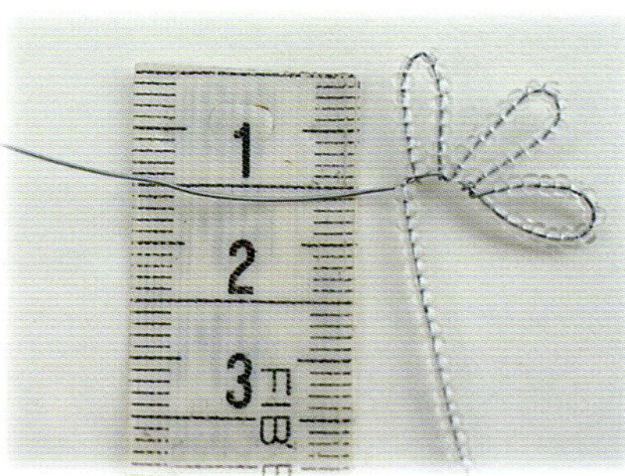

6. *Insert the pistils at the center of each flower. To make the pistils, you may use darker pink beads instead of clear ones. The flower will have more contrast, but will lose in luminosity.*

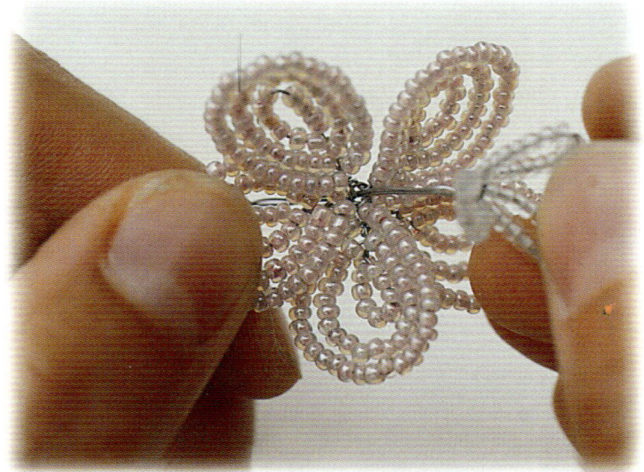

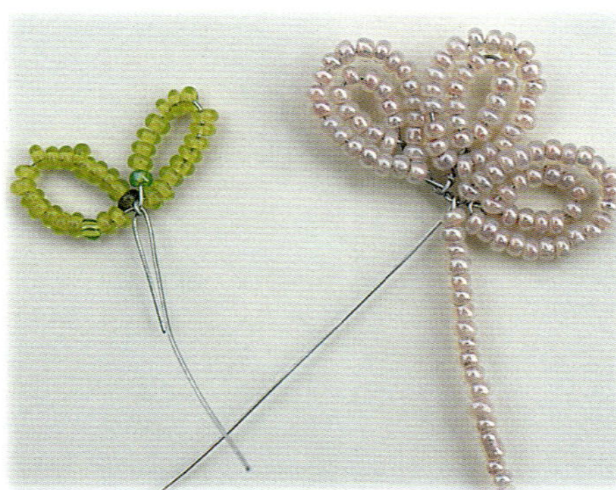

7. *Follow the same technique to make the buds; each bud has three petals. The central loop of each bud is 1/3 to 1/2 of an inch long. You will need only two rounds of string for each bud. Bend the petals slightly inward to create the bud effect.*

8. *Add two small green leaves at the base of each bud—these are the integuments—making sure that the open end wires are securely fastened to the bud's wire. You will need six buds for a full branch.*

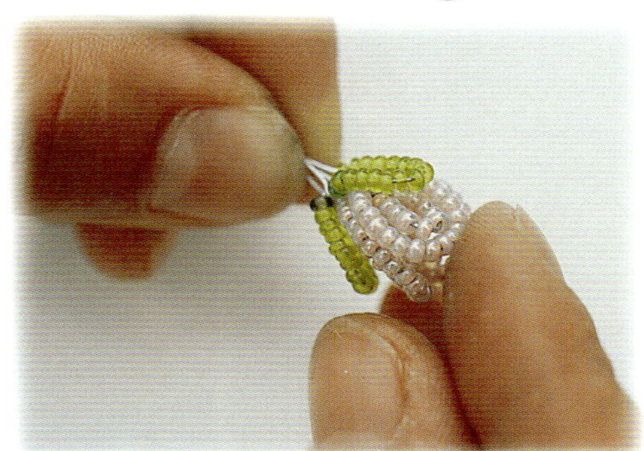

9. *All along the lateral branches you may add small gemmae—the closed buds—and small, tender green leaves. The closed buds are made by shaping a small length of pink beaded string into a walnut shape and covering it with two small green leaves. To do this, make a 1/2 inch loop with a pink string and another loop crossing over it.*

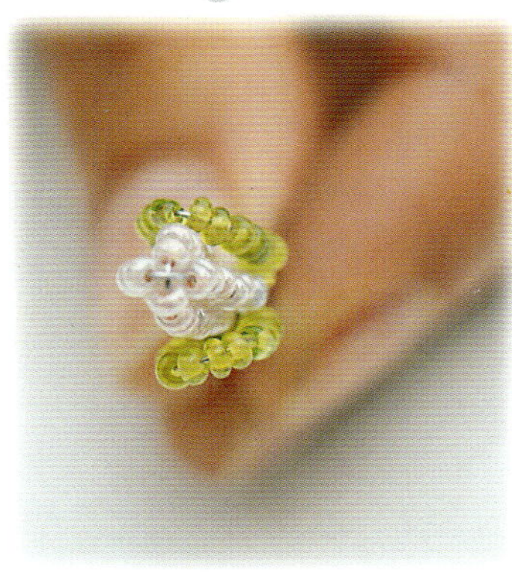

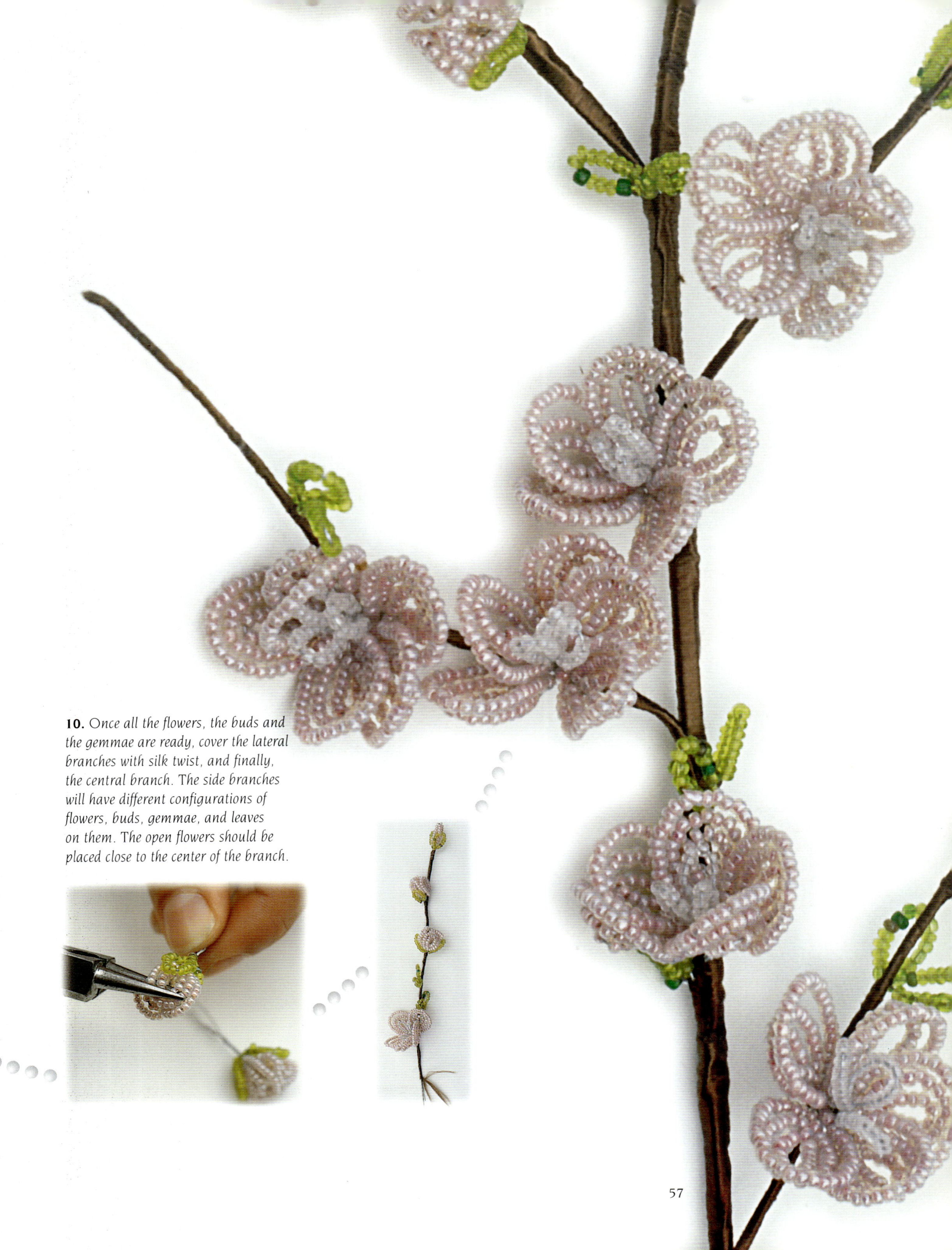

10. *Once all the flowers, the buds and the gemmae are ready, cover the lateral branches with silk twist, and finally, the central branch. The side branches will have different configurations of flowers, buds, gemmae, and leaves on them. The open flowers should be placed close to the center of the branch.*

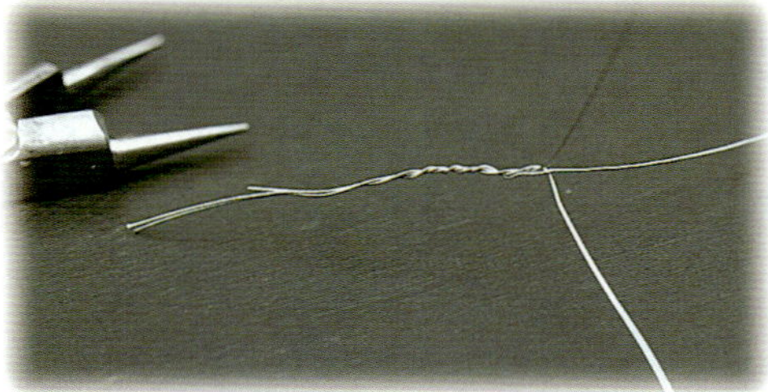

1. *Making this flower requires an entirely different technique from those we have used so far. Cut three 24 or 26 gauge wires, each 3½ inches long, and twist them together for about half their length, opening the opposite ends wide apart in three directions, in the shape of a pyramid.*

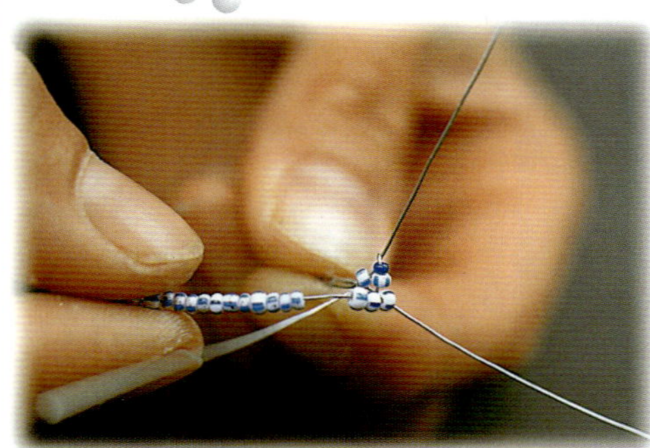

2. *Take one beaded string and tie it around the three wires at the tip of the pyramid where the twisting stops. Bead by bead, wind the string in a circular movement around the three wire cores, creating gradually wider circles. At each crossing, twist the string to the core wire so that the twist is visible only in the back.*

The Morning Glory

Making this flower requires a rigorous, innovative technique and great care in choosing the beads: for the best results choose enamel beads, because this is a small flower that needs visibility. The striking final effect is given by the airy design of the branch, with its many vine shoots ready to attach themselves to neighboring stems and to the compact shape of the flower, which consists of a single funnel-shaped corolla. Finally, the buds are twisted.

3. *Five or six full rounds will make a flower; cut the three wire extremities and turn the tips under with the pliers to secure them. Make five flowers in all.*

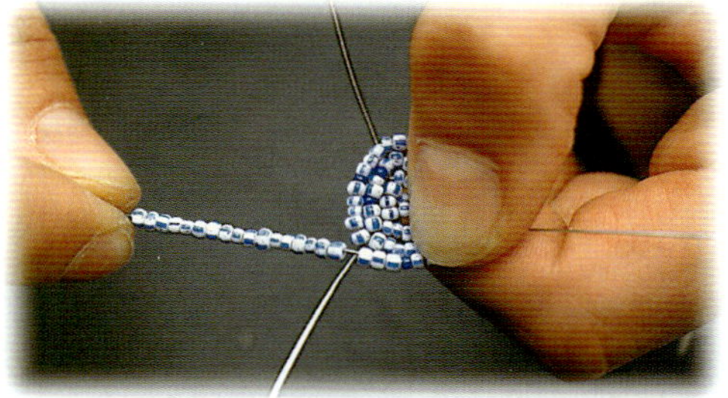

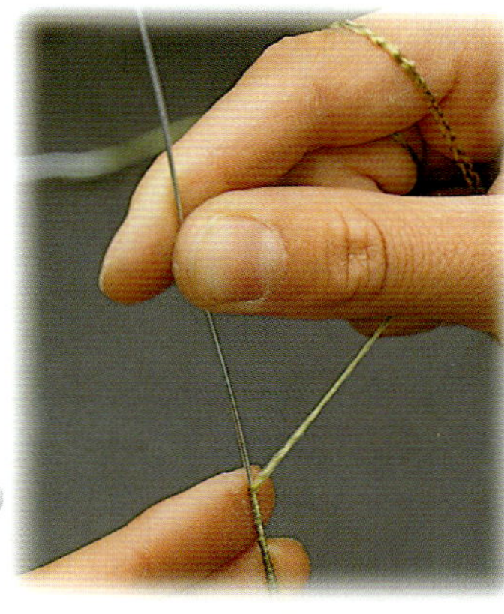

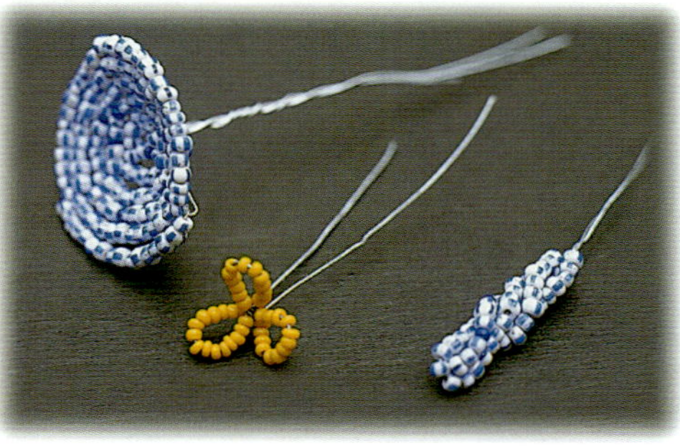

4. *To make a morning glory bud, you need only one string of beads. Create a 1¼ inch loop and then a second, perpendicular loop that crosses over the first; secure the end wire with the pliers, then gently twist the bud until you have the desired shape. For the intense yellow pistils you need one string of beads: make three loops of the same size with it.*

5. *To make the vine shoots, take a 20 gauge wire, cut a length of 12 inches, and carefully cover it with silk twist for about 10 inches ; use pale green silk. Remember to use vinyl glue to secure the silk both at the beginning and the end.*

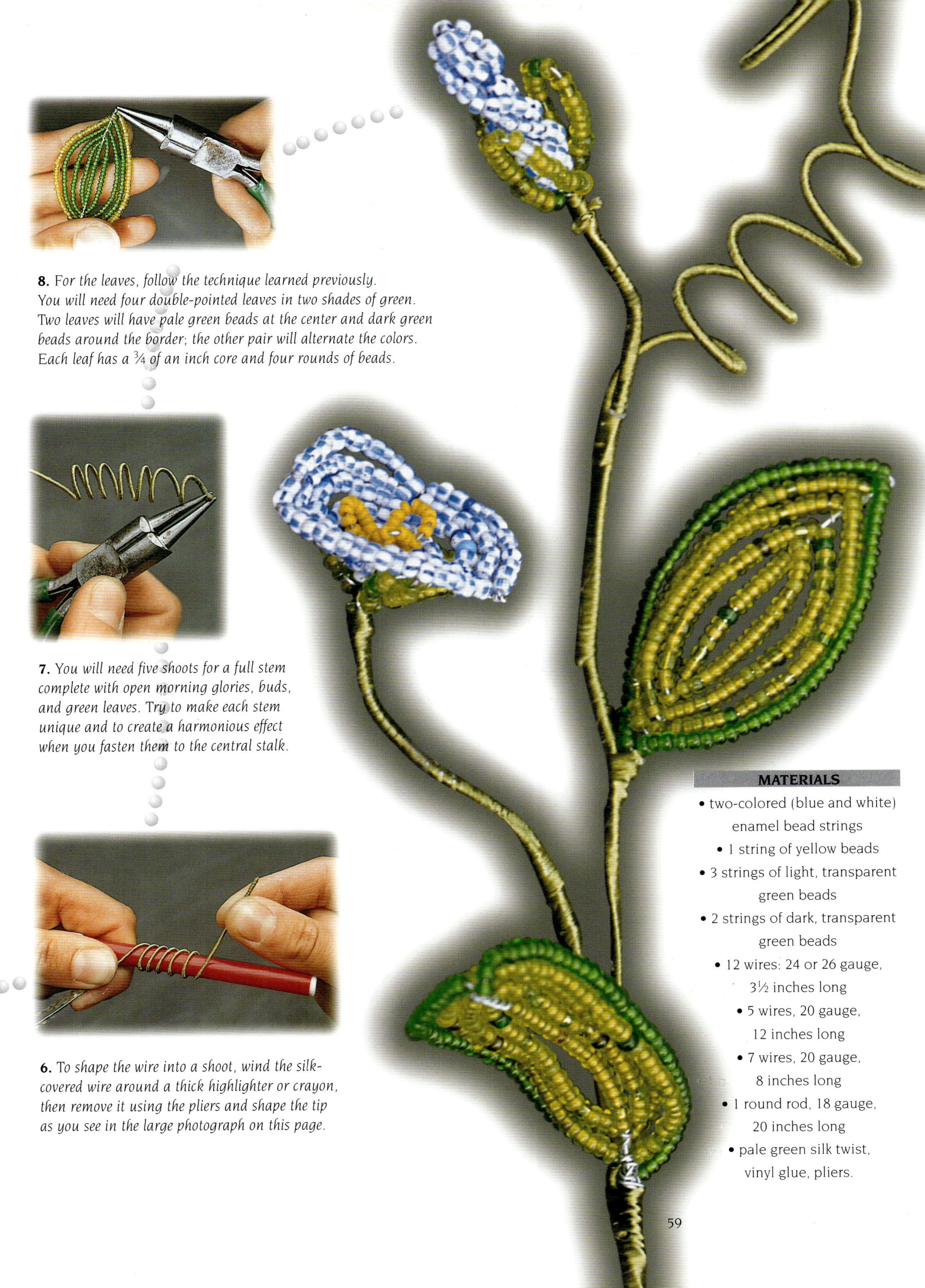

8. For the leaves, follow the technique learned previously. You will need four double-pointed leaves in two shades of green. Two leaves will have pale green beads at the center and dark green beads around the border; the other pair will alternate the colors. Each leaf has a ¾ of an inch core and four rounds of beads.

7. You will need five shoots for a full stem complete with open morning glories, buds, and green leaves. Try to make each stem unique and to create a harmonious effect when you fasten them to the central stalk.

6. To shape the wire into a shoot, wind the silk-covered wire around a thick highlighter or crayon, then remove it using the pliers and shape the tip as you see in the large photograph on this page.

MATERIALS

- two-colored (blue and white) enamel bead strings
- 1 string of yellow beads
- 3 strings of light, transparent green beads
- 2 strings of dark, transparent green beads
- 12 wires: 24 or 26 gauge, 3½ inches long
- 5 wires, 20 gauge, 12 inches long
- 7 wires, 20 gauge, 8 inches long
- 1 round rod, 18 gauge, 20 inches long
- pale green silk twist, vinyl glue, pliers.

The Hyacinth

Making a hyacinth with glass beads is a pleasant task. This flower is composed of about ten equal florets that are fairly easy to make. The effect is given by the choice of colors and by the arrangement with other hyacinths. You should choose a container that is proportional to the length of the flower, which is about eight inches, such as a ceramic, porcelain or silver bowl.

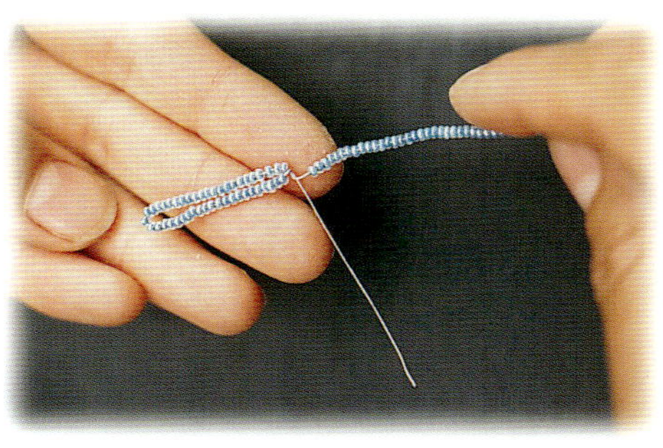

1. *Start by using the string in the darker shade of blue. Make five loops, each one ¾ of an inch long. Hold the wire downward as shown in the photograph at left: the beads will slide more easily.*

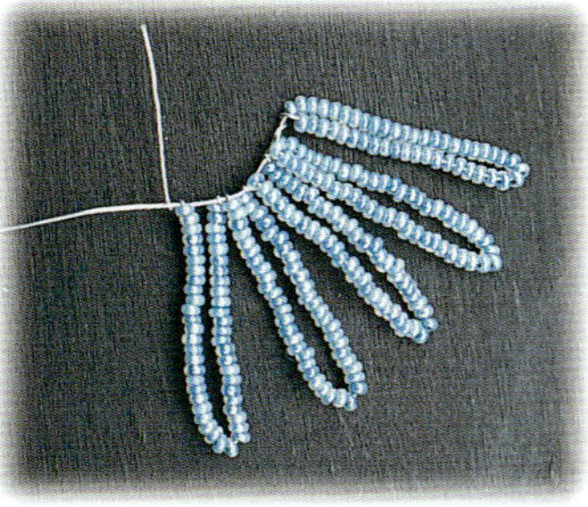

2. *Using the light blue string, add a second loop to each of the five dark blue loops, crossing each loop at the top. Make sure the beads are evenly spaced so that there are no empty spaces on the string.*

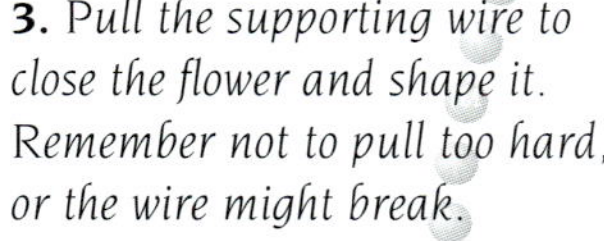

3. *Pull the supporting wire to close the flower and shape it. Remember not to pull too hard, or the wire might break.*

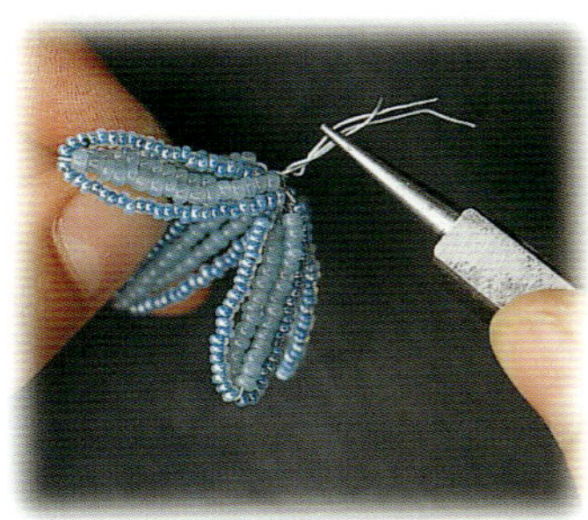

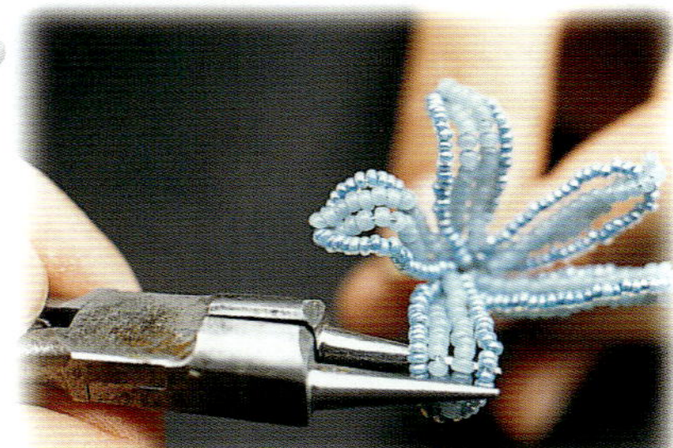

4. *Shape the petals using the pliers, gently arching them outward. For a rich hyacinth stem you need five ¾ of an inch and five 1 inch long flowers.*

5. *Using the technique we learned for the previous flowers, create two double-pointed green leaves with a 1½ inch core and a 1¼ inch width. Using two different shades of green will create a more interesting leaf.*

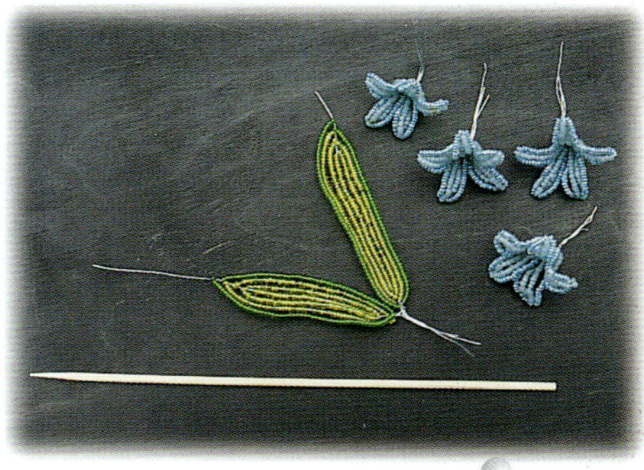

MATERIALS

- 3 strings of azure blue beads
- 3 strings of blue beads
- 2 green wires
- 1 wooden stick, 8 inches long
- pale green silk twist, vinyl glue, pliers.

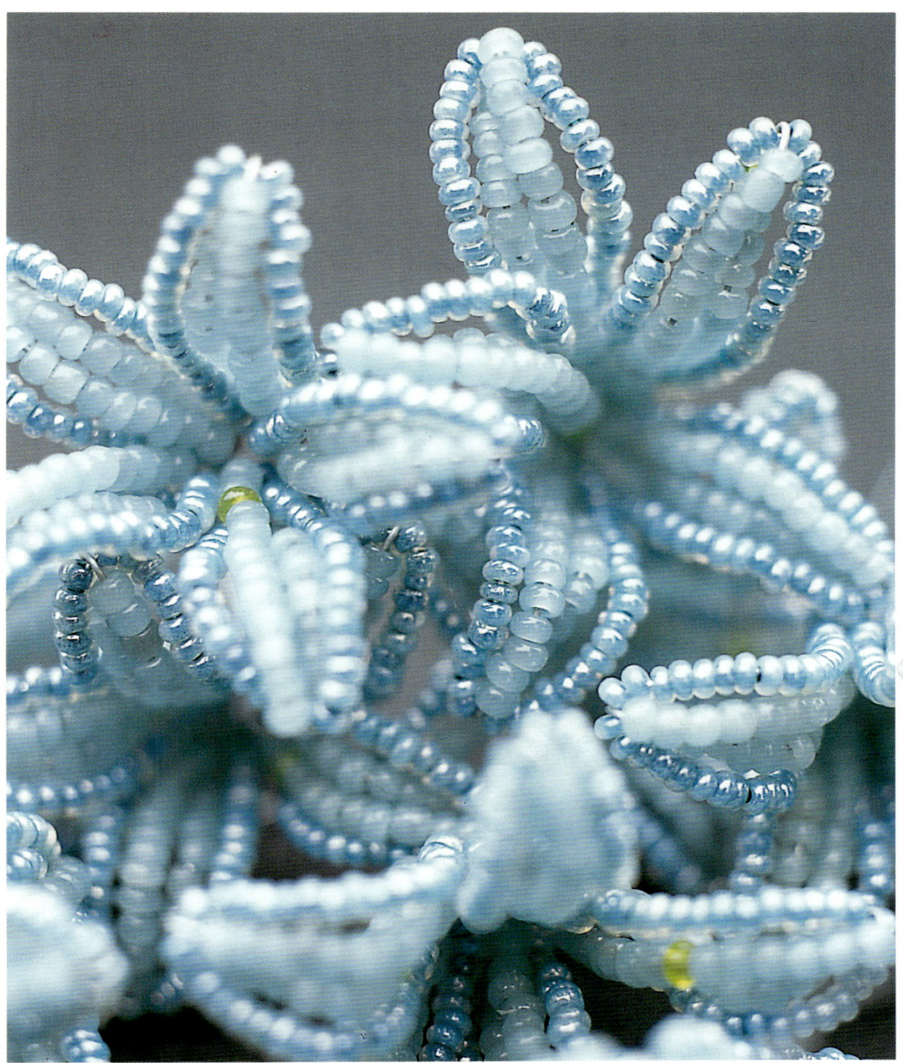

8. *The hyacinth stem, complete with flowers, has a majestic quality to it. The lighter blue should always be on the inside, and the darker hue on the outside. Other color combinations are pink on pink, white on pink, or mother-of-pearl white on white enamel paste.*

6. *Take a wooden stick, 8 inches long, and fasten the first flower at the top; pair the other flowers, each pair at the same height but oriented in opposite directions, down the stem at a distance of 1 inch each.*

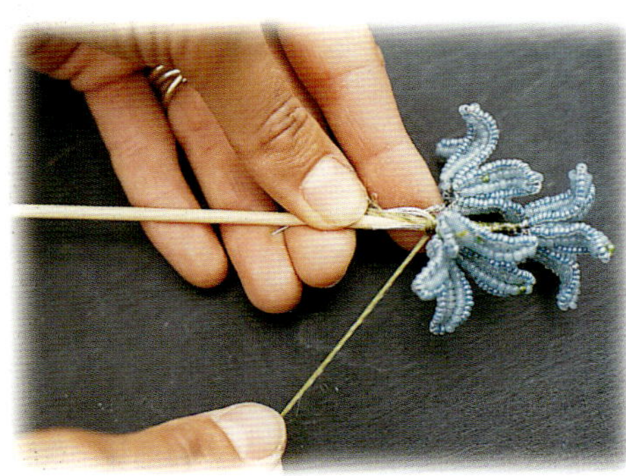

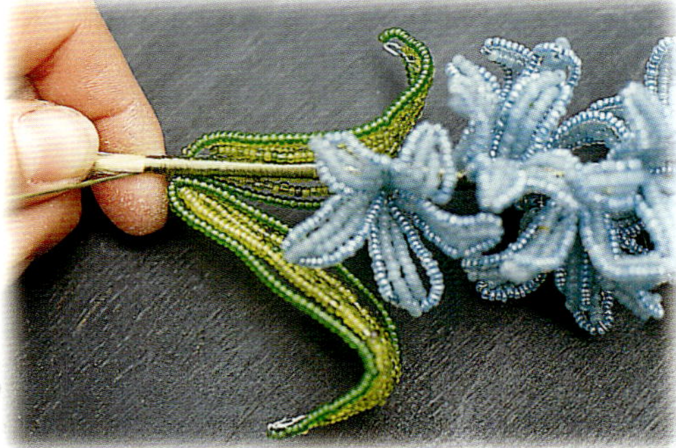

7. *About 1½ inches below the last flower fasten the two green leaves at the same height, then continue covering the stem with silk twist.*

The Daisy

Is there anyone who as a child has not counted the petals of a daisy? This flower has always been the plain, spontaneous flower of love, celebrated in countless poems and songs and reproduced in countless paintings. In spring bouquets the field daisy is very attractive, especially when contrasted with other flowers such as violets and, in the summer, poppies and stalks of wheat.

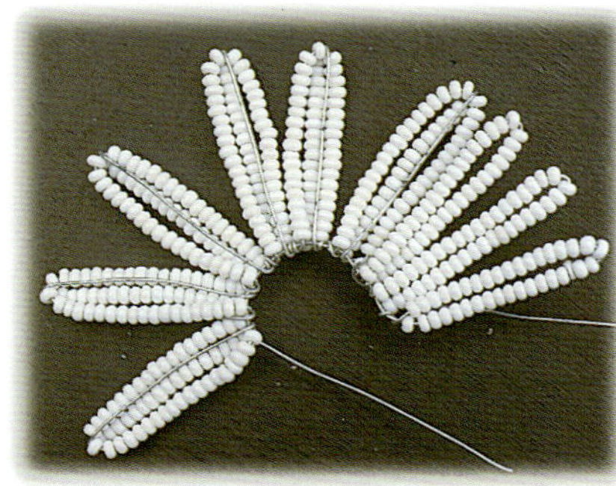

1. *The same technique used for the hyacinth will also be used to create the daisy. Take one string of white beads and make eight loops, each 1 inch long, and cross over each loop with another loop of the same size and perpendicular to it. For the second crossover loop, use beads in front only, to keep the design light and airy.*

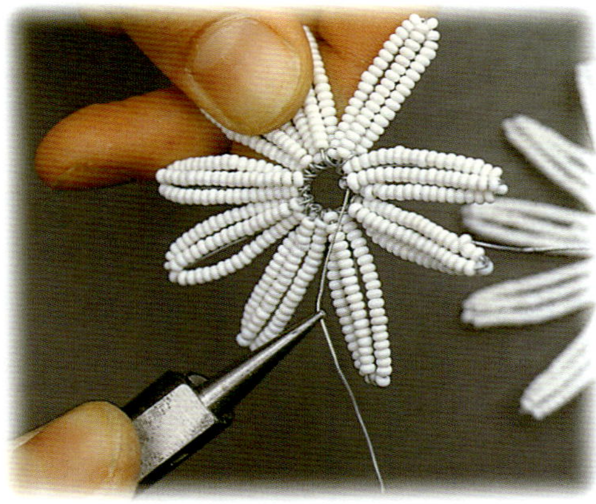

2. *With the pliers, pull the wire that supports the petals tight, giving them a curled look. Do this gently to avoid breaking the wire.*

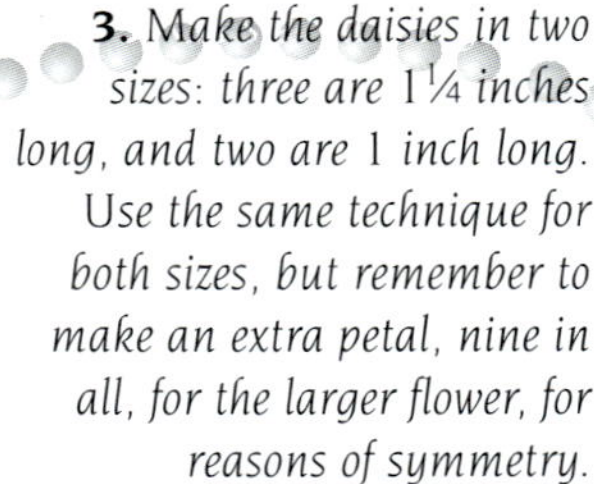

3. *Make the daisies in two sizes: three are 1¼ inches long, and two are 1 inch long. Use the same technique for both sizes, but remember to make an extra petal, nine in all, for the larger flower, for reasons of symmetry.*

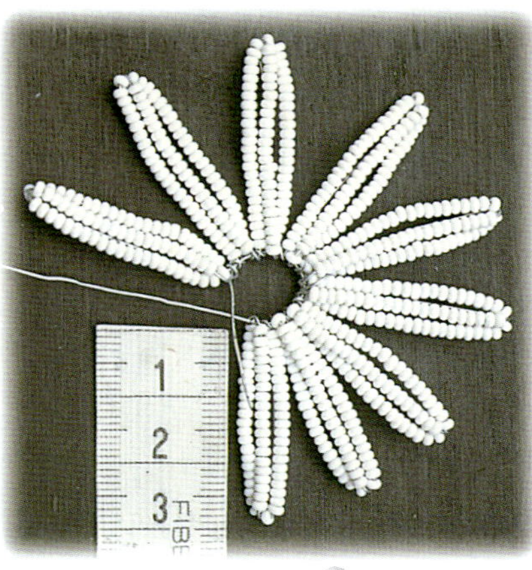

4. *Choose an intense, loud yellow for the daisy's centerpiece, to create a pleasing contrast with the white petals and the green stems. Use a 22 gauge wire; slide ⅕ of an inch of small yellow beads onto it; then take the beaded string and create a small leaf by turning it twice around the core.*

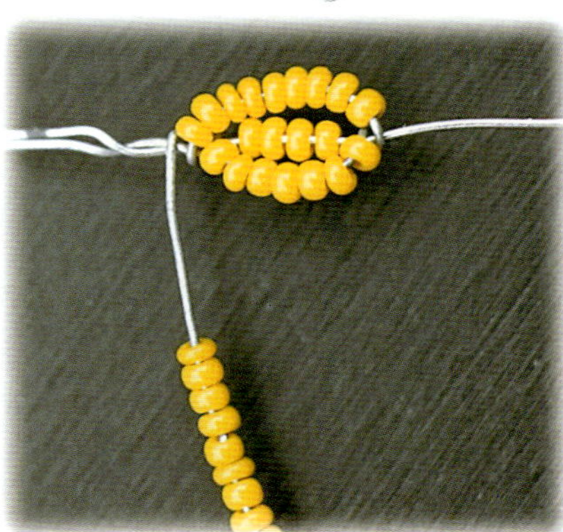

MATERIALS

For each daisy you will need:

- 6 strings of white beads
- 1 string of yellow enamel beads
- 2 strings of green beads
- 5 22 gauge wires, 3 inches long
- 5 wires, 20 gauge, 12 inches long
- 1 18 gauge stem wire, 12 inches long
- pale green silk twist, vinyl glue, pliers.

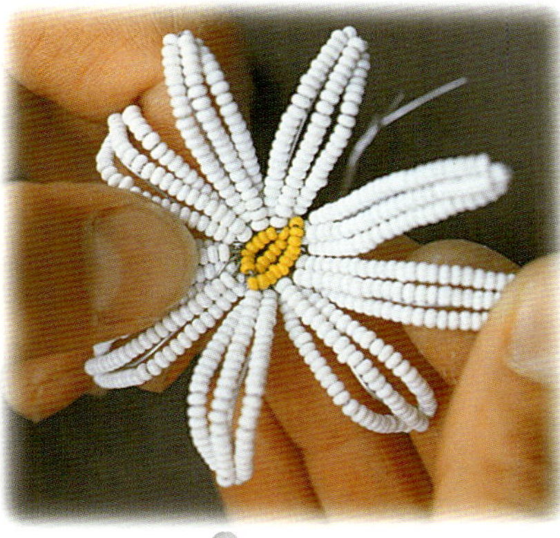

8. Create the typical serrated daisy leaf by making about seven loops with green beads. Make the central loop 1 inch long: this will be the center of the leaf; below it, make two slightly smaller loops, ¾ of an inch long, oriented in opposite directions.

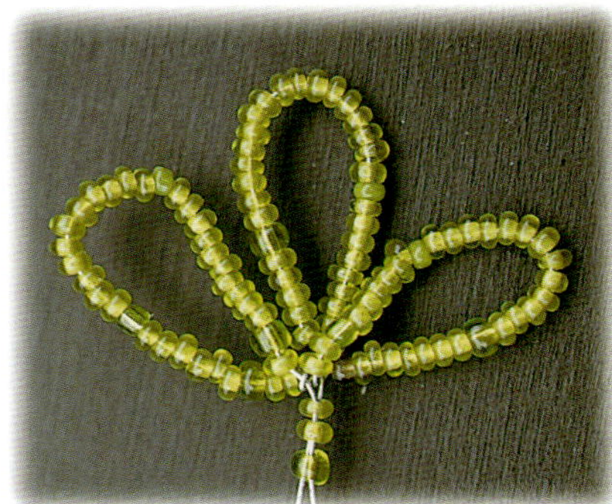

7. Gently shape the petals. The choice of opaque beads makes this a worthy flower for arrangements, as it provides a strong color and a soft shape.

6. In this photo you can see how the daisy looks from the back. The petals' wires make up the peduncle. Using silk twist, fasten the peduncle to the thicker wire (20 gauge and 12 inches long) that will be the stem; use one stem for each flower.

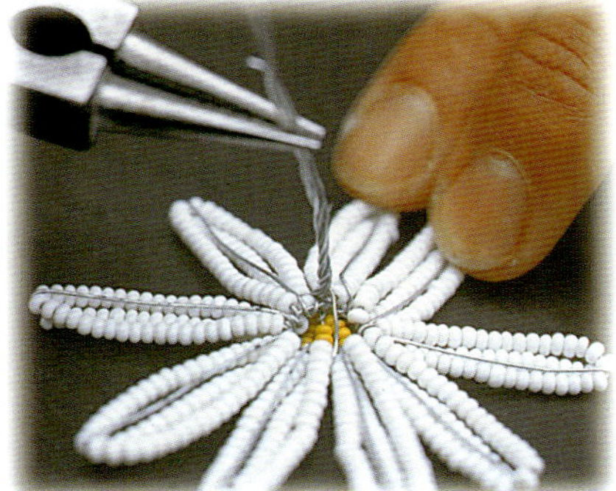

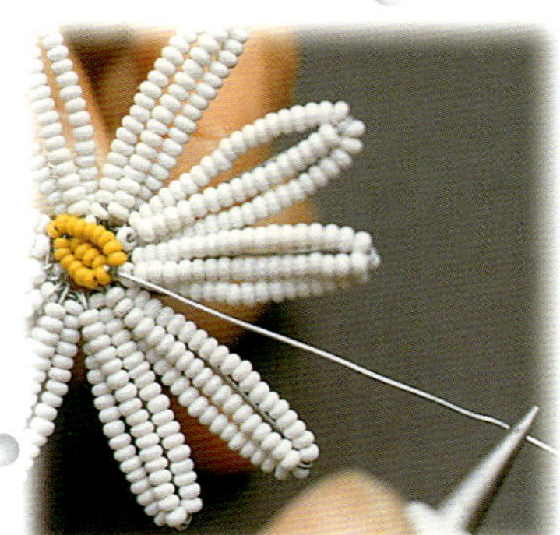

5. Insert the centerpiece at the center of the daisy petals and twist the end wires on the daisy's wires.

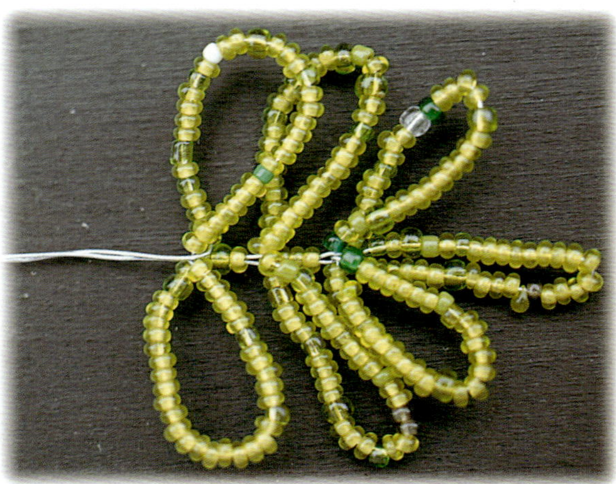

9. *Continue making two more loops of 1 inch each, separating them from the previous pair with three beads. Below them, make two additional loops, ¾ of an inch long. Close the leaf by twisting the wires together. Make three more similar leaves.*

10. *Insert each daisy on a 12 inch stem, twisting the pale green silk yarn around each stem.*

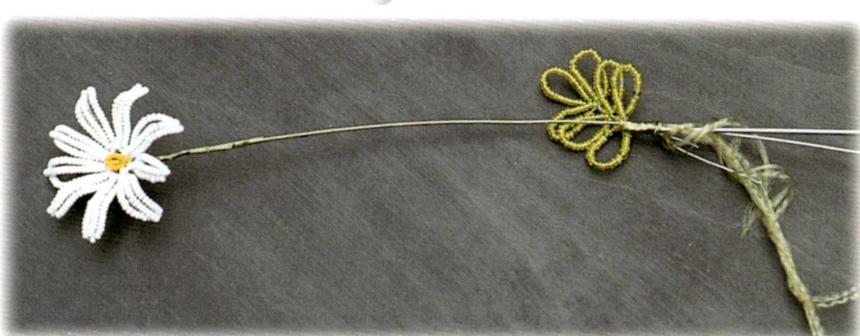

12. *Daisies can be either white or pale pink. It is usually best to use enamel paste beads, however if the bouquet is in a strong light you may also use tosca beads which are transparent on the outside and colored on the inside.*

11. *Fasten the stems to an 18 gauge rod, the central stalk. Fasten two green leaves—one on each side—to hide the place where the stem joins the central stalk.*

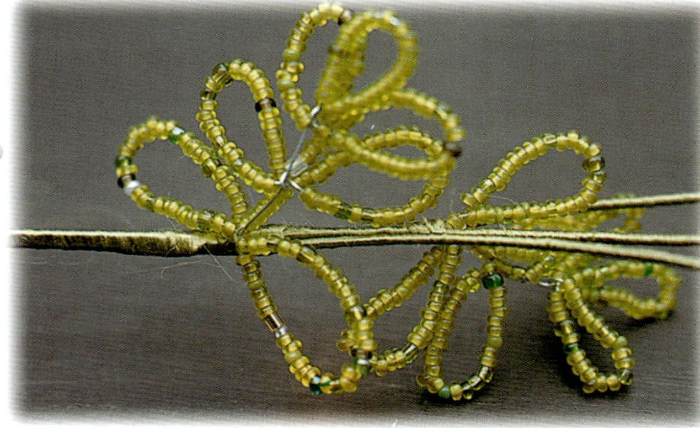

The Bluebell

The bluebell is a delightful flower whose blue, azure and rose flowers blanket sunny summer pastures and steep, rocky hillsides. Bluebells also grow along country roads and in sparse, sunny woodland. Reproducing them with beads is quite easy. For the flowers, you will need opaque beads in various shades of blue; for the leaves, you will need both pale and dark green beads.

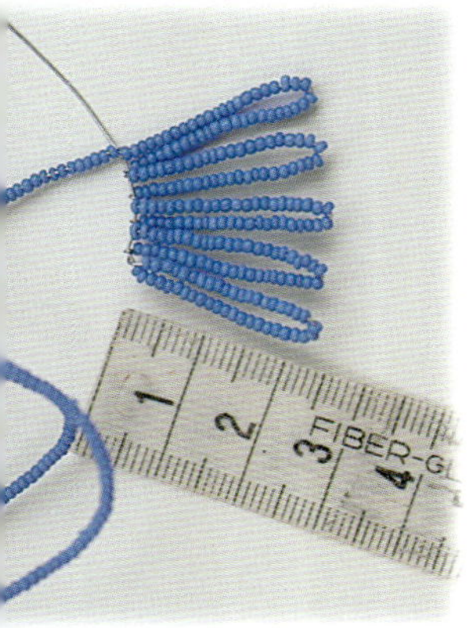

1. *Using the daisy technique, make five individual loops, each about ¾ of an inch long. Make sure the petals are all of the same length, for uniformity is important to achieve the best results for this simple flower.*

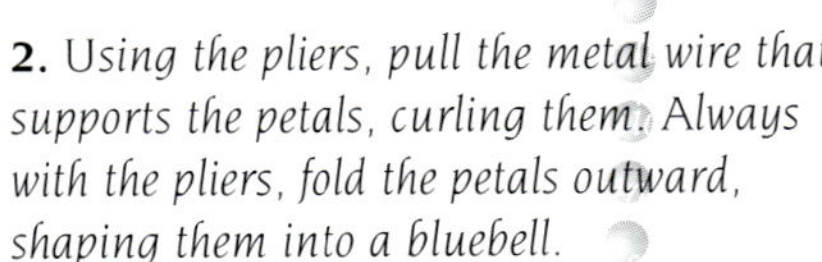

2. *Using the pliers, pull the metal wire that supports the petals, curling them. Always with the pliers, fold the petals outward, shaping them into a bluebell.*

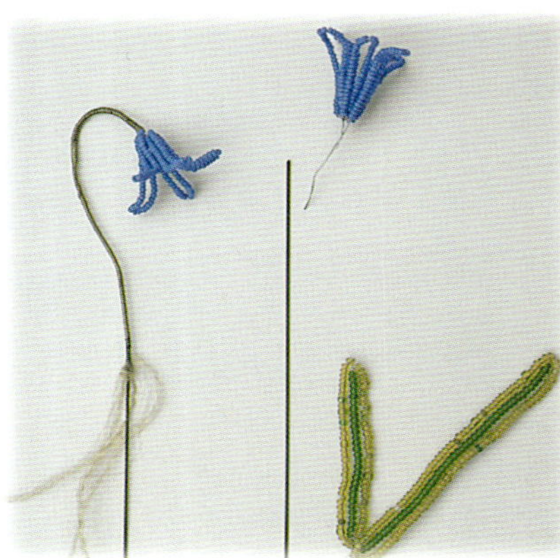

3. *Make the green leaves using the core technique; the core should be 1½ to 2 inches long. Take a string in a different shade of green beads and wind it once around the core, creating a top-pointed leaf.*

4. *To assemble the flower, fasten each bluebell to the top of a 5 inch 22 gauge wire using silk twist, and continue covering the wire for about 4 inches. At this point, add the leaves and then finish the stem. Bend the bluebell upper stem to the shape illustrated in the photograph.*

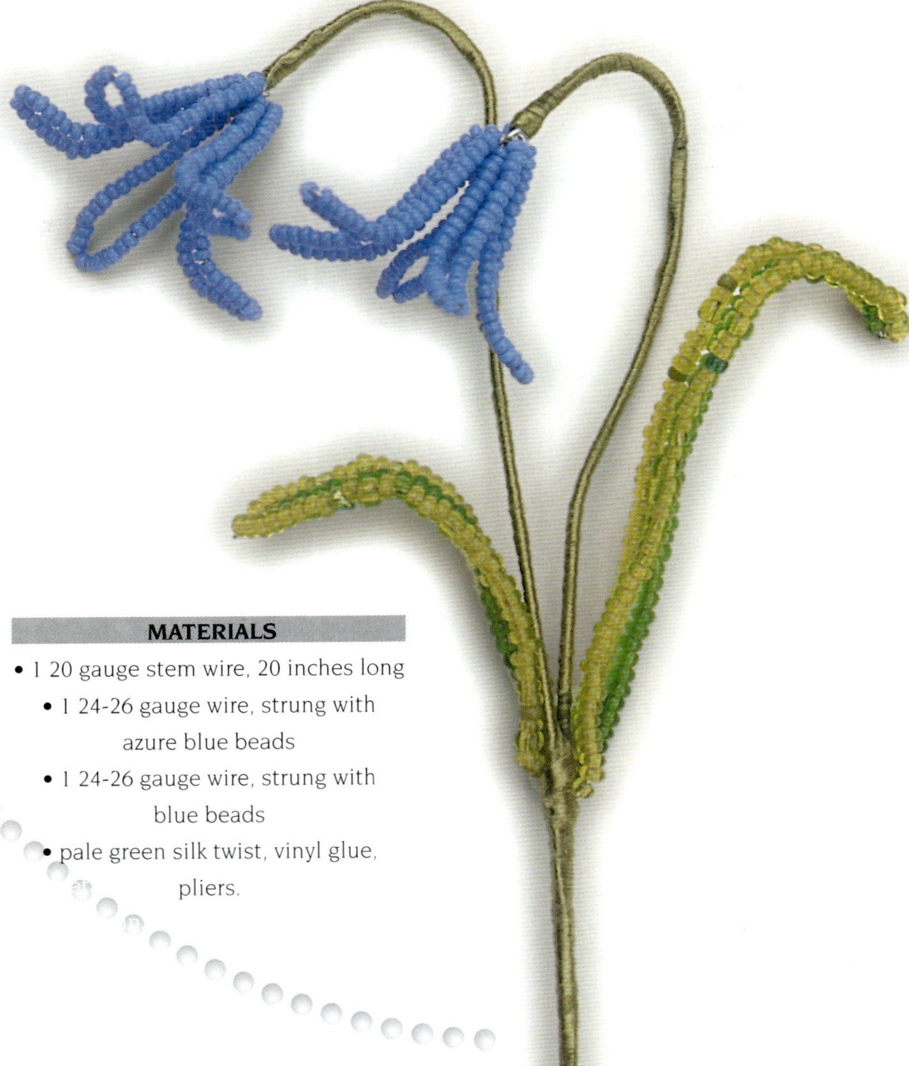

MATERIALS

- 1 20 gauge stem wire, 20 inches long
- 1 24-26 gauge wire, strung with azure blue beads
- 1 24-26 gauge wire, strung with blue beads
- pale green silk twist, vinyl glue, pliers.

The Lily-of-the-Valley

In the language of flowers, the lily-of-the-valley symbolizes the return of the good season, the freshness and sincerity of youth, and joyful love. The most appropriate beads for this flower and its symbolic meaning are bright white, opaque beads. For the foliage, pale green beads should be used, possibly with a mother-of-pearl finish to give more luminosity to the flower.

1. *Using the peach blossom technique, make four round petals with one round per petal plus an inner loop ⅓ to ½ inch long. Remember to twist the beaded string around the peduncle wire at every turn.*

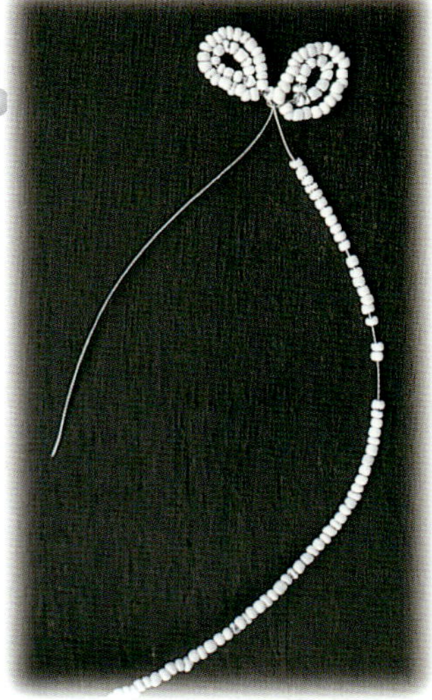

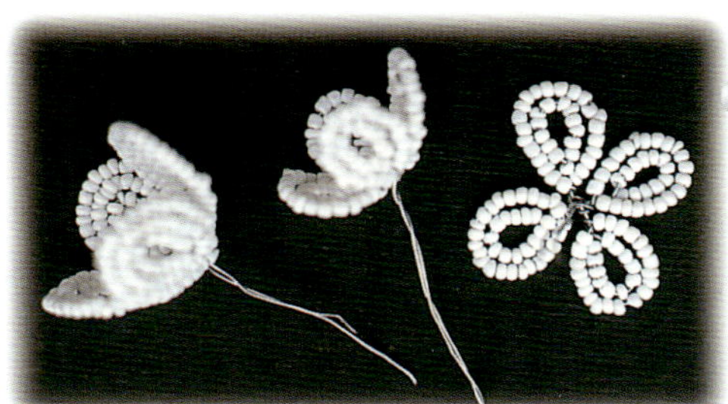

2. *For each main stem you will need three flowers with two-loop petals and four flowers with three-loop petals. Be careful to always work with the front of the flower, not the back.*

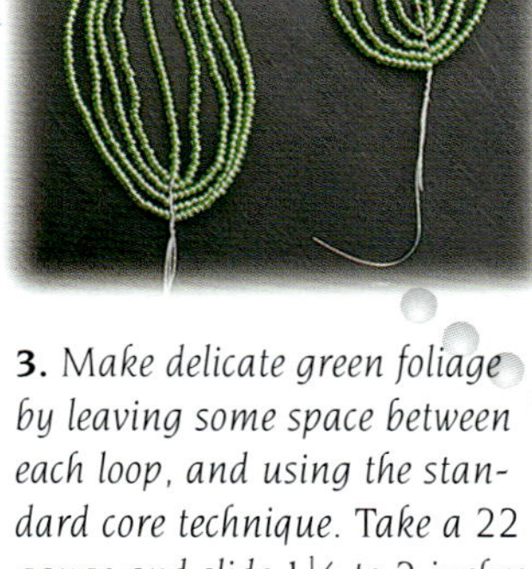

3. *Make delicate green foliage by leaving some space between each loop, and using the standard core technique. Take a 22 gauge and slide 1½ to 2 inches of green beads onto it; then take a beaded string of the same color and wind it four times around the core to make a leaf with a 1½ inch core; use five turns for a leaf with a 2 inch core.*

MATERIALS

For a lily-of-the-valley stem with 7 flowers you need:

- 2 24-26 gauge wires, strung with opaque white beads
- 2 24-26 gauge wires, strung with mother-of-pearl pale green beads
- 2 22 gauge stem wire
- 1 20 gauge stem wire
- pale green silk twist, vinyl glue, pliers.

4. *The flower is assembled on an 8 inch 18 gauge wire. First, cover the peduncle of each flower with silk twist for about ½ inch, then fasten each peduncle on the main stem.*

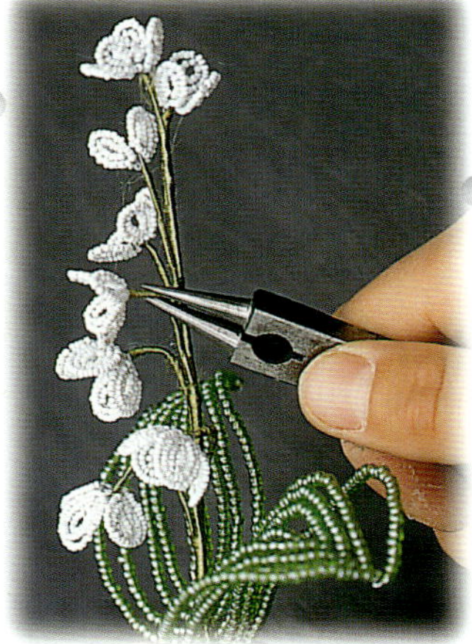

5. *Assemble the smaller flowers near to the top of the stem, the larger ones in the center and the leaves at the bottom. Leave about 3 inches of stem below the leaves so that it can be arranged in a vase.*

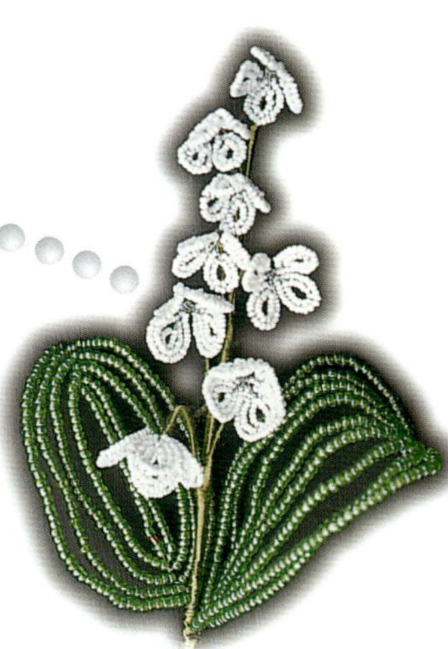

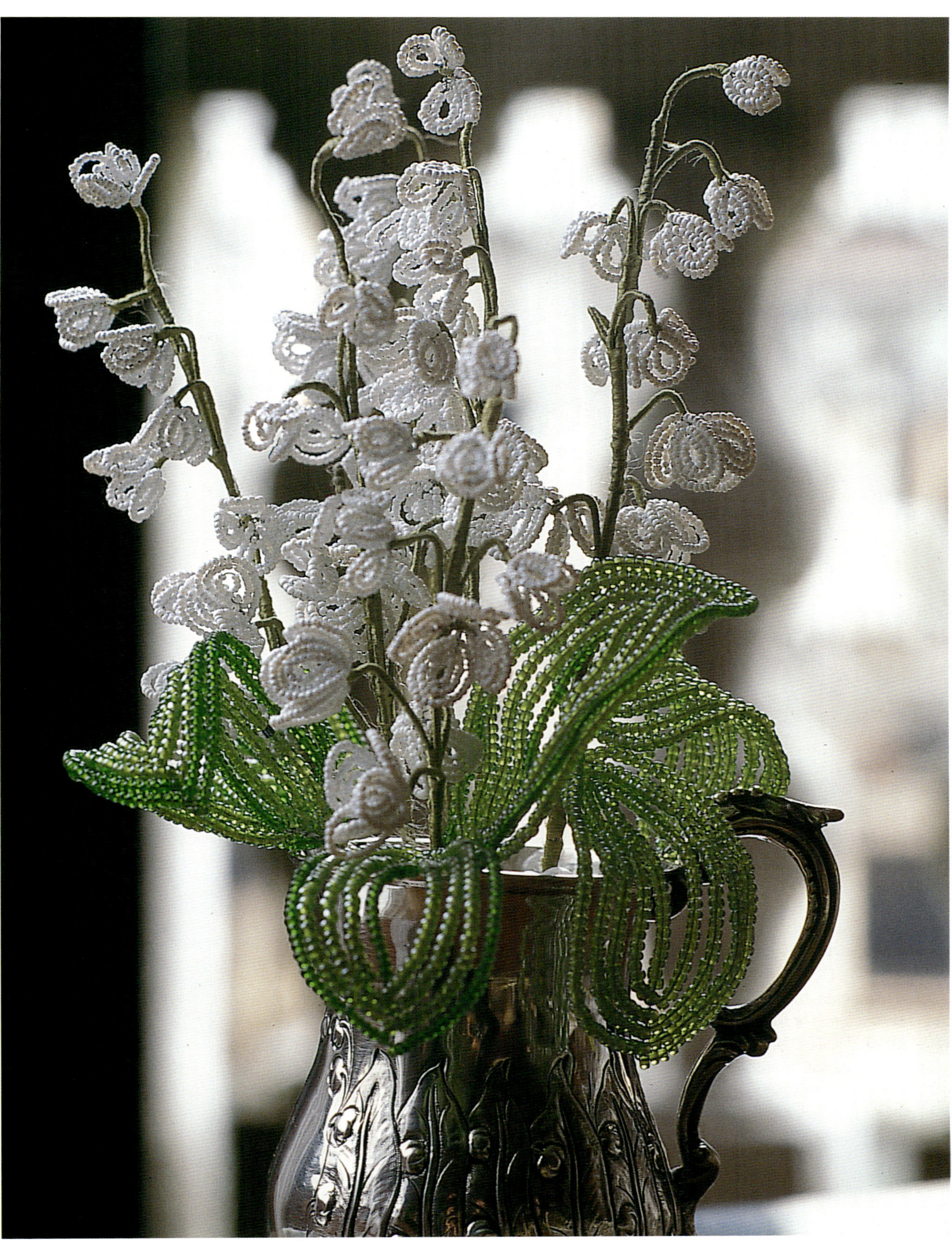

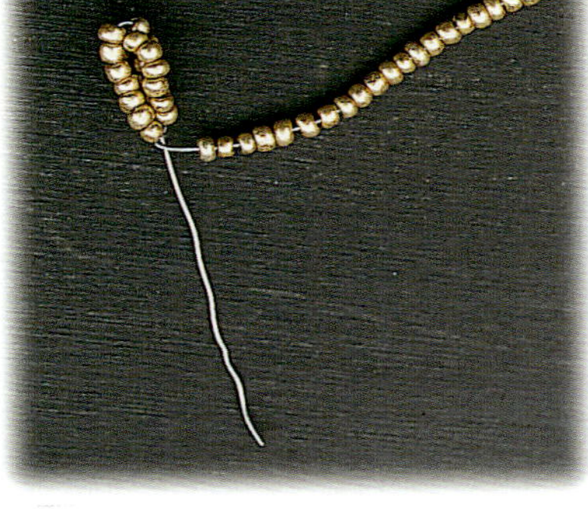

1. *A golden stalk of wheat contains 40 caryopses or spikelets—the clusters of grain with their husks—each one made individually. For each spikelet use a beaded string, measuring a 1/3 to 1/2 inch loop and then another loop that crosses over it at a right angle.*

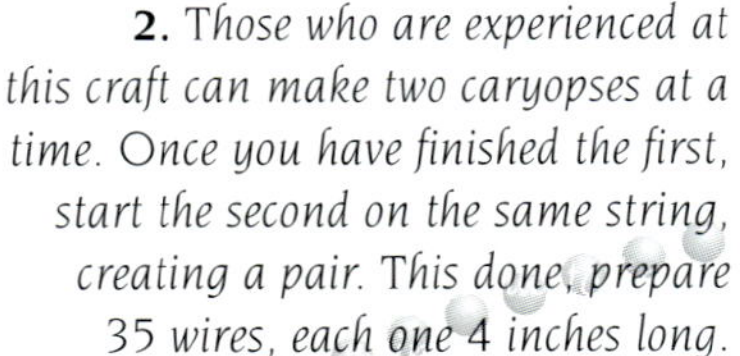

2. *Those who are experienced at this craft can make two caryopses at a time. Once you have finished the first, start the second on the same string, creating a pair. This done, prepare 35 wires, each one 4 inches long.*

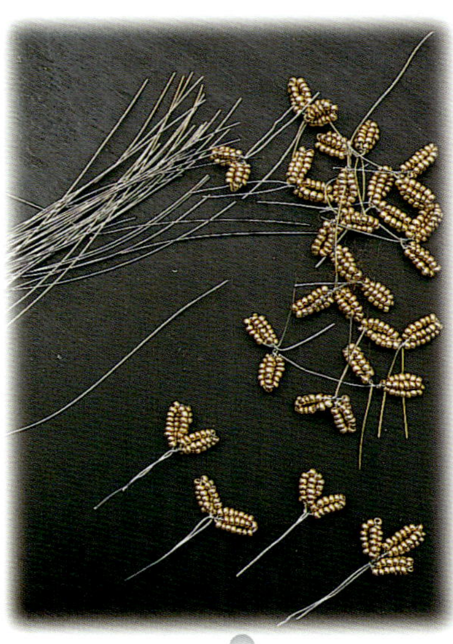

The Stalk of Wheat

Since earliest recorded history, golden wheat has been a symbol of fertility in all Western cultures. First a pagan, then a Christian symbol, it has accompanied the progress of humankind since the discovery of agriculture. Making a stalk of wheat with glass beads does not require any special skill, though you will need time and patience because of the small size of the caryopses.

3. *Assembling the stalk is the most difficult part of this project. After making all the parts, take a 20 gauge wire and fasten the first spikelet pair at the top using golden silk twist. Add the second pair about 1/5 of an inch below the first, facing in the opposite direction.*

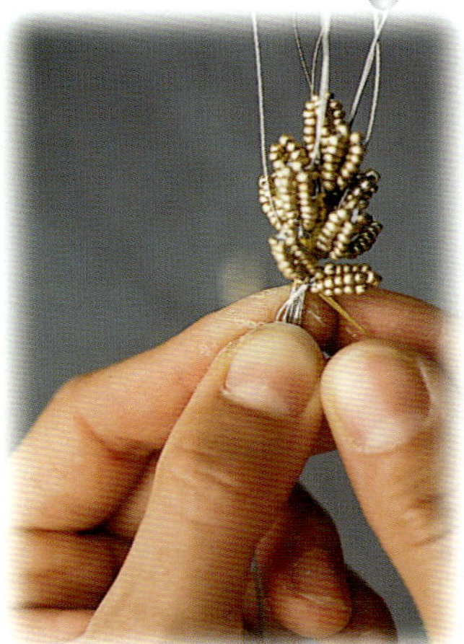

4. *Add the third pair about 1/3 to 1/2 an inch below the second, facing in the opposite direction. After about five pairs, insert the first pair of thin wires that recall the awns of the spikelet.*

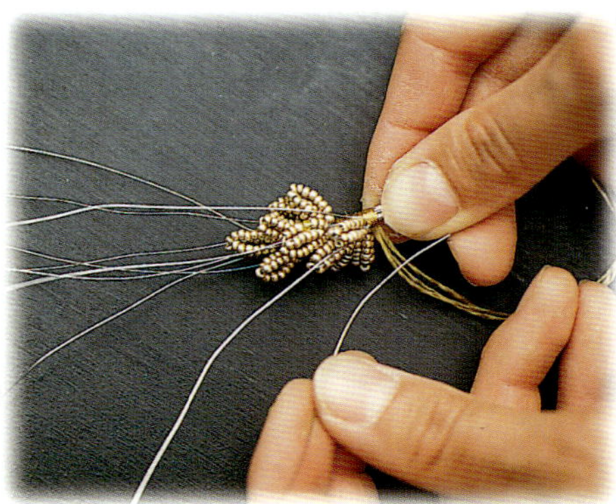

MATERIALS

For each stalk of wheat you will need:

- 3 wires: 24-26 gauge, strung with glossy gold beads
- 1 20 gauge stem wire, 7 inches long
- 1 18 gauge stem wire, 20 inches long
- 28-30 gauge wire for spikelets: 4 inches long
- dark gold silk twist, vinyl glue, pliers.

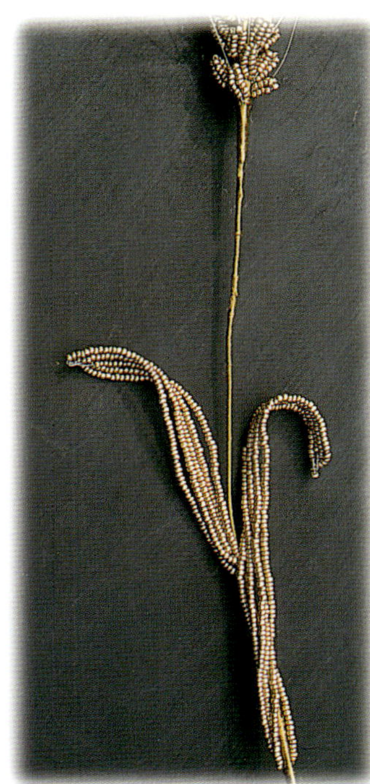

6. *Once the stalk is completed, prepare the leaves. Each stalk has two double-pointed leaves, made with the same golden beads used for the grains. One leaf has a 3 inch core and consists of two rows around the core; the second leaf has a 5½ inch core and the same number of rows.*

7. *Attach the first leaf about 5 inches below the last spikelet and the second leaf another 4 to 5 inches below, then continue covering the stem with the silk twist. These wheat spikes create a marvelous effect in bouquets of daisies, poppies, blue morning glories, and sunflowers.*

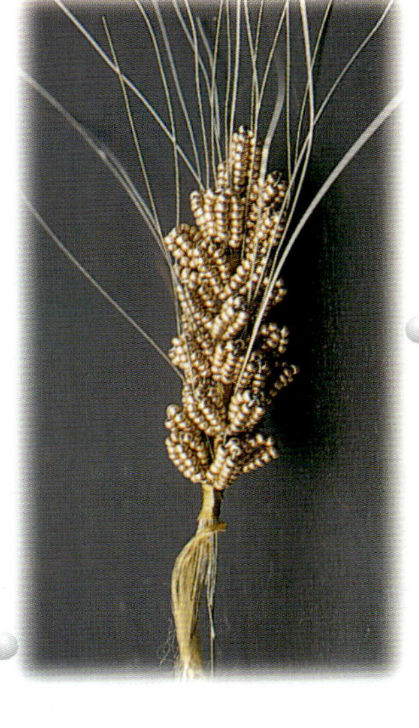

5. *Finish assembling the stalk carefully, distributing each pair of spikelets regularly down the stem, with an awn for each spikelet pointing upward.*

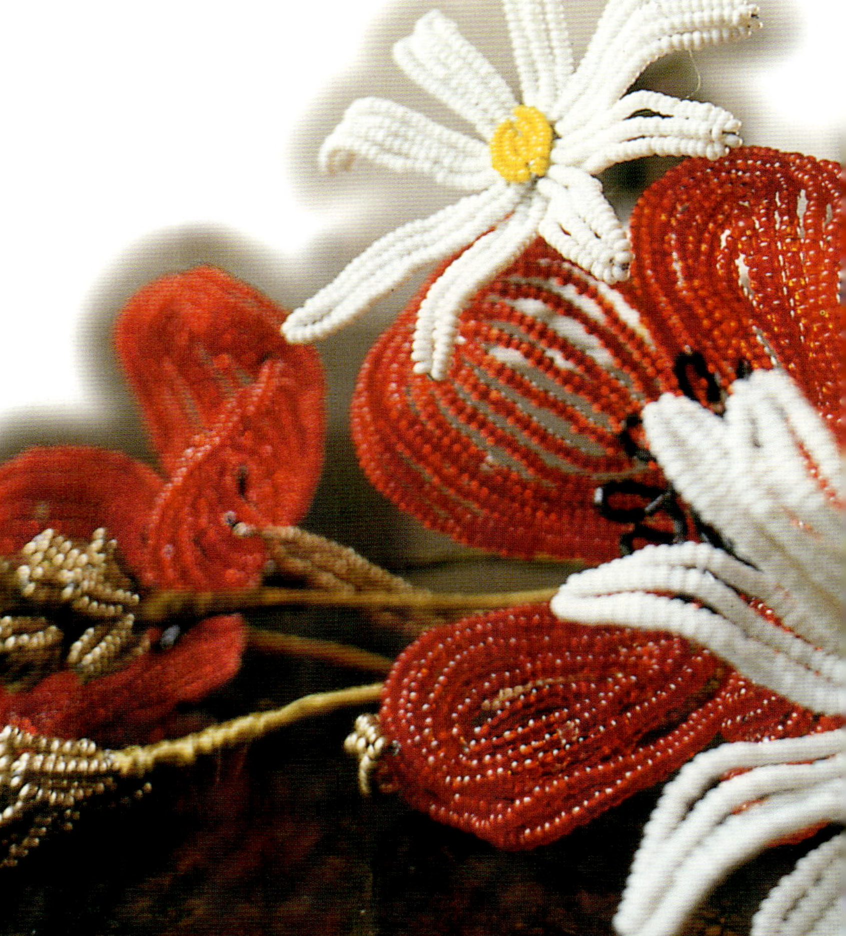

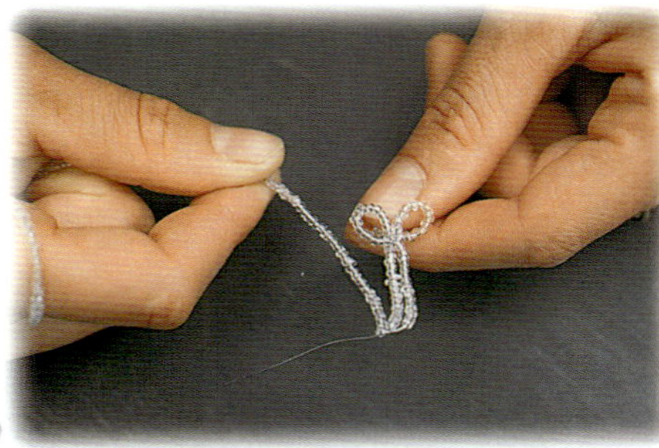

1. *This flower consists of several clusters joined at the base. Measure a 1½ inch length of white beaded string, then make three small loops ⅜ of an inch each; measure another 1½ inches of beads and tie the wire below the first 1½ inches of beads. This is the first floret.*

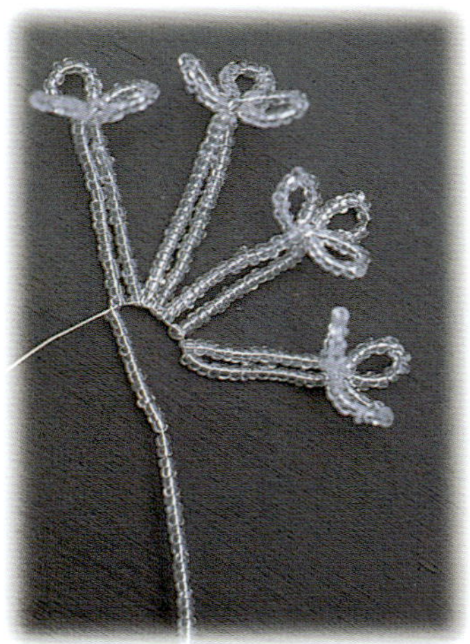

2. *Repeat three more times, then pull the wire that supports the florets, curling them and completing the first cluster. For a full African lily you will need a total of eight clusters of four florets each. For optimum results, make sure the length and the size of each floret are uniform.*

The African Lily

The African lily (Agapanthus africanus), known as the flower of love, is native to Southern Africa. The wild African lily has a lovely, pale blue umbrella-like shape, while the cultivated variety has white and blue umbrella-like flowers. The white African lily is particularly suited for spring bouquets that are light and airy. It is a bright flower with a charming shape. To make it, use transparent or iridescent white beads.

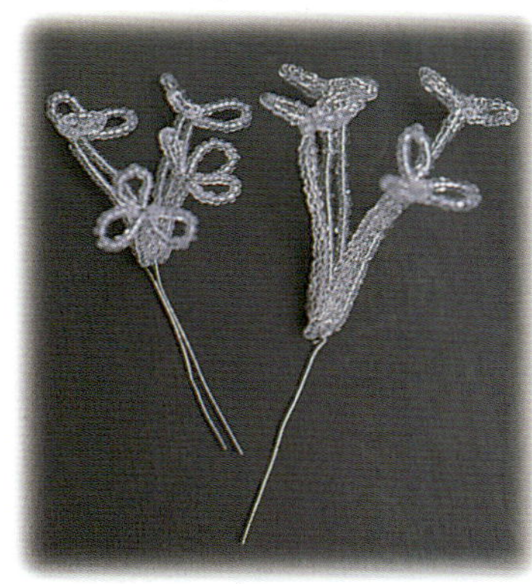

3. *Now make four smaller clusters to be attached below the larger clusters. Two clusters will be 1¼ inches long and the other two, ¾ of an inch long.*

4. *Attach three long, ribbon-like green leaves to the stem and wind them gently around it. Each leaf is double pointed and constructed following the core technique. The first leaf is 4 inches long, the second 5 inches , and the third 6 inches long. Each leaf consists of one round of beads around the core.*

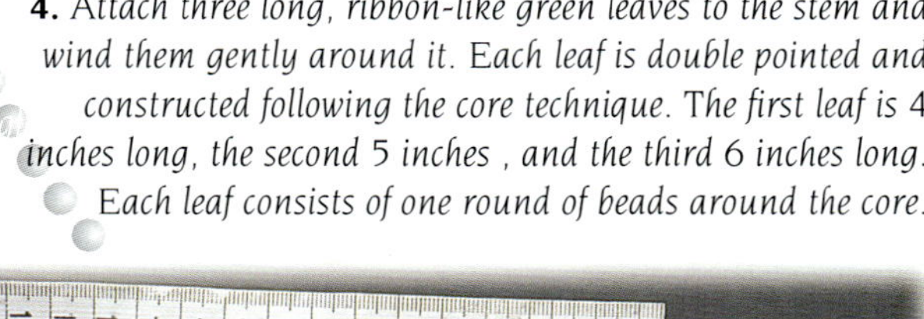

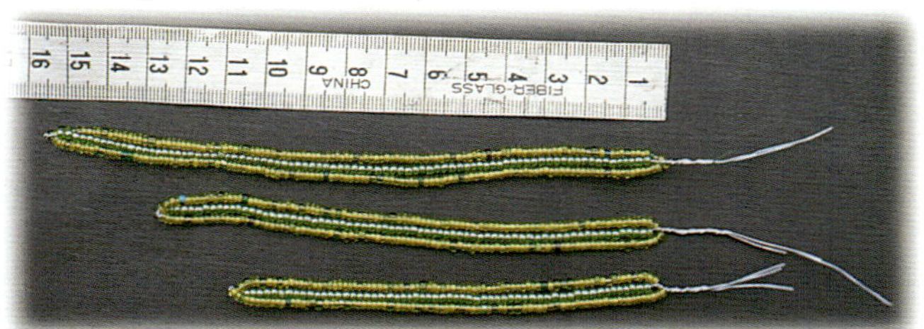

5. *Assembling this flower is easy. Take a 20 inch long, 18 gauge stem wire and attach the first four clusters at the top, then the smaller ones just below, creating one flower.*

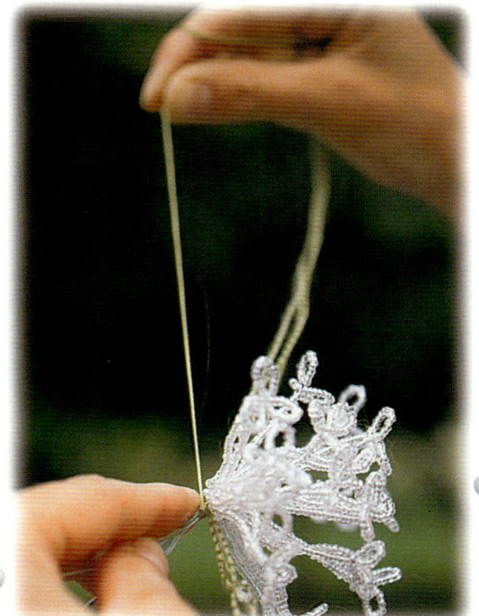

MATERIALS

- 10 strings of white iridescent beads strung on 24-26 gauge wire
- 3 strings of green transparent beads strung on 24-26 gauge wire
- 18 gauge stem wire
- pale green silk twist, vinyl glue, pliers.

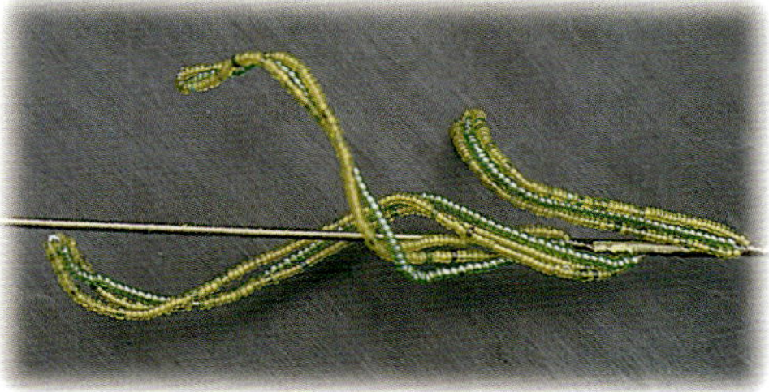

7. *Add the leaves about 10 inches below the flower. Each leaf should be at a distance of about 1½ inches. Wind them gently around the stem.*

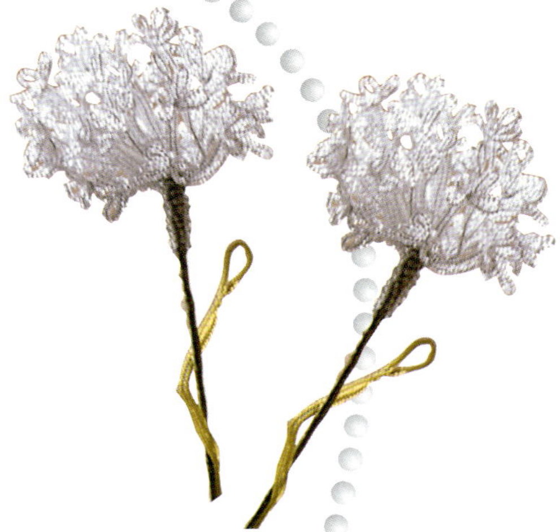

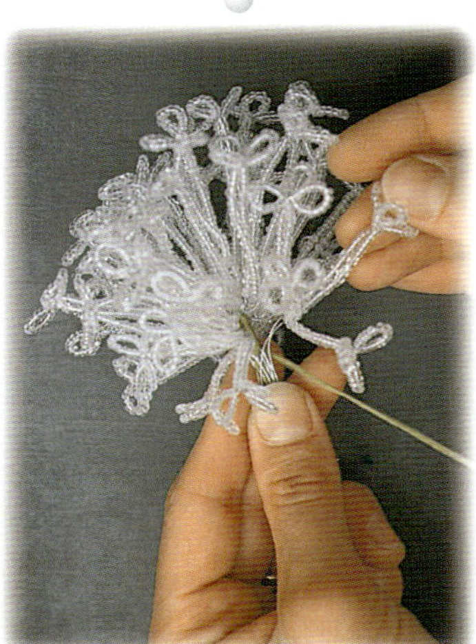

6. *Cover the stem with silk yarn for about 4 inches, then open the flower gently with your fingers, giving it the desired shape. Each floret should be opened in the same fashion. The type of beads used will give different effects of brightness and luminosity.*

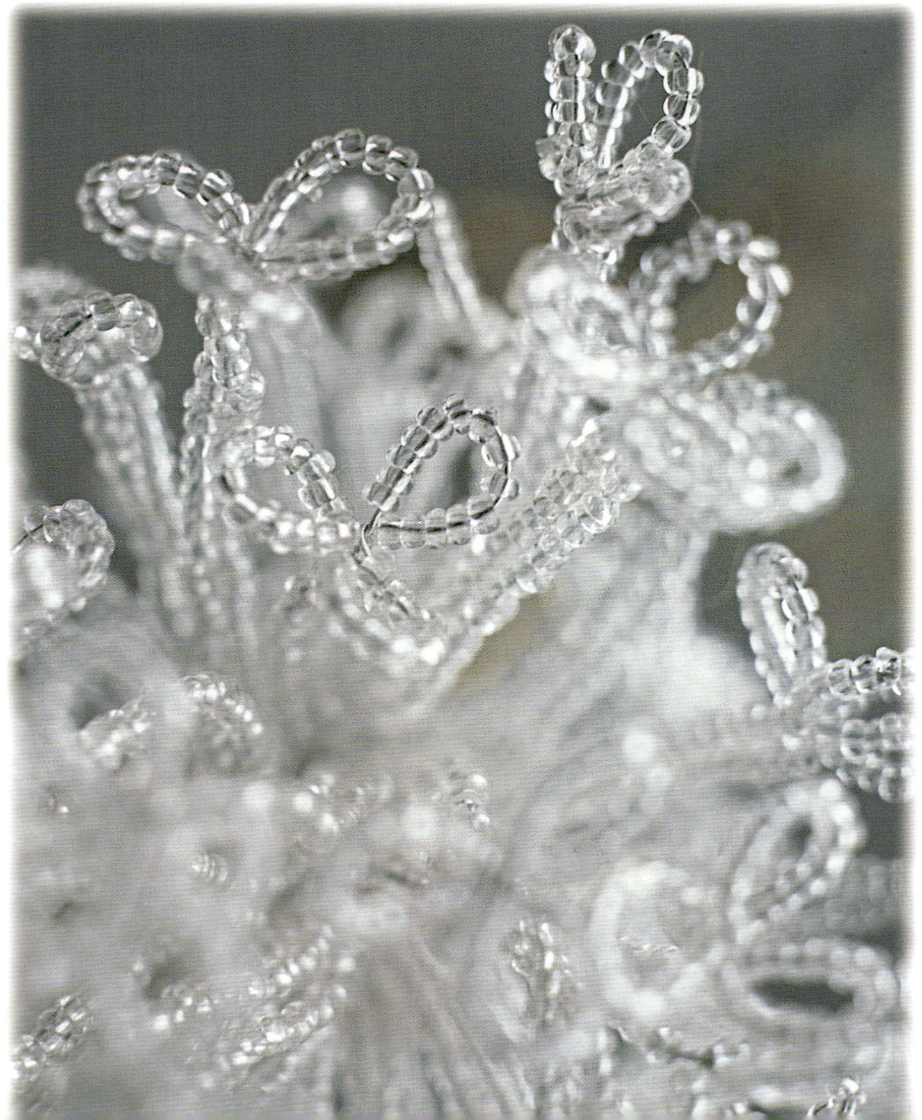

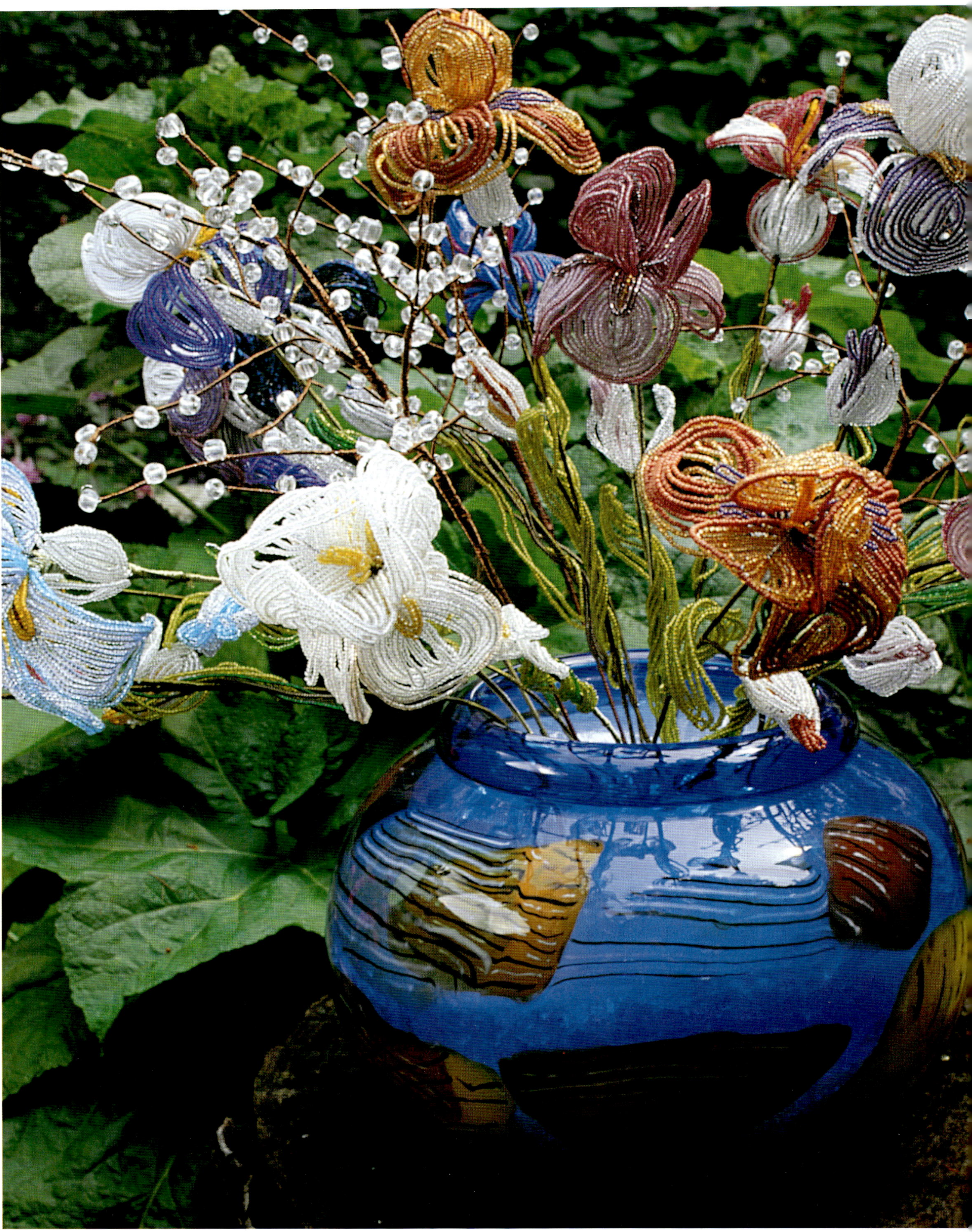

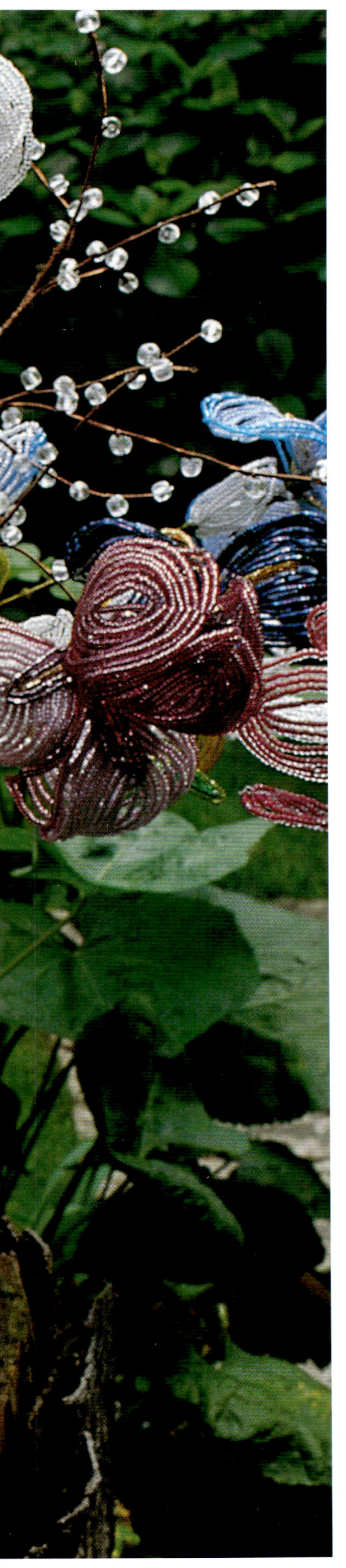

4 CHAPTER

Bouquets and Arrangements

Now that we have learned how to construct each single flower, the next step is to learn how to arrange them in pleasing bouquets and compositions. Creativity plays an important part in this pleasant task, so do not be afraid to follow your own unique style. Beaded flowers, being stiff by their very nature, need warm, spontaneous arrangements. Luckily, nature comes to our aid with all the splendor of the different seasons. One suggestion is to collect the most beautiful flowers of each season and reproduce them, creating bouquets that will survive many seasons.

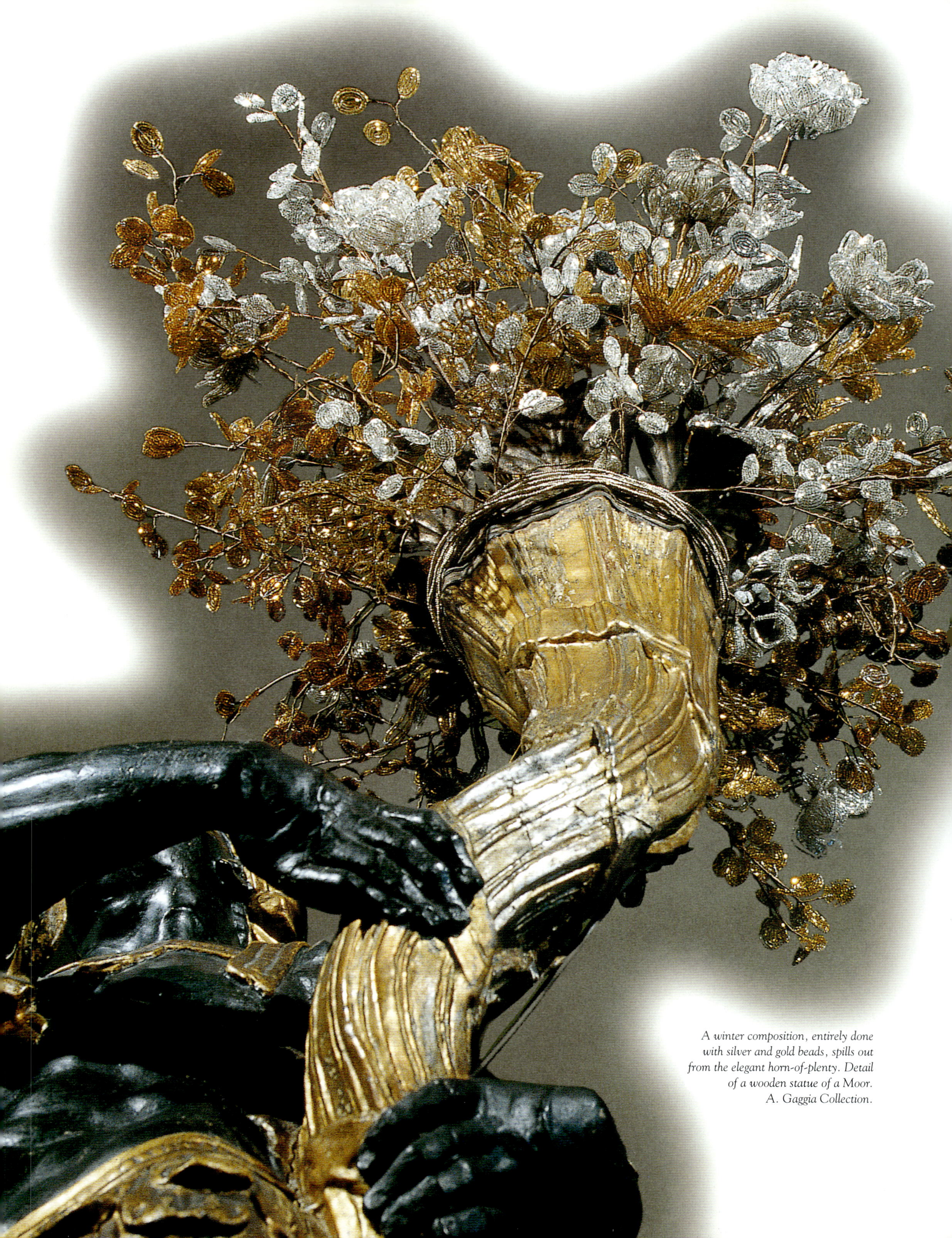

A winter composition, entirely done with silver and gold beads, spills out from the elegant horn-of-plenty. Detail of a wooden statue of a Moor. A. Gaggia Collection.

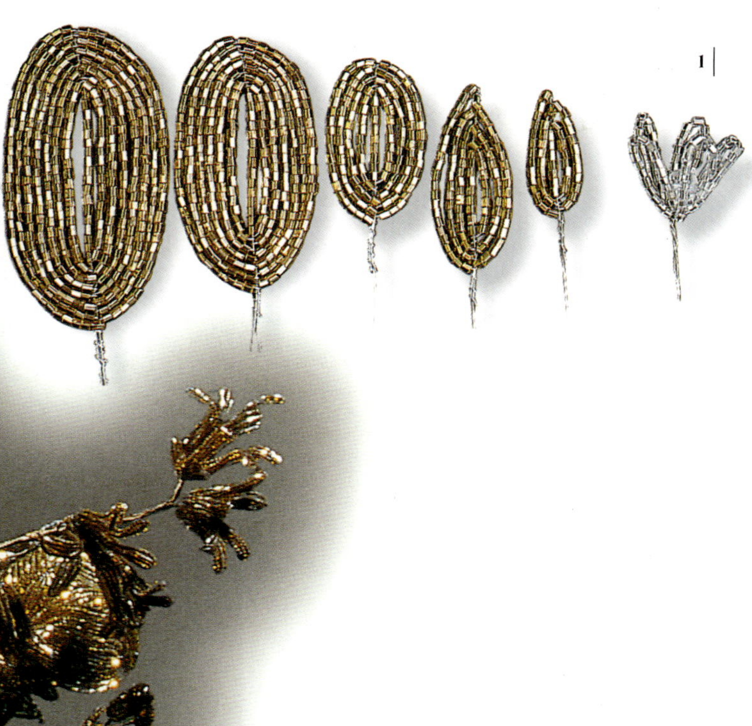

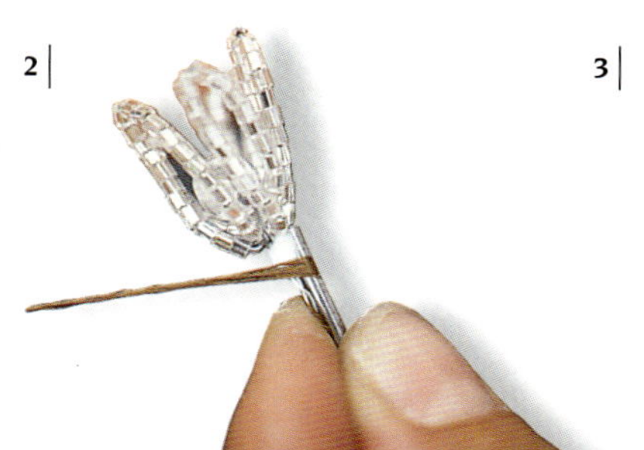

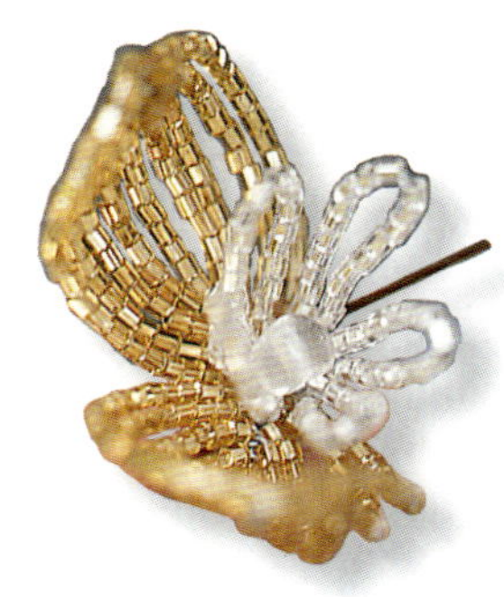

Silver and Gold Flowers

Of all the compositions made with beaded flowers, the gold and silver bouquet is the most typically Venetian. They are truly small, authentic, personal treasures, full of light and magic. The ideal flowers for these bouquets are roses, together with ethereal satinpods, and lilies and irises that reflect the light well.

The ideal containers for these flowers are clear crystal or golden amber vases, placed against a dark background that plays up the flowers, or against a wood-paneled wall that adds warmth to the composition.

Materials | For each rose you will need:

- *10 strings of gold (or silver) beads*
- 28, 22 *gauge stem wires,* 5 *inches long*
- 2, 20 *gauge stem wires,* 8 *inches long*
- 18 *gauge stem wire,* 20 *inches long*
- *dark brown silk twist, vinyl glue, pliers.*

PREPARATION

1 | Like the red rose, the corolla of the golden rose consists of 13 petals of three different sizes: four small, four medium, five large, plus the flower's heart. In addition, the rose has five pointed sepals composing the calyx.

2 | As usual, assemble the flowers starting from the top and working towards the bottom. Take an 18 gauge stem wire and attach the small light-colored central button to it. Before starting the assembly, we suggest you fasten the silk yarn to the rod with a little glue.

3 | Fasten the four small gold petals at the same height, shaping them gently with your fingers before attaching them to the stem.

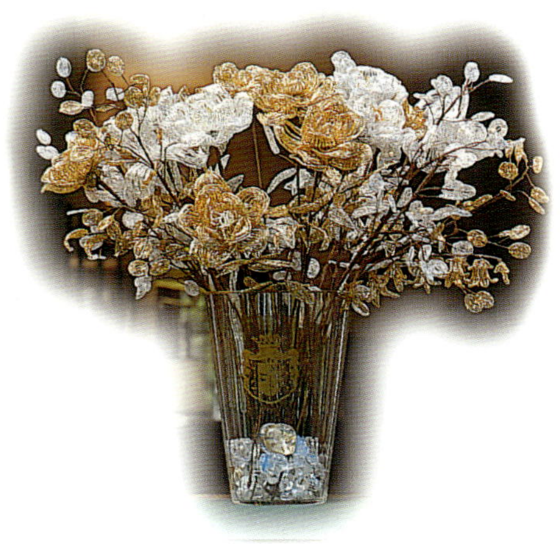

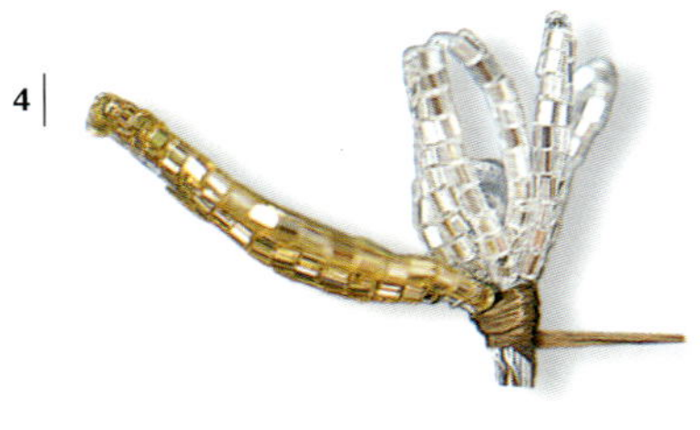

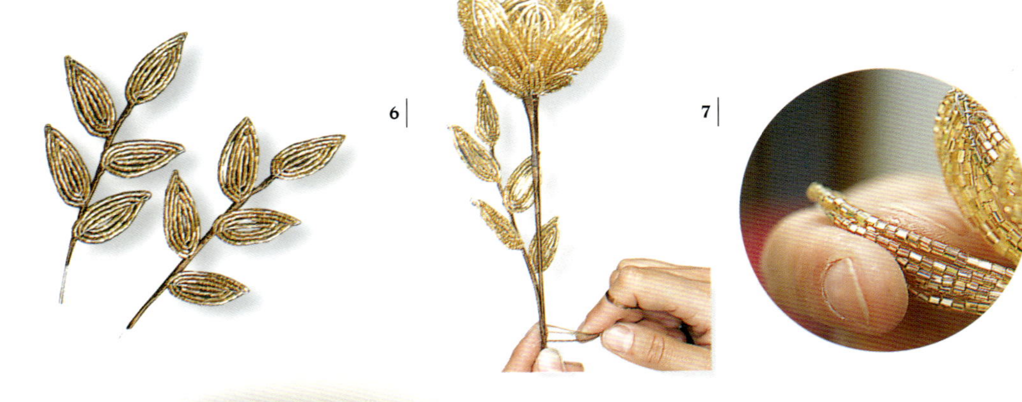

4 | Add each petal to the flower by attaching it firmly to the stem with silk twist. After fastening the small petals, add the medium ones and finally the large ones. Each series of petal must be inserted at the same height.

5 | At this point you are ready to prepare the two small lateral branches that complete the rose. Make five small, pointed leaves for each branch, inserted at a distance of about ½ inch each. Cover the small branches with dark brown silk first, and then add the leaves.

6 | To complete the rose, add the five sepals below the corolla, attaching them firmly with silk twist. Then, about 6 inches below add the first branch and a few inches below the second one facing in the opposite direction. Both are attached to the center stem with silk twist.

7 | Curve the five small sepals downward using your fingers or the pliers, to give the flower a natural look.

8–9 | Carefully shape the flower petal by petal with your fingers, opening it up, then with your index and thumb slightly turn the point of the petals downward.

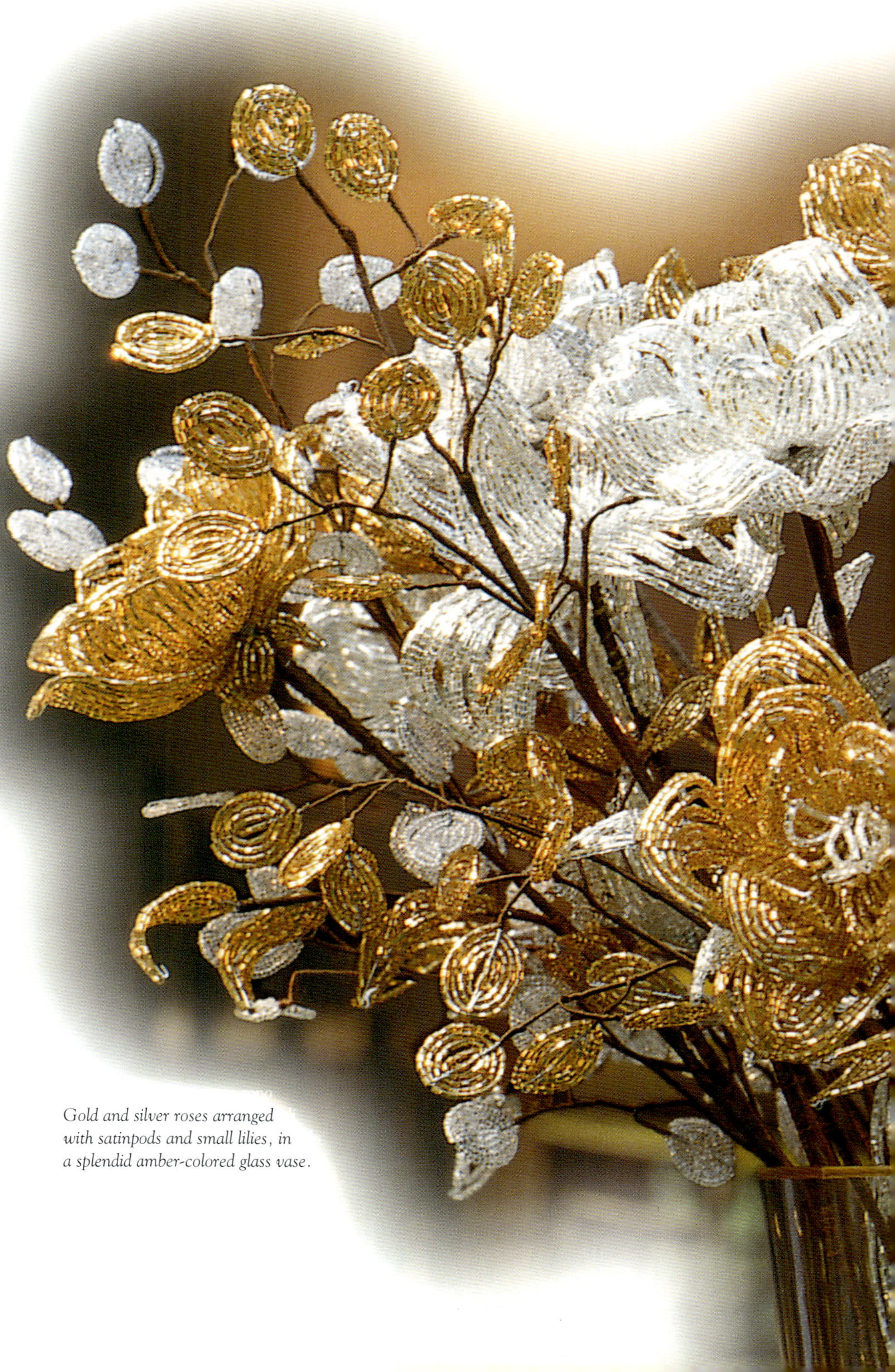

Gold and silver roses arranged with satinpods and small lilies, in a splendid amber-colored glass vase.

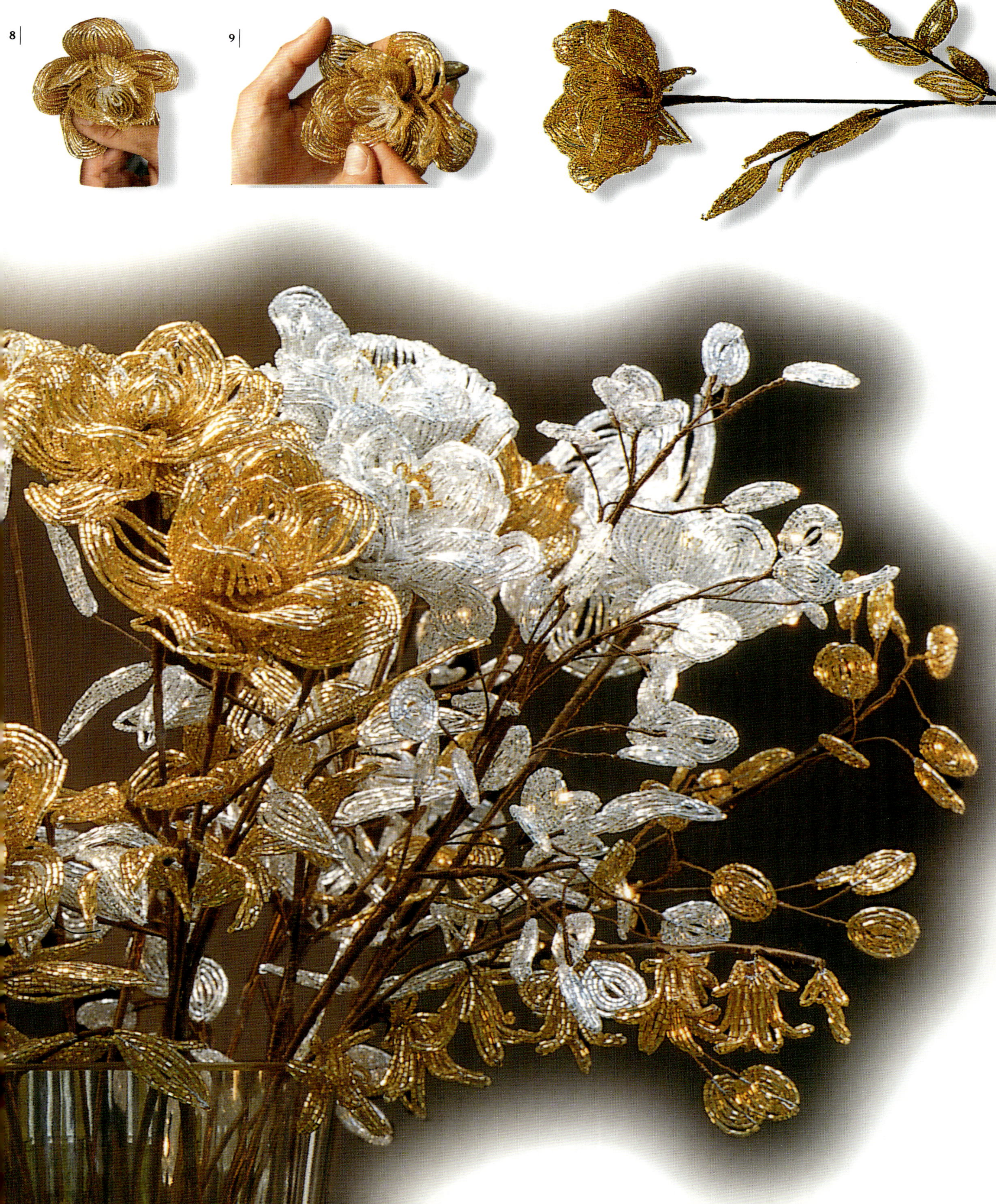
8
9

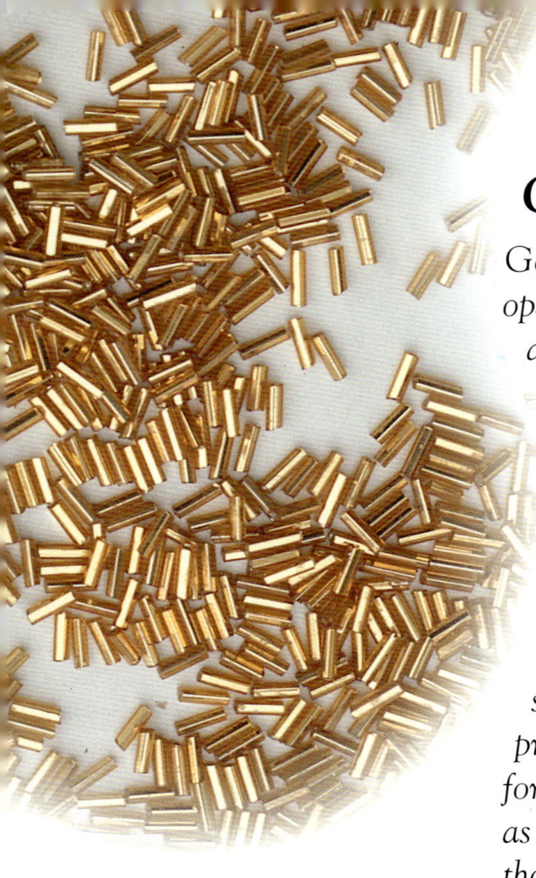

Old Gold

Gold and silver beads that have become opaque as a result of long exposure to the air are ideal for creating attractive compositions where time's patina is the true celebrity.

For these compositions, you need suitable containers such as antique vases that because of their delicate nature should not be used for freshly cut flowers, or vases decorated with gold and silver highlights that can be displayed preeminently in the house. The techniques for making old gold flowers are the same as those for regular gold and silver flowers, though you should be careful not to twist the wires too much, as due to oxidization within the bead, the old glass has become more fragile.

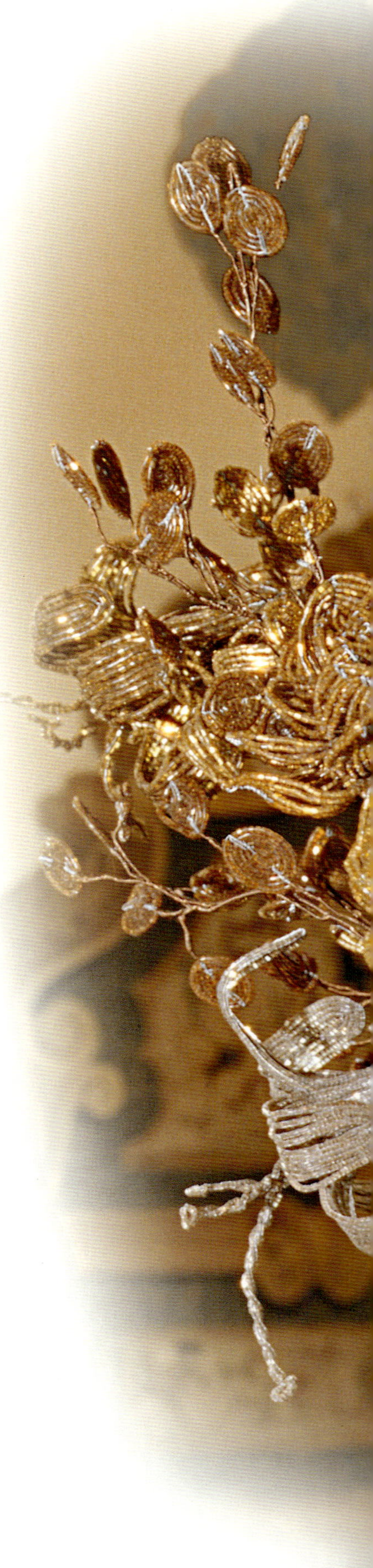

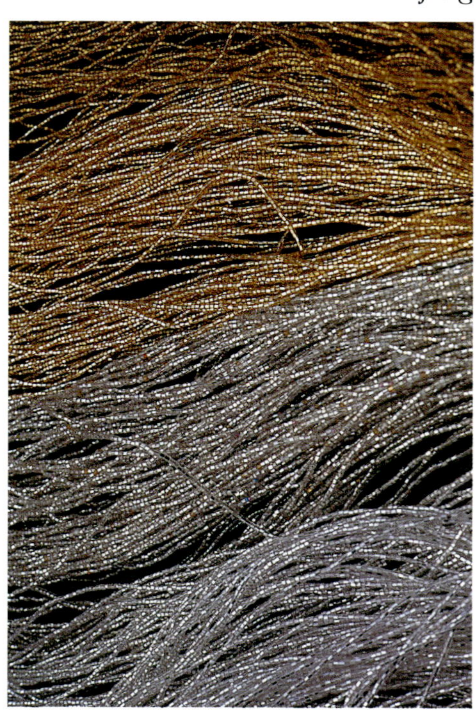

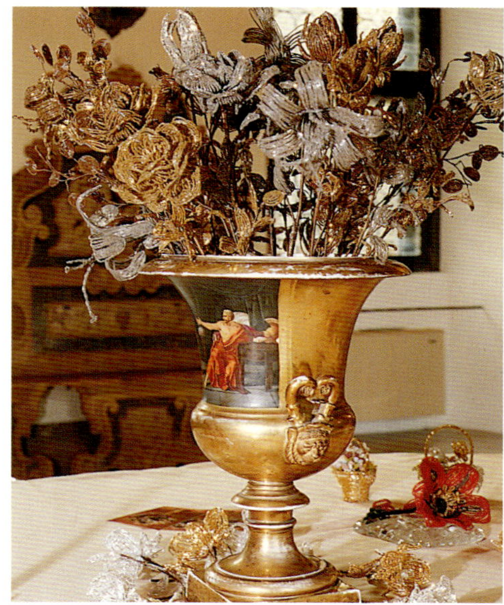

A bouquet of flowers made with old gold beads is enhanced by a lovely vase in a neoclassical style and shape.

1

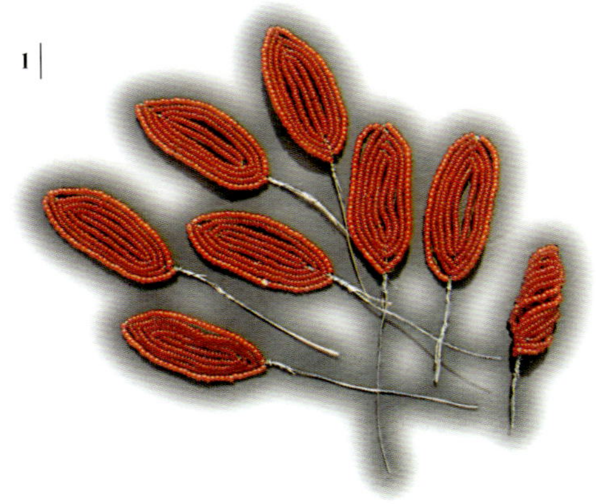

2

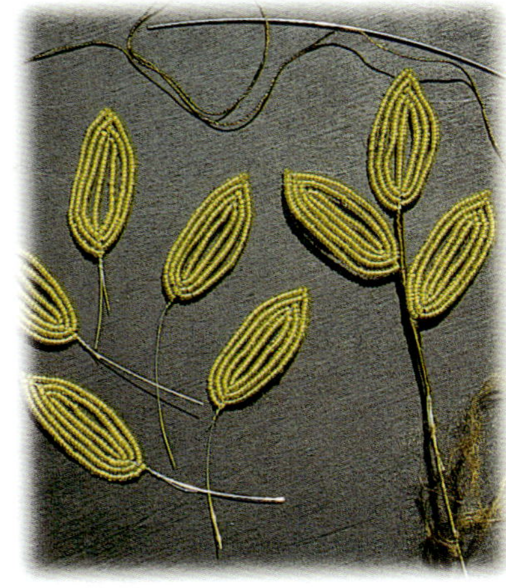

3

A Brightly Colored Bouquet

Sometimes we are so attracted to compositions of freshly cut flowers in strong, contrasting colors that we wish we could recreate them, suspending time. We can create our bouquet whenever we want, one flower at a time, whenever we find a flower whose colors we particularly like, or whose form we find particularly attractive, or that reminds us of someone dear to us or of a happy time. We can make a bouquet using flowers that we are already familiar with, adding maybe a rose bud or a white and blue tulip.

Materials | For each rose bud you will need:

•

4 strings of clear red beads

•

2 strings of red corniola *beads (white hearts)*

•

3 strings of clear green beads

•

22 gauge stem wire

•

20 gauge stem wire.

Procedure | To make a rose bud, prepare the red petals first, then the foliage, and finally assemble the flower.

THE ROSE BUD

1 | In the photos above you can see the petals that make up the rose bud. For the corolla, we need seven double-pointed petals with a 1½ inch core and three rounds of transparent red beads, plus one final round of red *corniola* (white hearts), beads to outline it. Curl one petal on itself to create the heart of the flower.

2 | There are eight double-pointed stem leaves. Make each leaf by measuring 1¼ inches of transparent green beads for the core, and wind three full rounds around it to complete the leaf. For the collar, you will need five double-pointed green leaves with a ½ inch core and two rounds of green beads.

3 | In the photograph above, you can see how we curled one petal around itself to create the bud's center. Curl it around your finger in a spiral movement. The petal is double pointed, has a 2 inch core, three rounds of transparent red beads, and one outer round of red *corniola* beads.

4 | Assemble the flower starting from the corolla. First attach the heart of the flower with green silk and vinyl glue at the top of a 20 inch, 18 gauge stem wire, then add the petals one by one.

5 | Immediately below the red petals add the collar sepals. There are five of them and they must be attached all at the same height.

6 | Now prepare the two small branches, using two 20 gauge wires, 8 inches long. Assemble three leaves on one branch and five on the other. The branch with three leaves should be higher up on the stem than the other.

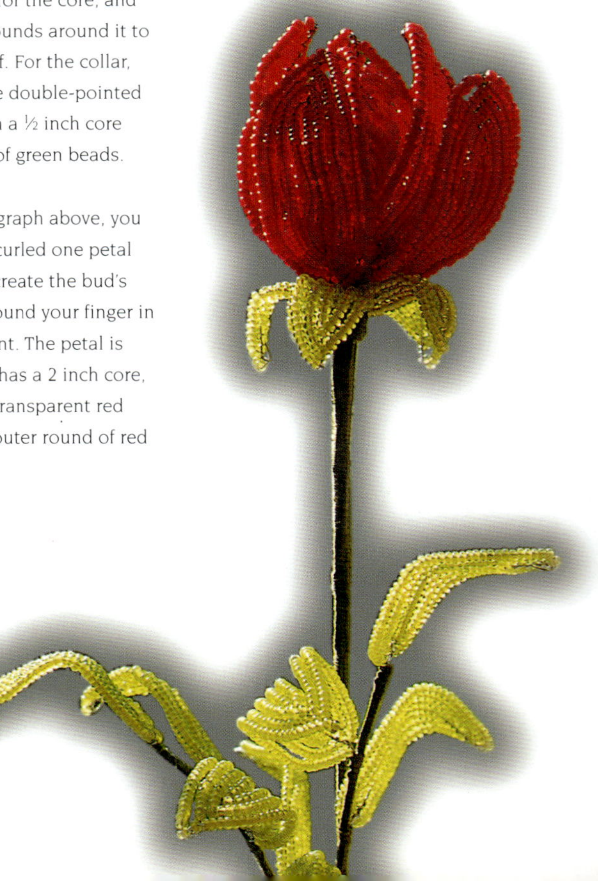

4

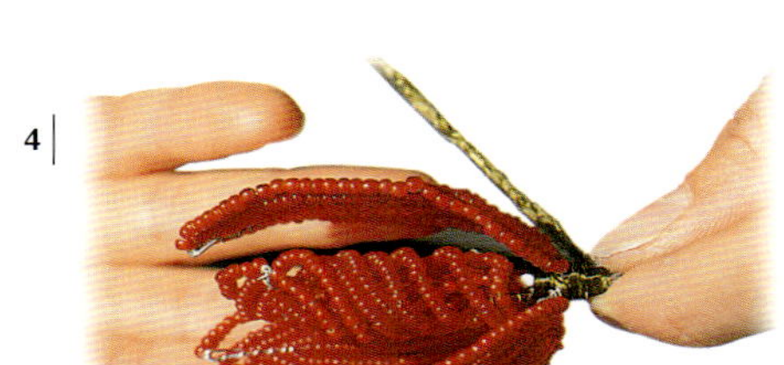

5

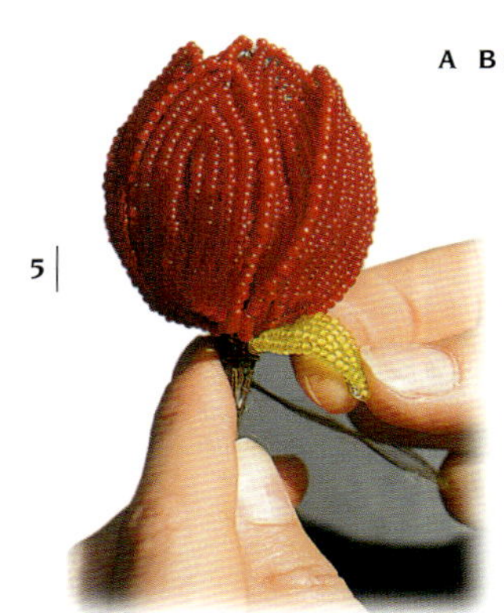

6

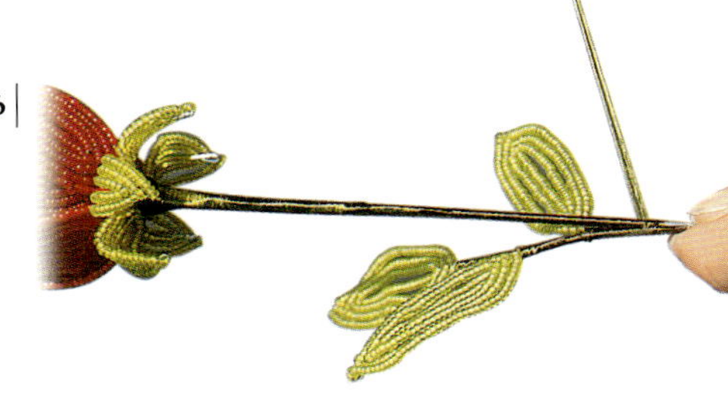

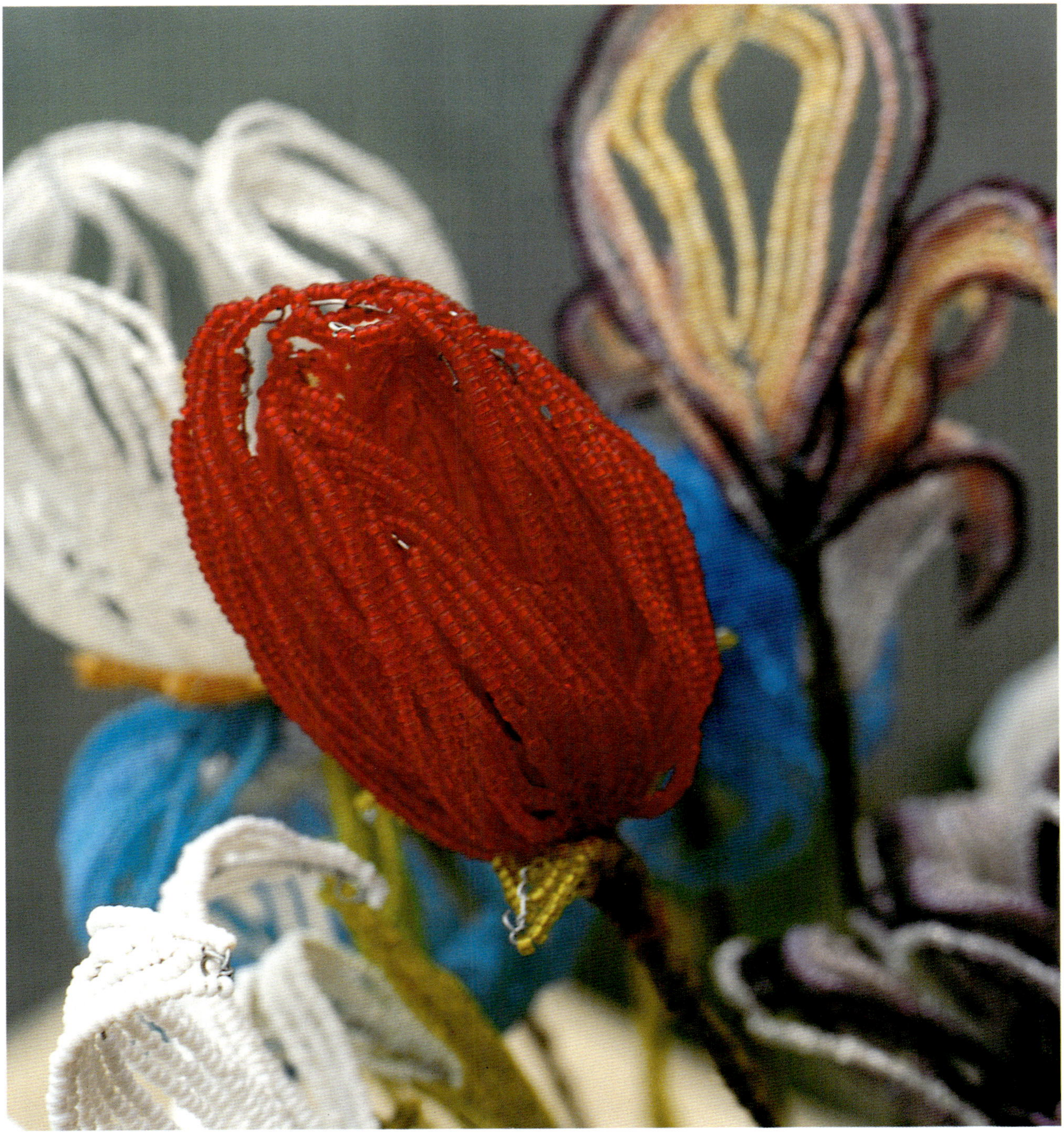

1

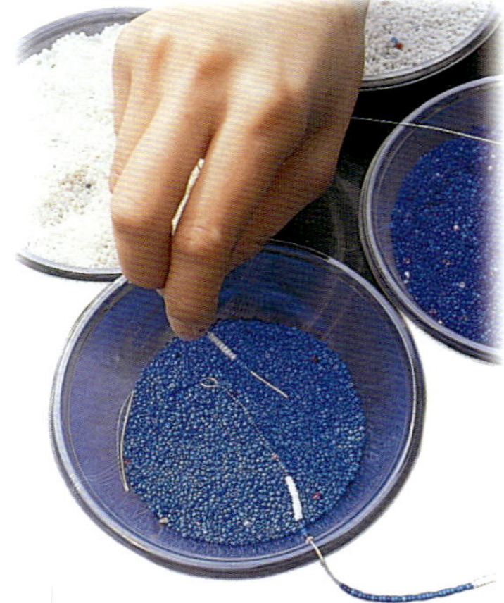

2

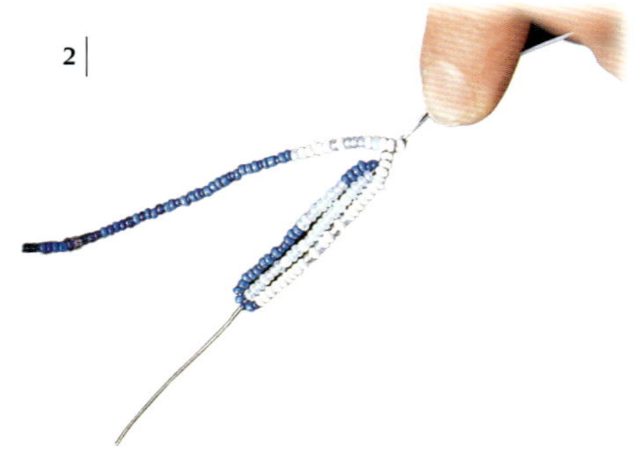

3

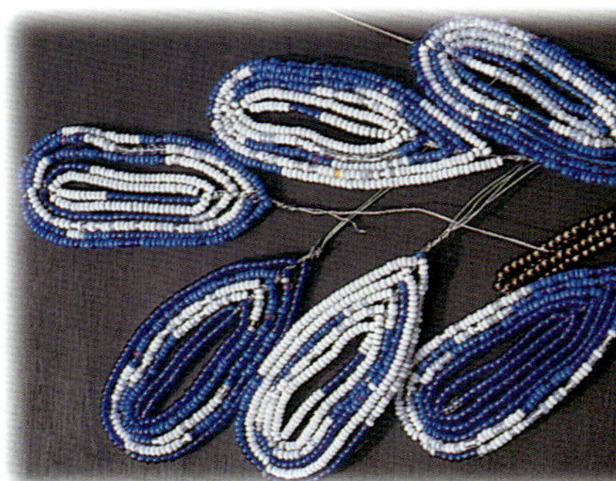

THE BLUE AND WHITE TULIP

1 | Prepare several bowls full of beads in different shades of white and blue (at least two of each color) and string six separate strings by dipping them into the bowls in random fashion.

2 | Shape the six petals that make up the tulip. They are pointed at the bottom and rounded at the top, with a 1 ½ inch core and five rounds of beads.

3 | You can see the petals of one tulip in the above photograph. Note, in particular, the pistil made with a 1¼ inch double loop of copper-colored beads.

4 | Cover the stem with the silk twist starting from the top. Fasten the pistil first, then the petals at the same height.

5 | To the stem add one double-pointed green leaf, about 7 inches long, shaped as you see in the photograph on the top right.

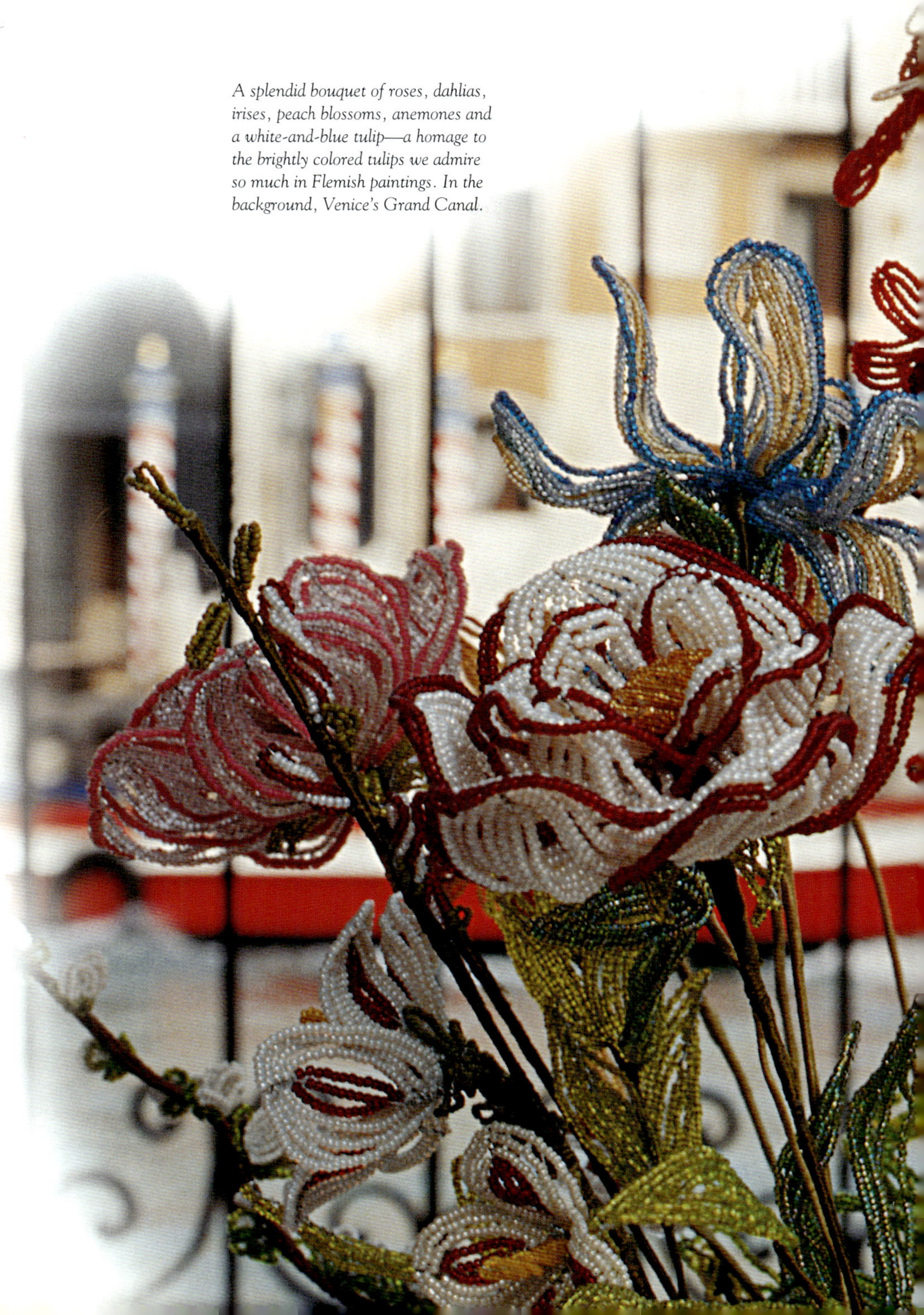

A splendid bouquet of roses, dahlias, irises, peach blossoms, anemones and a white-and-blue tulip—a homage to the brightly colored tulips we admire so much in Flemish paintings. In the background, Venice's Grand Canal.

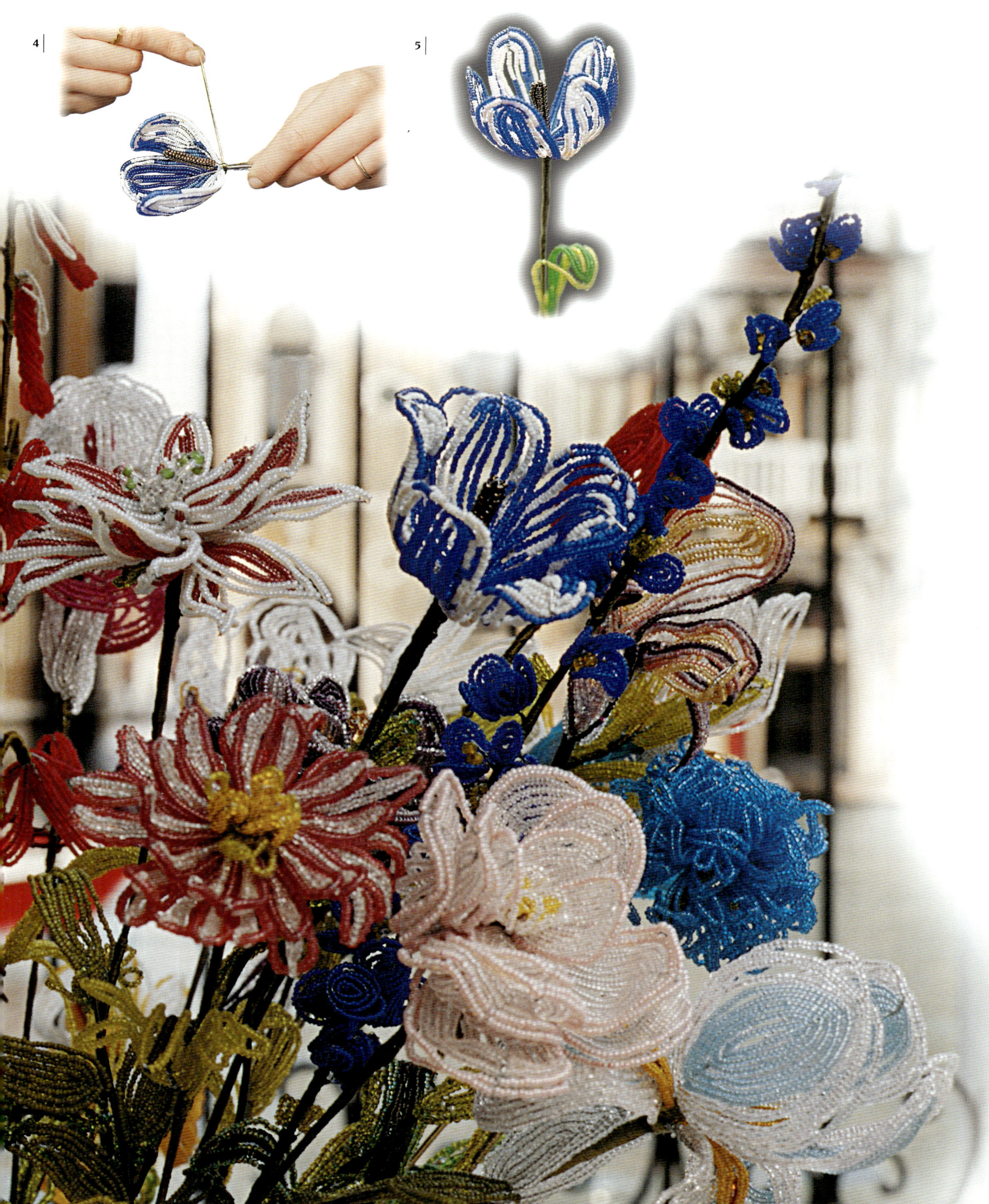
4
5

A Spring Arrangement

At the end of winter, the narcissus start blooming along with bushes of golden forsythias and the first, shy tulips appear. They are the first flowers to drive away winter and revive the garden and the home with their colors.

Materials | For a white and red tulip you will need:

- *1 string of bronze colored beads*
- *2 strings of white beads with a mother-of-pearl finish*
- *2 strings of transparent red beads*
- *22 gauge stem wire*
- *18 gauge stem wire*
- *dark green silk twist, vinyl glue, pliers*

For each forsythia branch you will need:

- *6 strings of transparent yellow beads*
- *18 gauge stem wire*
- *brown silk twist, vinyl glue, pliers.*

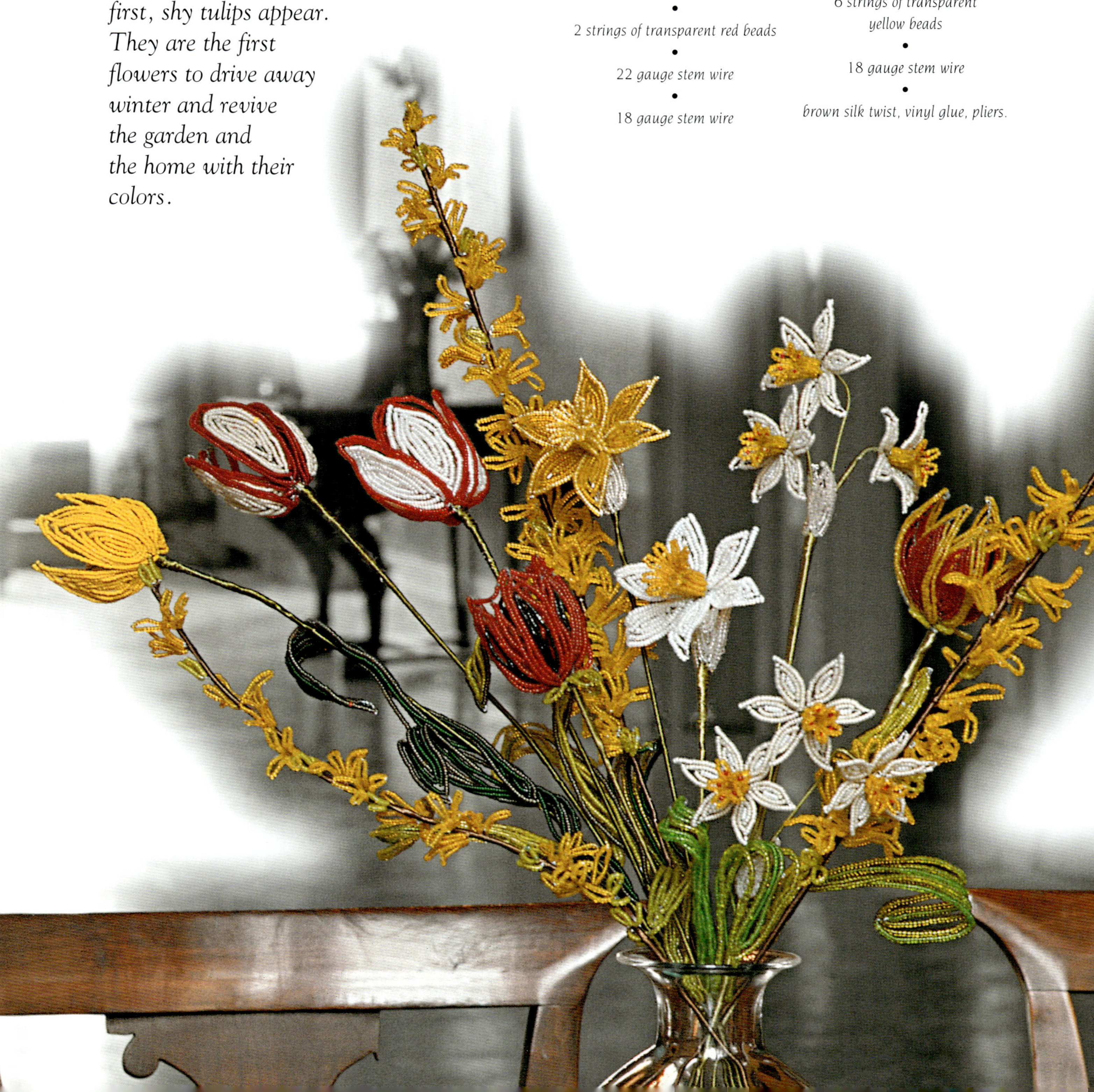

1

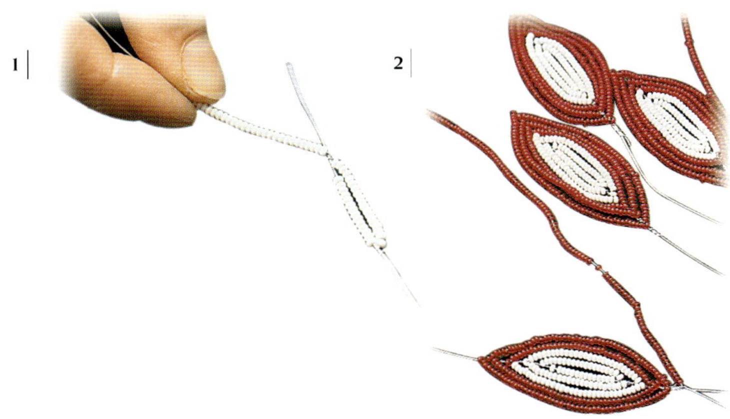

2

3

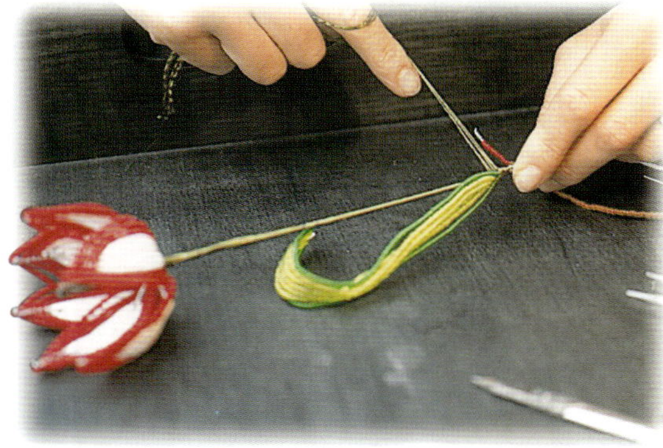

4

THE WHITE AND RED TULIP AND THE FORSYTHIA

1 For an open tulip we need six white and red petals. Each petal has a ¾ of an inch white core with two rounds of white beads around it.

2 Each petal is completed by three more rounds of red beads. The pistil consists of a double loop of bronze-colored beads, 1¼ inches long.

3 Build the tulip starting from the pistil, adding the petals and then one green leaf to the stem. The leaf is double pointed and about 6 inches long.

4 The forsythia consists of about 18 florets of four petals each. Build each floret by making four small, equal loops about ½ inch long and curl them to give them the proper shape. Alternate at random with slightly larger florets of ¾ of an inch loops.

5 Assemble the forsythia by attaching the florets to the stem in a uniform manner, being careful not to leave too many empty spaces.

6 You may also add tiny green leaves to the forsythia, signifying that truly spring is just around the corner. And tulips, as we know, come in many different colors.

5

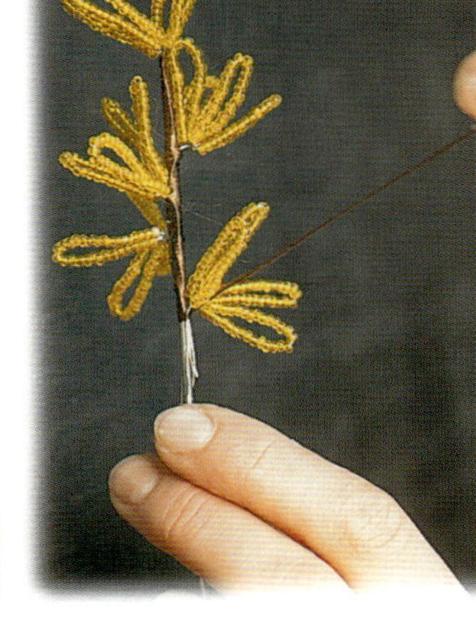

6

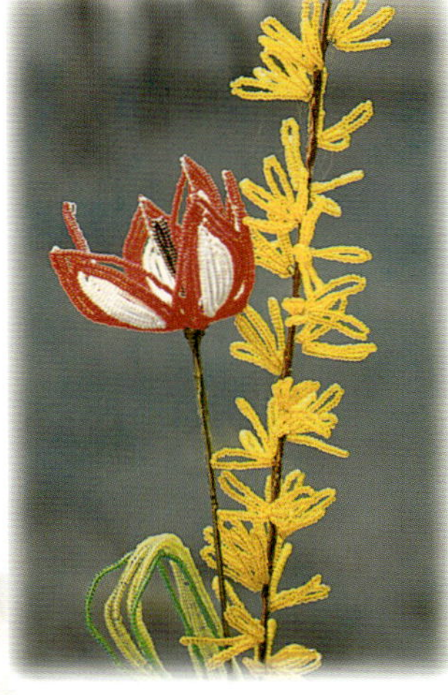

A Summer Arrangement

In summer, the sunflowers obediently turn their heads to follow the sun. When the plains are blanketed with them all the way to the horizon, we are in the dog days of summer, in hot July, and we look for the cool of the shade. Sunflowers, large white daisies and red poppies are the protagonists of summer field flower bouquets. For an ideal composition, arrange them in metal containers of bronze or copper, or maybe in a plain straw basket.

Materials For each sunflower you will need:

- *10 strings of transparent yellow beads*
- *4 strings of transparent green beads*
- *4 strings of bronze beads*
- *45 wires: 24 or 26 gauge, 4 inches long.*
- *3 wires: 22 gauge, 8 inches long*
- *1 wire, 20 gauge, 8 inches long*
- *1 18 gauge stem wire, 20 inches long.*

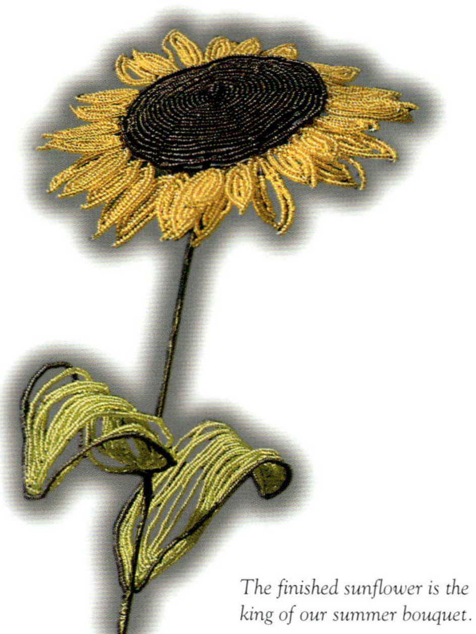

The finished sunflower is the king of our summer bouquet.

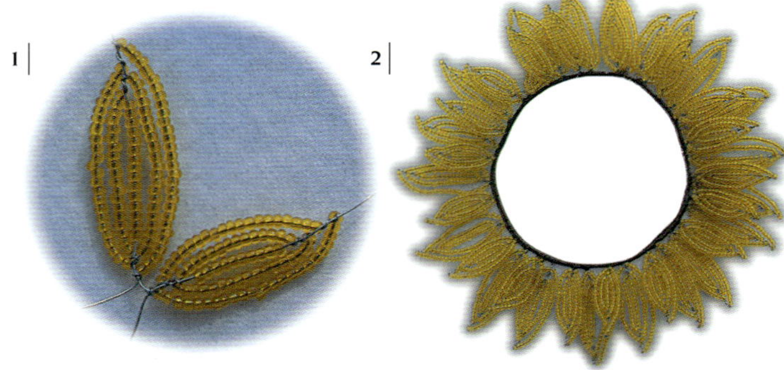

1 | 2 |

THE SUNFLOWER

1 | Make 40 yellow, double-pointed petals in two different sizes: 20 with a ½ inch core and 20 with a 1 inch core. In addition to the core, each petal consists of two rounds of yellow beads.

2 | Use brown silk twist to add each petal to the 18 gauge stem wire, alternating a large petal with a small one. The final result will be a ring of yellow petals.

3 | With the bronze beads make a large, flat disc of the same size as the inside ring of yellow petals. Start by crossing three 8 inch long wires together. See illustration. Once the disc is ready, do not cut the open end wires.

4 | Place the bronze disc in the center of the yellow ring. Use the disc's three wires to fasten it to the ring.

5 | Attach two large green leaves to the stem of the sunflower. Use two shades of green, light green and olive, to approximate the real colors. The leaves have a 5 inch core and eight or more rounds of beads.

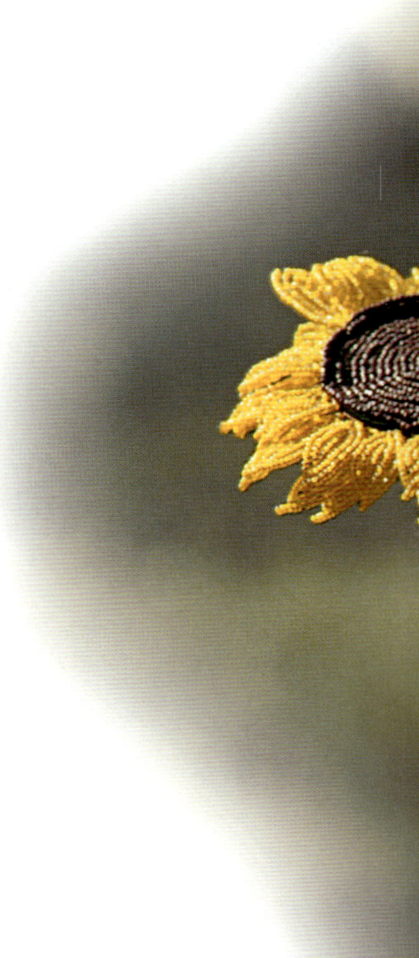

3

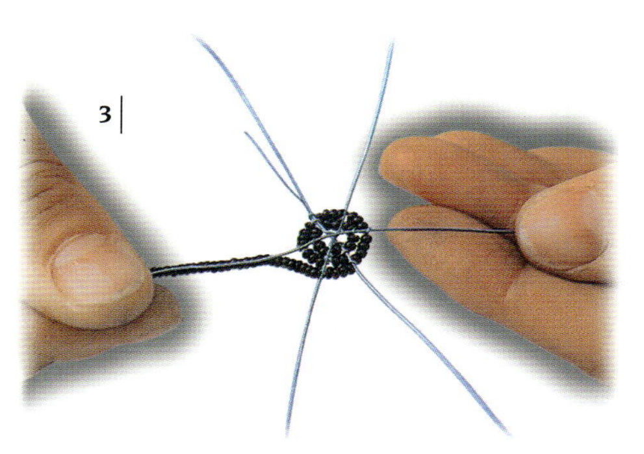

4

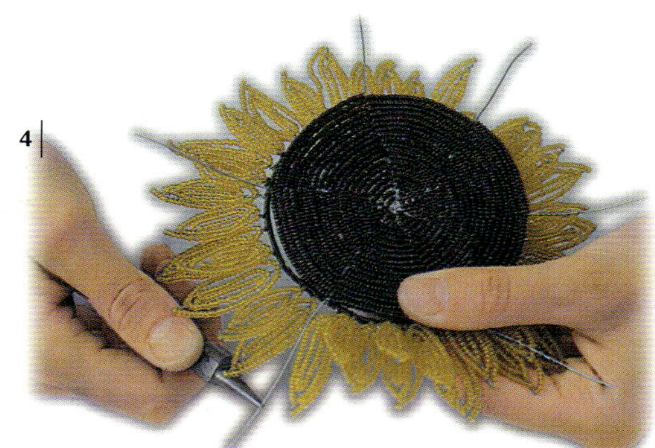

5

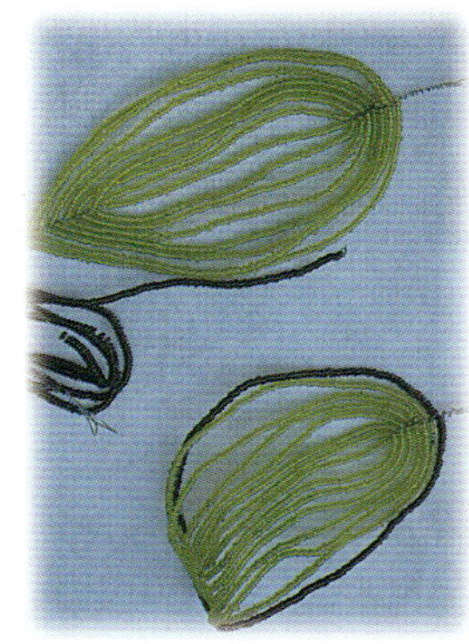

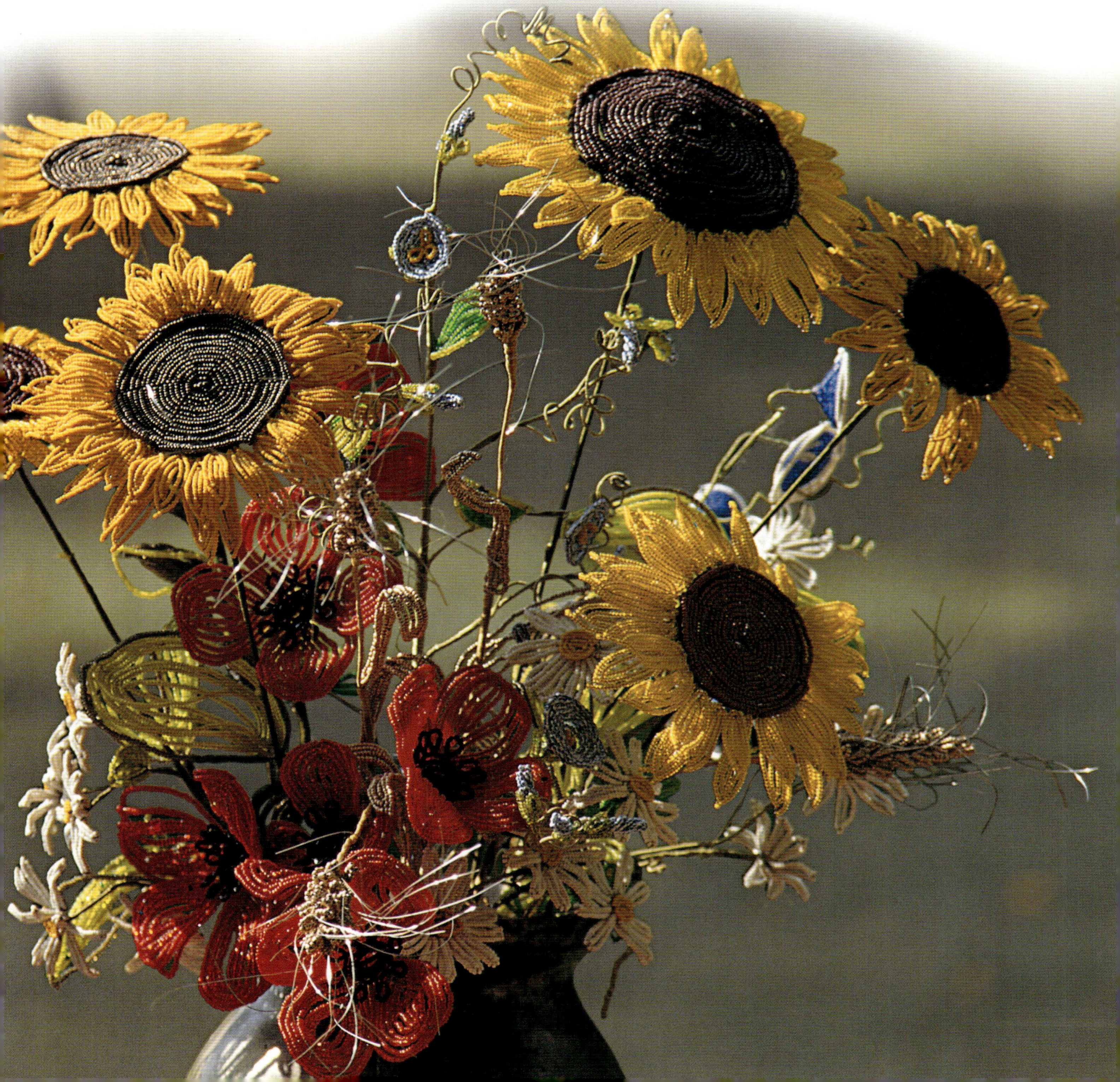

1 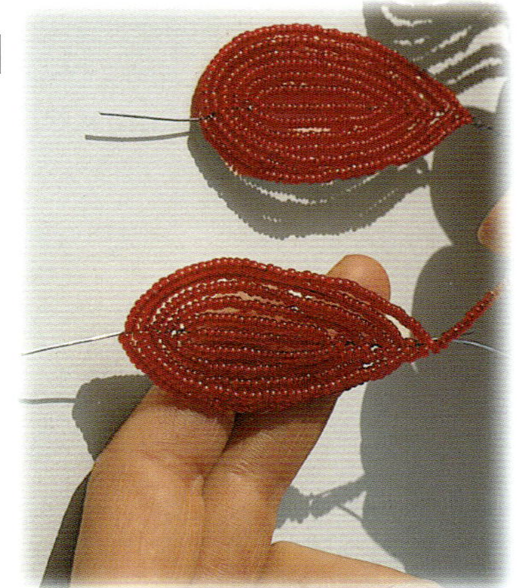

2 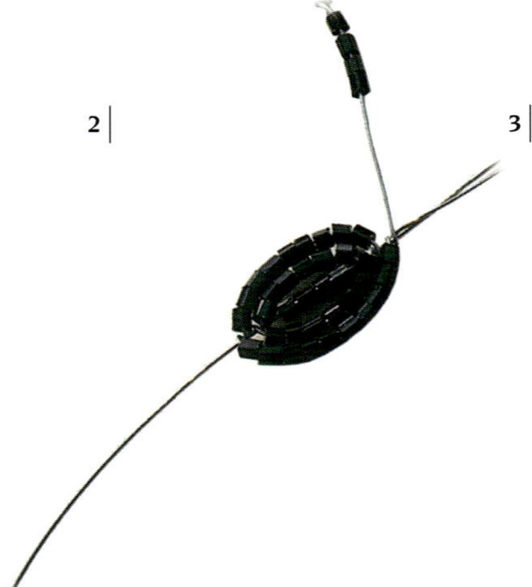

3

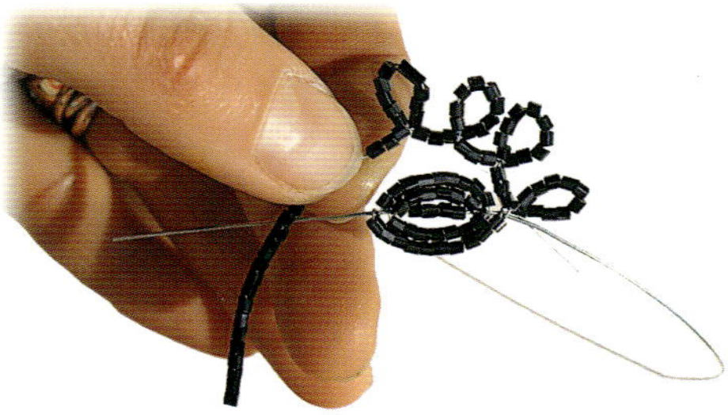

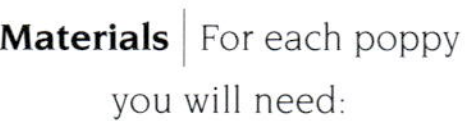

Materials | For each poppy you will need:

•

2 strings of dark red beads

•

2 strings of light red beads

•

2 strings of black beads

•

3 wires, 20 gauge, 10 inches long

•

1 18 gauge stem wire, 12 inches long

•

12 wires: 22 gauge, 5½ inches long

•

3 wires: 24 or 26 gauge, 3 inches long.

THE POPPY

1 | Each poppy stalk carries three flowers of four petals each. Use two different shades of red for a more interesting effect, with the darker shade inside the flower near the black pistils. Each petal has a 1 inch core and a pointed bottom; it is completed by three rounds of dark red beads and three of lighter red beads.

2 | Make the black pistil as if you were making a small, round petal with a ⅜ of an inch core and two rounds of beads.

3 | Complete the pistil by adding all around it a ring of small loops,

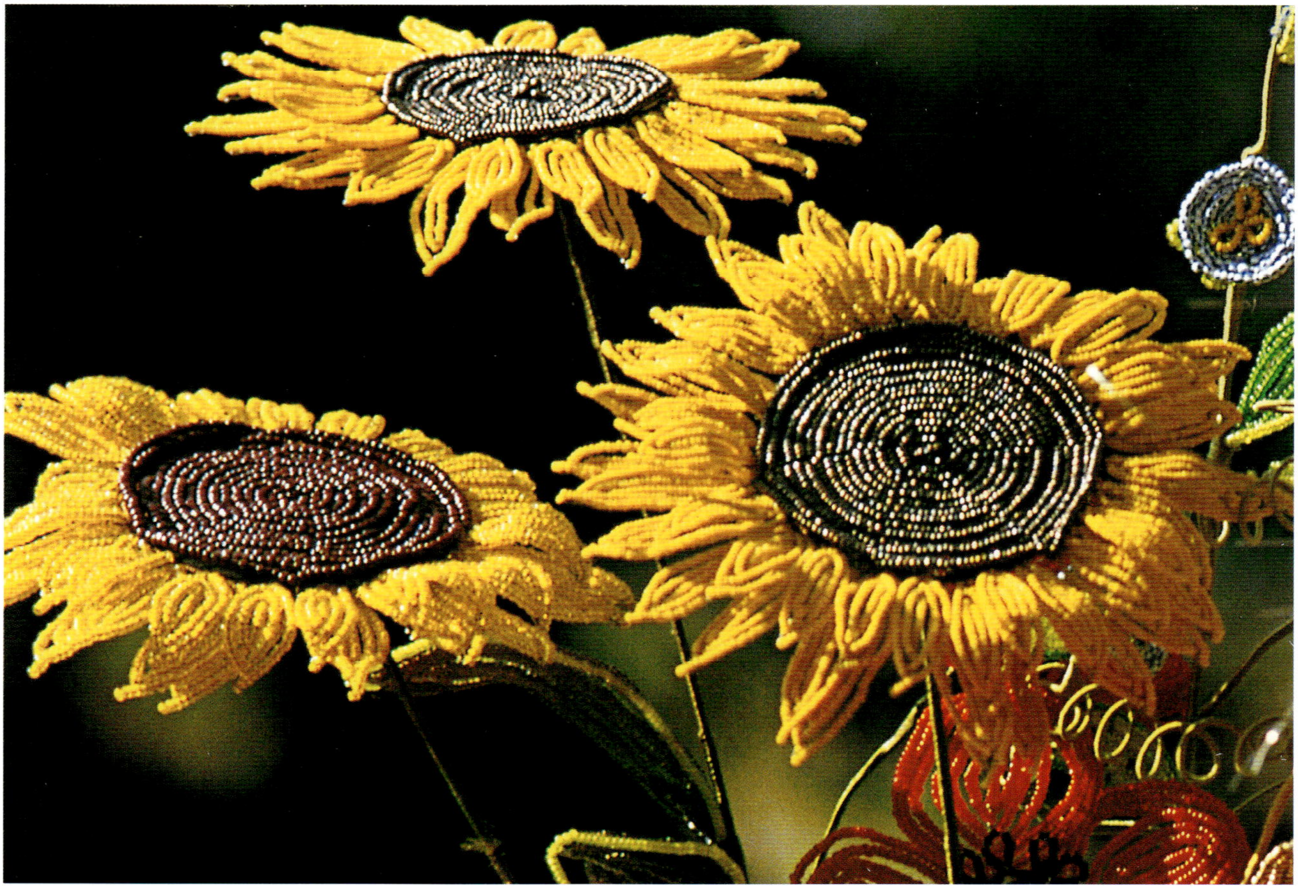

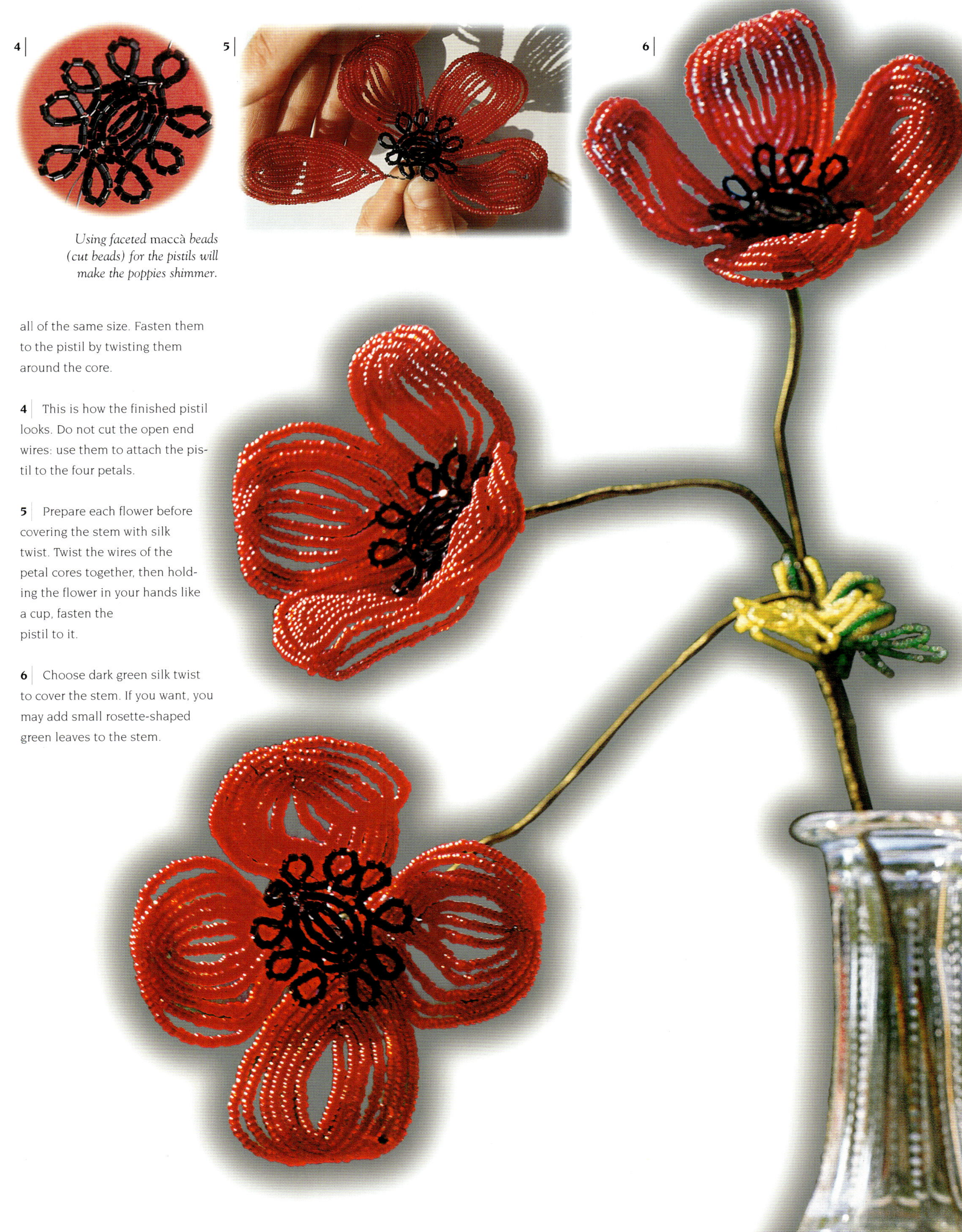

Using faceted maccà beads (cut beads) for the pistils will make the poppies shimmer.

all of the same size. Fasten them to the pistil by twisting them around the core.

4 | This is how the finished pistil looks. Do not cut the open end wires: use them to attach the pistil to the four petals.

5 | Prepare each flower before covering the stem with silk twist. Twist the wires of the petal cores together, then holding the flower in your hands like a cup, fasten the pistil to it.

6 | Choose dark green silk twist to cover the stem. If you want, you may add small rosette-shaped green leaves to the stem.

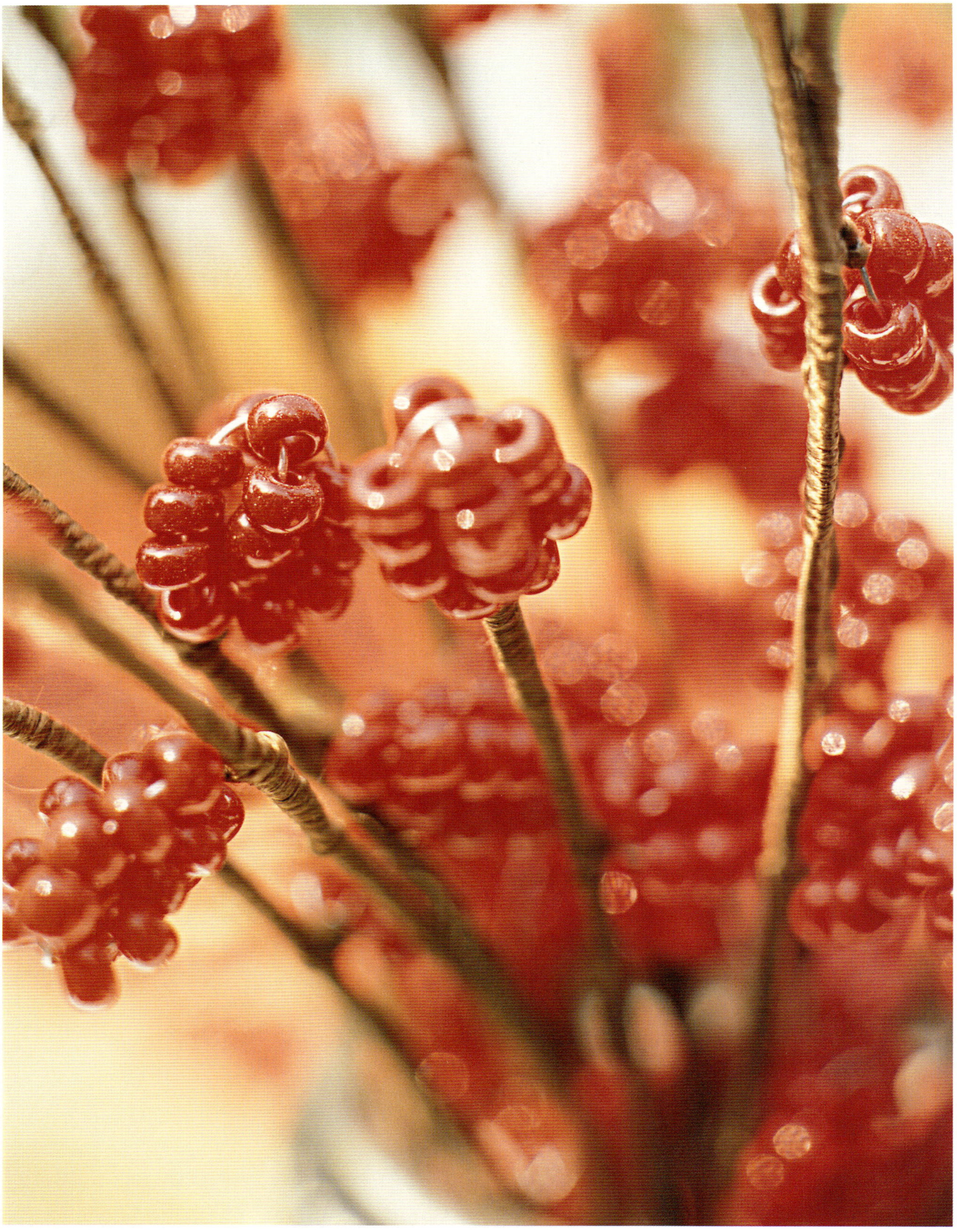

An Autumnal Arrangement

When the leaves start to turn yellow, gold, and deep flaming red, when the crisp air causes the petals of the last, lingering flowers to fall, and the nights grow cold, it's berry time. Red, orange, festive berries: surrounded by small, dark green leaves or sitting alone on bare brown branches, resist the coldest temperatures.

Red berries combine beautifully with white branches that shimmer with dew drops; together they form a light, luminous bouquet. But you should remember to place the vase in the sunlight, otherwise the dew drop crystals will not glitter; in this case, it is better to only use red berries.

Materials | For each dew-drop branch you will need:

- *100 grams of crystal beads, size 5°, 6°, or E*
- *2 yards of 24 gauge wire*
- *20 wires, 20 gauge, 8 inches long*
- *18 gauge stem wire, 20 inches long*
- *brown silk twist, vinyl glue, pliers.*

THE BRANCH WITH DEW DROPS

1 | Take a 24 or 26 gauge wire, cut four pieces, each 20 inches long, and string on each of them about 6 inches of beads.

2 | Using brown silk yarn, fasten the beaded string to a 20 gauge wire, positioning the beads at a uniform distance from each other. Cover the stem with the silk carefully, especially around each dew drop.

3 | Make many small branches in different sizes, in lengths from 2½ to 6 inches ; some branches can be attached together for an even fuller effect.

4 | Fasten the plain branches first to the central branch, then the fuller ones. Try not to make too regular an arrangement, or the result will be stiff and lack spontaneity.

1 |

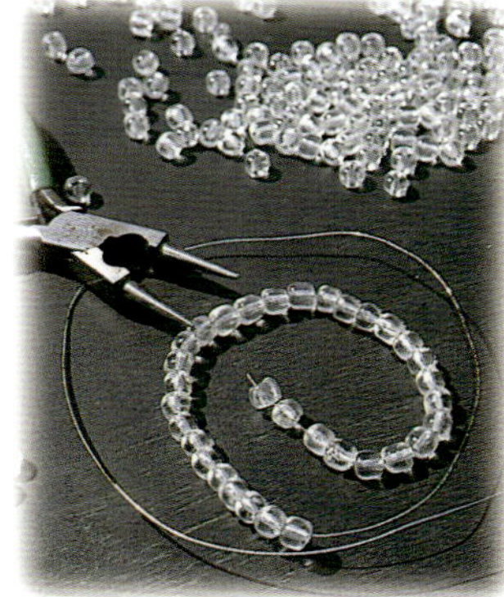

2 |

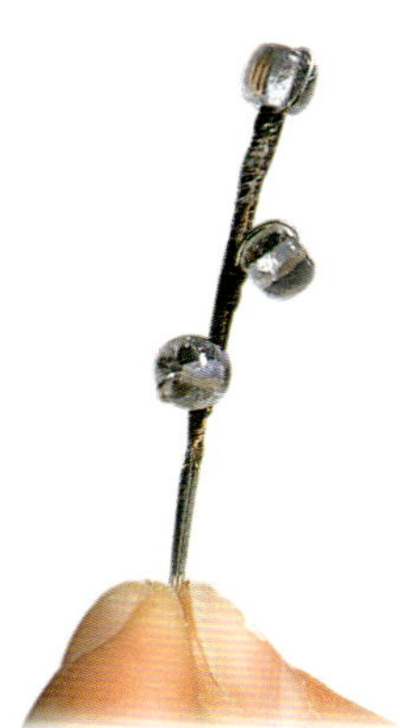

3 |

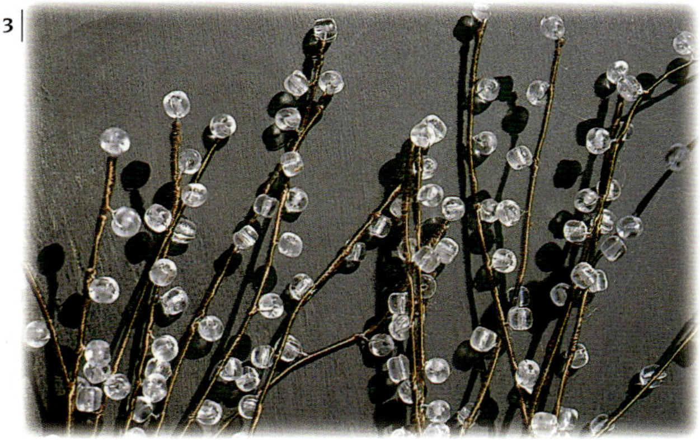

4 |

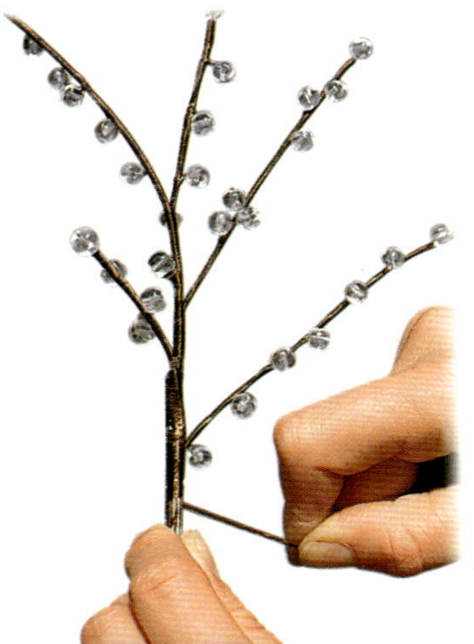

1 |

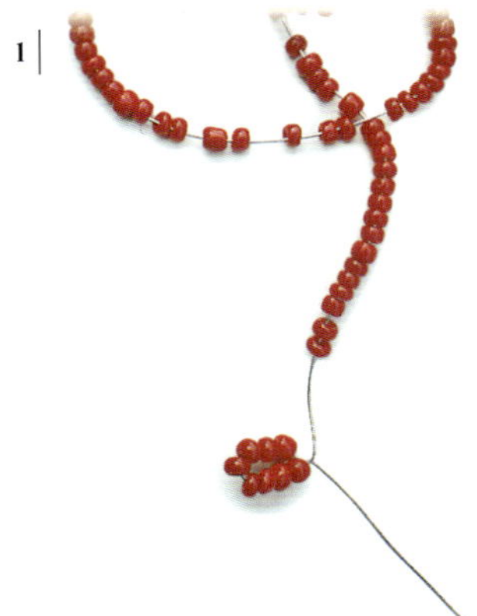

2 |

3 |

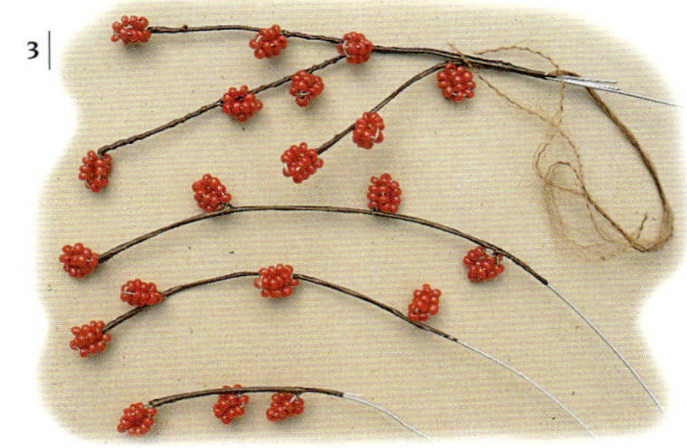

4 |

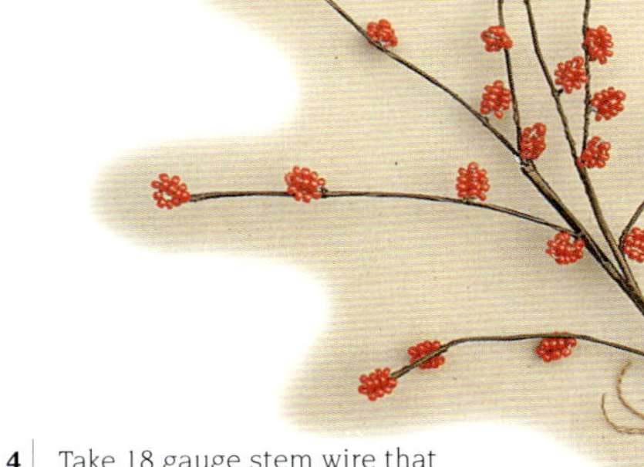

THE BRANCH OF RED BERRIES

Materials | For each branch of red berries you will need:

•

200 grams of red opaque beads, size 9° or 10°

•

24 gauge wire

•

20 wires, 20 gauge, 8 inches long

•

18 gauge stem wire, 20 inches long

•

brown silk twist, vinyl glue, pliers.

1 | Take 24 or 26 gauge wire and cut four lengths of 1 yard each; string about 20 inches of red beads on each of them. Shape a small loop with eight beads and cross it over with another one of the same size, then twist the wires to secure the berry in place.

2 | Keep making berries on the same wire, as shown in the photograph. Make several yards of them.

3 | Prepare a few branches covered with silk twist, some 1½, some 2½, some 3 inches long; attach some together for a more complex effect, in random fashion.

4 | Take 18 gauge stem wire that will serve as the main branch and fasten the branches to it. Remember not to make the central branch too heavy. It is better to leave some space between the branches.

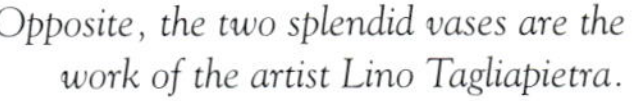

Opposite, the two splendid vases are the work of the artist Lino Tagliapietra.

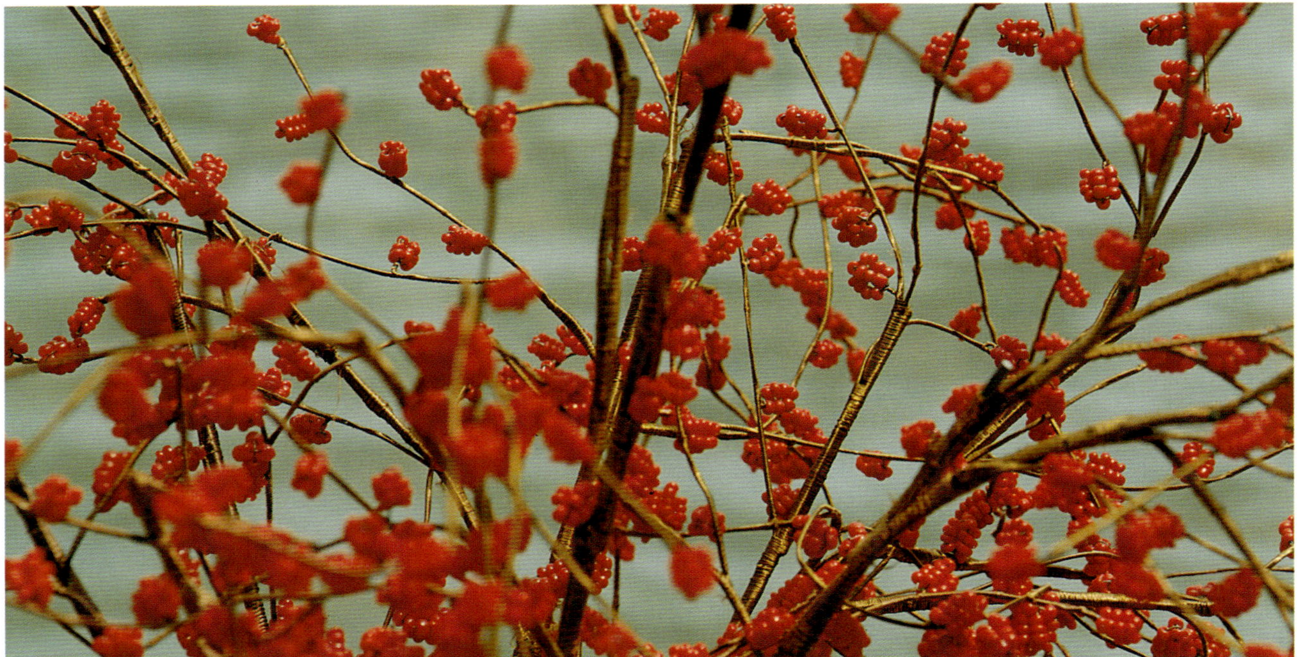

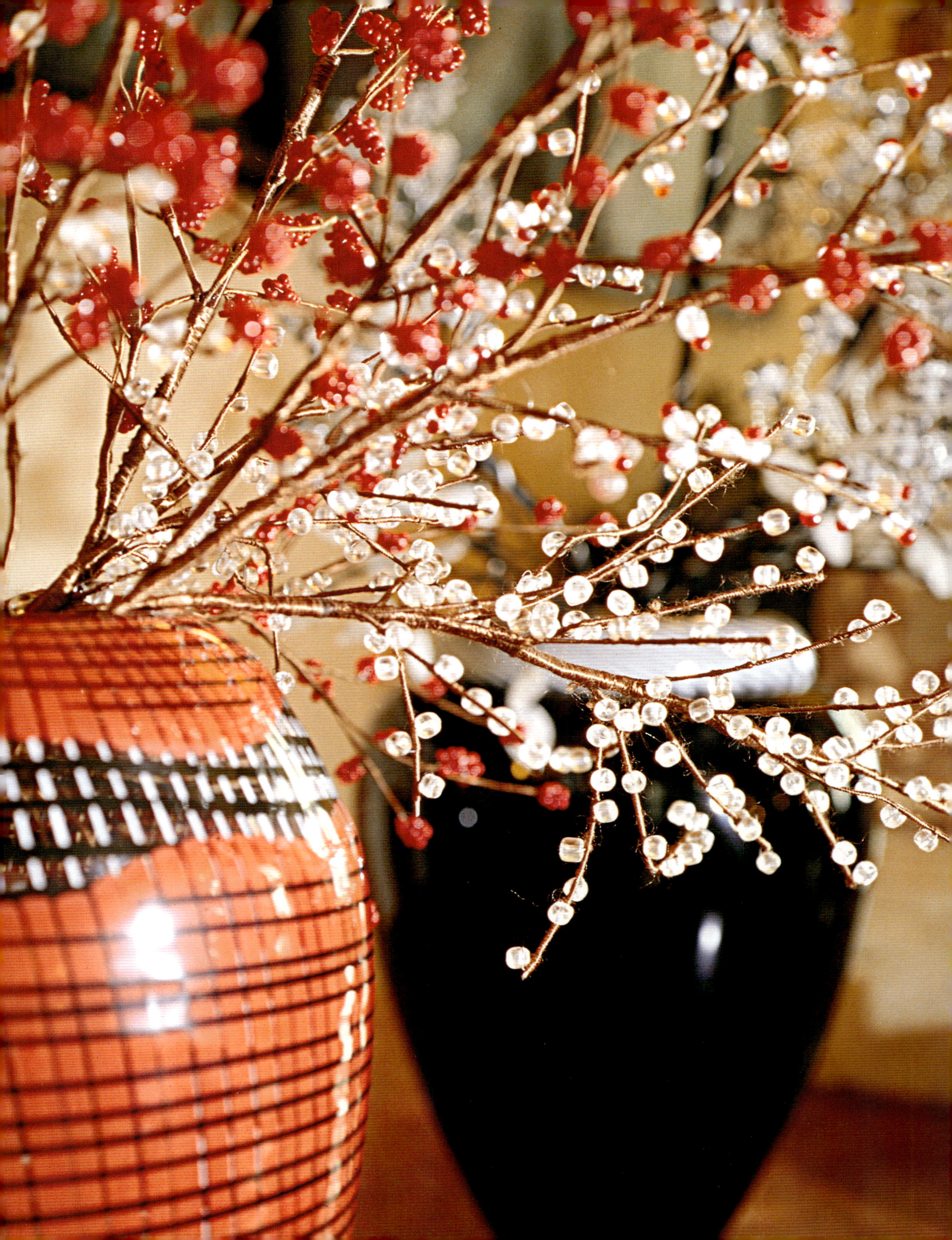

Ice Flowers

We are now in winter, and in a secret corner of our garden the first frost has suddenly turned the virgin's bower (Clematis vitalba) *into brilliant crystalline clusters. These flowers of great luminosity and beauty are easy to reproduce. The most important items are the beads, which must be the Venetian half-line silver* pivette, *(a size ½ or 1 silver or silver lined bugle should be close). More than any other type of bead, these capture the light and reflect it in all directions.*

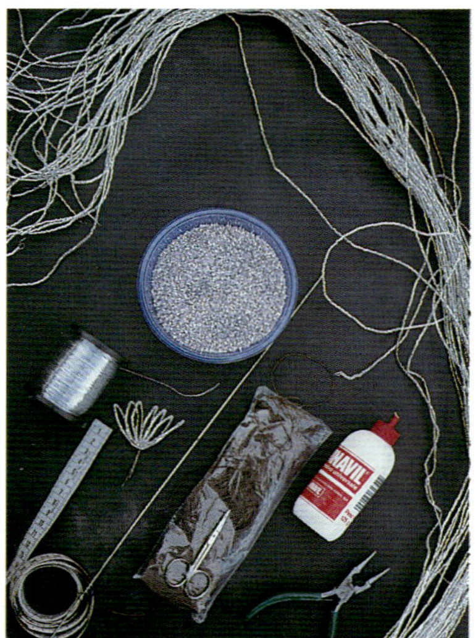

The materials needed to make ice flowers: about ten strings of silver beads, brown silk twist, glue, pliers, and scissors.

Materials | For each virgin's bower you will need:

•

10 strings, 52 inches long, strung with silver pivette *beads for about a yard. Leave the remaining 12 inches of wire empty, you will need it to build the flower*

•

1 18 gauge stem wire, 20 inches long

•

10 24 or 26 gauge wires, each about 10 inches long

•

brown silk twist, vinyl glue, pliers.

Procedure | First prepare ten "ice clusters," then assemble the flower.

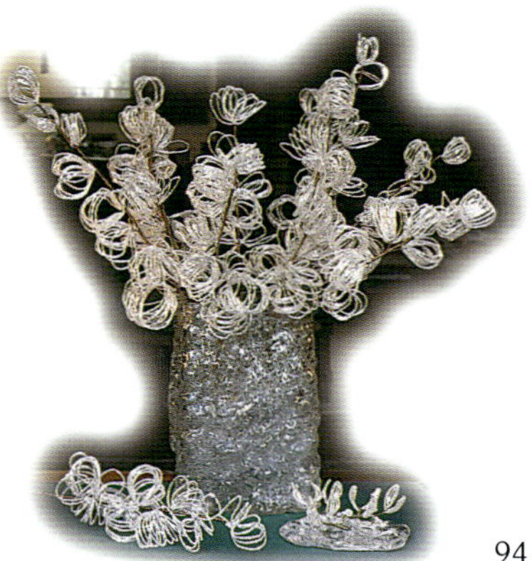

THE VIRGIN'S BOWER

For each flower cluster you will need one beaded string 1 yard long and one wire, 10 inches long. This may require smaller gauge wire as some bugles have rather small holes.

1 | Take 24 or 26 gauge wire, 10 inches long, and string about 5 inches of beads on it.

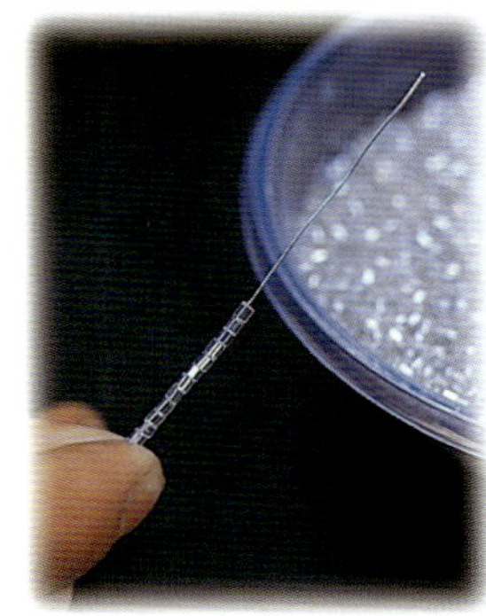

2 | Hold the shorter wire with the 5 inches of beads on it with the left hand and with the right take the longer beaded string; hook them together following the round leaf technique.

3 | Hold the wires on the top with your left hand and slide the beads of the long wire down to the same length of the shorter wire. Make sure the two wires are even. Then with your right hand twist the long wire around the short one, immediately below the 5 inches of beads. Now most of the work is done! Twist the long wire around the short one about six times. If you don't have enough beads on the long wire, string some more on it. Make sure you create a uniform structure and that you keep the flower open with your fingers.

4 | After finishing one flower, fold the ends of the supporting wire under and tighten them with the pliers, giving a ring shape to the cluster. Widen each strand delicately with your fingers, opening the cluster. Do the same with the other clusters.

ASSEMBLING THE FLOWER

5 | Assemble the clusters on the stem, starting from the top. Use 18 gauge stem wire, brown silk twist and vinyl glue; fasten the first cluster and then the other nine, adding them one by one in a light spiraling arrangement.

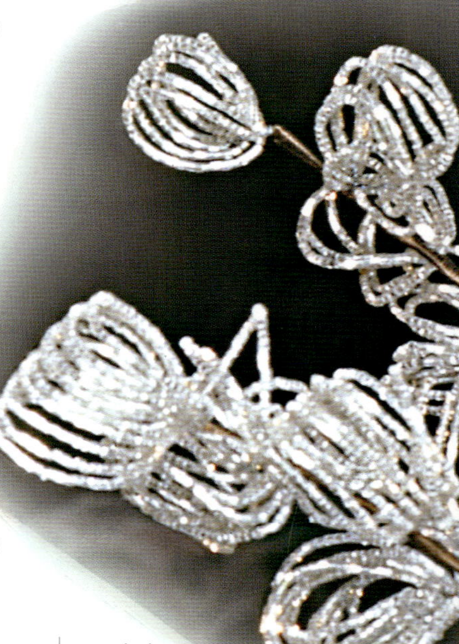

6 | Attach the clusters to the stem for a length of about 12 inches and cover with silk the remaining 8 inches of stem. We suggest you place the smaller flowers at the top first, then attach slightly larger flowers as you move down the stem.

2

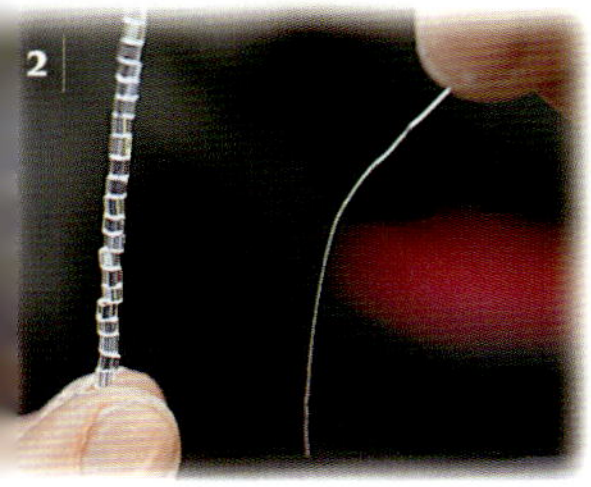

3

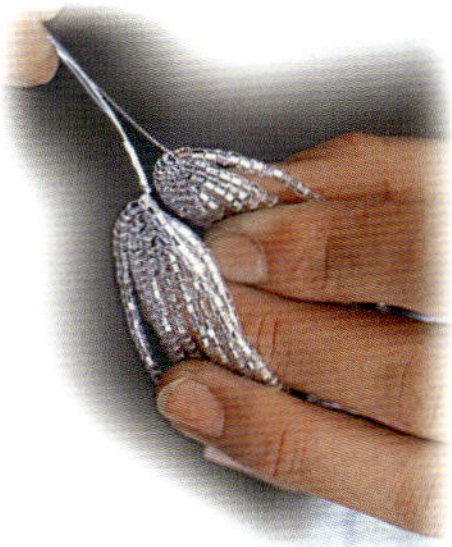

4

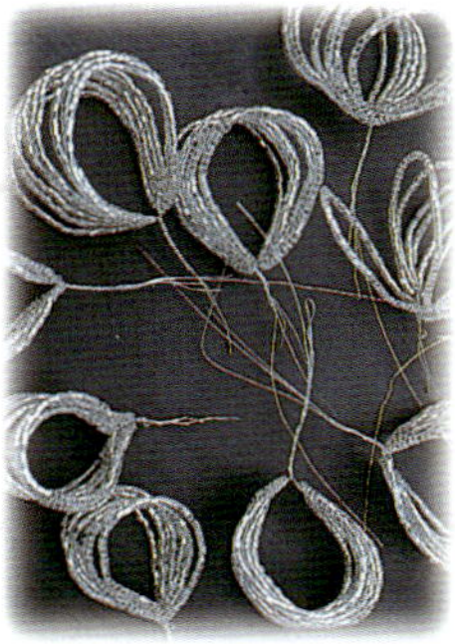

5

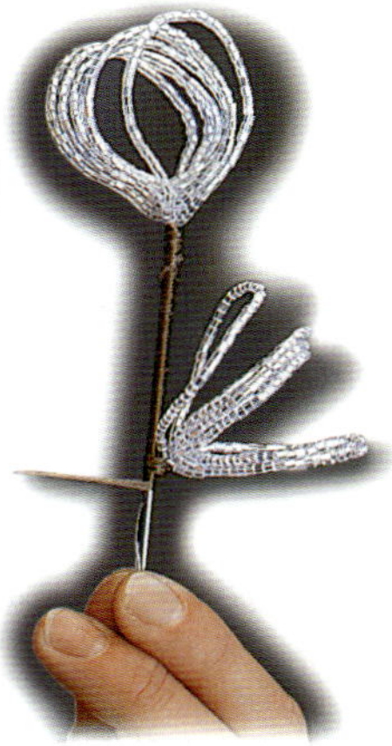

6

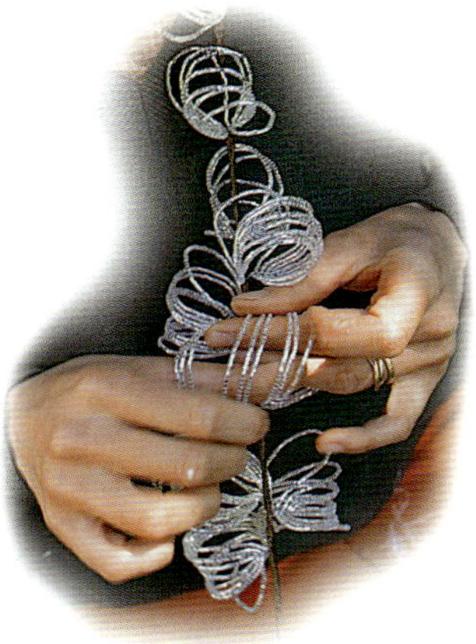

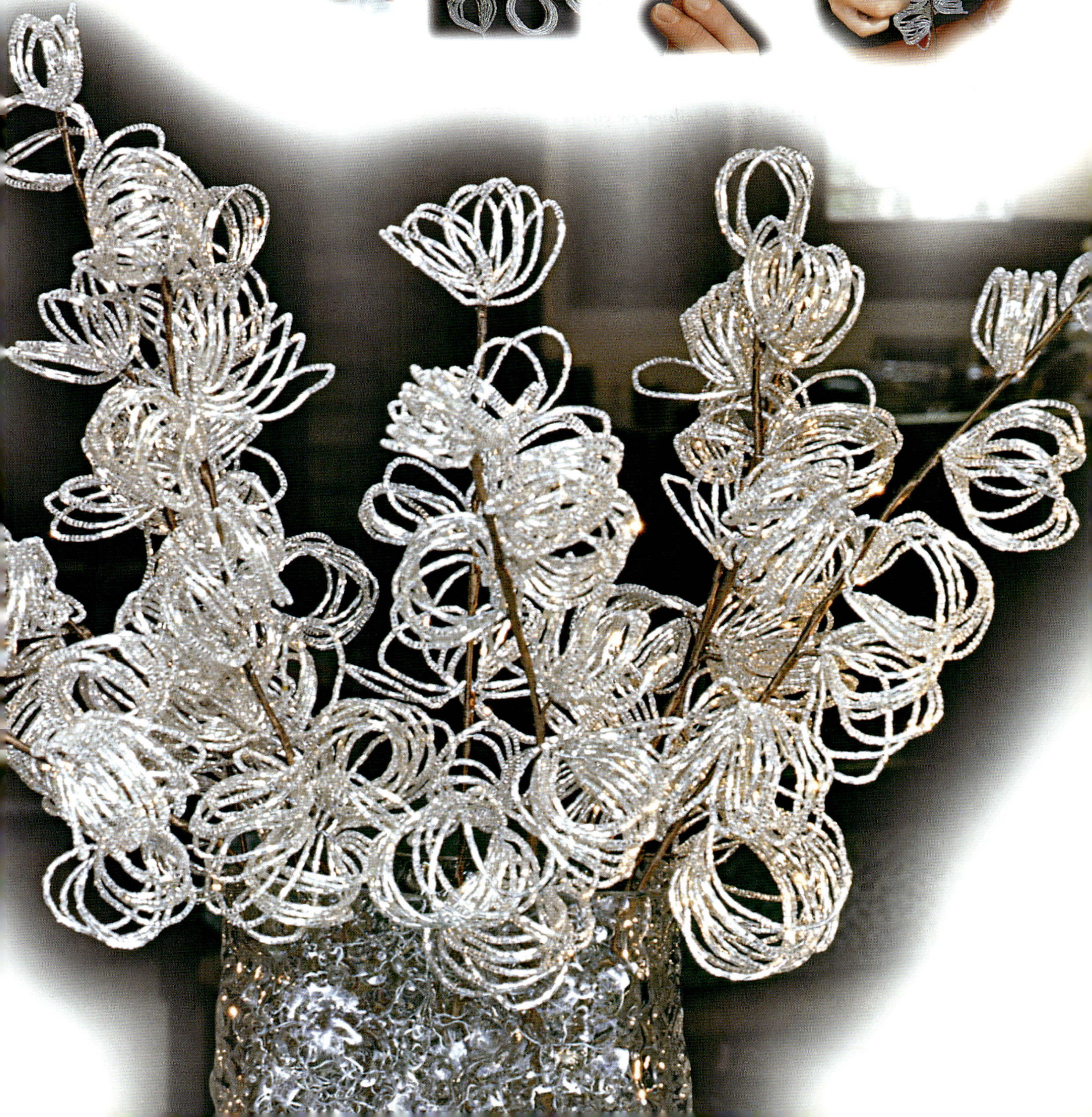

A Mountain Bouquet

At the edge of the pasture fields, where the woodland begins and small, wild flowers grow in meadows safe from the scythe, there is an extraordinary richness of colors and scents. Buttercups, small lilies, wild orchids, perfumed cyclamens, blue hepatica, pink pillows of alpine asters: we can reproduce them all with beads.

Materials | For each cyclamen you will need:

- *many strings of pink beads in different shades*
- *1 string of loden green beads*
- *1 string of pine green beads*
- *1 string of grass green beads*
- *1 20 gauge wire, 6 inches long for each flower*
- *dark green silk twist, vinyl glue, pliers.*

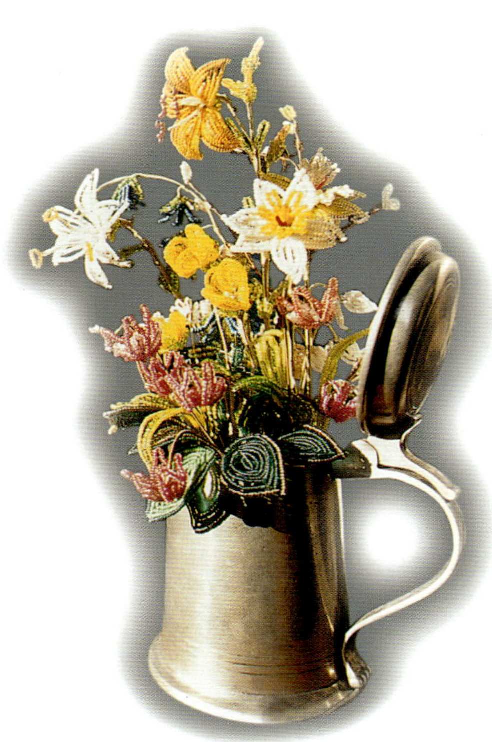

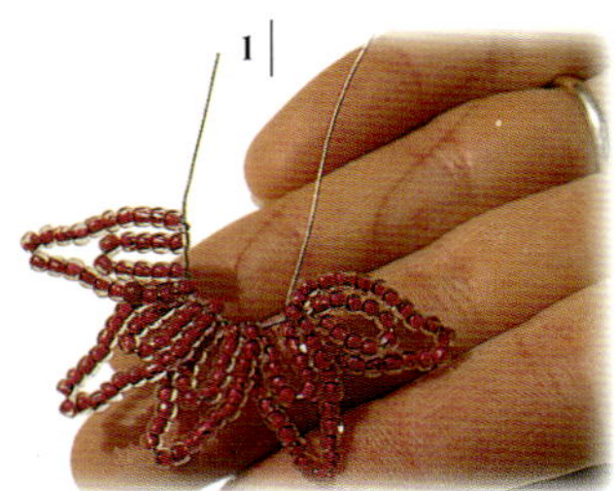

1

THE CYCLAMEN

1 | Using a string of pink beads, make five equal loops, each ⅓ of an inch long. With the same string, make five more loops superimposing them on the first and giving them a pointed tip, as in the photograph above.

2 | Join the flower to the stem—20 gauge stem wire—using green silk yarn. For the foliage, use different shades of green; they are round at the bottom and pointed at the top, with a ⅜ of an inch core.

3 | Use the pliers to give the flower its typical cyclamen shape. The beauty of these flowers lies in their many shades of red, white and pink. Since you need only a small amount of beads, you can recycle here all the leftover beads from other flowers.

4 | Place the cyclamens in a pewter tankard, inserting them into a polystyrene base that's been covered with beads.

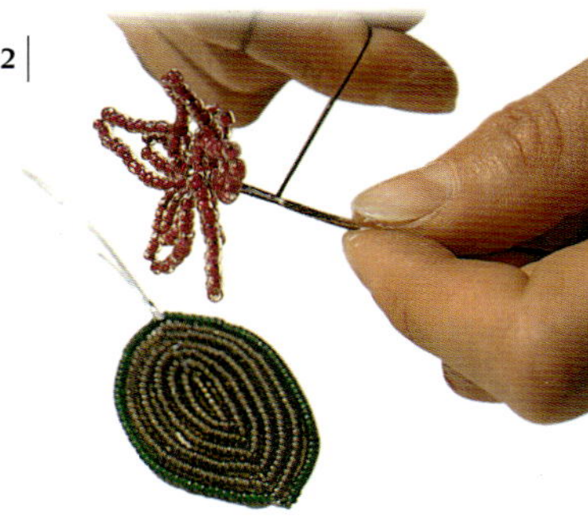

2

Materials | For each buttercup you will need:

- *2 strings of yellow beads*
- *1 string of dark green beads*
- *a few green beads, size 5°, 6° or E*
- *1 20 gauge wire*
- *dark green silk twist, vinyl glue, pliers.*

THE BUTTERCUP

5 | Using the peach blossom technique, build a small, five-petal flower, a green collar of three loops each ¼ of an inch long, and a small rosette-shaped green leaf consisting of five equal loops. Add one center pistil to each buttercup, using a large green bead, size 5°, 6° or E.

6 | Join the flower and the leaf to the stem.

7 | Cluster at least three small flowers of the same color together, otherwise they will be hardly visible.

3

4

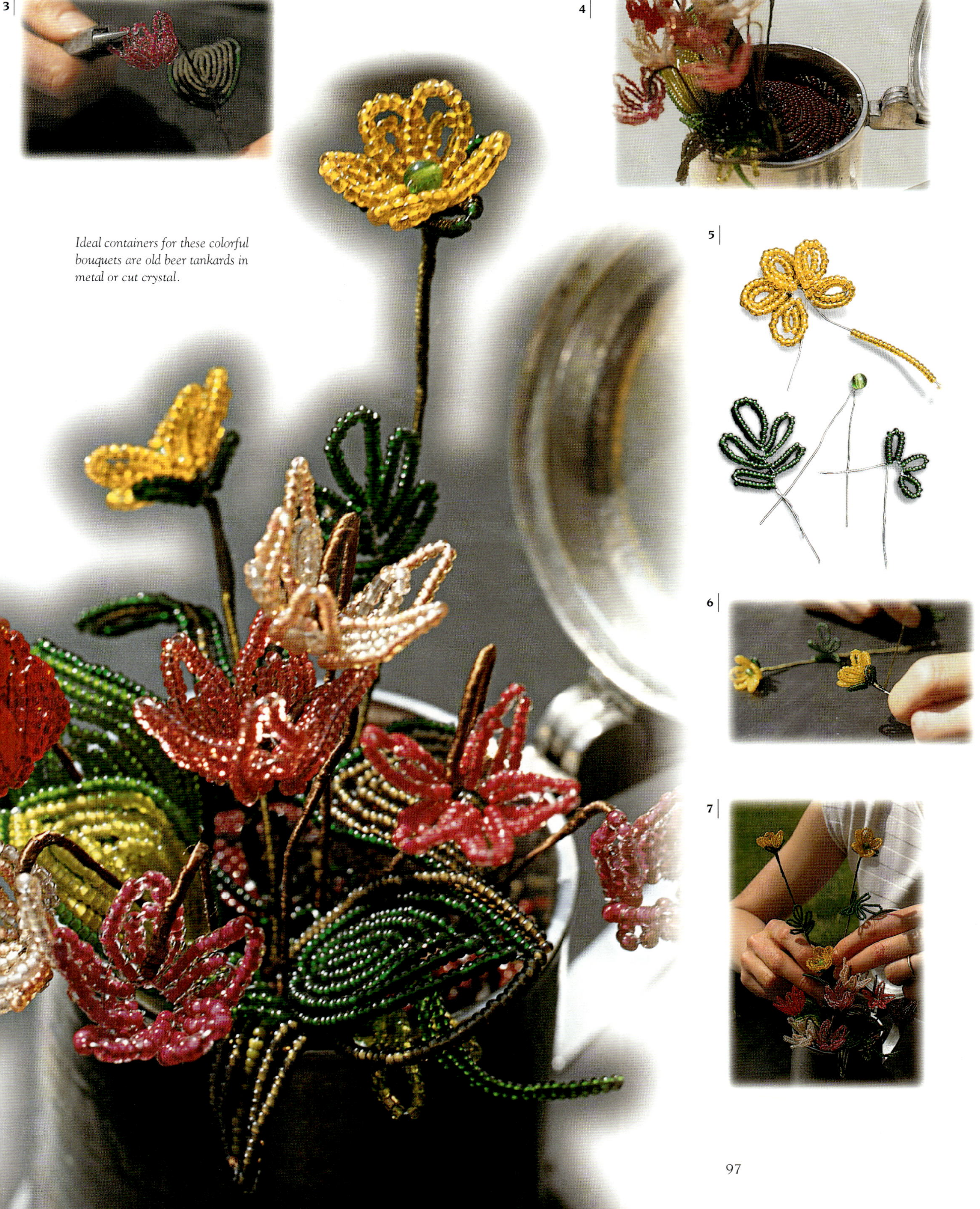

Ideal containers for these colorful bouquets are old beer tankards in metal or cut crystal.

5

6

7

A Round Bouquet

A footed bowl of ceramic or silver is an ideal container for elegant round compositions. The beads will enhance the preciousness of the vase and complement its shape, adding light and color. Choose flowers that complement the size, shape, and color of the vase as well as the surrounding ambiance. Here we show you how to prepare the base for the bouquet.

1

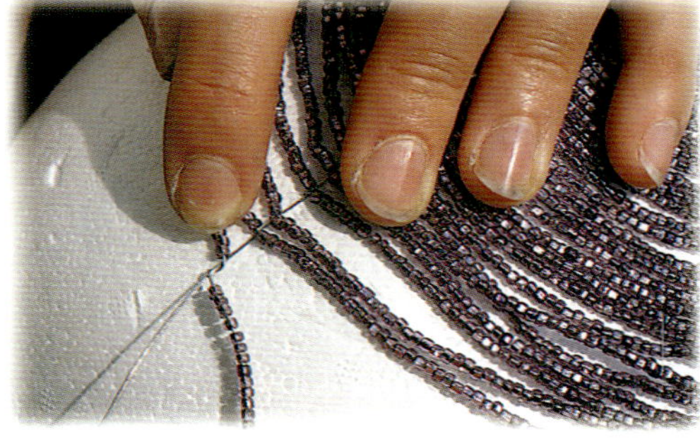

2

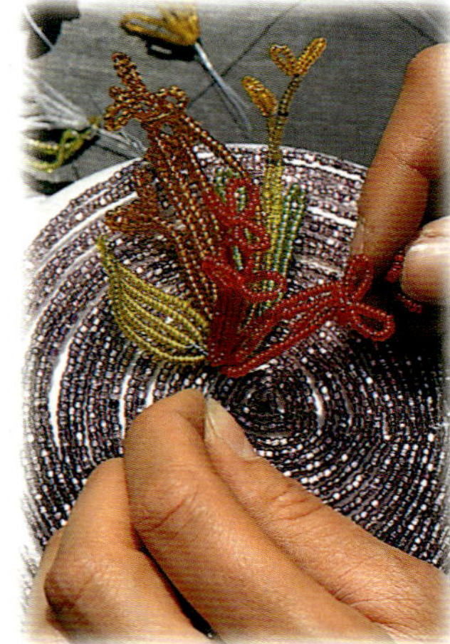

Materials | For each base you will need:

- *1 hollow polystyrene ball, 8 inches in diameter*
- *30 strings of silver-washed lilac beads to cover the ball*
- *3 wires: 22 gauge, 14 inches long*
- *to cover the ball, make flowers and small leaves using the techniques shown on the preceding pages*
- *dark green silk twist, vinyl glue, pliers.*

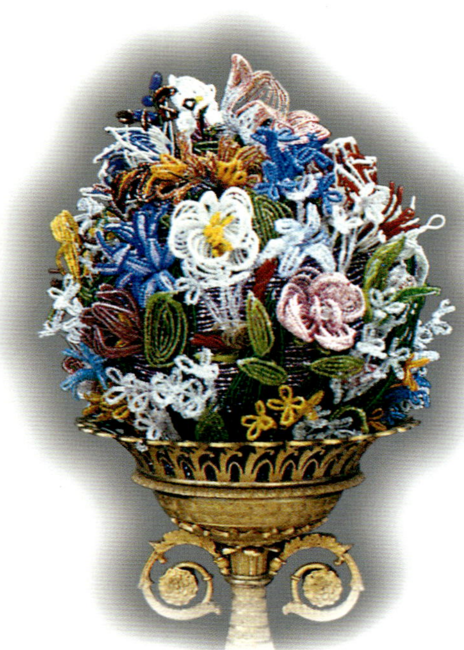

HOW TO MAKE THE BASE

1 | Join three 14 inch long wires and start weaving a disc around them using the lilac colored string. Place the 3 inch diameter disc on the polystyrene ball and continue. You may use pins to fasten the disc to the ball.

2 | Once you have covered the whole ball, add the flowers by inserting the stems into the ball and securing them to keep them in place.

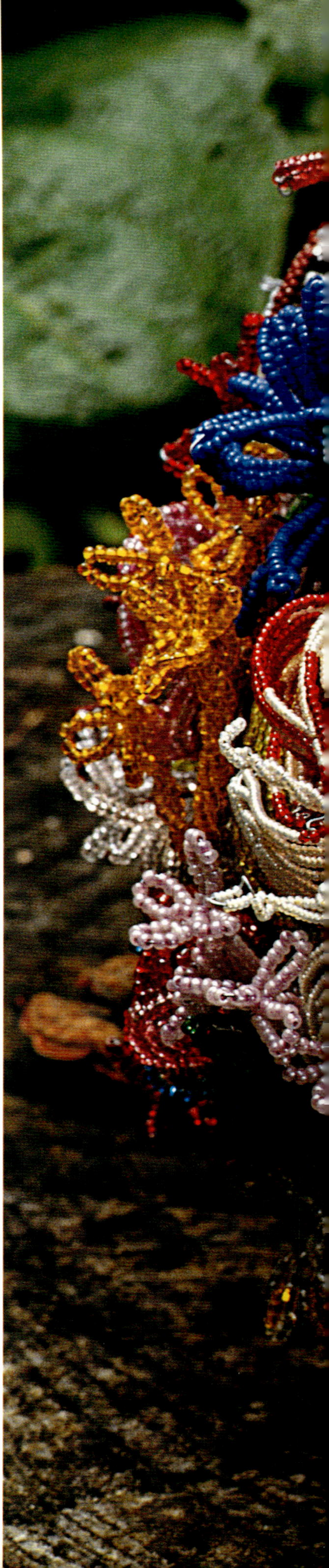

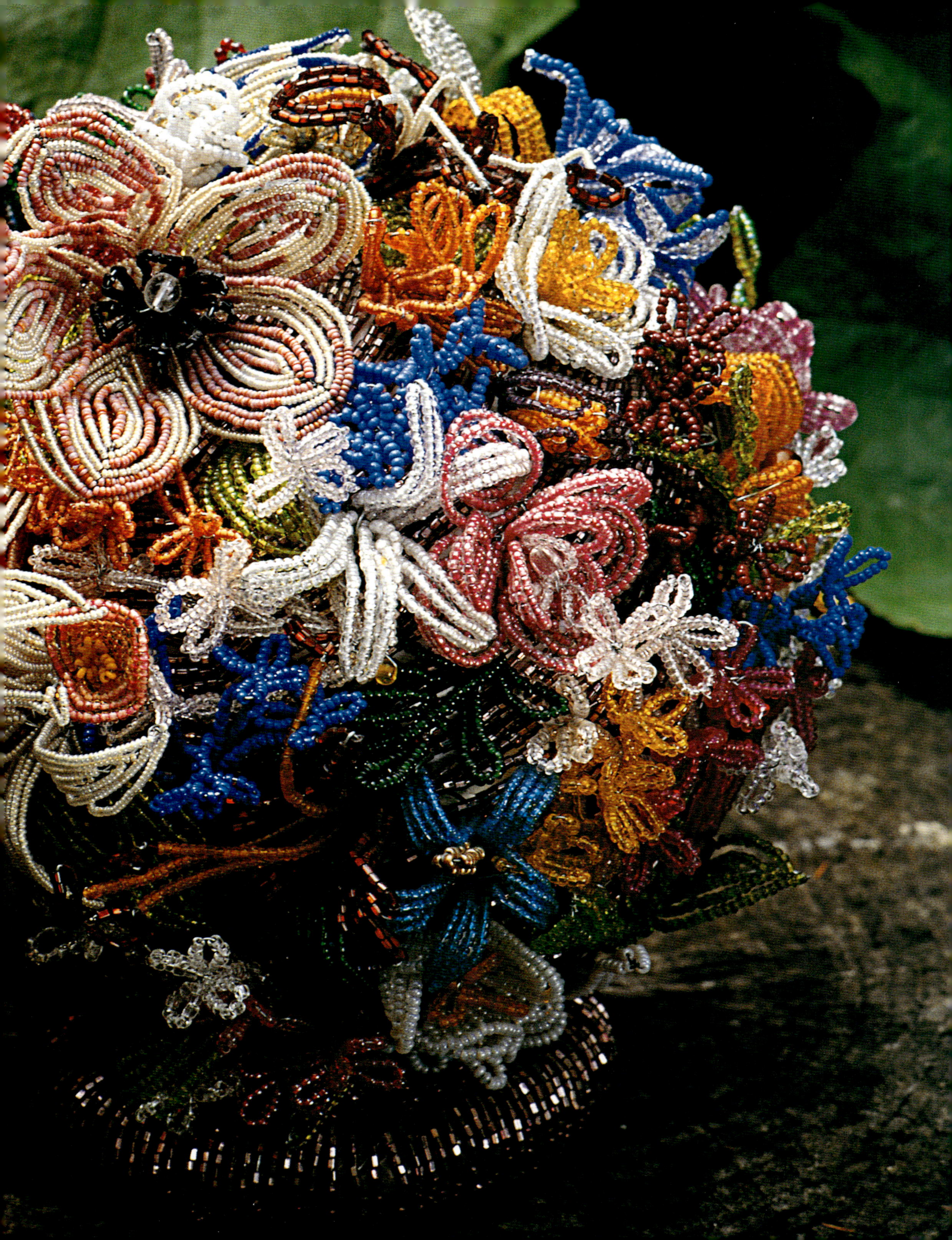

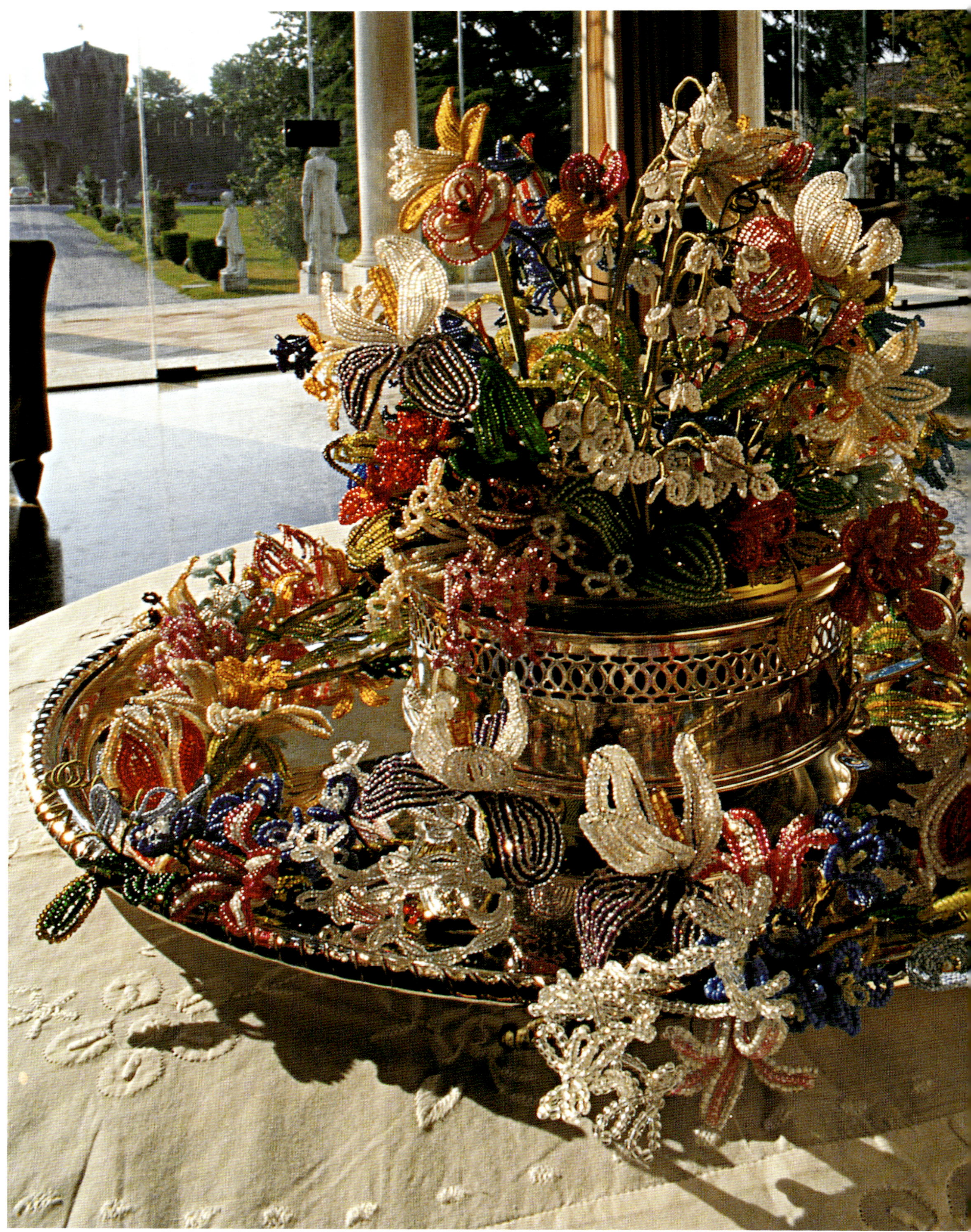

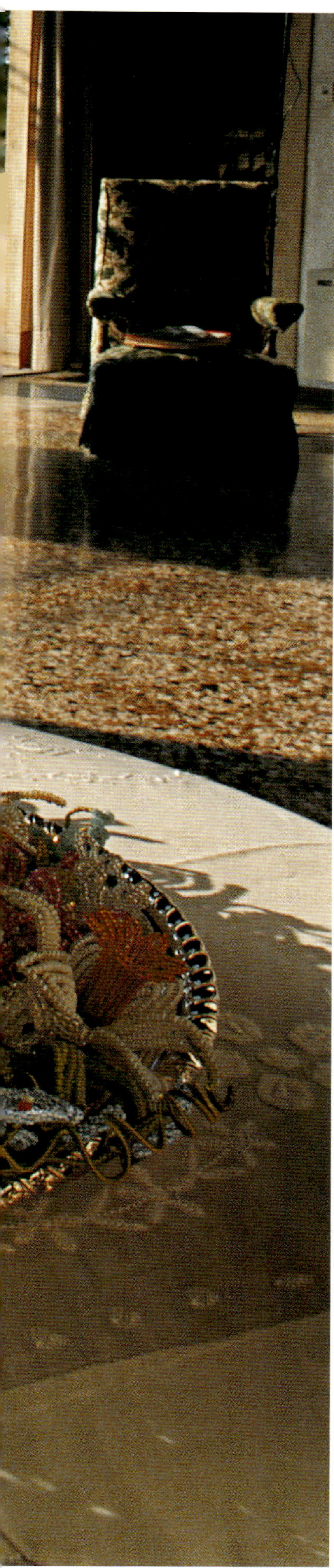

5 CHAPTER

Other Decorations

Glass-bead flowers can be used to decorate many parts of your home, even the least likely corner, and to invent special objects for special occasions. You can create a center piece for an important dinner, for Easter or Christmas, a bridal bouquet, festive wreaths for flower girls, a mirror frame, a lampshade, or curtain tiebacks. Even dresser and armoire keys can be embellished with soft beaded fringes. Finally, for a magic Venetian Carnival, a beaded mask is a must!

1 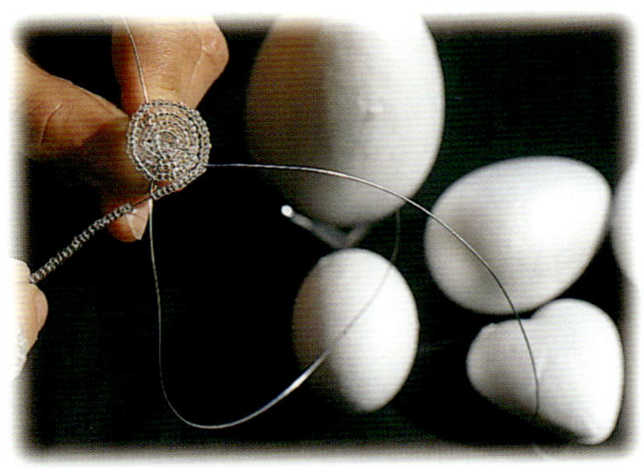

2 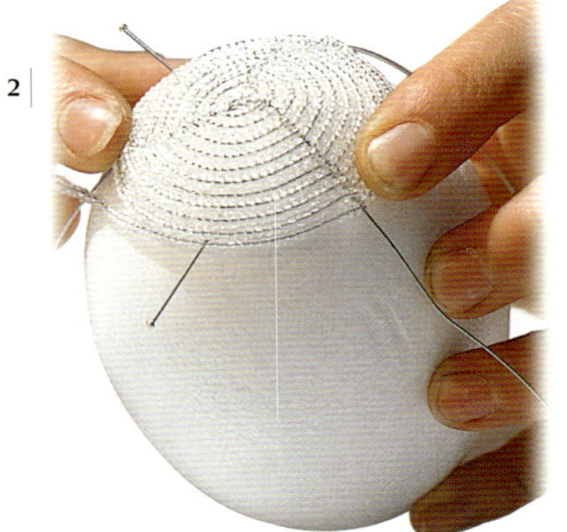

3 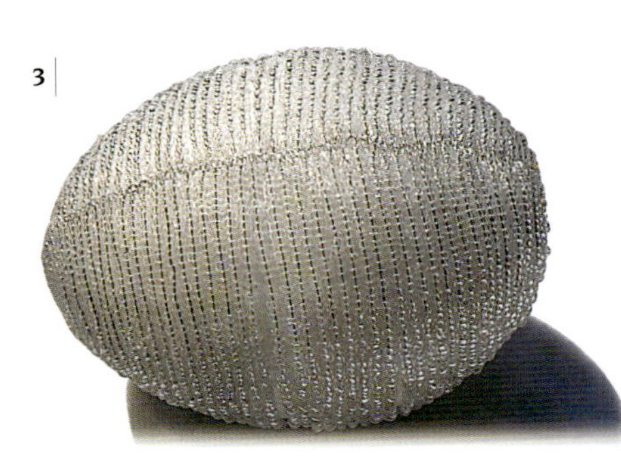

Easter Eggs

In the Christian tradition, the egg is a symbol of Easter. Easter eggs can be made with precious materials (such as Fabergé's creations), or they can be real eggs, hand decorated at home with the children and placed at the center of the Easter table, together with olive branches or palm leaves.

A whole array of materials can be used to make Easter eggs: marble, wood, glass, fabric, and of course . . . glass beads! We can use the beads to cover polystyrene eggs and decorate them with small flower bouquets, love knots or monograms.

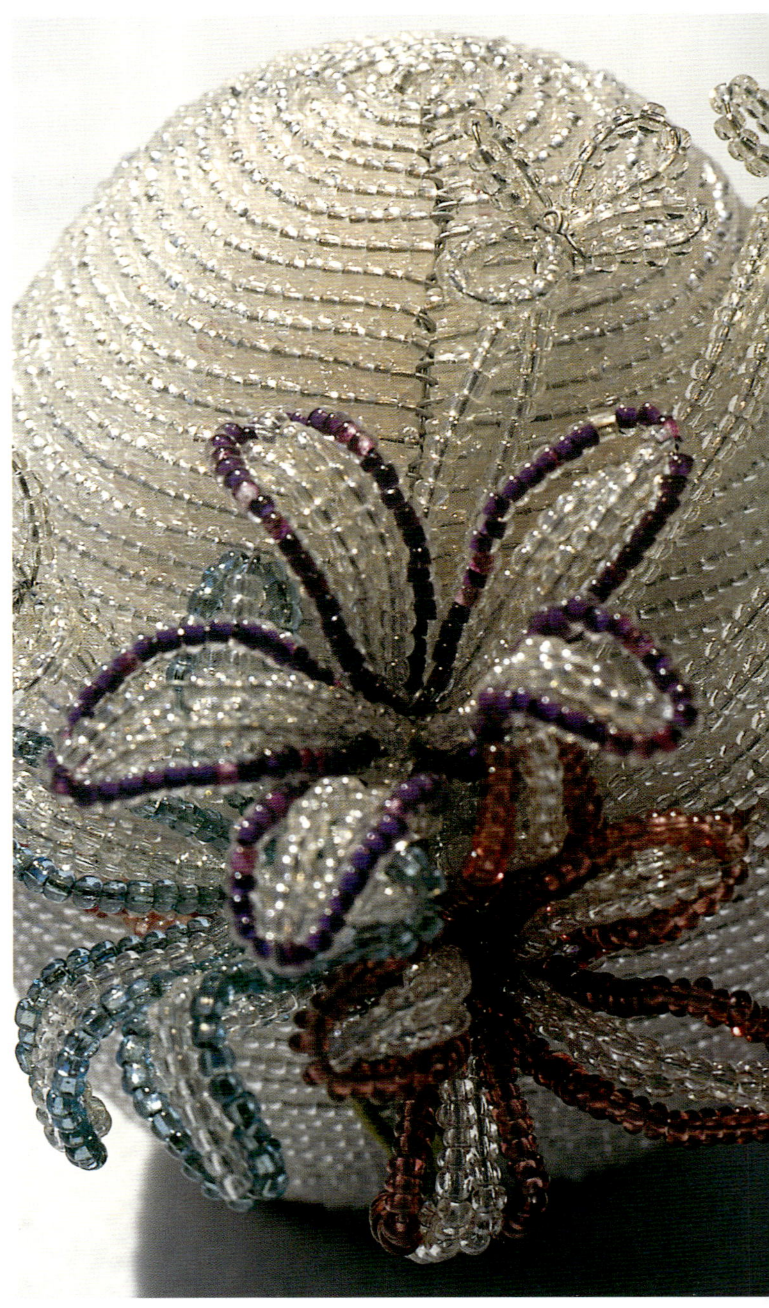

Materials | For each Easter egg you will need:

•

1 polystyrene egg, 4 inches long

•

3 22 gauge wires, 9½ inches long

•

8 strings of crystal beads

•

For the ribbon:

•

1 string of white beads

•

1 string of pink beads

•

1 string of cyclamen beads

For the flowers:

•

1 string of azure blue beads

•

1 string of pink beads

•

1 string of lilac beads

•

1 string of crystal beads

•

pale green silk twist, vinyl glue, pliers.

4 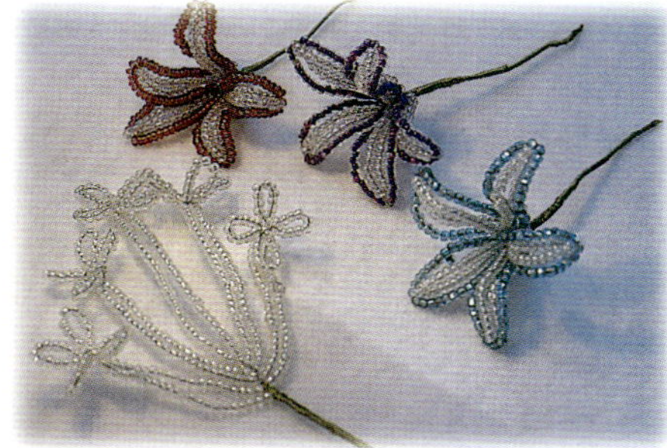

5 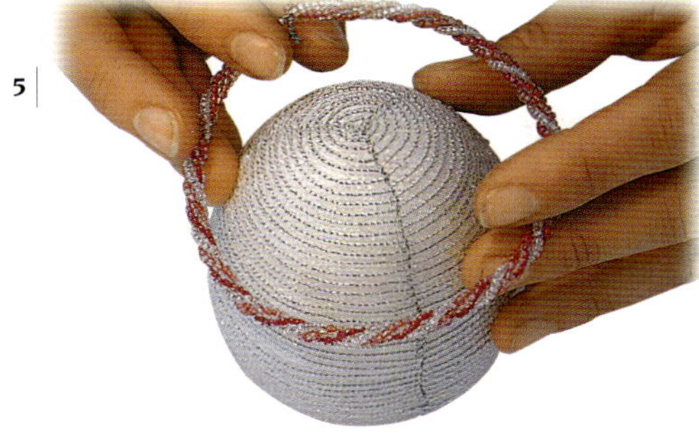

6 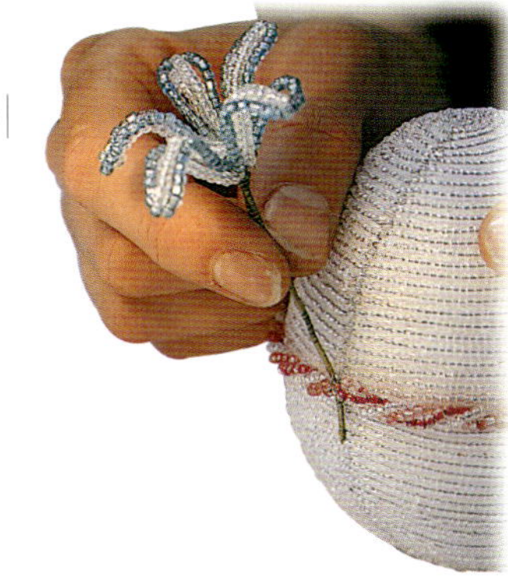

HOW TO MAKE AN EASTER EGG

1 Join three 9½ inch, 22 gauge wires together and start weaving a string of crystal beads around them to make a cap.

2 When the cap is about 1½ inch in diameter, fasten it to the top of the polystyrene egg. Continue making the cap, i.e. covering the egg, being careful to make uniform rounds and attaching it to the egg with pins.

3 Try to achieve a uniform, homogeneous result; if you want to cover the cap completely with small flowers, however, you don't need to be so precise in making the cap.

4 For the bouquet you will need three small lilies—one light blue, one lilac, one pink; a small African lily completes the bouquet. Make the lily petals using five double loops, 1¼ inches long.

5 Place a decorative ribbon at the center of the egg; use the ribbon to attach the bouquet. To make the ribbon, twist three beaded strings together to a length of about 3¾ inches.

6 Insert the three lilies with the stem covered in pale green silk at the point where the ribbon is attached to the egg.

7 To complete the decoration, add the African lily to cover any flaws and give a softer look to the egg.

7 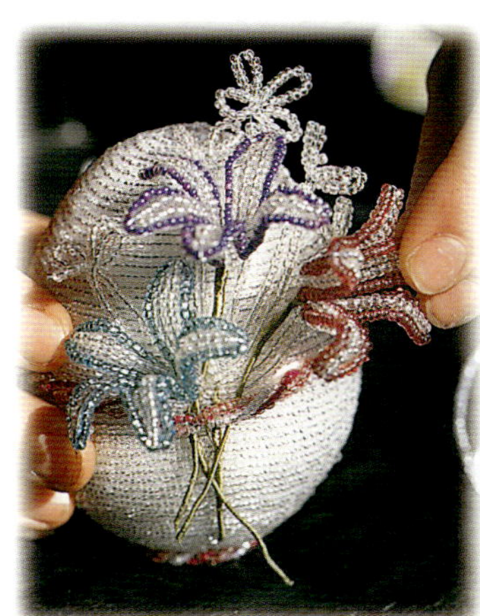

Below, another decorated Easter egg.

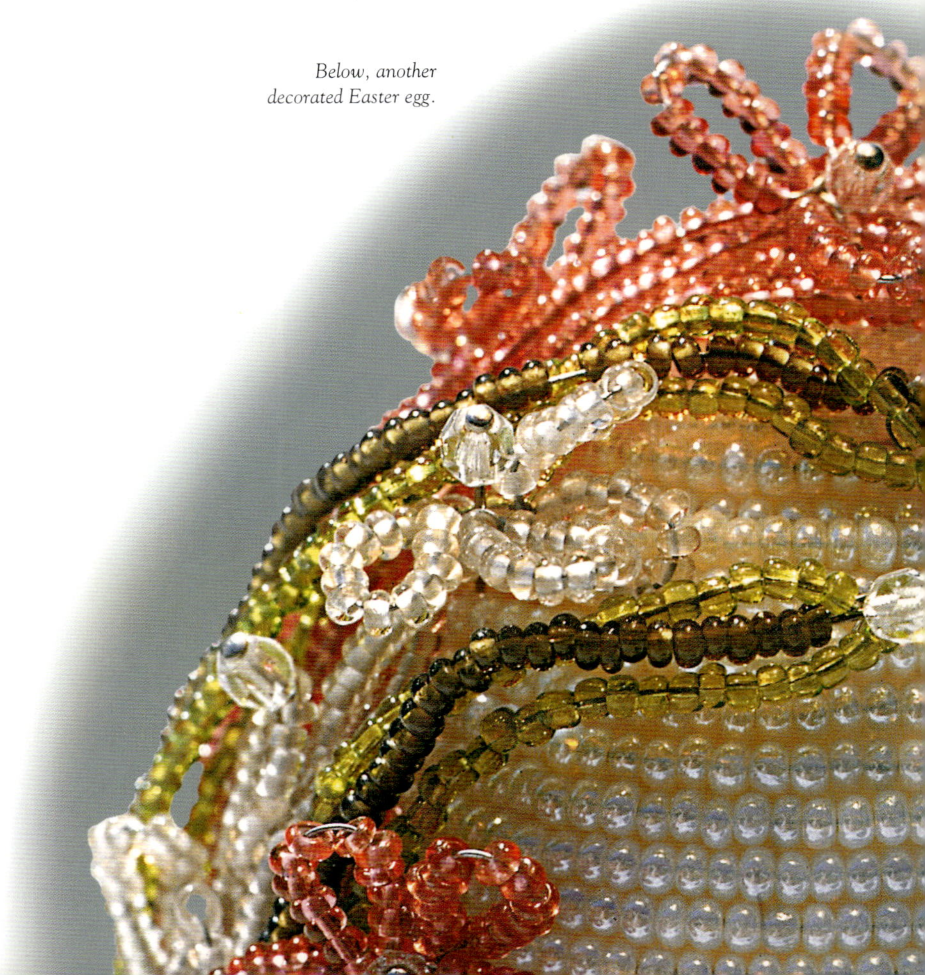

Gift Boxes

Once you have mastered the art of handling beads and wires and your hands work easily with these materials, you are ready to make tri-dimensional objects such as small boxes, which require very accurate craftsmanship. For the boxes reproduced in these pages we have chosen colors inspired by Venetian mosaics. However, even a completely white box, decorated with just a single flower on the cover can be very attractive and useful for countless occasions.

Materials *You need stiff wires for the frame and thinner wires for the sides. As for the beads, choose a size that complements the size of the box. You may decorate the box by placing an ammonite or other semiprecious stone in the bottom center.*

•

Procedure Start with the container, then make the cover.

PREPARATION

For best results, use different kinds of beads: transparent, opaque, shiny, silver-washed.

MAKING A ROUND BOX

A round box is the simplest shape to make. Make a disc and create the bottom by folding the disc at straight angles, then continue to build the sides.

To make the cover, prepare a frame by crossing at least three rather stiff wires.

Starting from the center, weave the beaded string around the wires, as if building a spider web.

Be very careful when you weave the sides; you want to achieve a uniform effect.

Start with small boxes, or use more wires for the frame, and always choose very stiff wires.

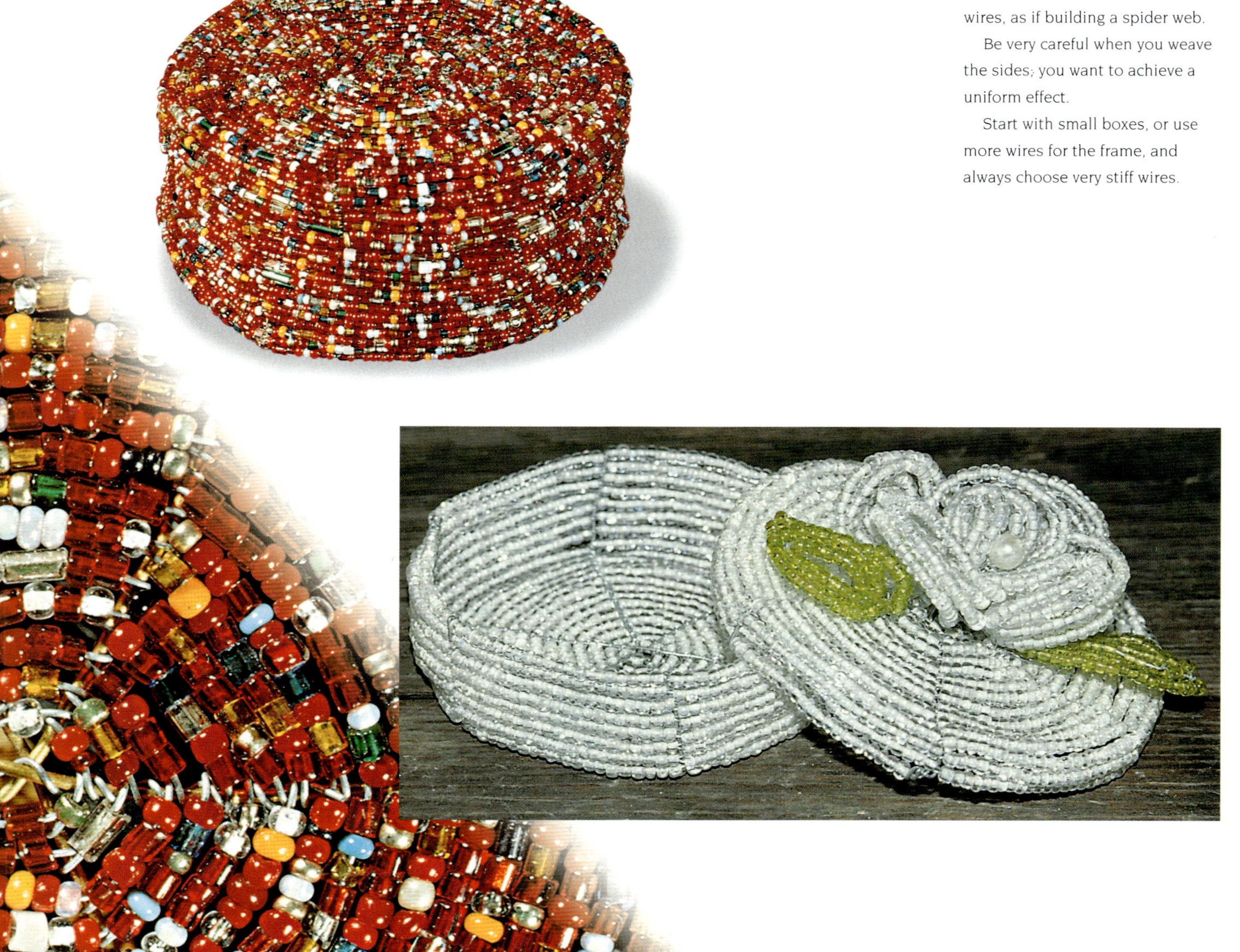

OTHER SHAPES

You can make square, oval, or triangular boxes by changing the shape of the frame. For small boxes, choose thin wires and small beads; the opposite for large boxes. Avoid using wires that are too stiff, otherwise bending them will be difficult.

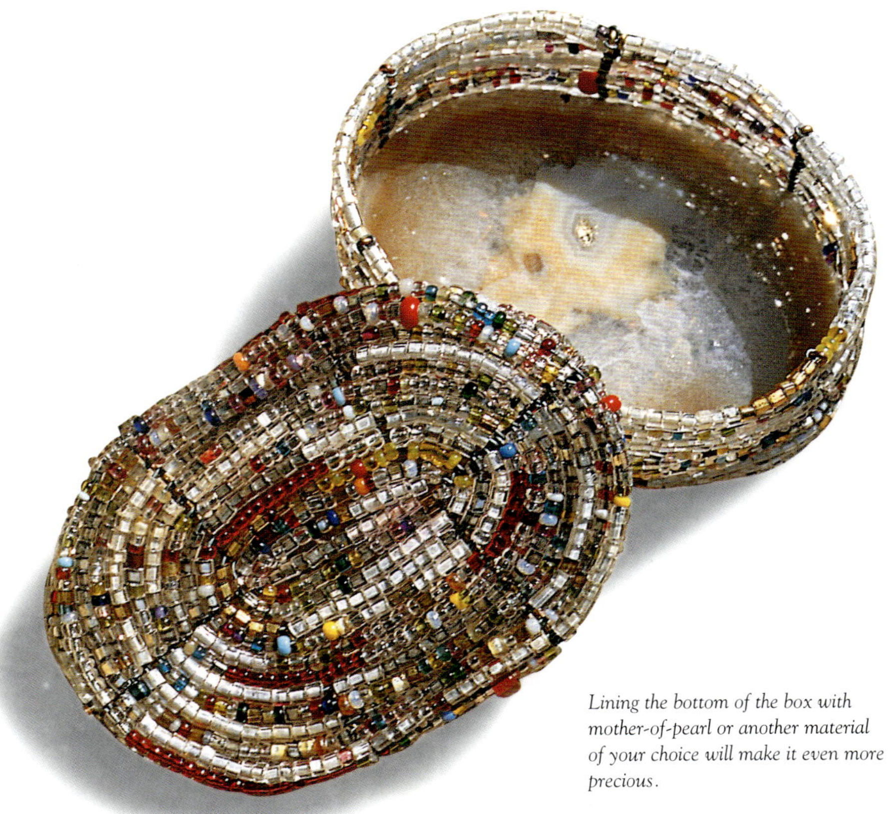

Lining the bottom of the box with mother-of-pearl or another material of your choice will make it even more precious.

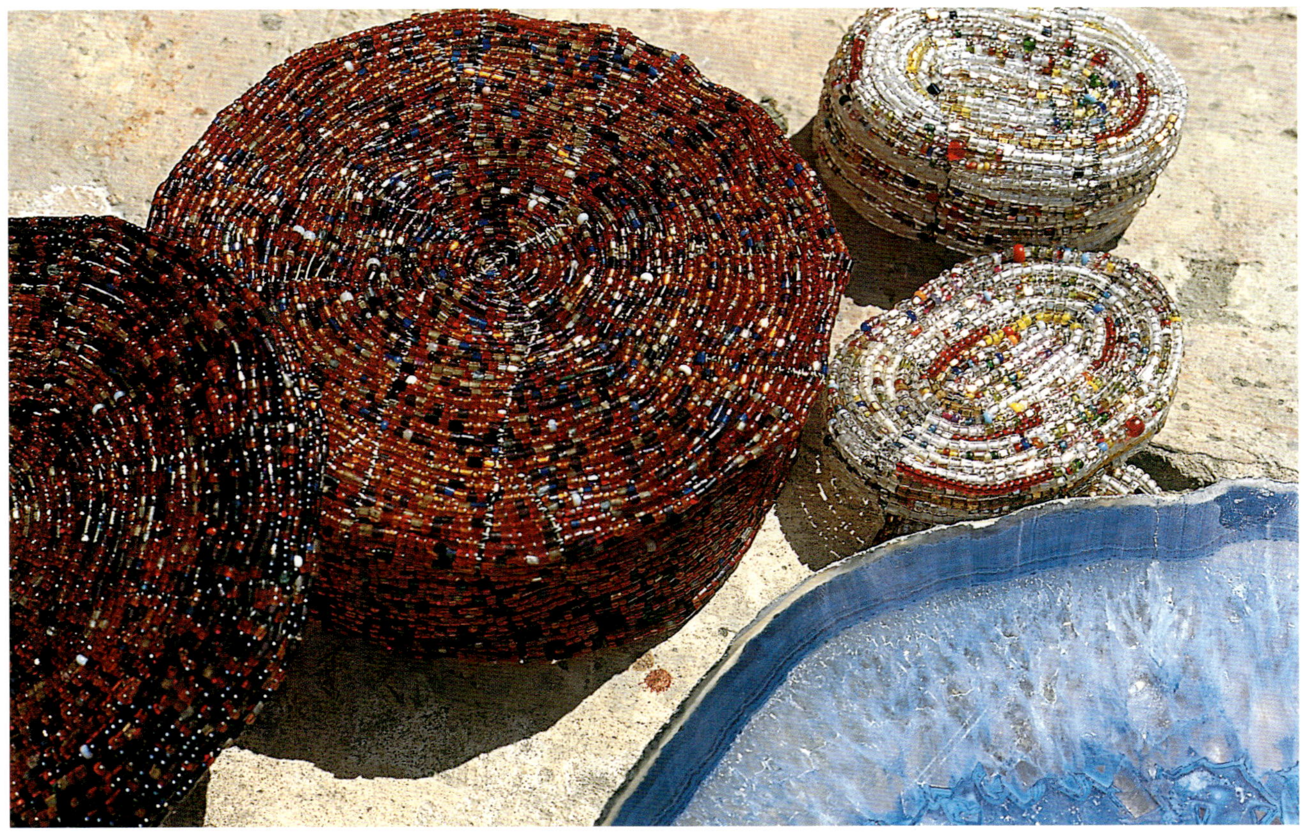

Primrose place holders

When primroses first appear in flower shops, filling them with all their colors, we know spring cannot be far behind. Red, white, yellow, pink, blue—every color is represented in a stunning, inviting palette. We can recreate the same effect with glass beads, using several small vases and a good selection of colors. With a little effort, we can create an original center piece for the dining room table and coordinated place holders. The vases can be of different materials: metal, porcelain or glass, depending on the table's decor; in these photographs we use silver vases because we like its luminosity and the way it enhances all the objects surrounding it.

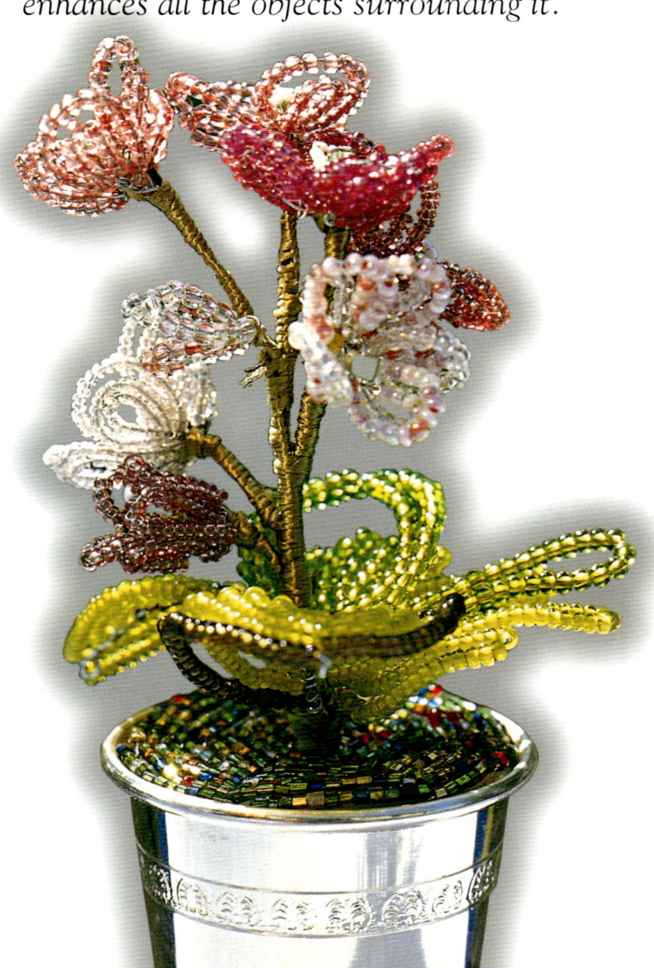

1

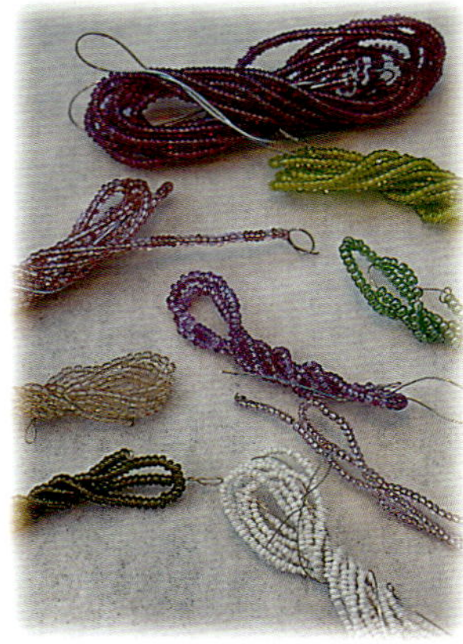

2

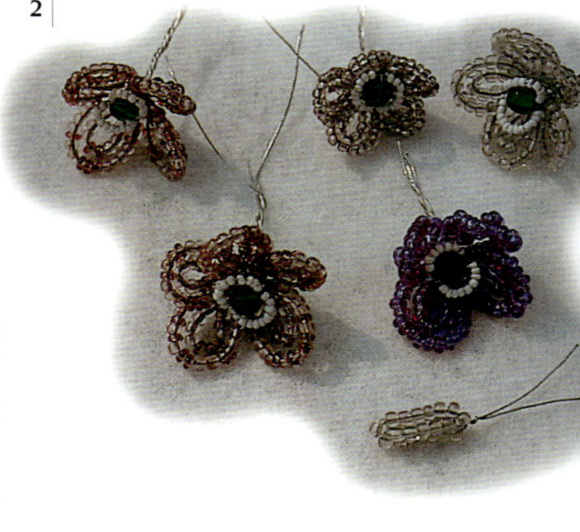

Materials | For each vase of primroses you will need:

•

3 strings of pale green beads

•

1 string of mixed color beads

•

1 string of olive green beads

•

1 string of pale pink beads

•

1 string of rose beads

•

1 string of cyclamen pink beads

•

1 string of white opaque beads

•

5 green beads, 1/8 inch diameter

•

6 20 gauge wires

•

non-hardening modeling clay such as plasteline or floral clay

•

pale green silk twist, vinyl glue, pliers.

HOW TO MAKE A PRIMROSE

1 | Because primroses are small flowers, you will only need a small quantity of beads. You can recycle leftover beads from other flowers.

2 | Prepare five primroses and their pistils using different colors. Each primrose has five petals constructed with the peach blossom technique. Adding some buds creates an interesting effect.

3 | Using silk twist, attach each flower to the stem, 22 gauge wire; make short peduncles for the buds also.

4 | As with the flowers, make the leaves in several sizes and shades of green, for the more varied, the more interesting the bouquet.

5 | Add the flowers to the central stalk, creating a miniature tree.

Opposite, the variety of colors and shapes calls to mind a bed of spring flowers.

3

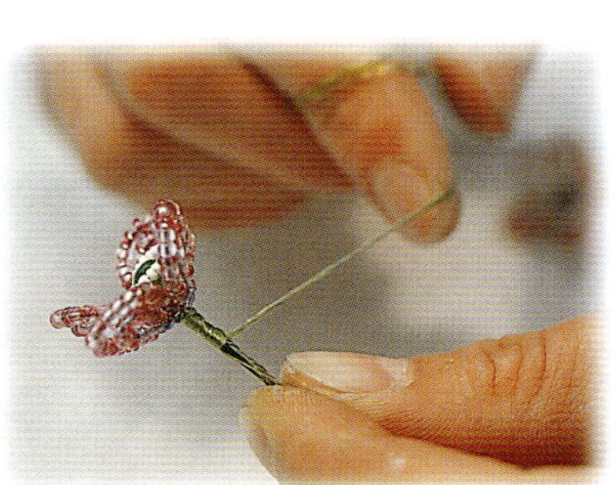

4

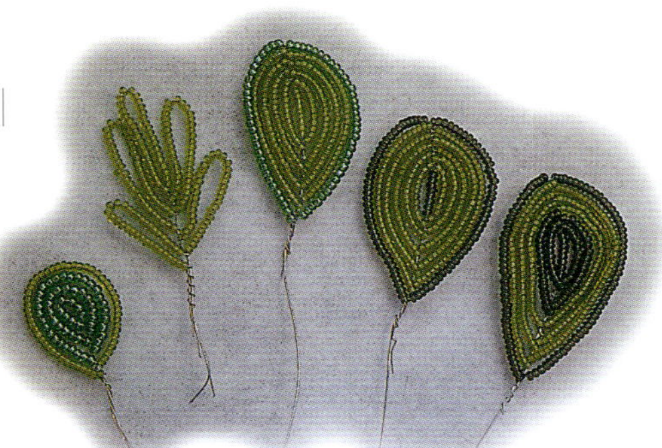

5

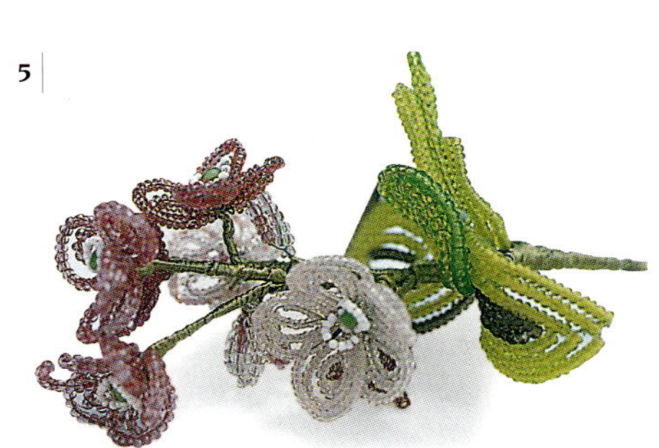

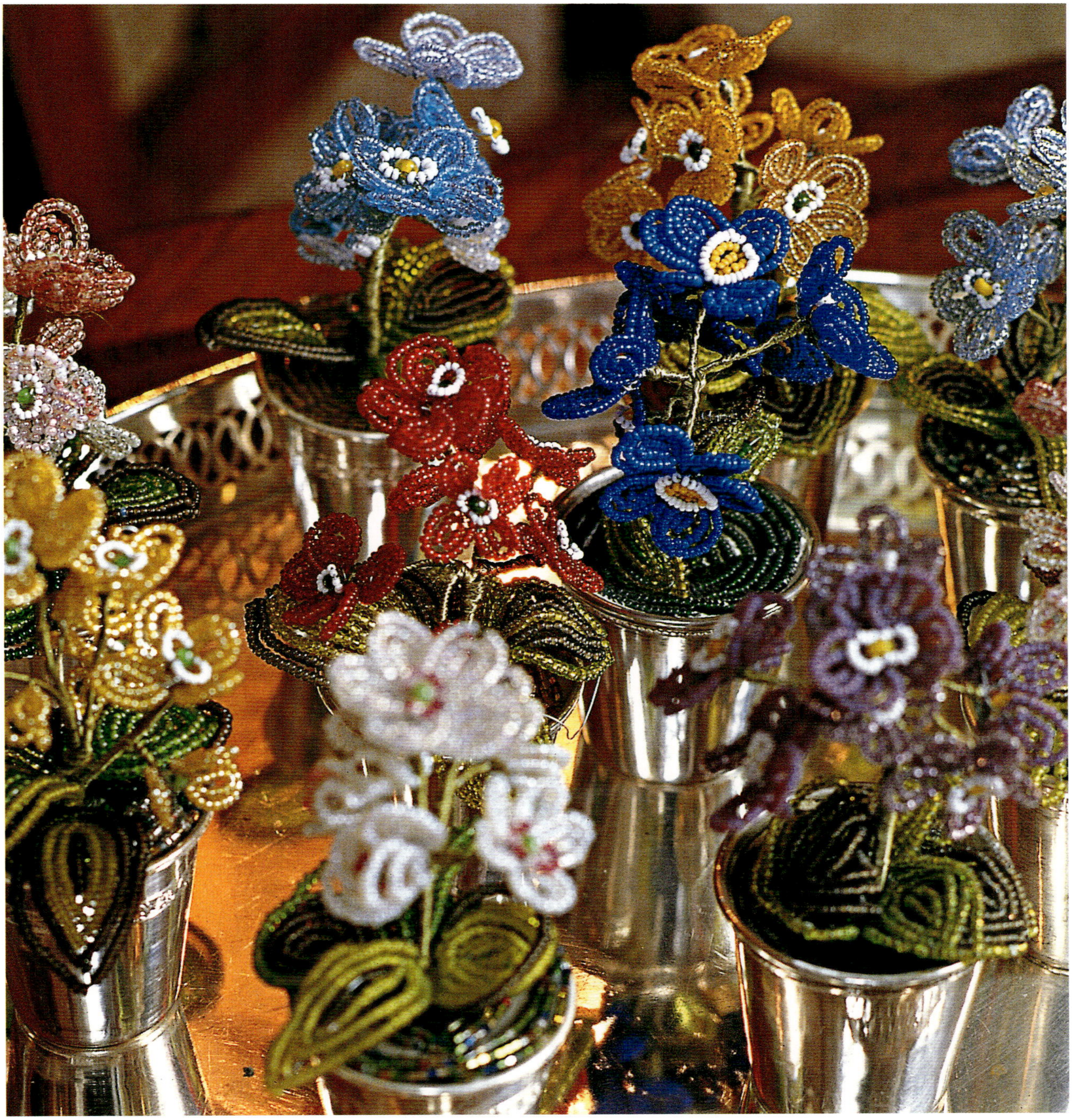

6

7

8

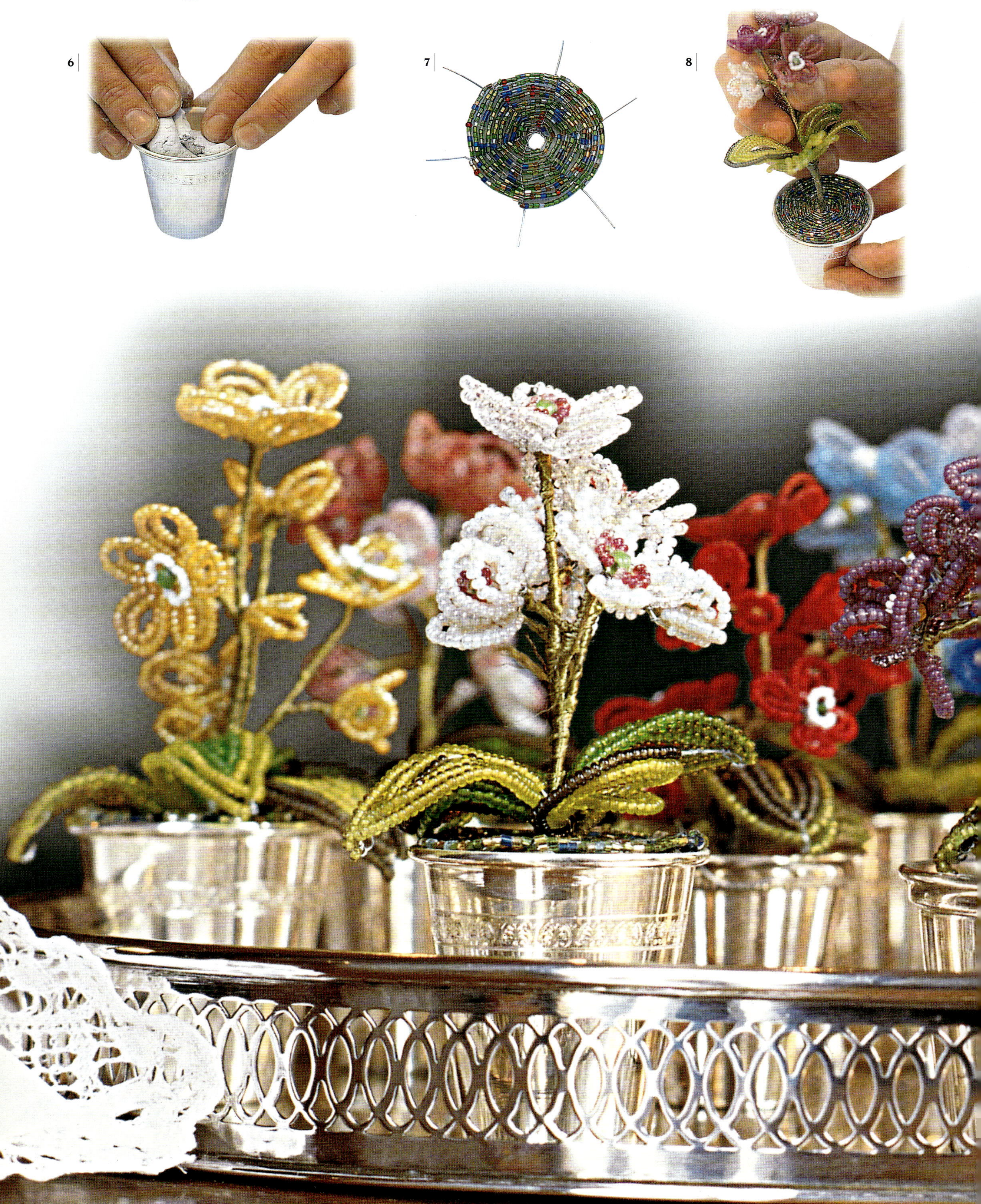

6 | Fill each small vase with plasteline (floral clay). Because this is a heavy clay, it will prevent the vase from tipping. Also, since it does not harden right away, errors can be easily corrected.

7 | Make a disc with beads of various sizes and colors, leaving a whole in the center. Make the disc as wide as the top diameter of the vase and place it on top of the plasteline (floral clay) in the vase.

8 | Assemble the miniature tree with all the flowers, buds, and leaves and insert it in the plasteline (floral clay).

The small vases can be inserted in a large center tray or arranged before each setting as place holders.

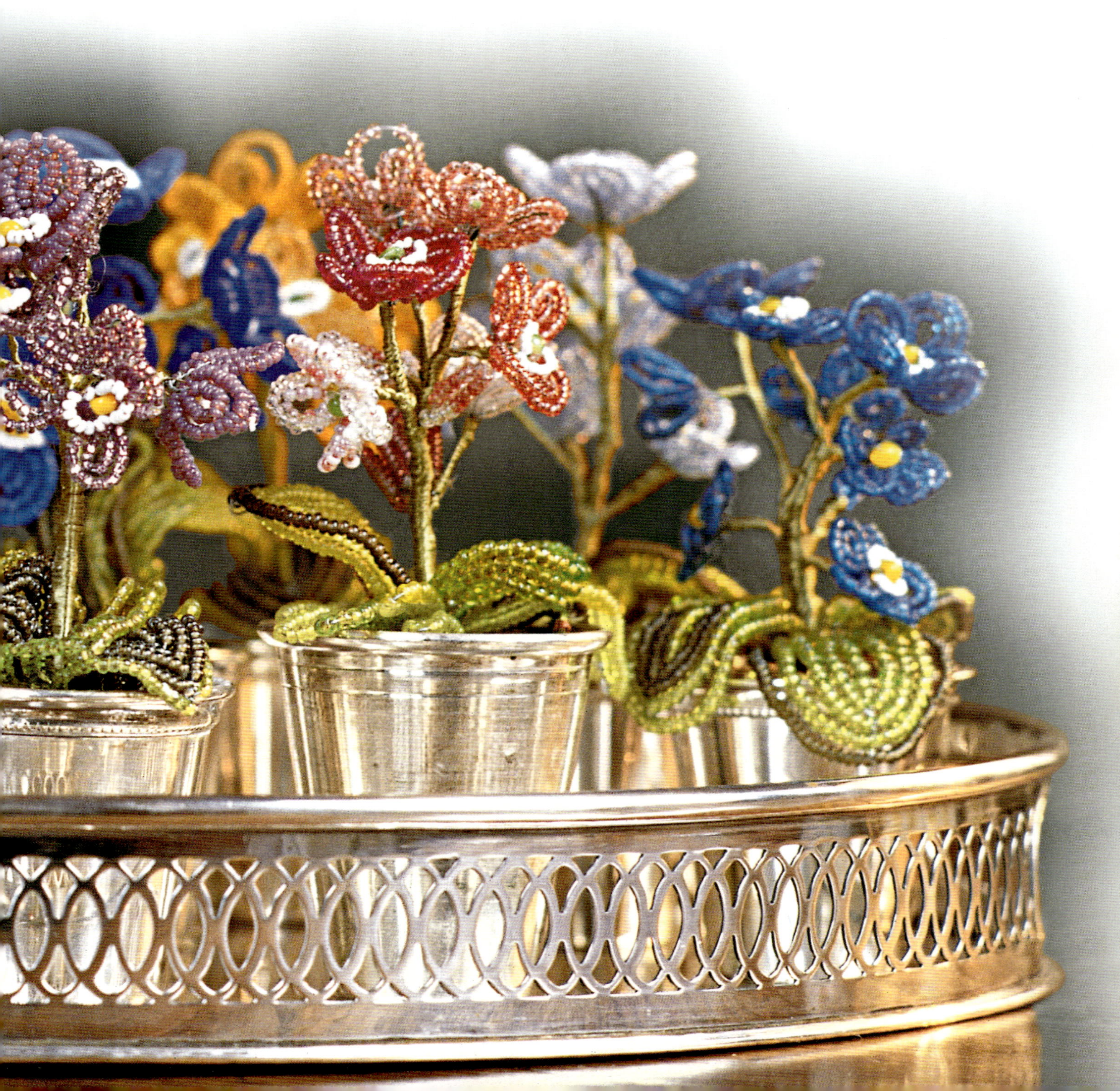

Center Piece

A cascade of glass bead flowers makes any table festive and is forever fresh and maintenance-free. Creating the center piece reproduced in these pages is time consuming because of the large number of flowers used, but the final result is spectacular. We suggest you arrange the flowers on a silver tray to enhance the effect. Placing some branches along the tray's border will further enhance the composition; for a small table, a beautiful bowl in the center will suffice.

HOW TO MAKE THE BASE

First prepare the base, then the flowers

1 | Fill a bowl or a vase of similar shape with a florist sponge; use a cutter to shape the sponge if necessary.

2 | Place a large beaded disc, the same diameter as the bowl or vase, on top of the sponge. Construct the disc in the usual manner, using three wires to build the frame. Because the disc will be hardly visible, it doesn't need to be flawless.

3 | Fasten the disc to the sponge using the end wires of the disc.

4 | Take a green florist wire and twist the four beaded strings around it, making a cord 20 inches long.

5 | Arrange the cord around the rim of the bowl and fasten it to the sponge to hide any defects.

6 | Now you may arrange the flowers in the vase. Don't use too many flowers, for each flower must stand out in all its splendor.

Materials | For one center piece you will need:

- *1 bowl, 6 to 8 inches wide*
- *1 synthetic florist sponge and 1 cutter*
- *10 strings of green beads mixed with other colors*
- *1 20 gauge wire*
- *1 string of silver beads*
- *1 string of silver-washed green beads*
- *2 strings of mixed green beads*
- *pliers*
- *beaded flowers on silk-covered stems*

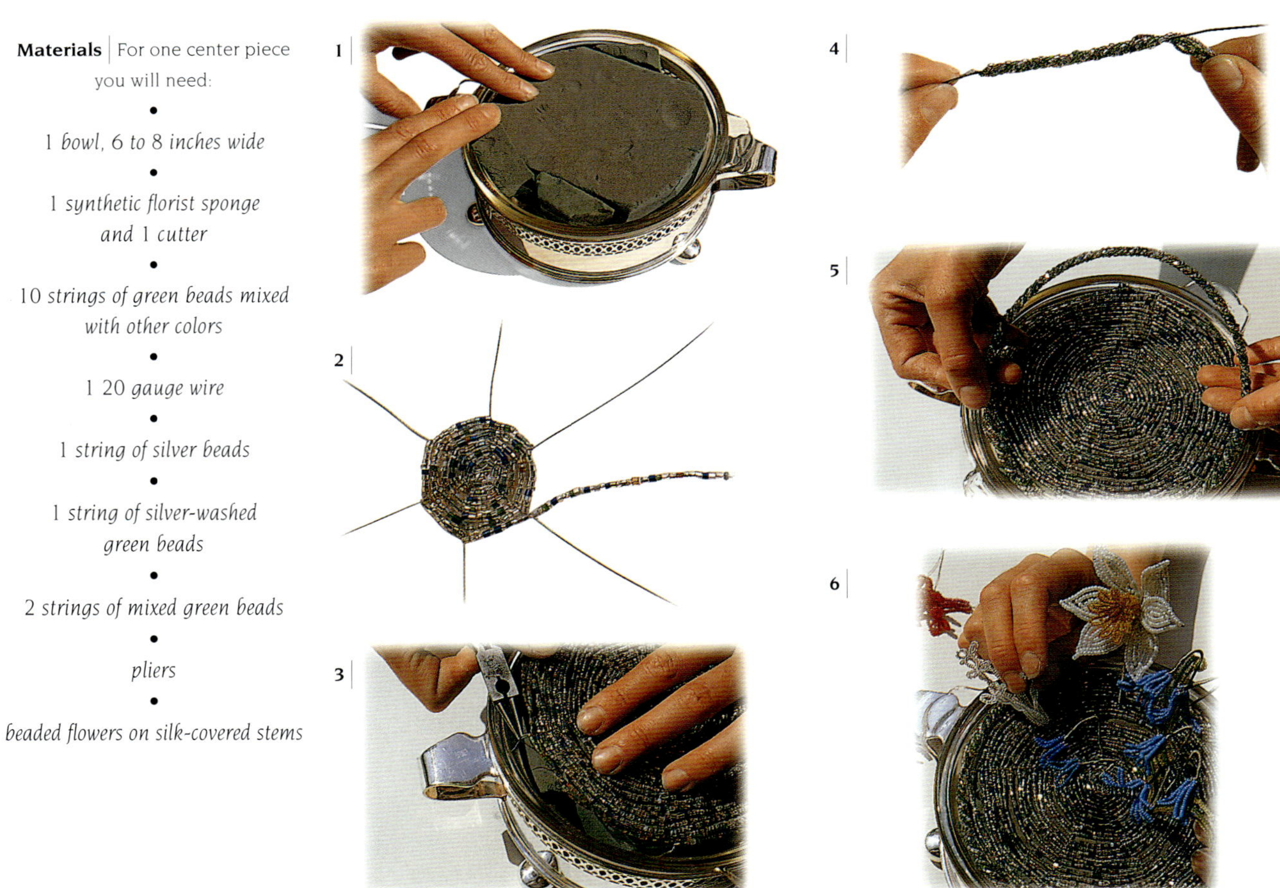

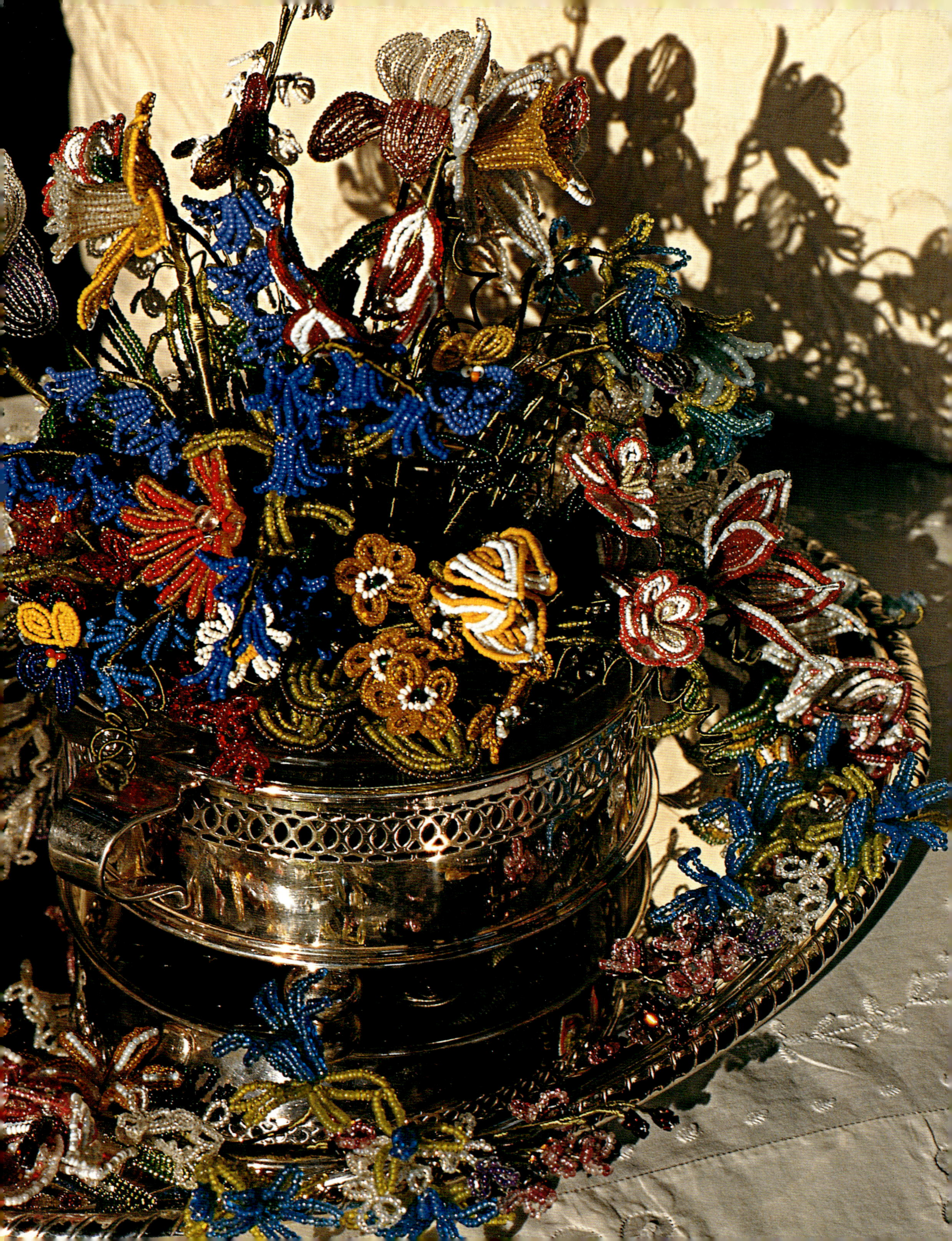

Candle Holder

1

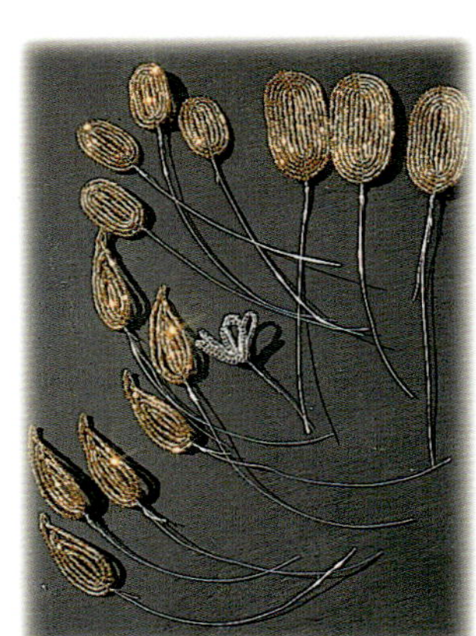

The idea of creating this candle holder came to us by looking at a pair of outdoor candle holders that had such a lonely air, even with the candles lit. Why not add beaded flowers at the base, to fill that emptiness? And so we created gold and silver roses and placed them at the bottom of the glass, adding an extra glow, heightened by the dancing reflections of the candle's flame. The precious beaded roses are preserved under glass, protected from the weather, like all beautiful and delicate objects of yore.

2

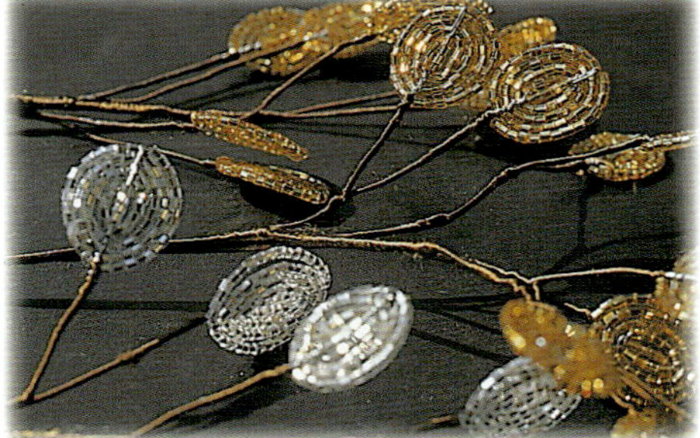

3

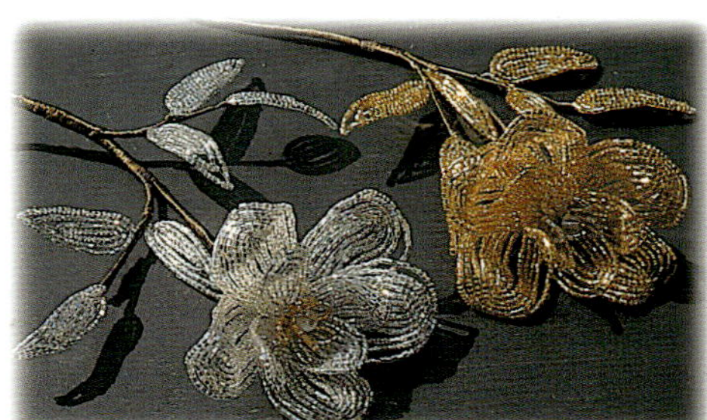

Materials | For each candle holder you will need:

•

20 strings of gold beads

•

20 strings of silver beads

•

10 wires, 20 gauge, 10 inches long

•

1 roll 22 gauge wire

•

brown silk twist, vinyl glue, pliers.

HOW TO MAKE A CANDLE HOLDER

Make four gold roses and four silver roses, four satinpod branches with 10 leaves each, and arrange them in two wreaths of four roses and two branches each.

1 | Create each rose by attaching to the stem 5 medium-size round petals, 4 small round petals, 6 pointed leaves for the stem, and one bud.

2 | For each satinpod branch you will need 10 gold leaves and 10 silver leaves. Prepare each leaf separately, and cover the branch with silk twist. Then assemble the branch.

3 | Each rose has a center bud of a different color: gold if the petals are silver, and vice versa.

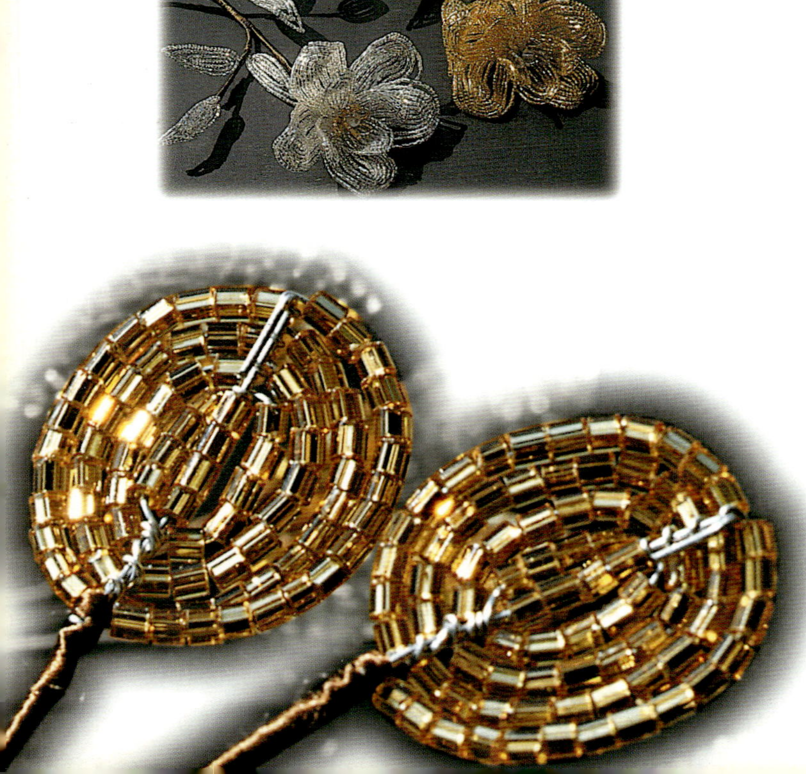

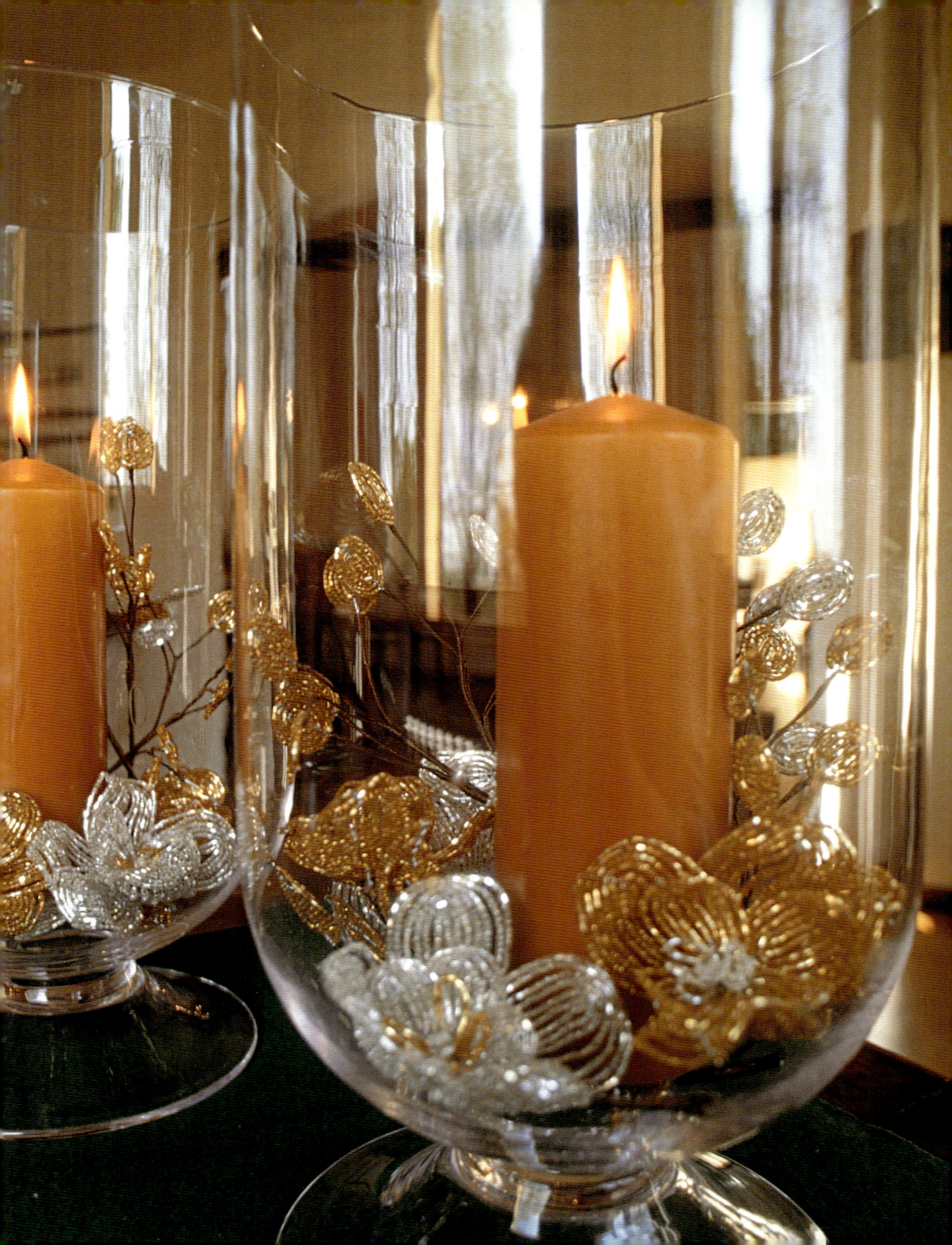

Miniature Christmas Trees

We can create an enchanted forest of miniature firs for a magic Christmas table setting. Making fir trees is fun: we can easily create the branches from strings of silver beads. Each branch is like a bright snowflake lit by the sun.

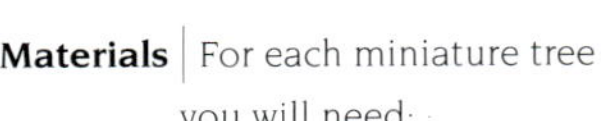

1

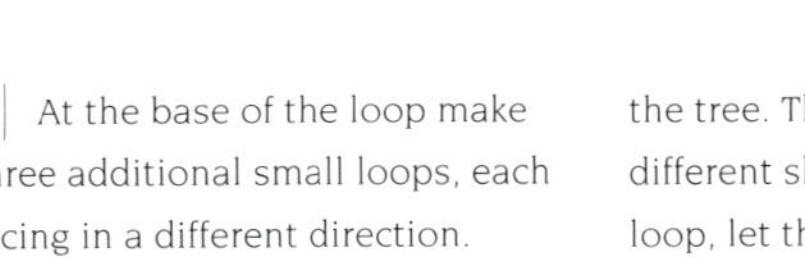

2

Materials | For each miniature tree you will need:

•

3 strings of silver beads

•

18 gauge stem wire, 3 inches long

•

4 wires, 20 gauge, 4 inches long

•

brown silk twist, vinyl glue, pliers.

HOW TO MAKE A MINIATURE CHRISTMAS TREE

First make the leaves, then the roots, and assemble them on the trunk.

1 | Make one beaded loop ¾ of an inch long, then a second loop crossing it over the first at a right angle.

2 | At the base of the loop make three additional small loops, each facing in a different direction.

3 | Bend the beaded string to make three small loops of equal size. These are the first leaves of the tree. The other leaves have a different shape: bend the first loop, let three beads slide, then make two equal loops facing in opposite directions.

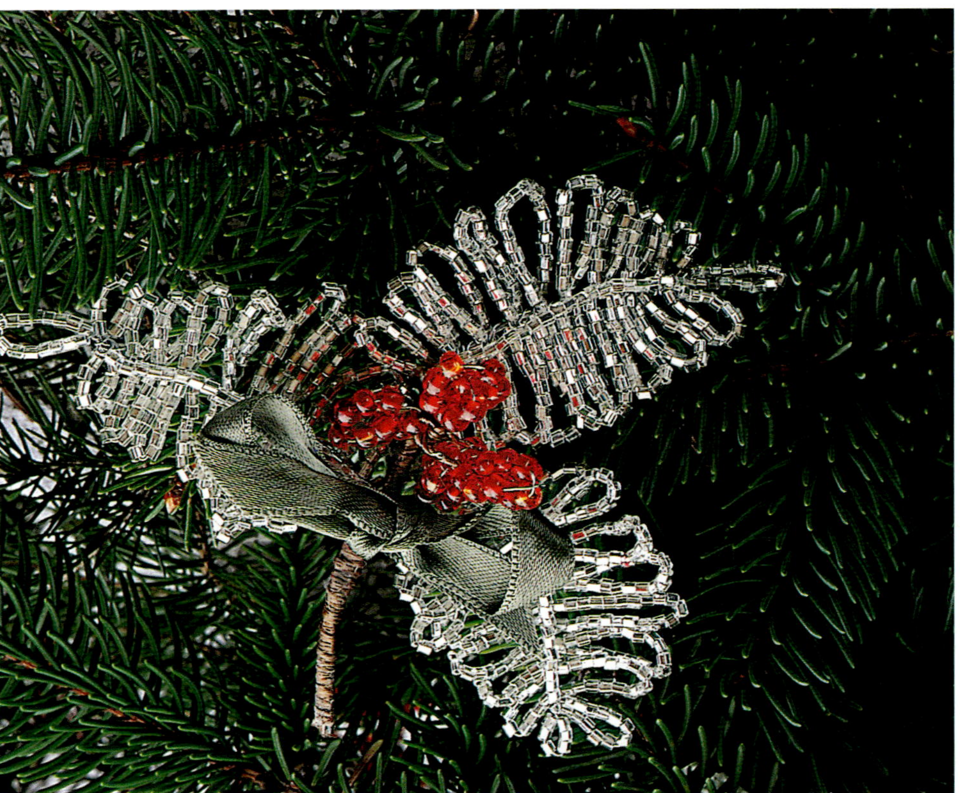

A glittering arrangement of three fir leaves used as ornament for our Christmas tree.

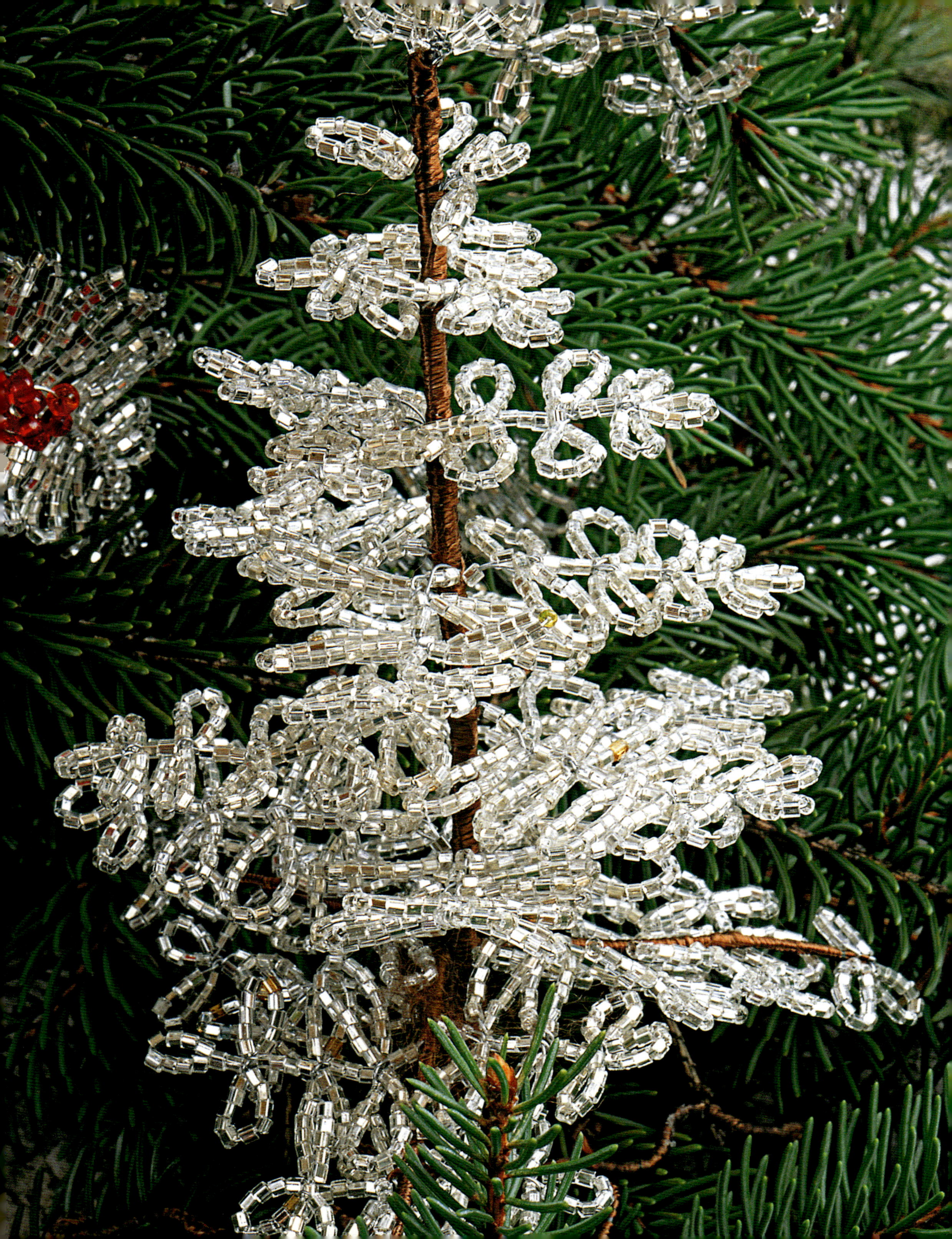

3

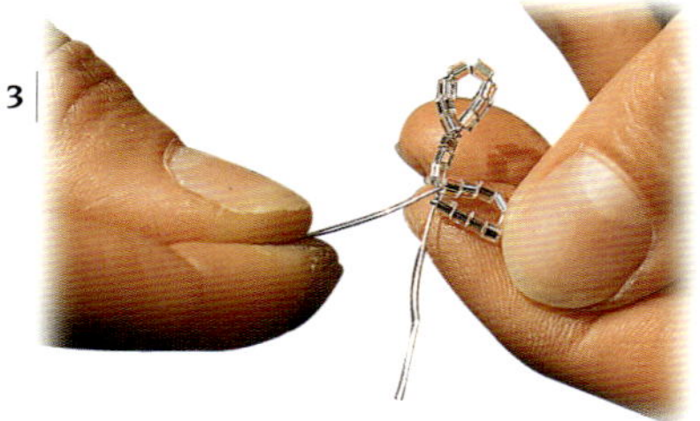

4

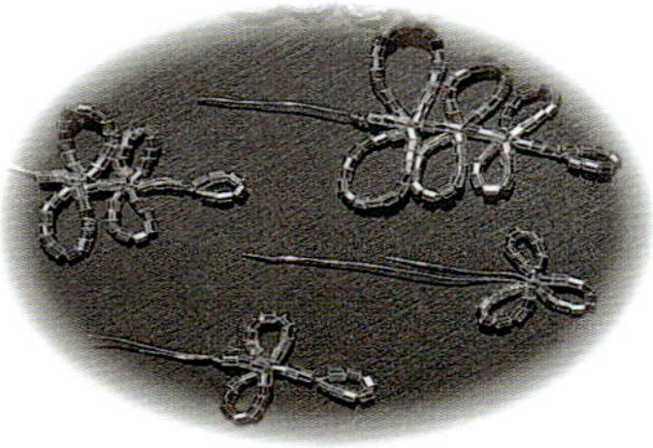

5

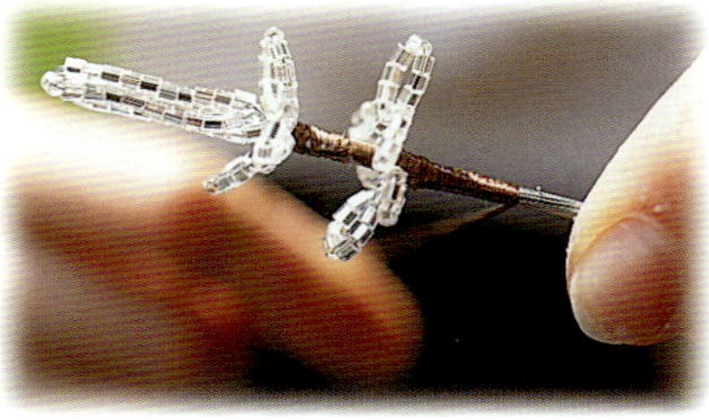

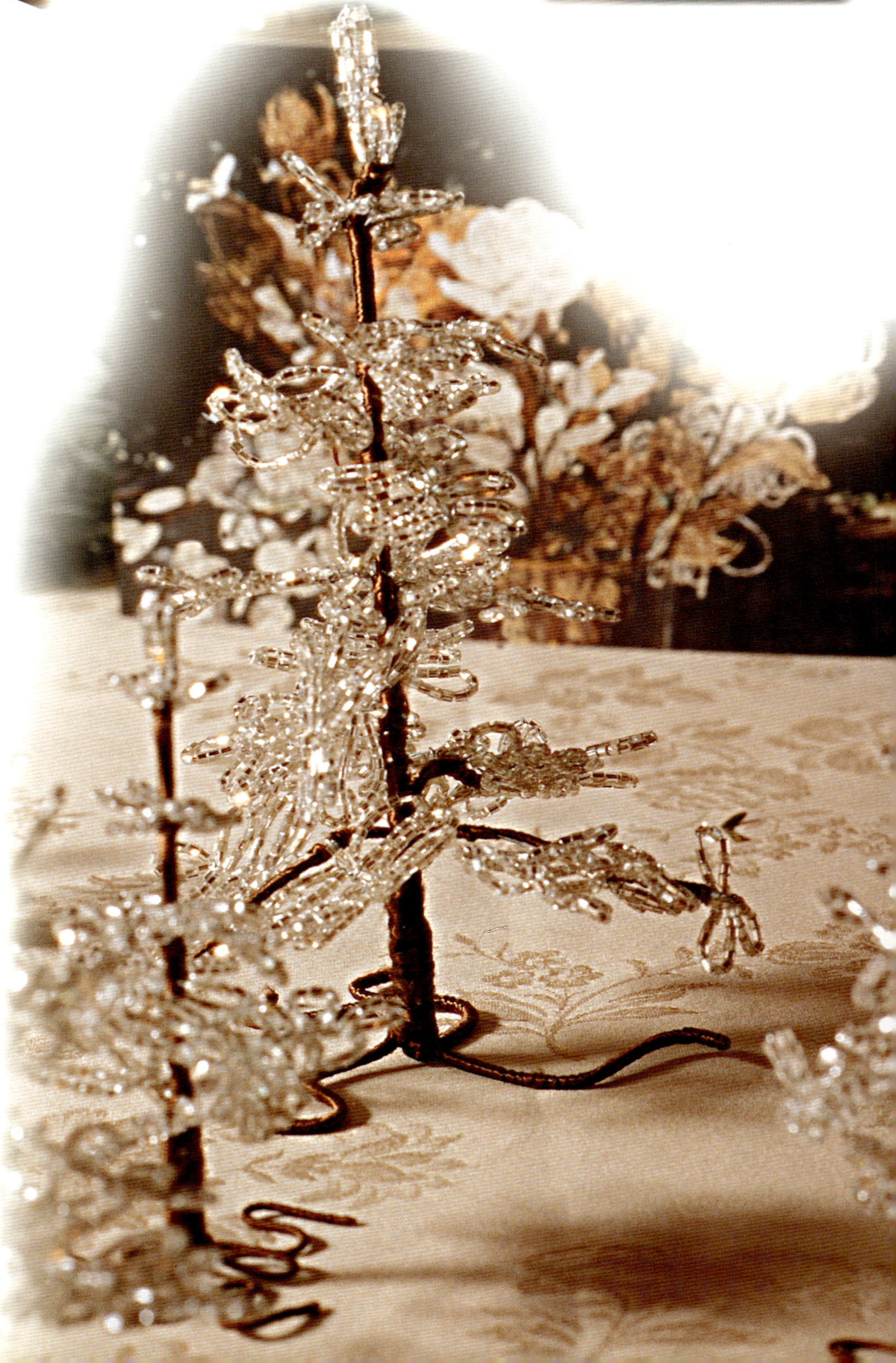

4 | There are four types of leaves in all: the two small ones have only three loops, then there are three longer ones with three loops each, three leaves with five loops, and finally three leaves with seven loops each.

5 | Start carefully assembling the tree. At about ⅓ to ½ inch from the top add the first two small leaves, then ⅓ to ½ inches below the three leaves made of three loops, another ⅓ to ½ inches below add the three leaves with five loops each, and at the same distance below add the large leaves.

6 | Each time you attach a set of leaves, make sure they are at the same height, but oriented in different directions.

7 | Prepare the roots separately. Take four 22 gauge wires, 4 inches long and cover them with silk for at least 3 inches of their total length. Attach them about 1¼ inches from the bottom of the trunk; cover and fasten them together with silk twist.

8 | Open the roots and shape them with your fingers, curving them as in the photograph at right. Open the leaves of the fir tree, filling the tree as much as possible. The final effect will be a miniature ice tree like those shown in the large photograph on this page.

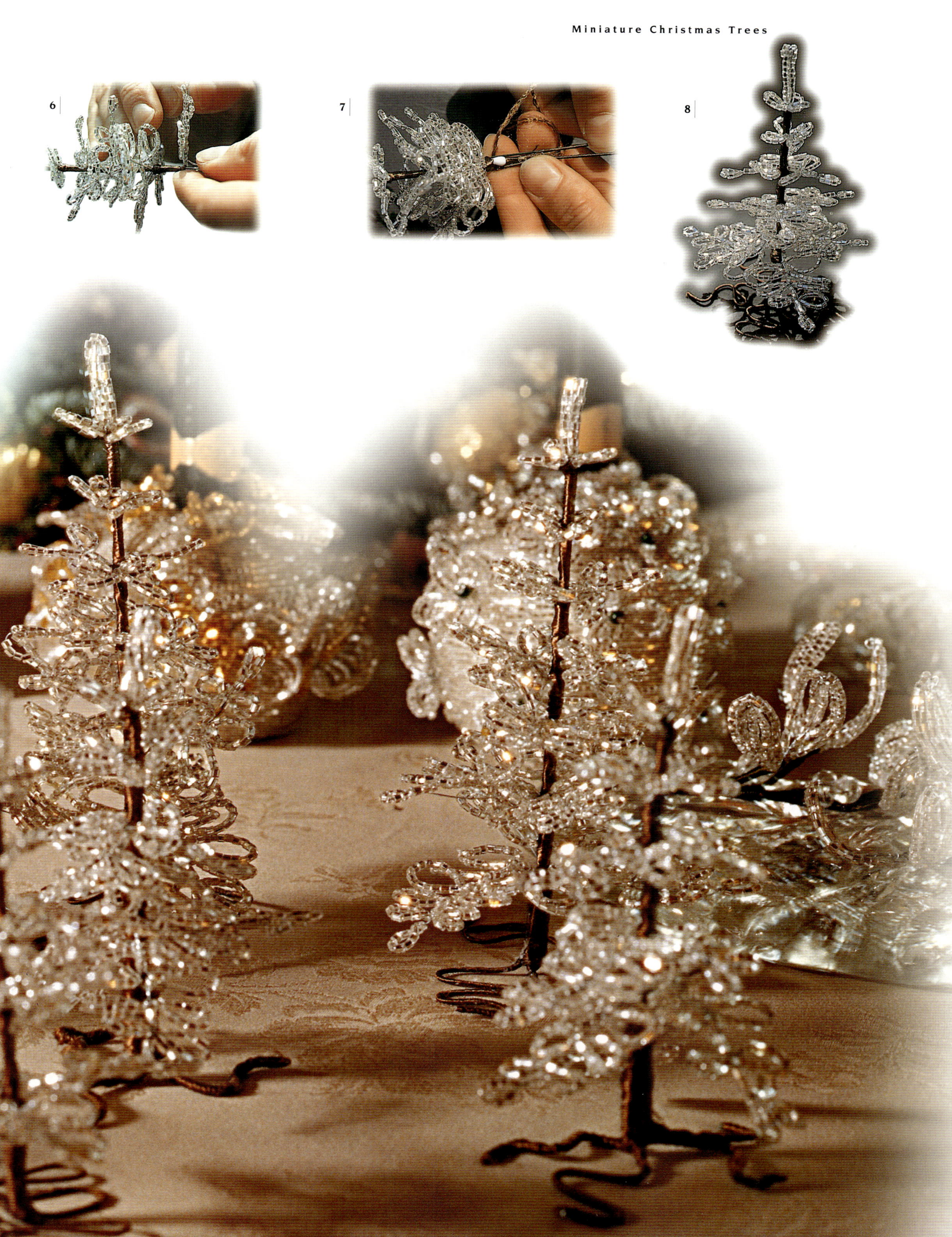

6

7

8

Curtain Tiebacks

We can create beaded curtain tiebacks in original shapes; they are fun to make and easy to clean. Making delicate wreaths that recall the colors of the curtains and the room's décor, or spring flower bouquets held by cords in coordinated colors is an easy project. If the drapes are in a flower pattern, we suggest you choose a cord in the same colors as the fabric.

HOW TO MAKE A TIEBACK

For each cluster you will need one 1 yard beaded string and one 11 inch wire.

1 | Each wreath consists of eight satinpods made with crystal beads, 10 colored lilies and one small rose in the center. The lily's petals are 1¼ inches long. The small rose has two rows of petals: an outer row of five pink petals consisting of rounds each, and an inner row of smaller crystal petals consisting of 2 rounds each; the heart of the rose is made with amber beads.

2 | The eight satinpods have a ⅜ of an inch core and 4 rounds of beads. They are arranged on a small branch and fastened with silk twist, four to a branch.

3 | Fasten the four satinpods to the top of a 6 inch wire, then add five assorted lilies, each one with its short peduncle.

Materials | For the flowers you will need:

- *7 strings of crystal beads*
- *3 strings of azure blue transparent beads*
- *3 strings of pink transparent beads*
- *3 strings of rose beads*
- *1 string of yellow beads*
- *1 wire, 20 gauge, 6 inches long*
- *1 string of amber beads*
- *pale green silk twist, vinyl glue, pliers*

For the cord:

- *2 strings of crystal beads*
- *1 string of pink beads*
- *1 wire, 20 gauge, 32 inches long*
- *2 crystal beads, ⅕ inch in length and width.*

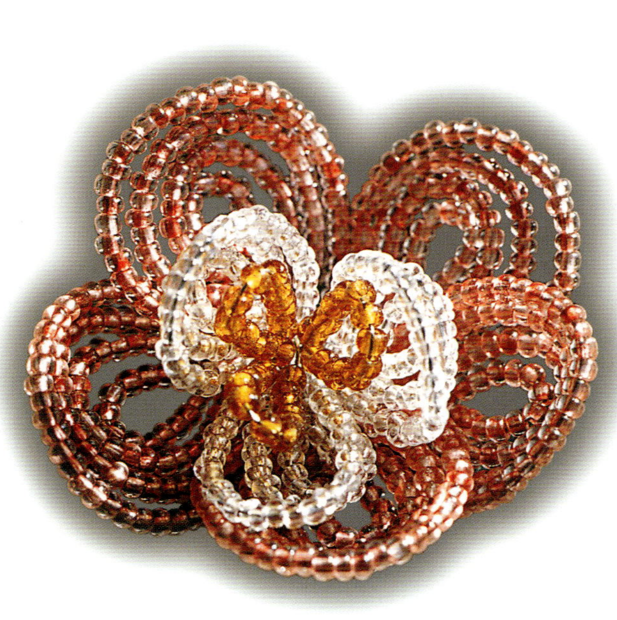

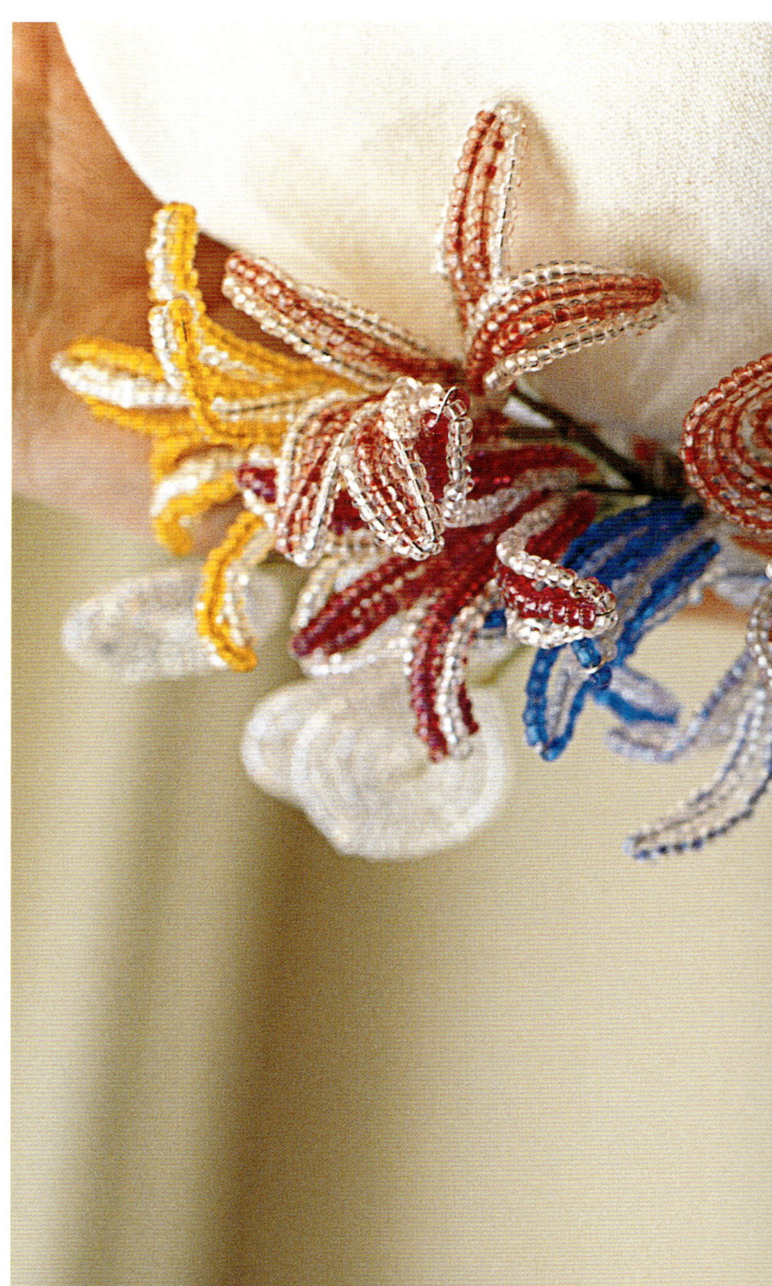

1
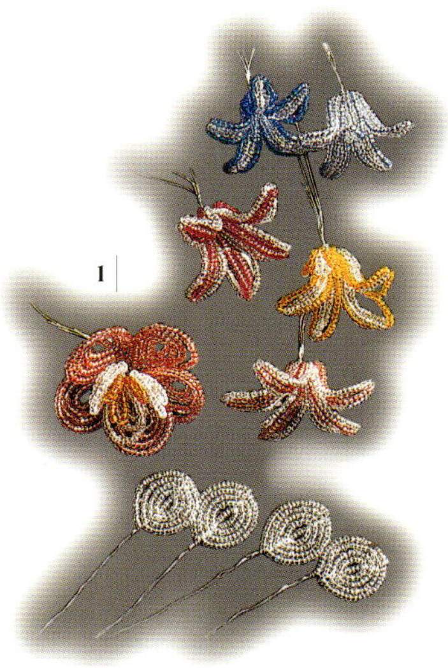

2
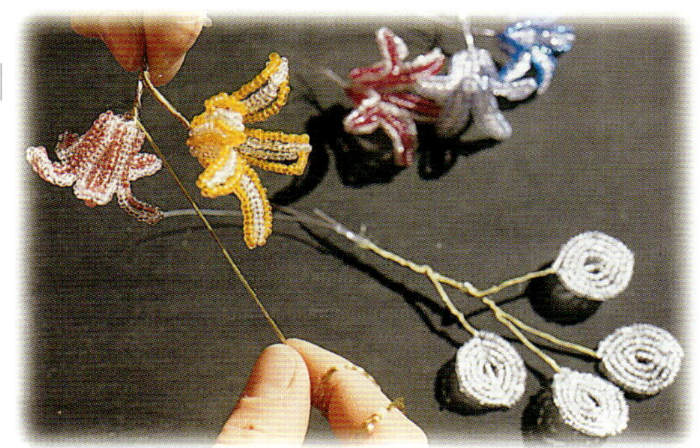

3
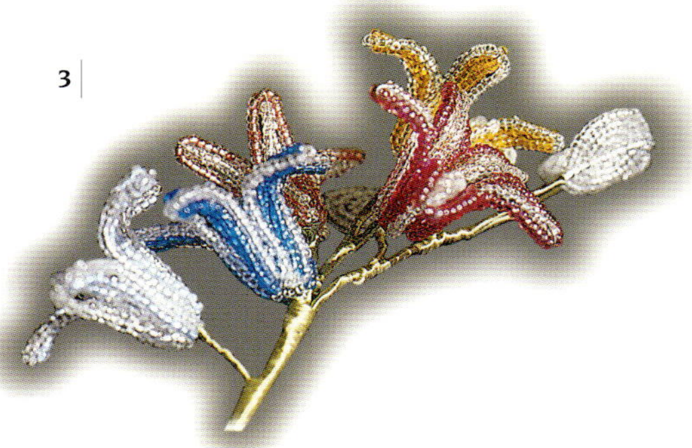

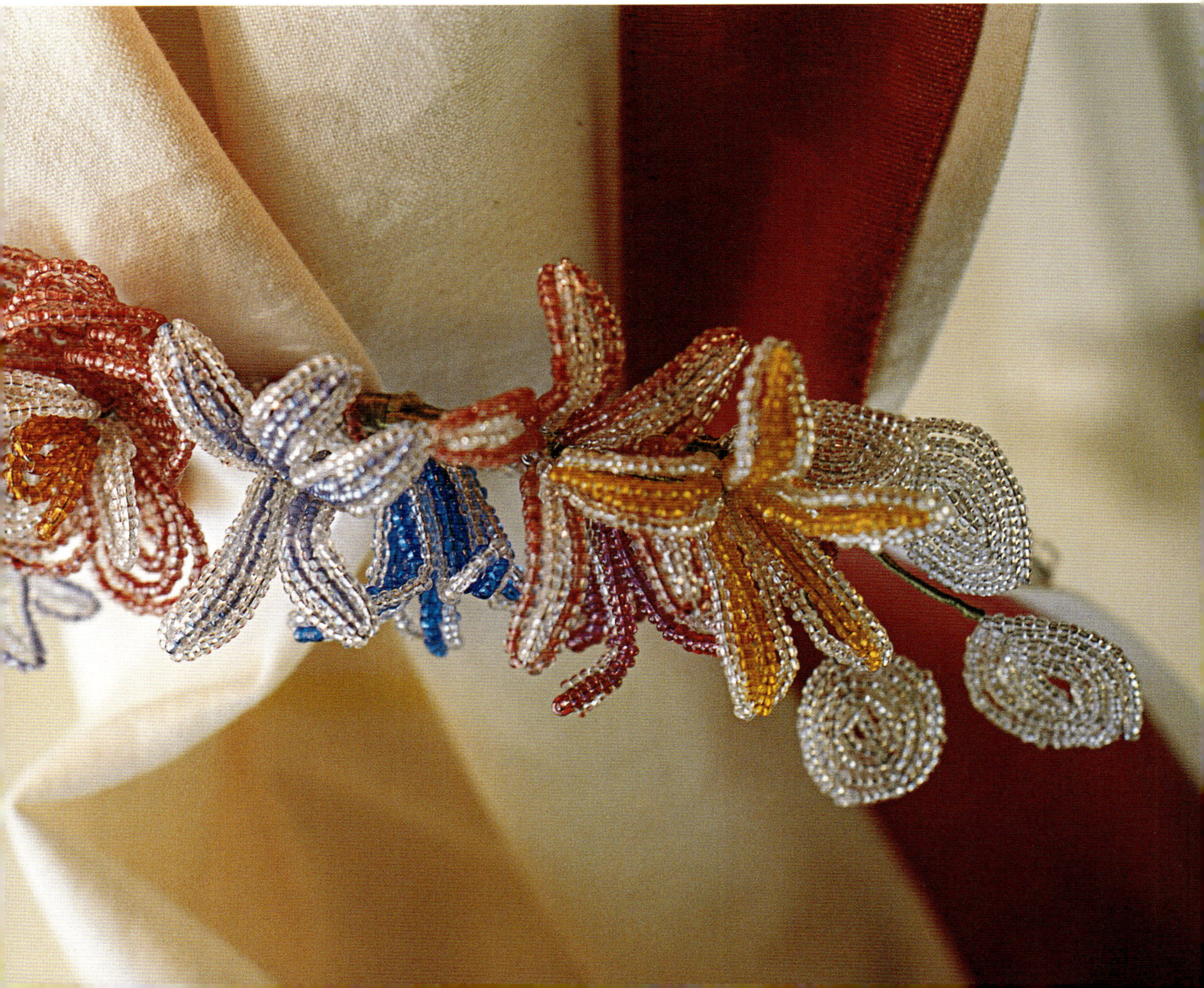

4

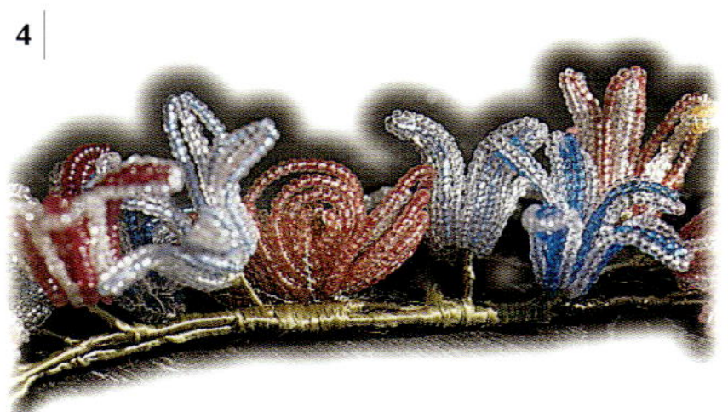

5

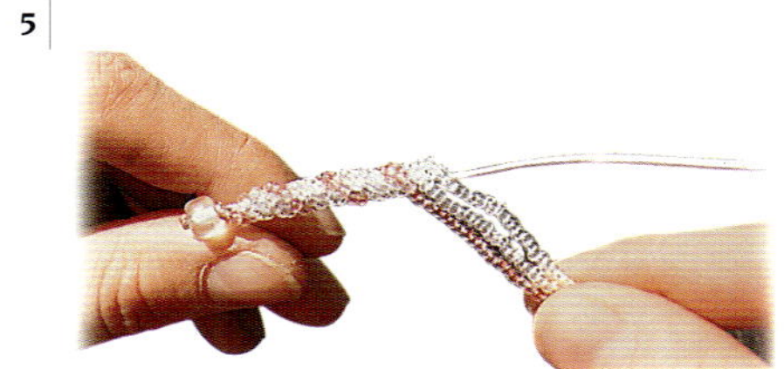

6

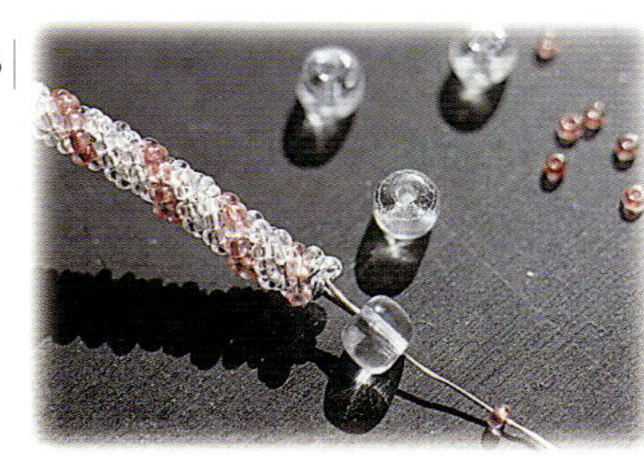

7

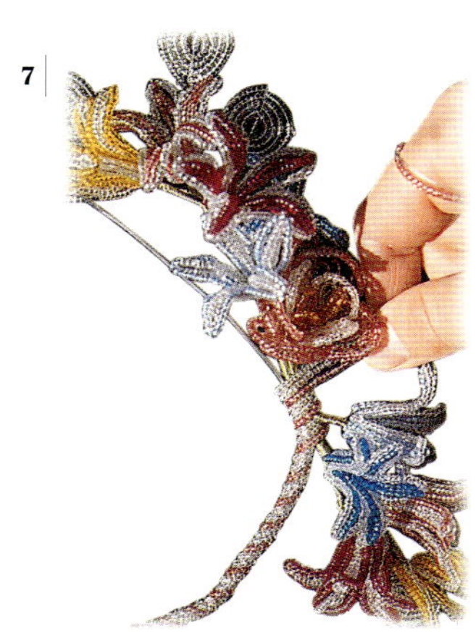

4 | Place the rose at the center of the wreath, making make sure the silk twist covers all of the wire as it attaches the flowers to it. Complete the branch symmetrically with five lilies and the second satinpod branch.

5 | Make a heavy tieback cord by twisting the three beaded strings around a 32-inch long wire.

6 | Add a large crystal bead, 1/3 of an inch diameter, at the beginning and the end of the tieback cord, to hide the wire.

7 | Fasten the flower wreath to the cord at about 10 inches from the top of the cord. Now continue covering the cord with the three strands of beads and finish with another large crystal bead and voila!, the tieback is ready.

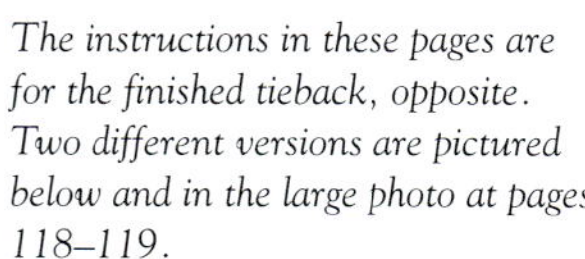

The instructions in these pages are for the finished tieback, opposite. Two different versions are pictured below and in the large photo at pages 118–119.

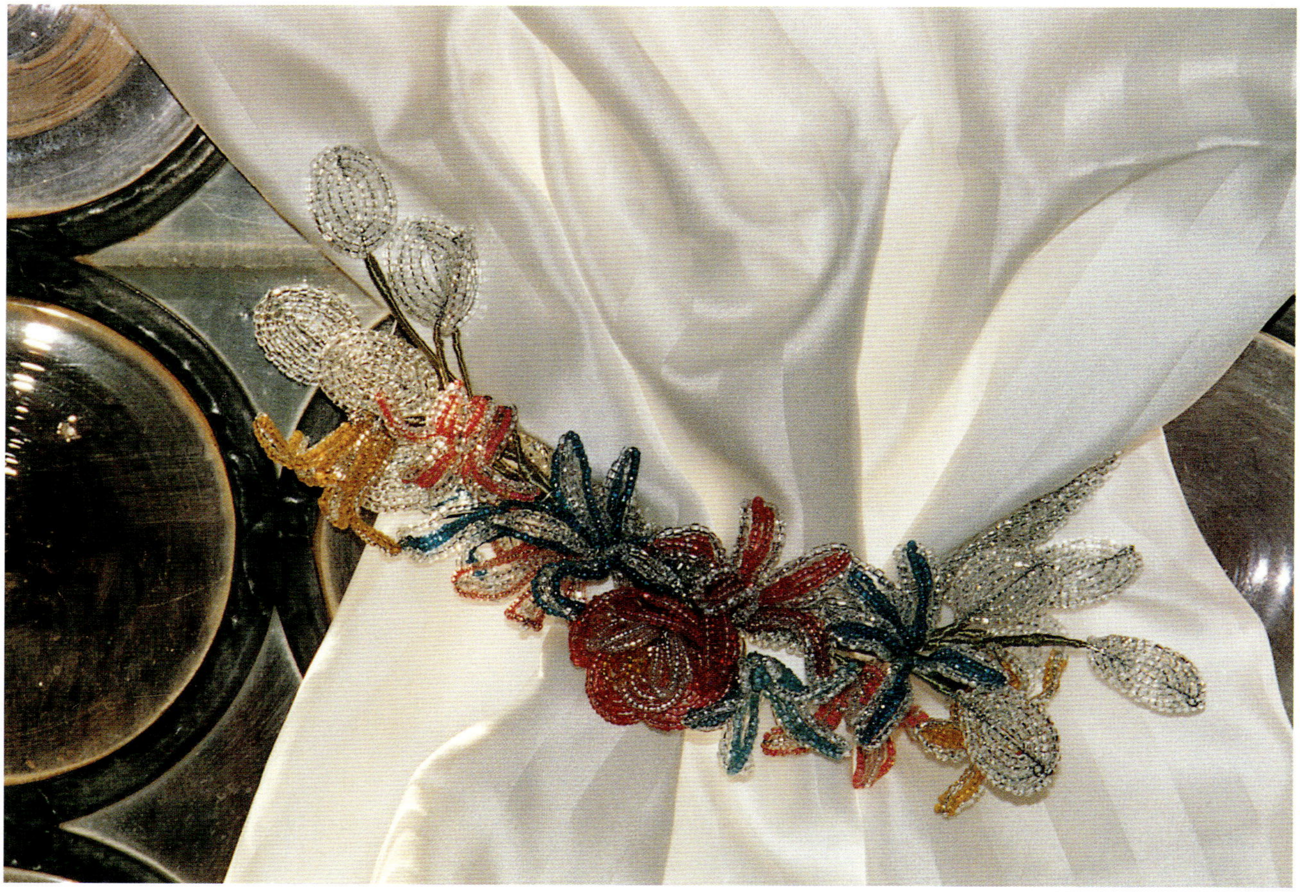

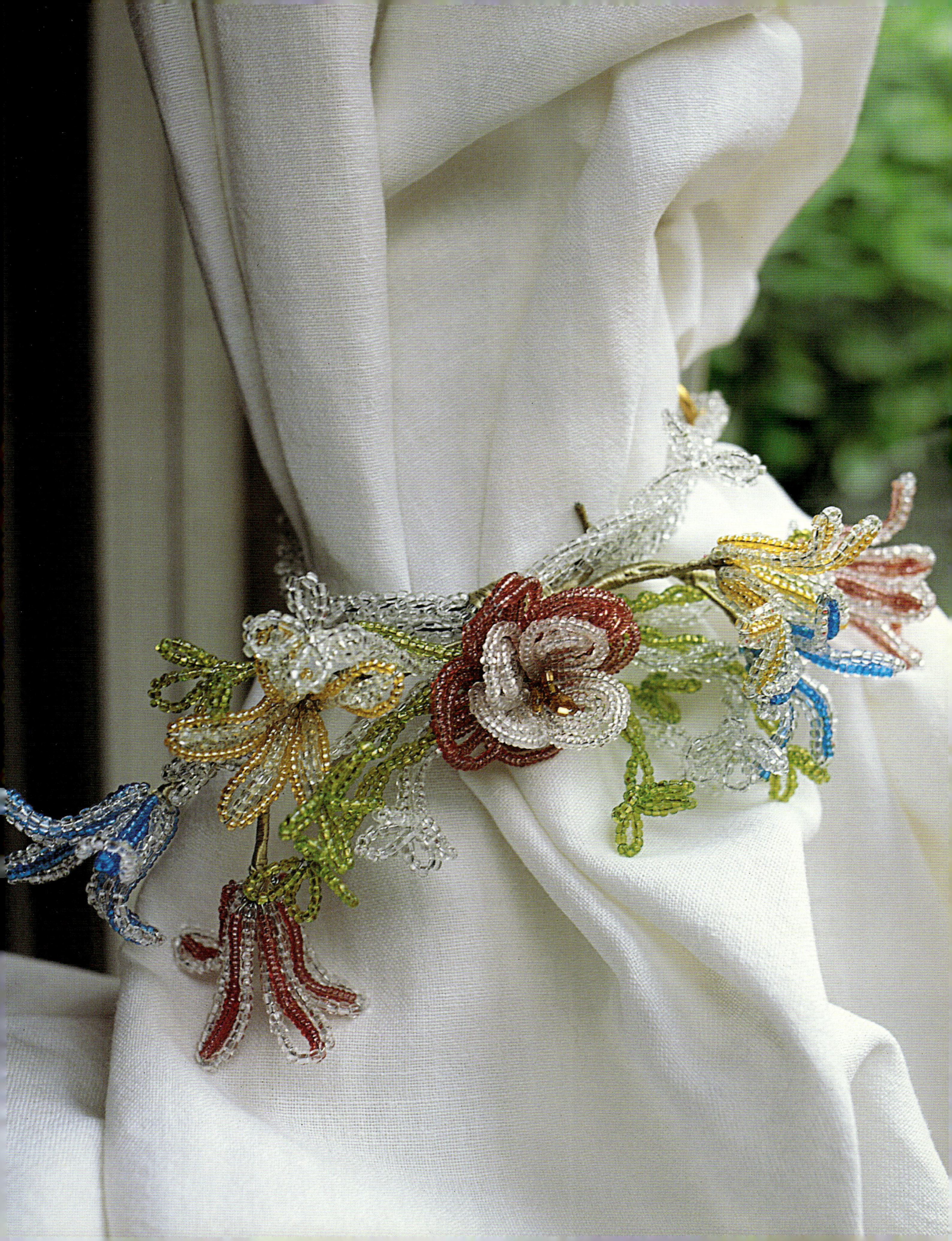

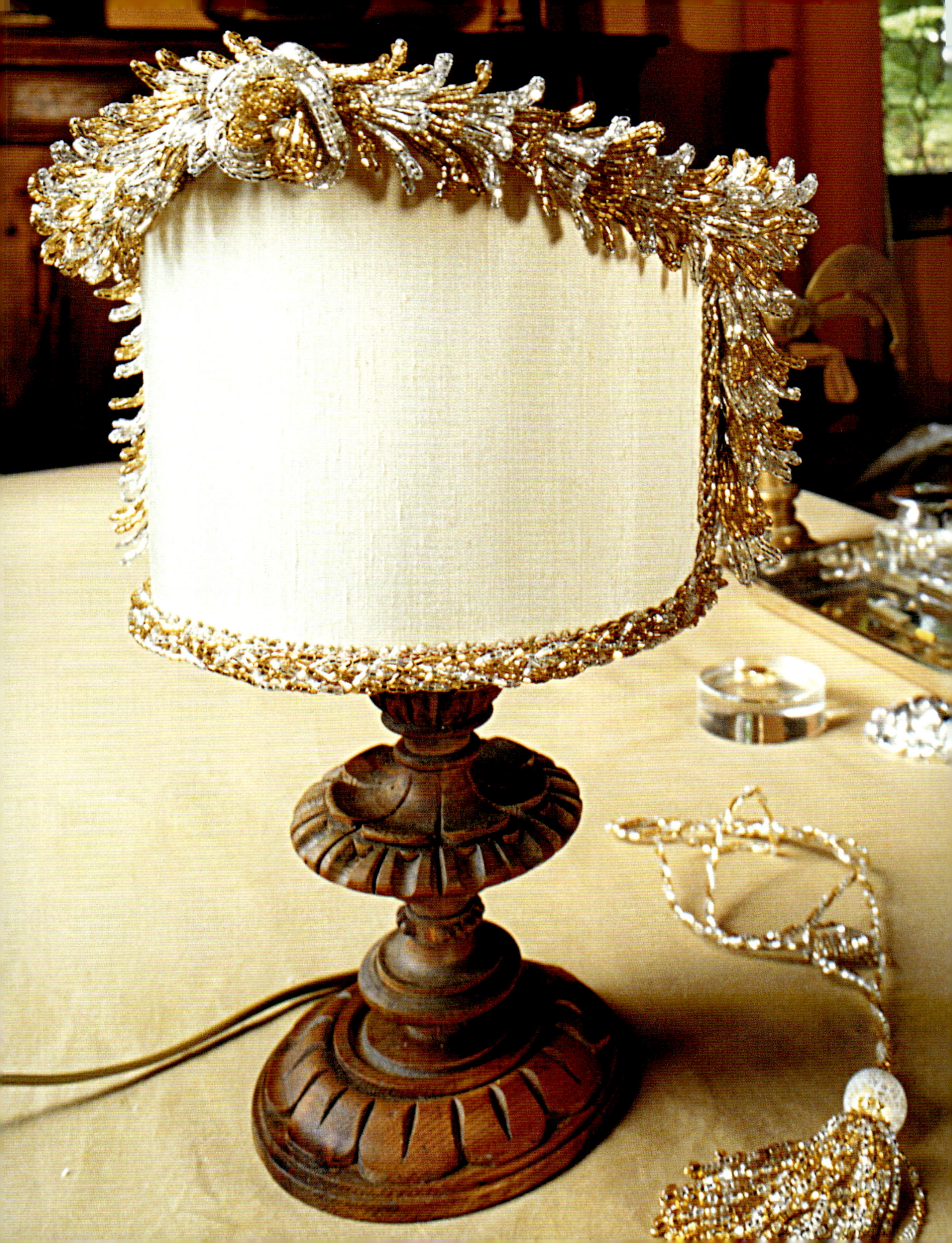

1

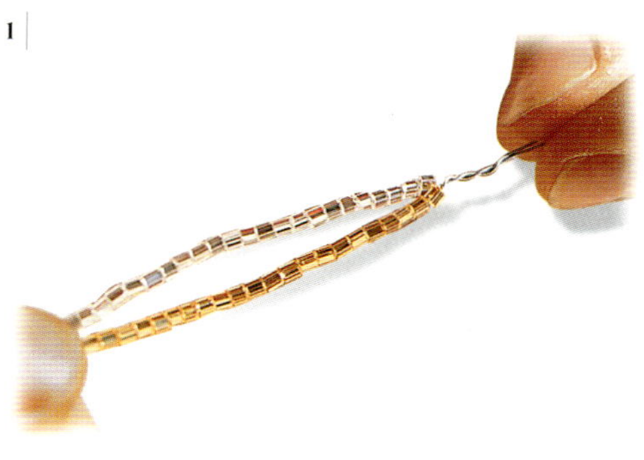

2

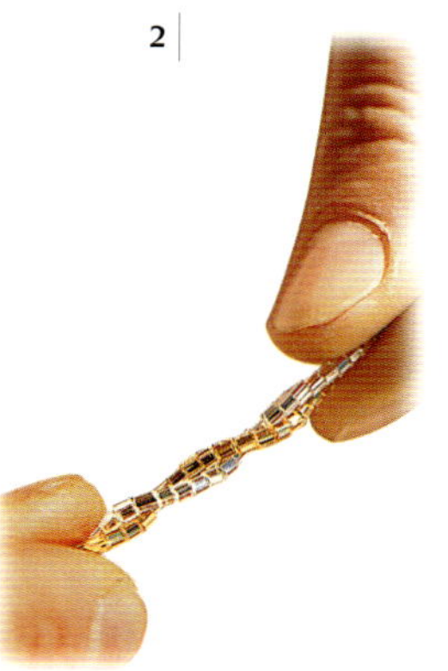

3

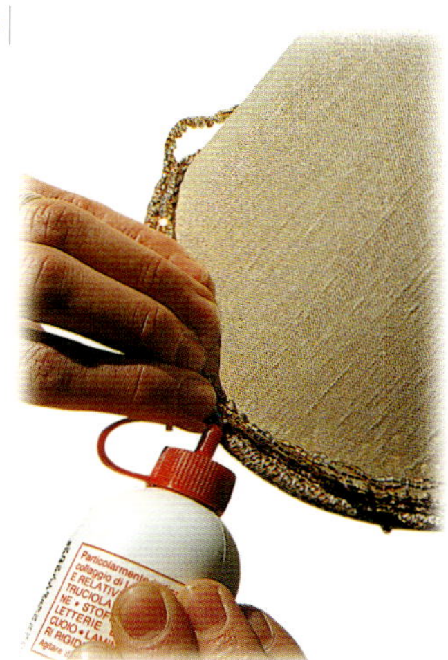

Decorated Lamp Shades

At the turn of the century, lamp globes made with large beaded flowers were very much in fashion: lilies, pansies, and irises were the preferred flowers. Today, we prefer warmer shades and a simpler design, and use the flowers only to decorate the outside border of lampshades. The effects created by the glass beads and the lamp light are both pleasing and intimate.

Materials | For each lampshade you will need:

•

1 lampshade, 6 inches wide

•

20 strings of gold beads

•

20 strings of silver beads

•

vinyl glue, gold silk twist, pliers, and pins.

HOW TO DECORATE A LAMPSHADE

1 | Prepare a cord of about 33 inches with one gold and one silver beaded string.

2 | Twist the cord gently. Gold and silver beads are fragile, therefore try to protect your eyes from any accidents.

3 | Glue the cord to the lampshade using vinyl glue. For the bottom border of the shade, use a four-string cord, using two gold and two silver strings.

Below, detail of the miniature gold and silver roses and lilies that decorate the shade's upper border.

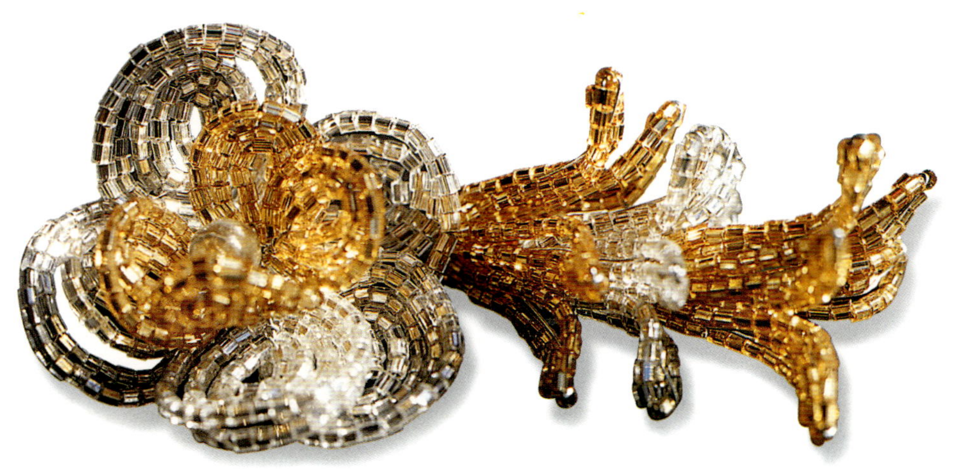

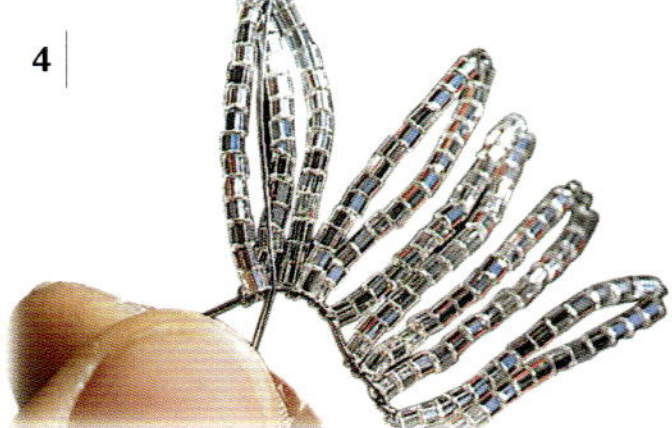

4

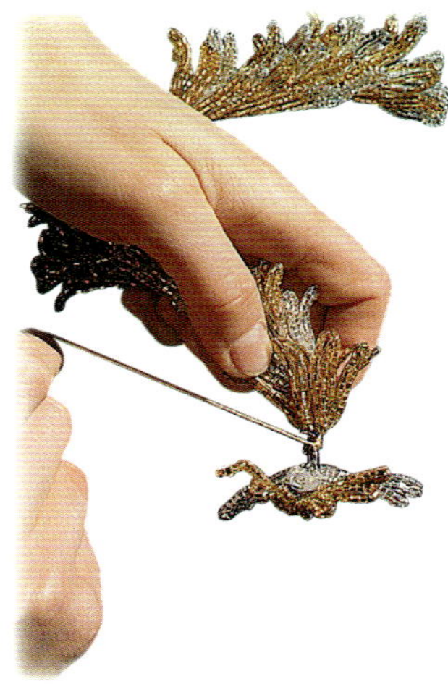

5

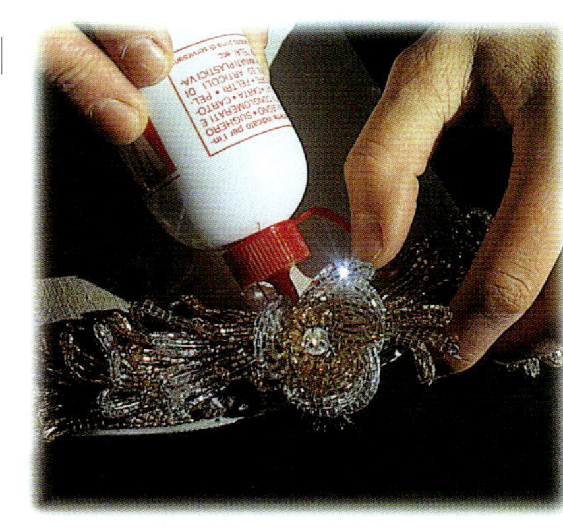

6

4 | To make a lily wreath you will need 22 gold lilies and 22 silver lilies. Make the petals with only three rounds of beads instead of four to lighten the arrangement.

5 | Using gold silk twist fasten the lilies to the wire, alternating a gold lily with a silver one. Make two wreaths, each one bearing 11 lilies. At the center of each wreath place a gold rose. The rose consists of two petal rings: and outer ring with five petals of 5 rounds of beads each, and a smaller, inner ring with four petals of 3 rounds of beads each. At the center of the rose place one crystal bead and some silver fluff.

6 | Use vinyl glue to fasten the wreath to the lampshade. Shape the lilies and the rose with the pliers, arching the petal points outward.

Opposite, another type of shade decoration, this one with white daisies.

A good time-saving method when making many identical elements (flowers and foliage of the same type), is to prepare long beaded strings. In this way, you do not have to repeat all the steps required for each flower or leaf.

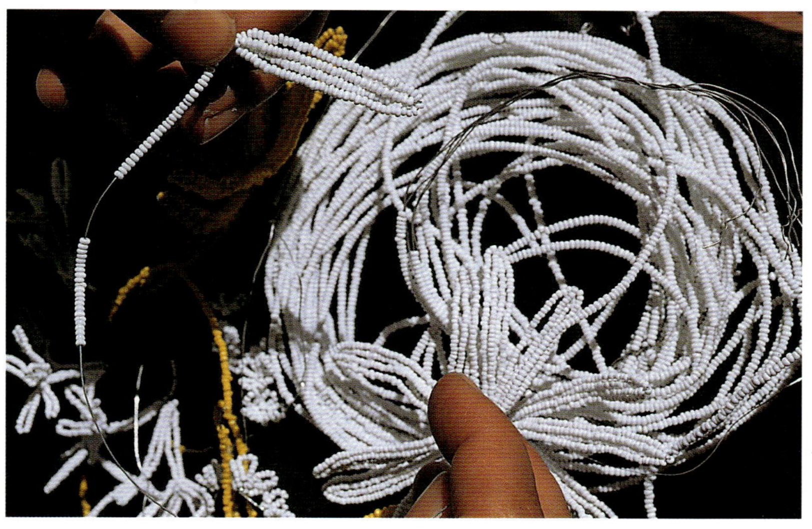

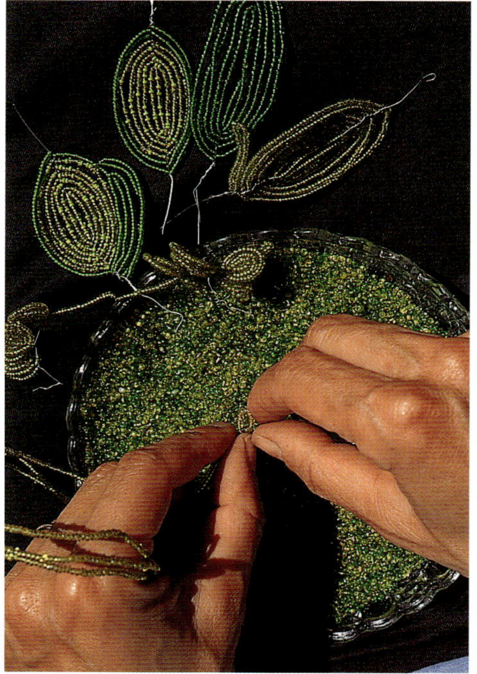

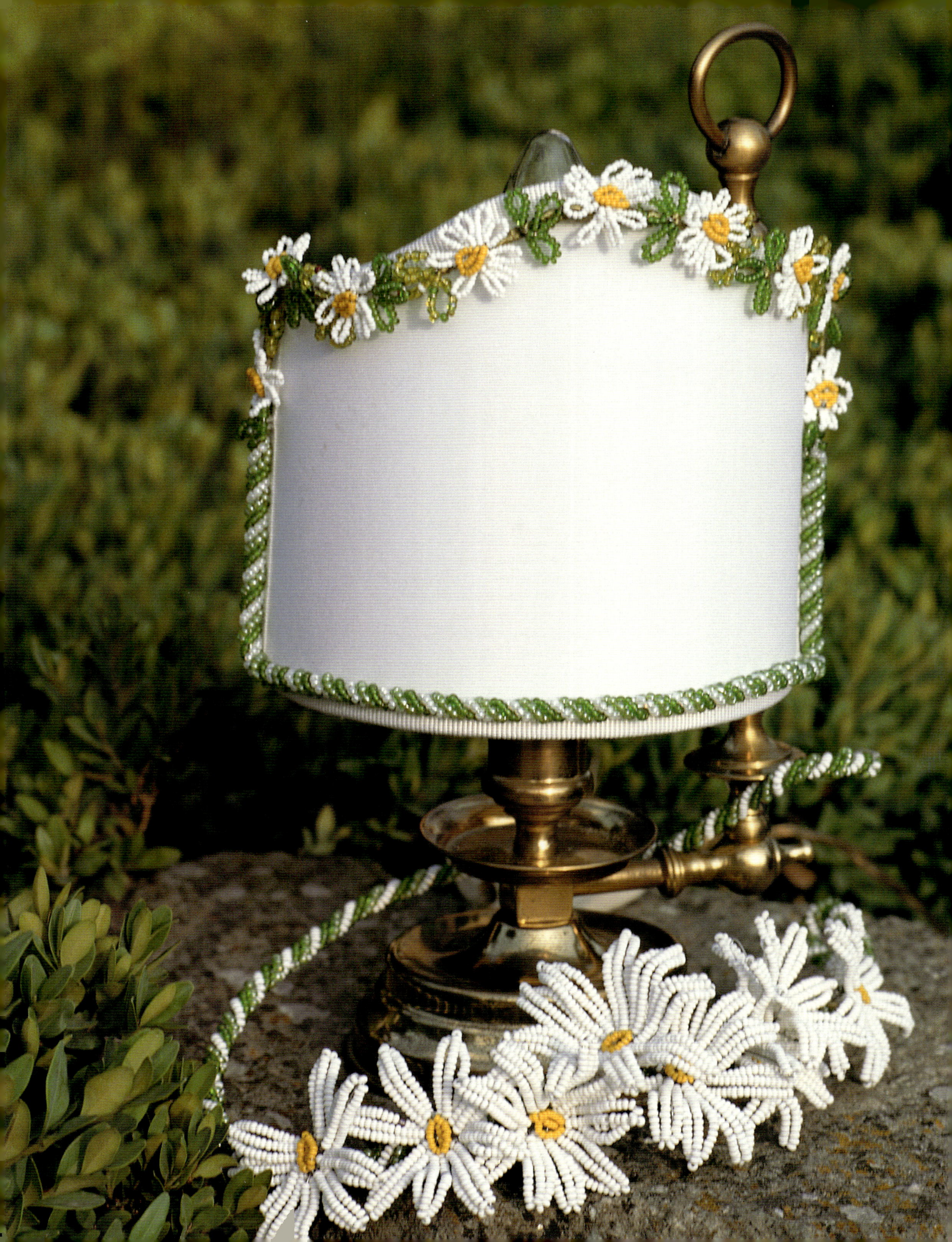

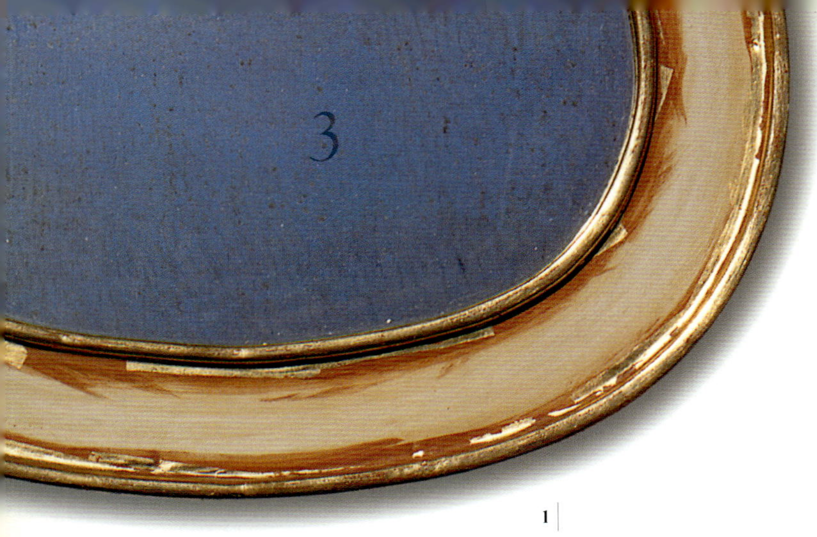

1

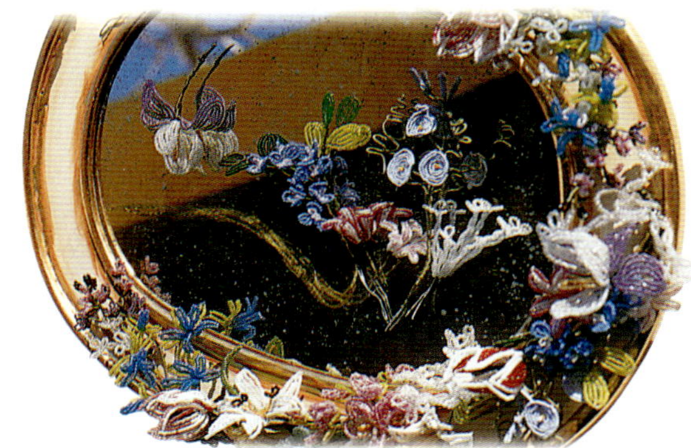

2

A Mirror Frame

The garland as a decorative motif lends itself to many different uses. In these pages, we show a garland framing a large antique mirror, creating suggestive reflections. This wreath can also be used to frame a painting or a portrait, or even as a precious center piece for a special occasion.

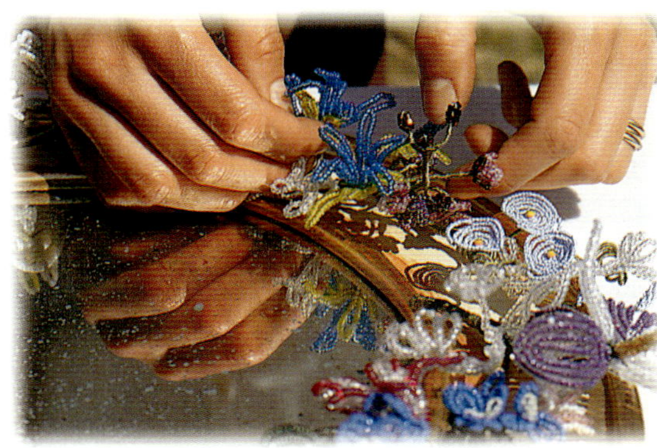

3

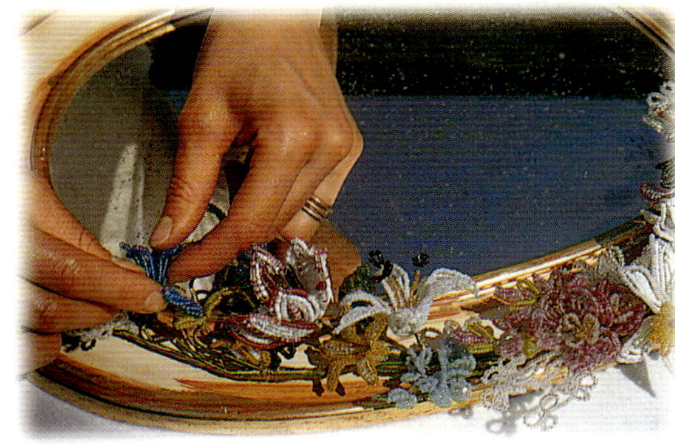

4

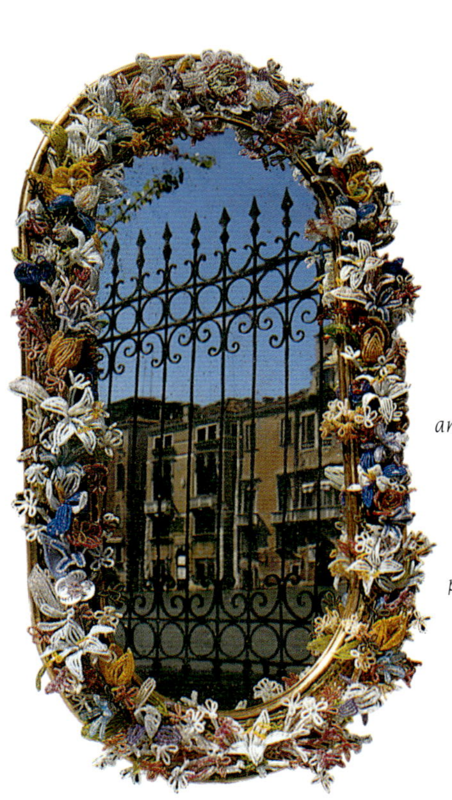

Materials | For each garland you will need:

•

an oval mirror with a gilded frame at least 2½ inches wide

•

many beaded flowers

•

pale green silk twist, vinyl glue, and pliers.

HOW TO MAKE A GARLAND TO FRAME A MIRROR

1 | For this project, it is best to use an antique mirror or, failing that, a mirror that has been "antiqued." Gild the inner and outer borders of the frame, leaving the center matte.

2 | Prepare the flowers, as many as you need to frame the mirror, and join them in two long, symmetrical garlands. You may add two large flowers at the bottom and top center of the frame.

3 | Try to arrange the flowers to achieve a light, airy effect. African lilies are ideal for this project, for they break up the uniform line of the more compact flowers.

4 | Fasten the two garlands to the frame with pliers and glue. This done, gently open the petals so that all the flowers are fully open.

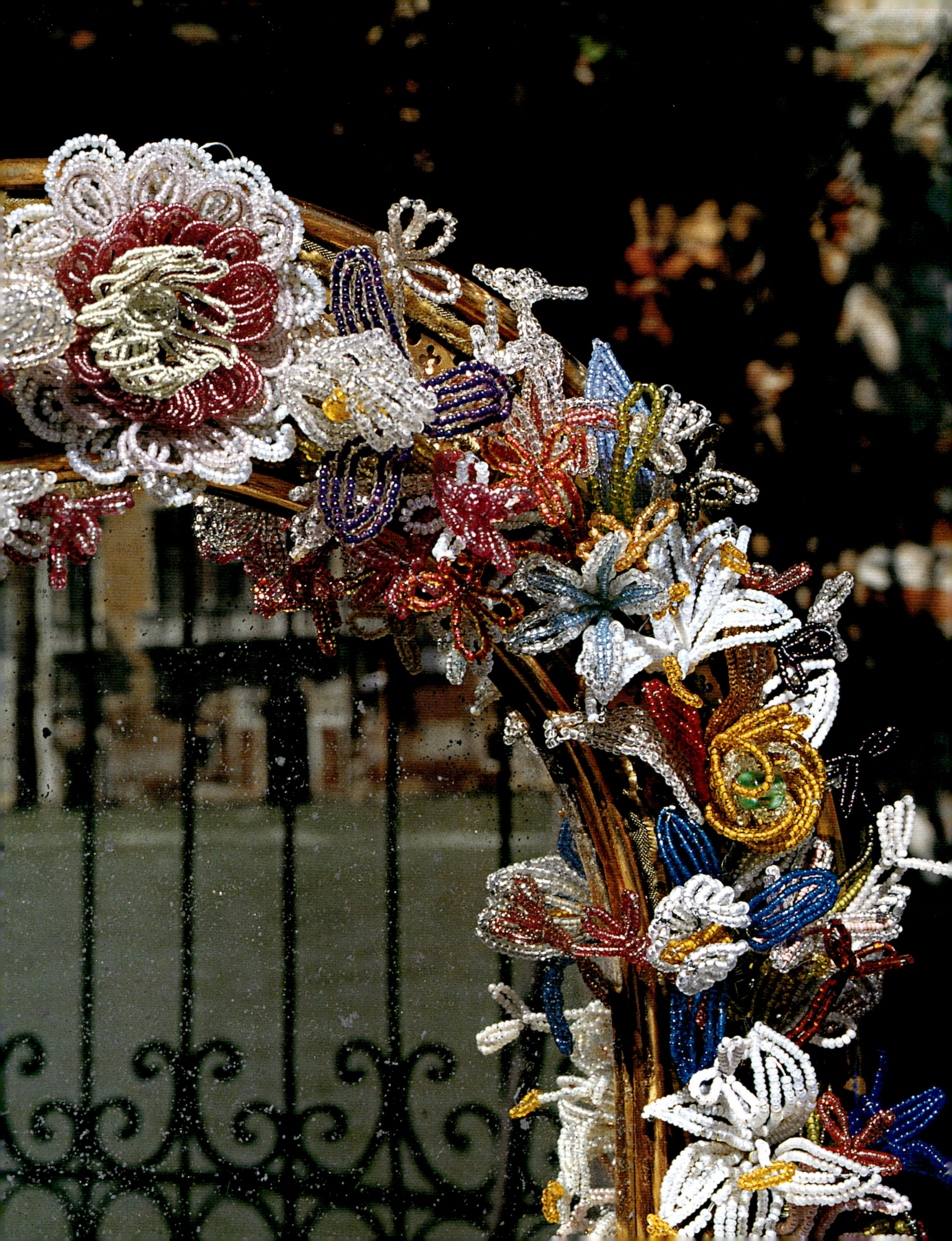

A Bridal Bouquet

The wedding bouquet is a cherished tradition, held dear by almost all the cultures of the world. Bouquets made with fresh flowers are lovely, but unfortunately have a very short life; other bouquets may be made with silk flowers or other materials. Here we show you how to create a bouquet of beaded flowers. As beautiful as the natural flowers, they resist time and can also be used by other couples, as a token and a promise of long-lasting happiness. Or they may be preserved as a memento of a very special and happy day.

1 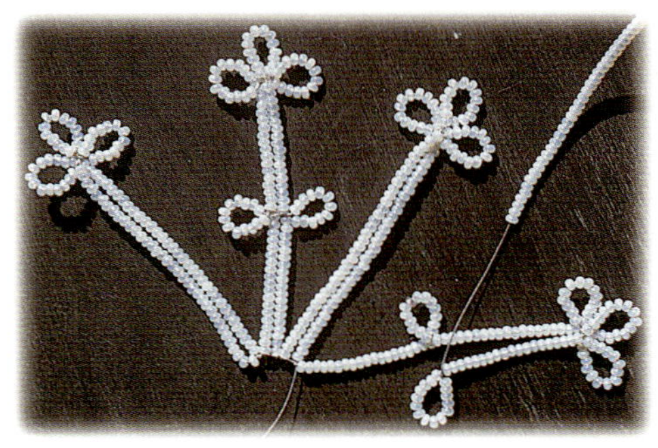

Materials | For each bridal bouquet you will need:

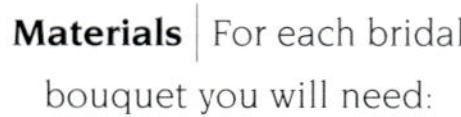

•

8 strings of white mother-of-pearl beads

•

2 strings of azure blue beads

•

2 strings of pink beads

•

1 string of green beads

•

8 20 gauge wires, 5 inches long

•

4 20 gauge wires, 3 inches long

•

pale green silk twist, vinyl glue, pliers.

Procedure | First we prepare the lace that holds the bouquet together, then the flowers, then we fasten the flowers to the lace and shape the handle.

HOW TO MAKE A BRIDAL BOUQUET

1 | Use a single strand of beads. Measure 2 inches of white mother-of-pearl beads and at that point shape a small, three-loop flower; now measure another 2 inches of beads parallel to the beaded string and return to the point of departure.

2 | Measure 1¼ inches of beads and at that point make one loop, then measure ¾ of an inch of beads; now make a three-loop flower, then repeat the same procedure (¾ inch of beads, then one loop, then 1½ inches of beads), back to the point of departure. The complete lace has 16 such pieces. Join all the pieces together with wire and you have the supporting lace.

3 | Follow the African lily technique to make four clusters, each one consisting of four 2-inch florets.

4 | Using silk yarn and a 3 inch long wire create peduncles for each cluster of florets.

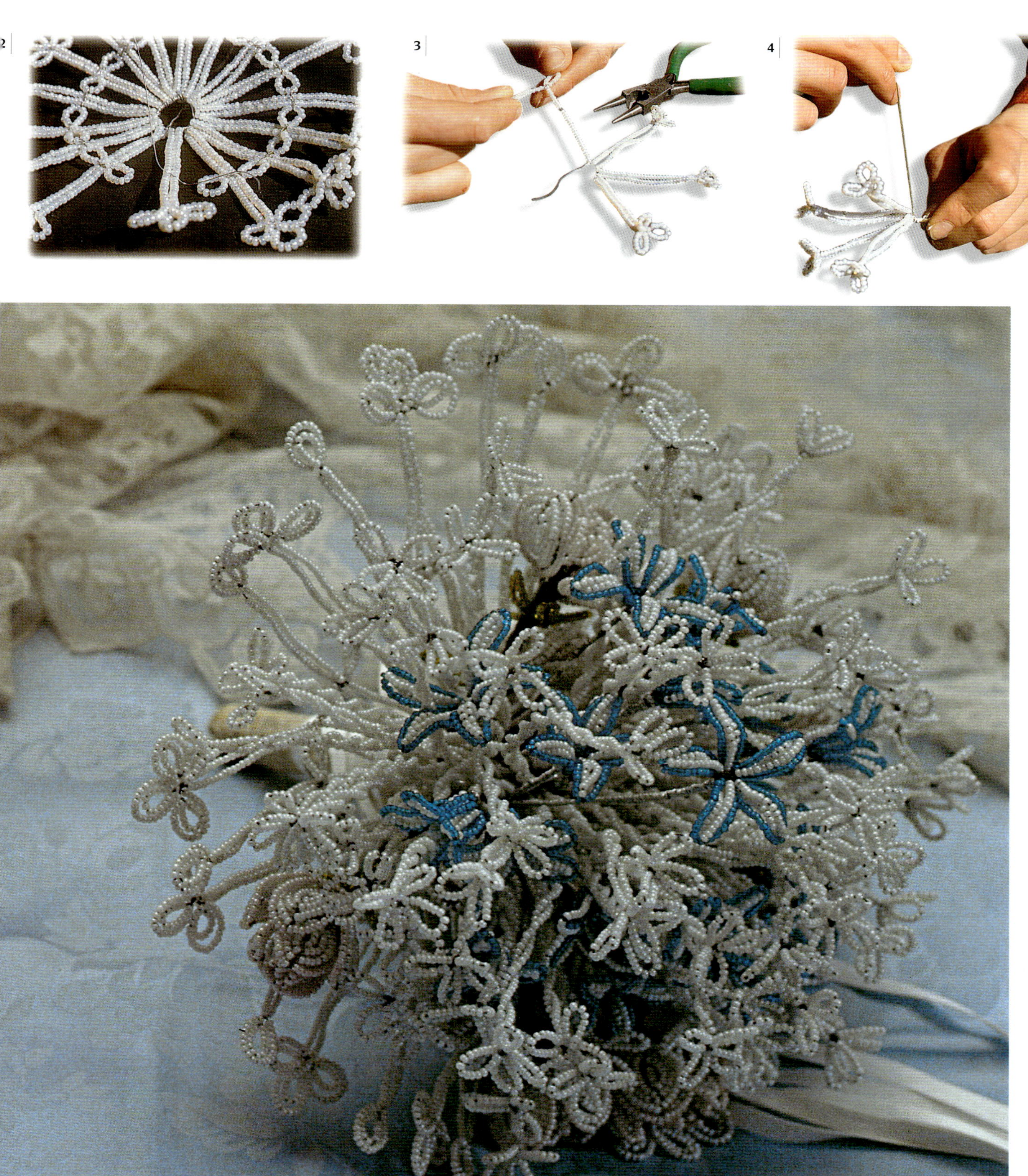
2
3
4

5

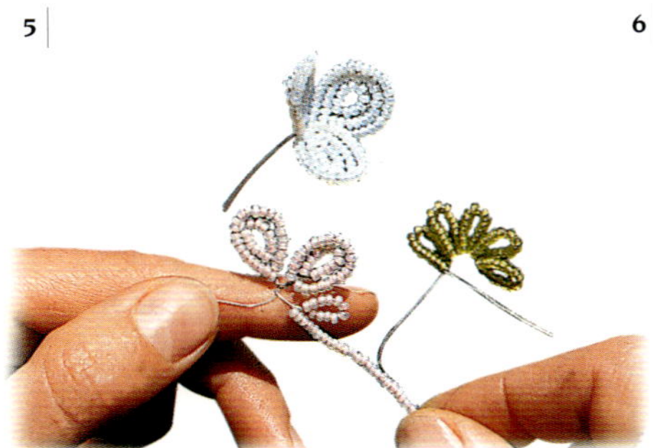

6

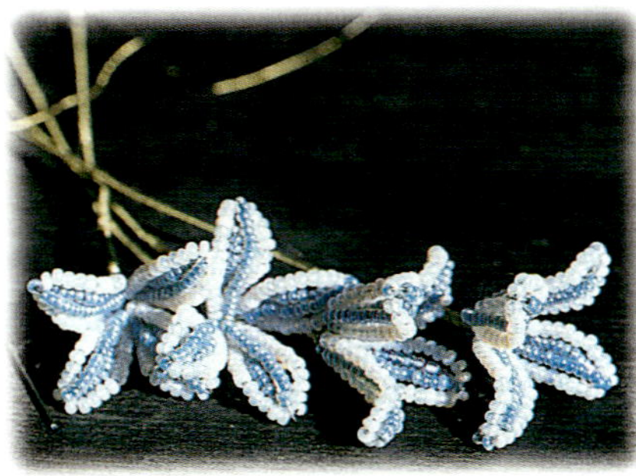

7

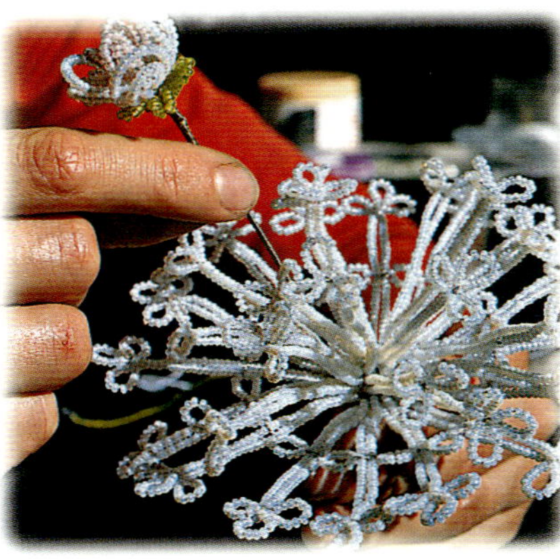

8

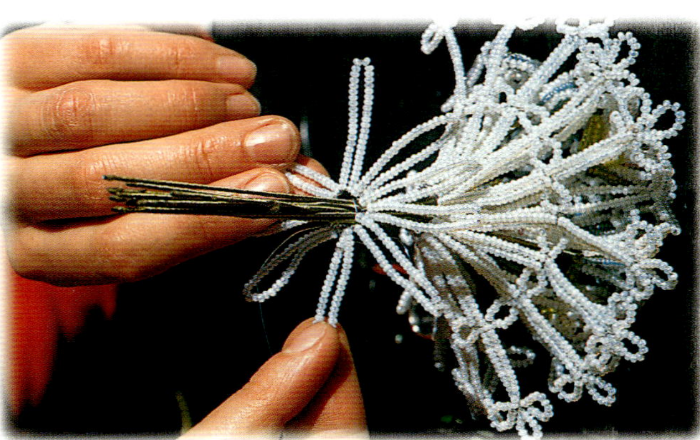

5 To create the bouquet shown in the photograph below, you need three small white and pink roses. Each rose has two rings of petals: the outer ring is white and consists of three petals of 3 rounds of beads each; the inner ring is pink and consists of two petals, each one with 2 rounds of beads.

6 The bouquet consists of five white and light blue lilies together with the roses and the African lily clusters. Lilies consist of four petals, each one ¾ of an inch long. The roses and the lilies are fastened with silk twist on a 5 inch stem wire.

7 To assemble the bouquet, first add the white clusters, then the roses, and finally the lilies.

8 Hide the stem of the bouquet by making six loops, each 1¼ inches long.

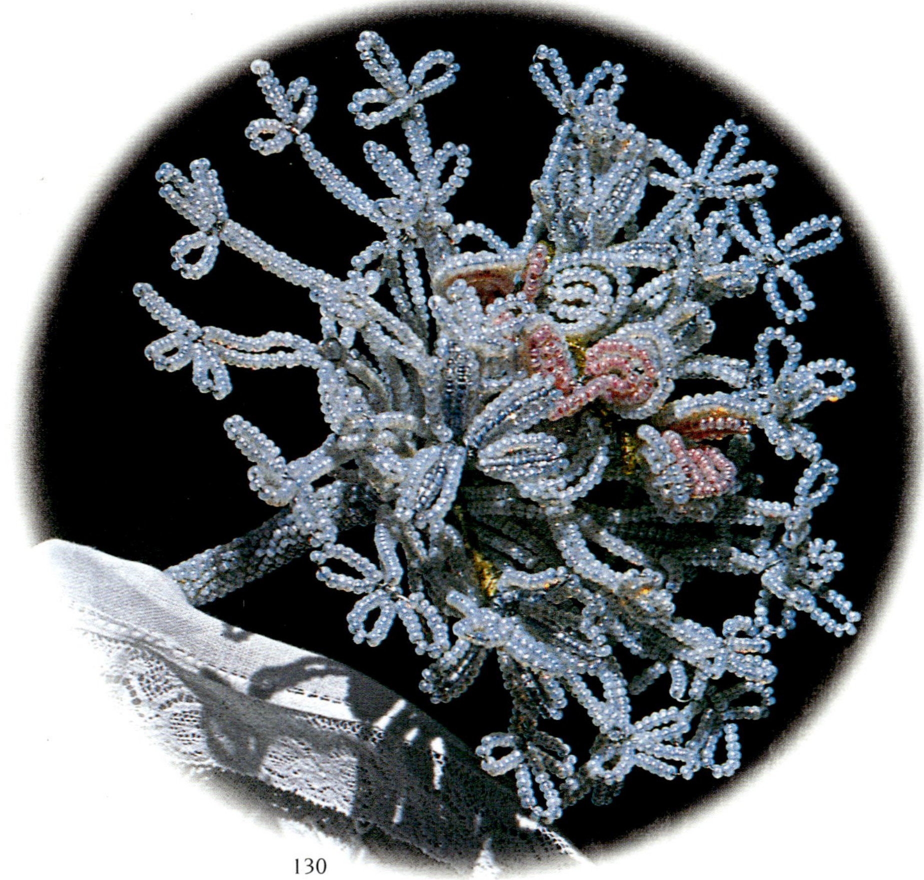

The bouquet's handle is covered with beads, making for a pleasant, easy touch. Opposite, African lily clusters used as graceful wedding favors.

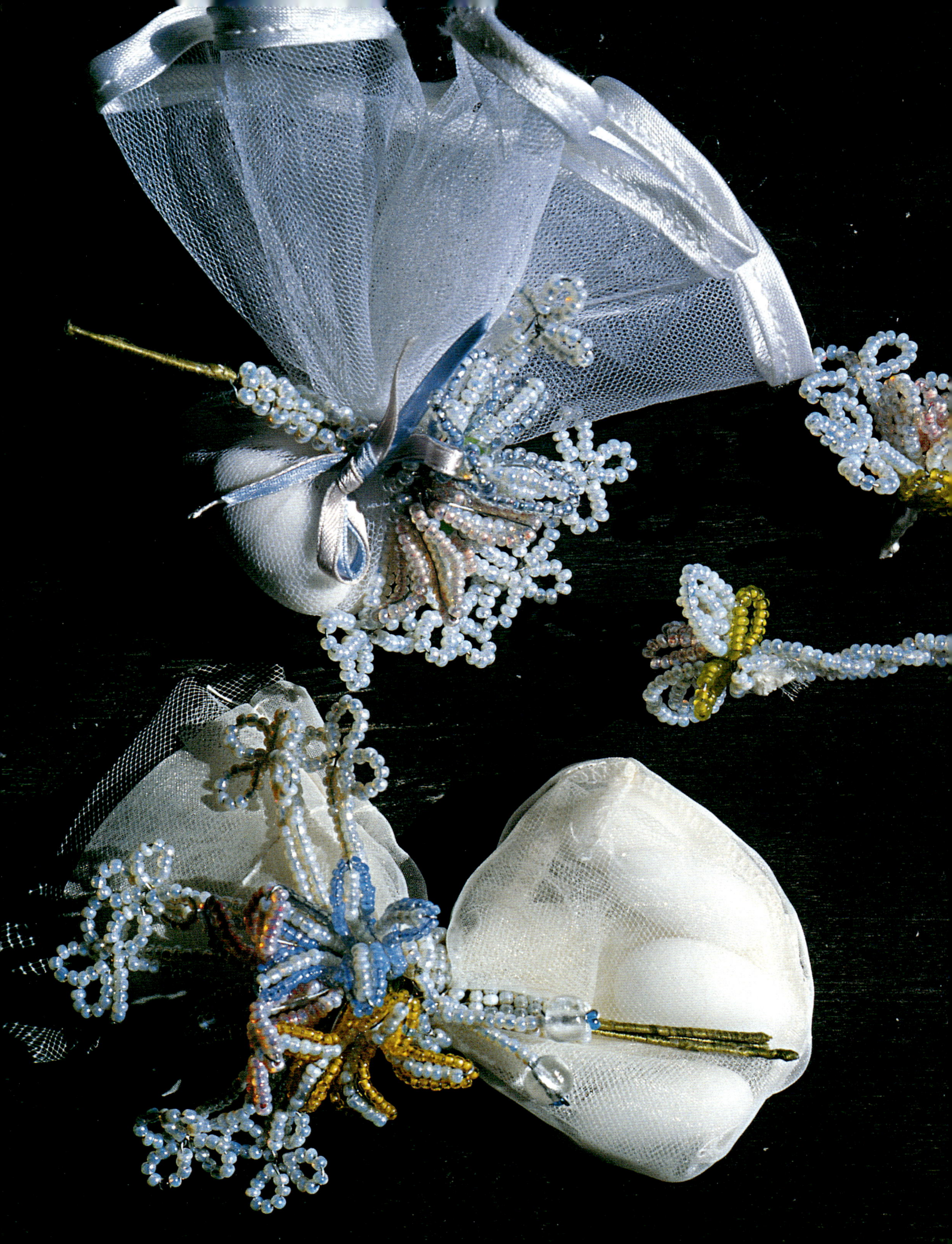

1 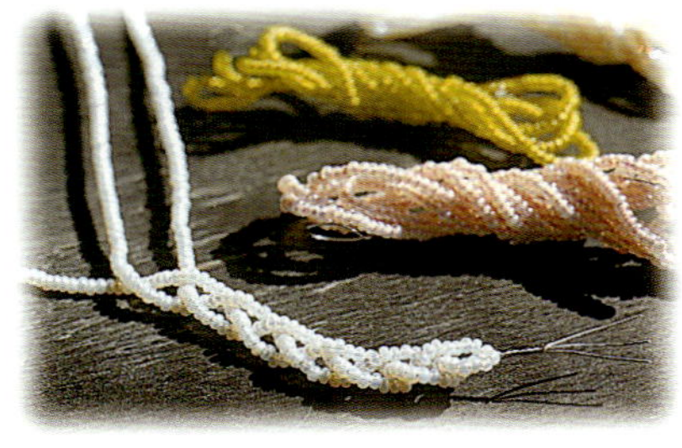

2 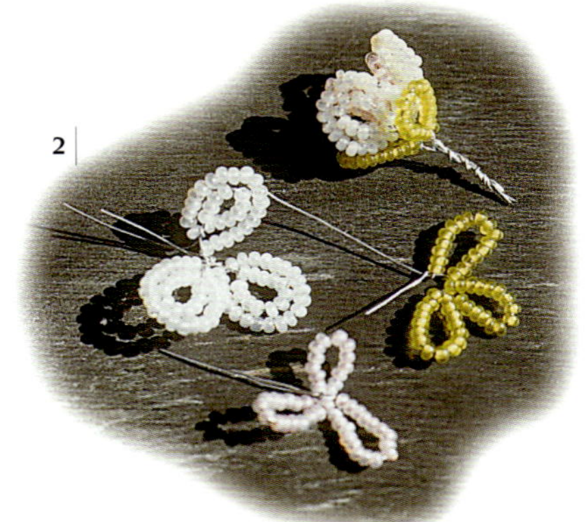

3 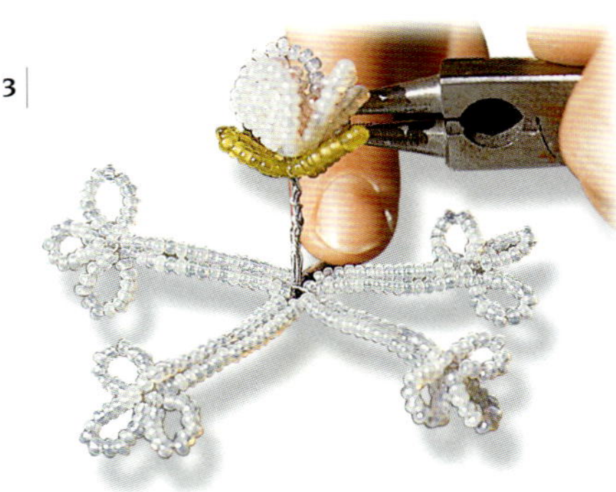

Flower Girl Wreath

Beads can also be used to make delightful wreaths for the flower girls who hold the bride's veil or carry the flowers or the pillow bearing the wedding bands. They can also be used to create original head pieces for the bride, using white roses, lilies, or African lilies to hold the veil, resting lightly on the hair. These wreaths should be light, soft, easy to wear; they may be all white or in pastel colors. They are usually complemented by satin ribbons.

4 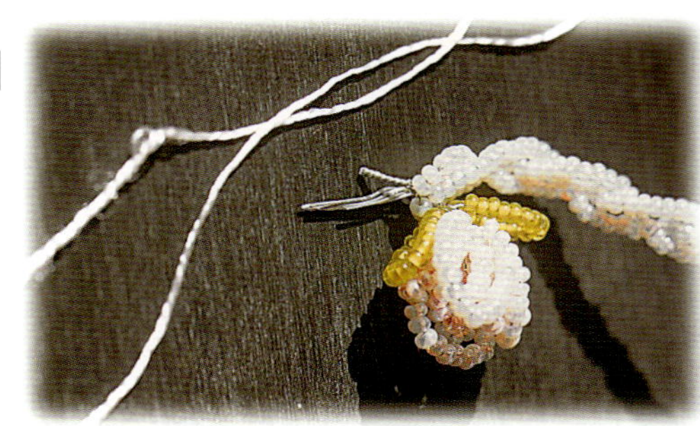

5 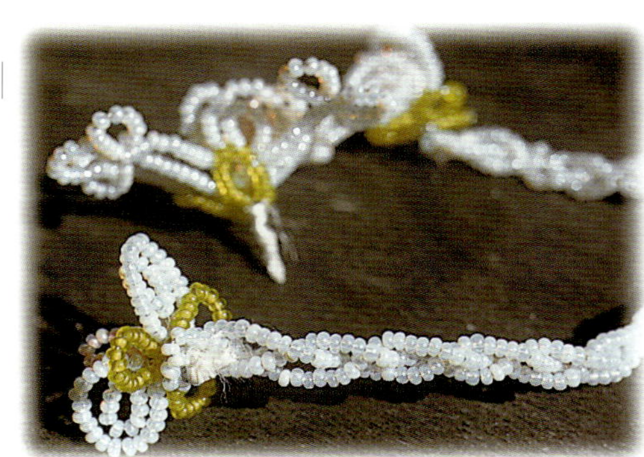

Materials | For each wreath you will need:

- *4 strings of white mother of pearl beads*
- *1 string of pink beads*
- *1 string of pale green beads*
- *1/5 inch wide satin ribbons*
- *pliers.*

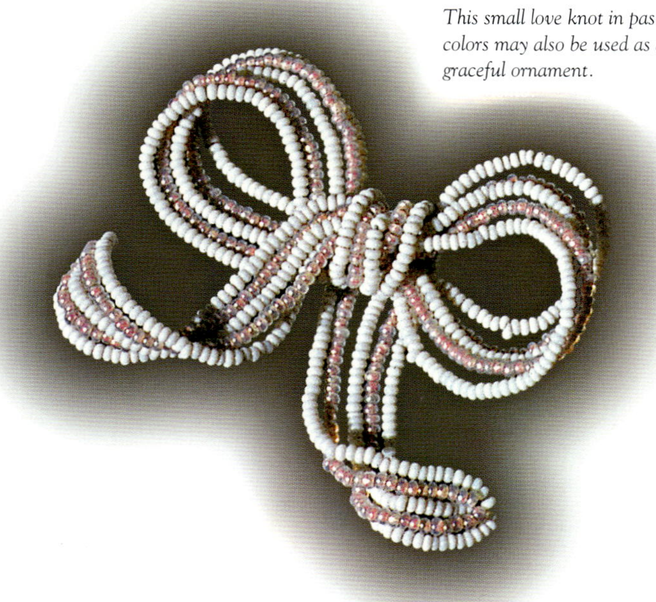

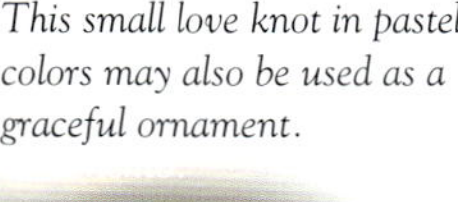

This small love knot in pastel colors may also be used as a graceful ornament.

HOW TO MAKE THE WREATH

1 | Using three strings of white beads make a braid 32 inches long.

2 | You will need five small pink and white roses. Each corolla has three white petals of 2 rounds of beads each and one pink pistil. Each rose has also a tiny green collar.

3 | Prepare three clusters of florets using the African lily technique. Each flower is ¾ of an inch long. In the center of each cluster insert a rose.

4 | The white braid is garnished with two roses at each end. Cover any wire that shows with white silk twist.

5 | Arrange the roses and the African lilies at the center of the wreath and the satin ribbons at the back.

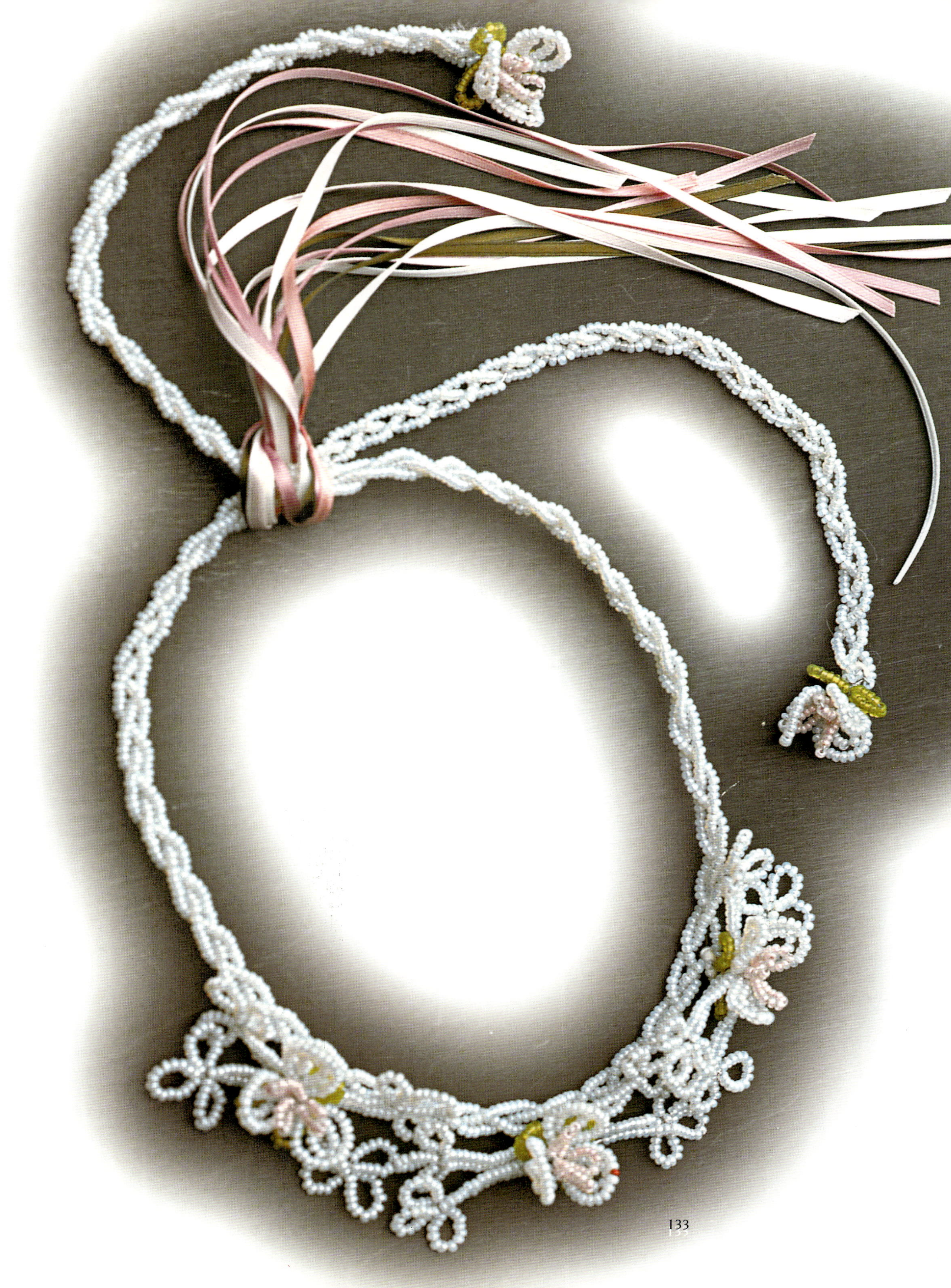

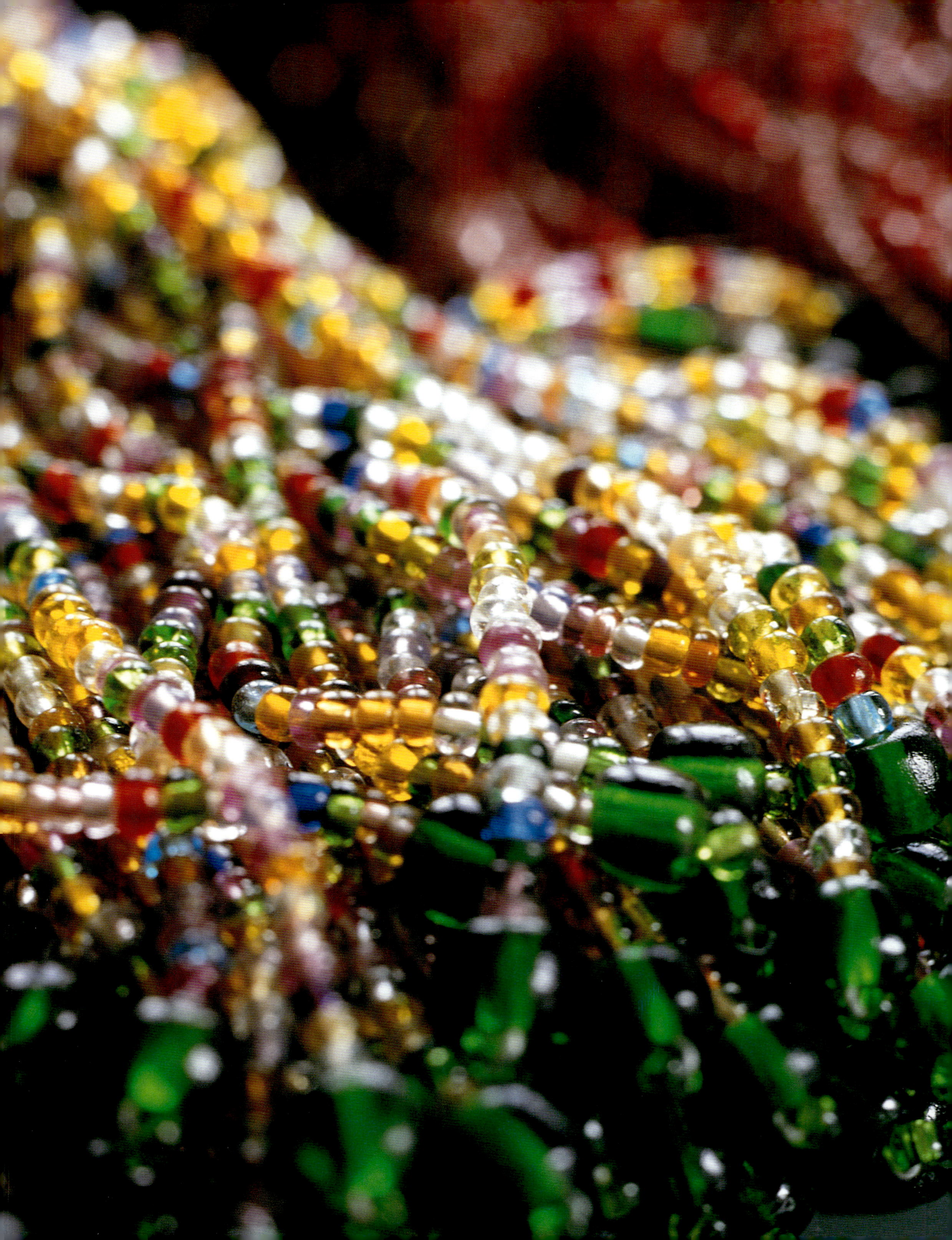

Multi-colored Tassels

Miles and miles of beaded fringes and tassels were produced from the second half of the nineteenth century to the beginning of the twentieth. They were used to embellish the interior of homes as well as for garments, and they came in many styles: in a single color or pattern, with flower transparencies, in geometric or animal patterns, opaque or shiny, very short for trimming small borders or very long to make long beaded curtains. Beaded tassels in all their variety are a typical Venetian story, and over the years special techniques were devised to simplify production.

When glass beads are threaded on a cotton string the effect is totally different than when they are strung on a metal wire: it's as if your hand was shifting sea sand. The beads slip away on every side, they come alive in your palm and make tiny noises. Strung on short cotton strings tied together in a soft tassel, they produce a different effect again, because to the pleasure of the touch is added the pleasure of sight, as the light plays magical effects on them as in a kaleidoscope. To make tassels, we string the beads on sorts of combs each composed of 20 to 30 needles, 8 inches long, connected to cotton strings. We immerse the comb in a container full of beads, feeding the needles so that the beads slide down on the cotton strings, which are then replaced by new strings. The beaded strings are then finished on a loom that weaves the tassel's edge, sealing it. In this way, each cotton string is secured together with the others and will not come apart.

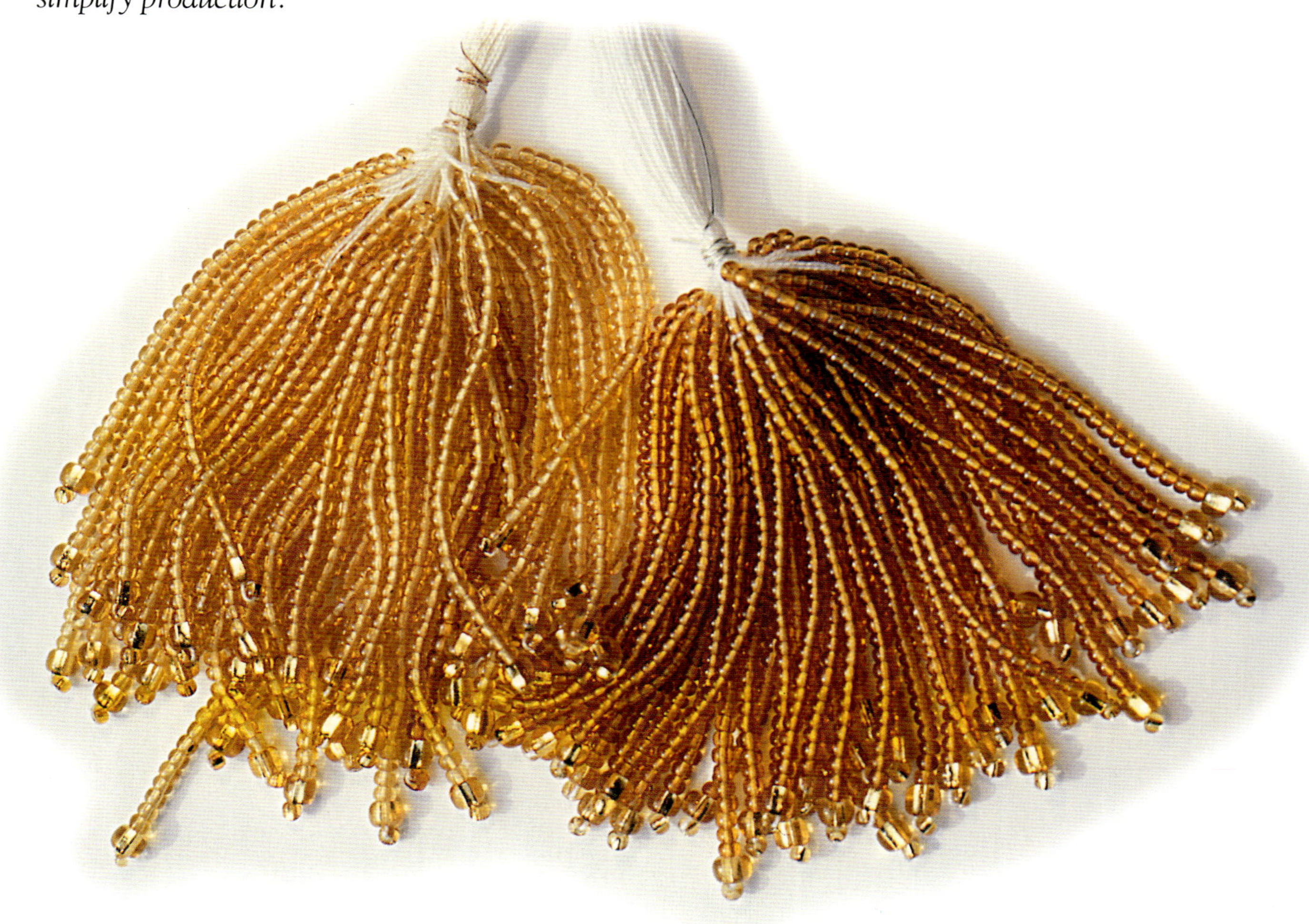

1

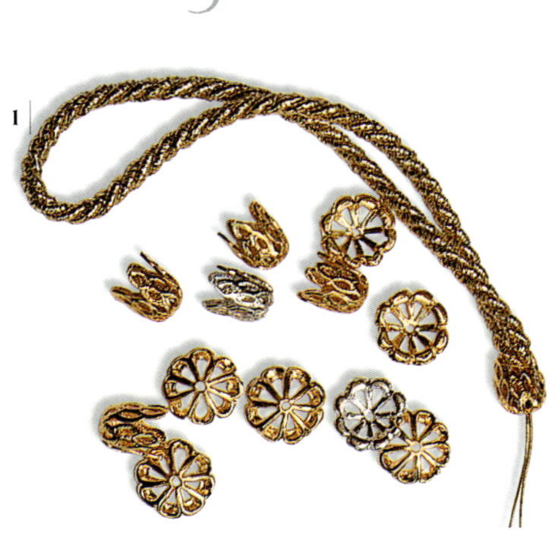

2

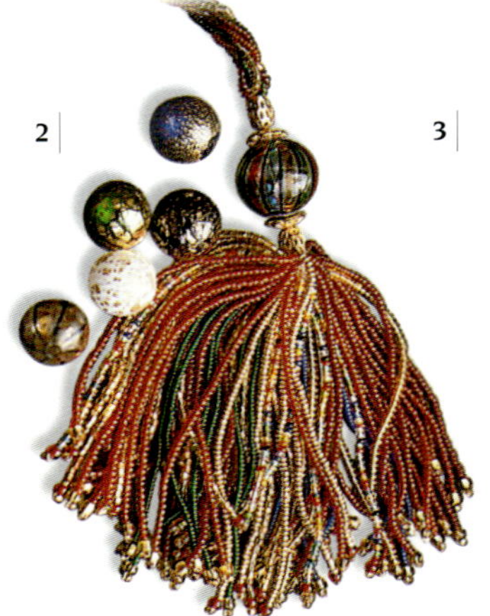

3

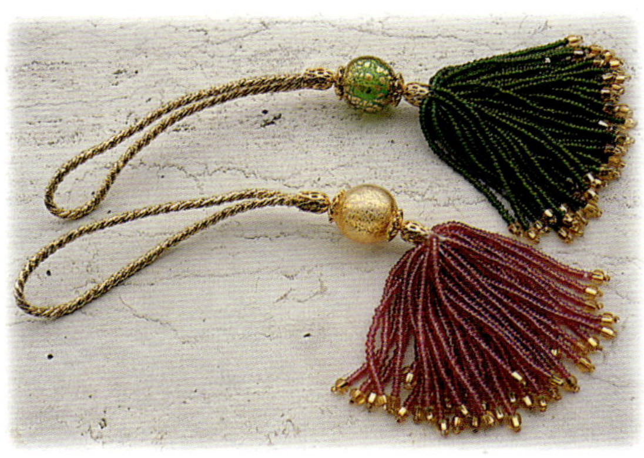

HOW TO MAKE A TASSEL

1 | For a tassel you need a thick silver cord and metal studs to cover the knots at the base of the strings.

2 | Tassels are more elegant and reflect more light if you add a large, transparent, decorated bead between the cord and the fringe.

3 | The finished tassel may be used for curtain pullbacks, or for the key of your most precious jewelry box.

Opposite, a suggestive image of brightly colored tassels made with large, precious transparent beads and tiny conterie *(seed) beads.*

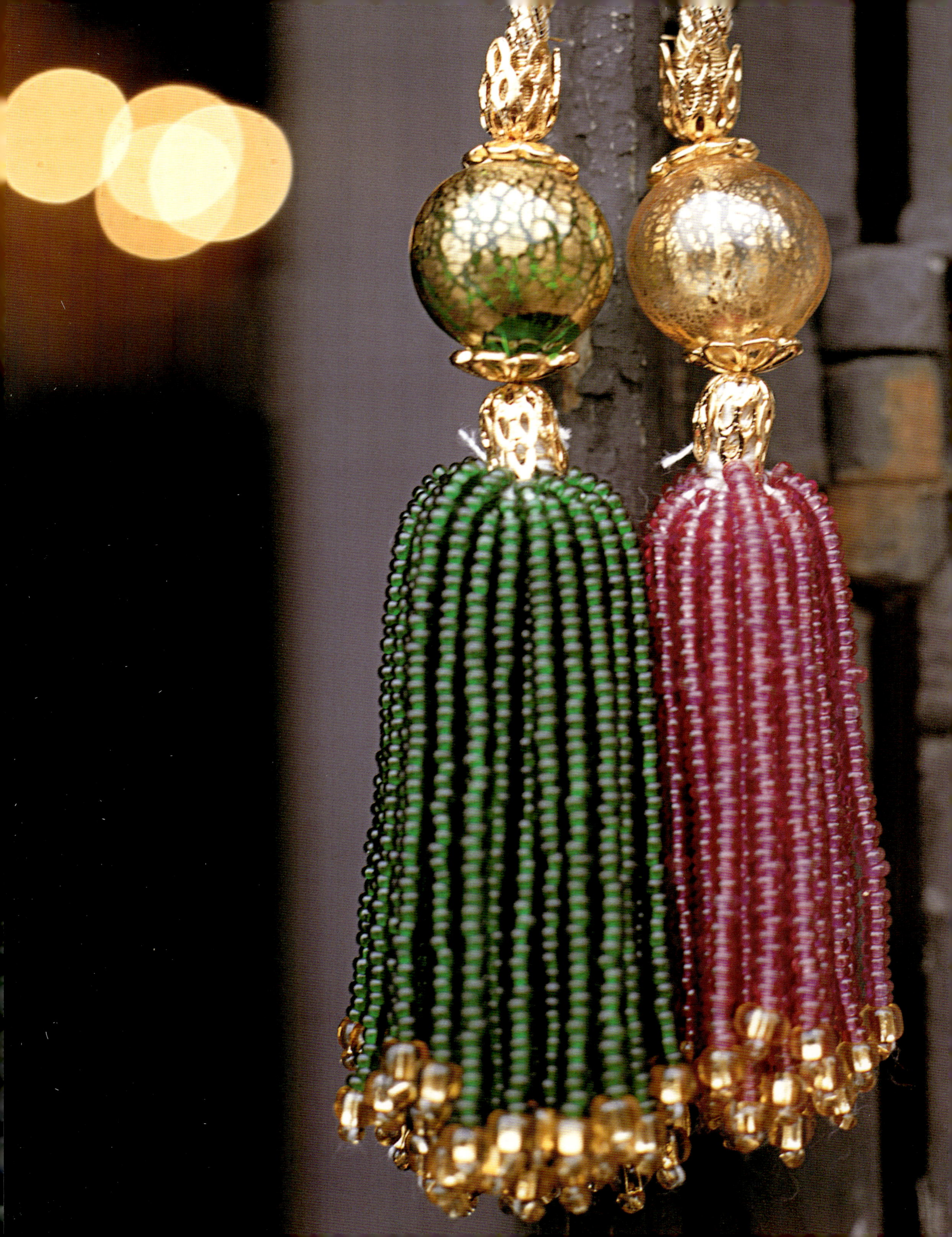

Carnival Masks

Masks can be made with beads also. In these pages we show you several types of masks of different colors and shapes, all unique Venetian designs.

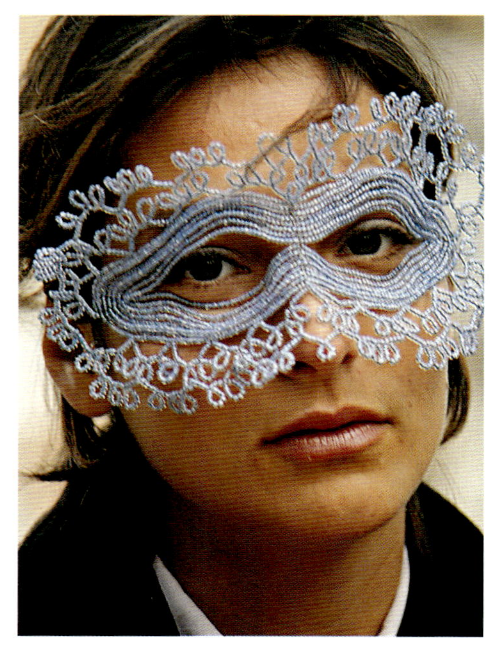

In recent years, the Carnival of Venice has been enjoying renewed popularity and international success, enlivening the city's narrow *calle* and *campielli*. There is great fun in the small neighborhood squares full of strolling masked revelers, in the crowded theaters, in the parties that bring ancient palaces back to life. The shops selling masks and costumes are full of customers and window shoppers from the four corners of the world. In past centuries, masks were worn on an almost daily basis: they served to guarantee anonymity to aristocrats, society ladies, spies, even charlatans. It was an efficient system used by anyone seeking protection from gossip and indiscreet eyes. The custom became so widespread that between 1339 and 1776—in an effort to protect the name and reputation of Venetian high society—the High Council, which was the legislative body of the Most Serene Republic of Venice, passed strict laws regulating the days and times when mask dressing was allowed and the proper manner of disguise. The frequency of these ever-changing decrees are evidence that Venetians disobeyed their government's restrictions often and with gusto.

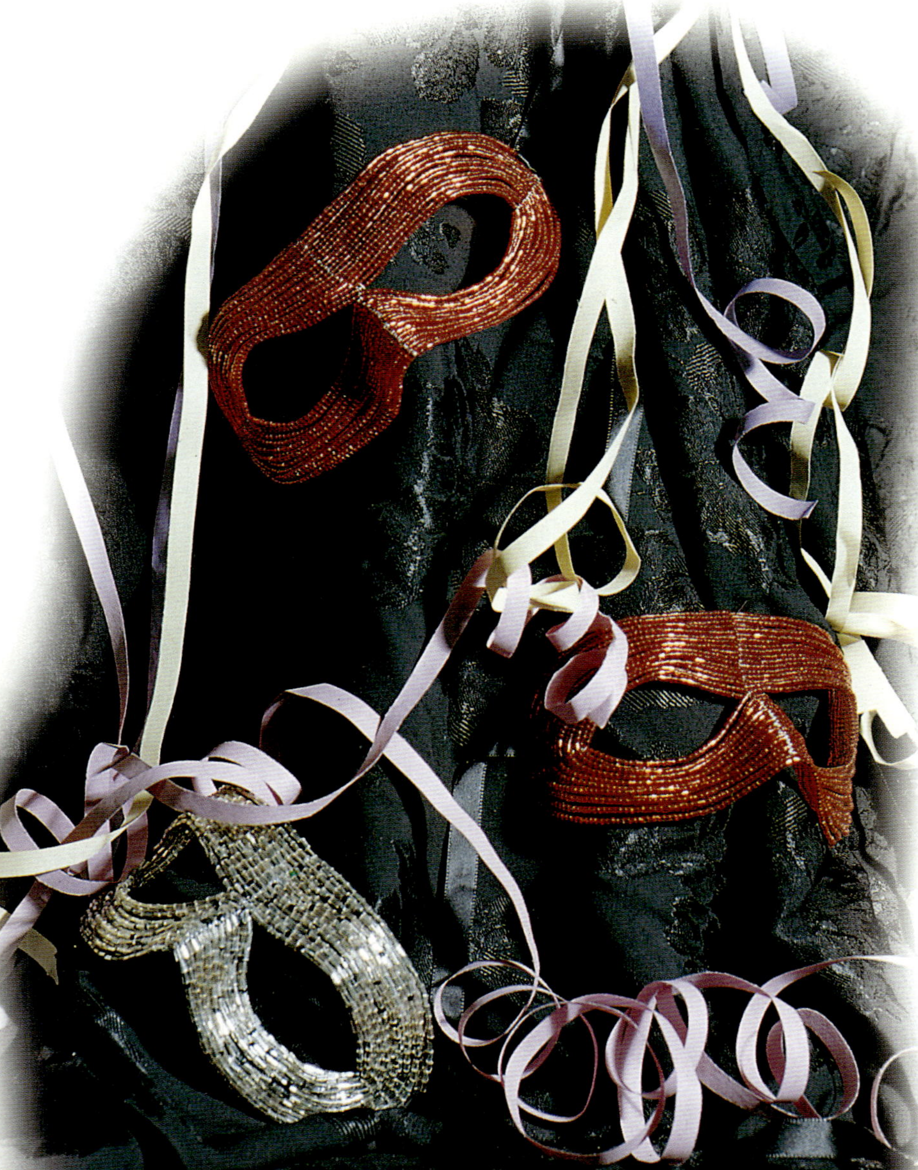

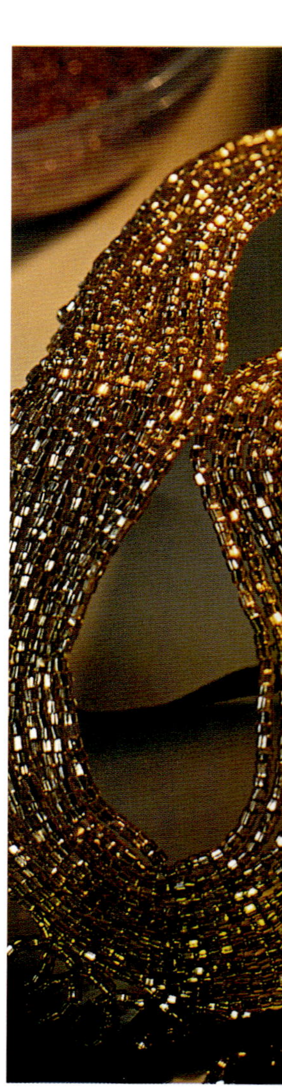

What follows is a brief description of the most popular traditional masks.

The *Mattaccino* was a clown costume; anyone wearing it was permitted to throw eggs full of rose water (or other liquids) to the ladies strolling in the streets. The *Mattaccino* moved about town with a retinue of egg sellers who assisted him and wore similar masks.

The *Bauta* was a noble, or "national" mask; it consisted of a short black cape that covered the shoulders and a white, almost ghost-like mask, called "larva" (zombie) or "volto" (face).

The *Moretta* was an oval black velvet mask that covered almost the entire face; it was worn by ladies and was held in place by a small button held between the lips.

The *Gnaga* was a costume worn by homosexuals and by men who liked to cross-dress.

However, the masks that gave Venice international recognition are those of the Commedia dell'Arte.

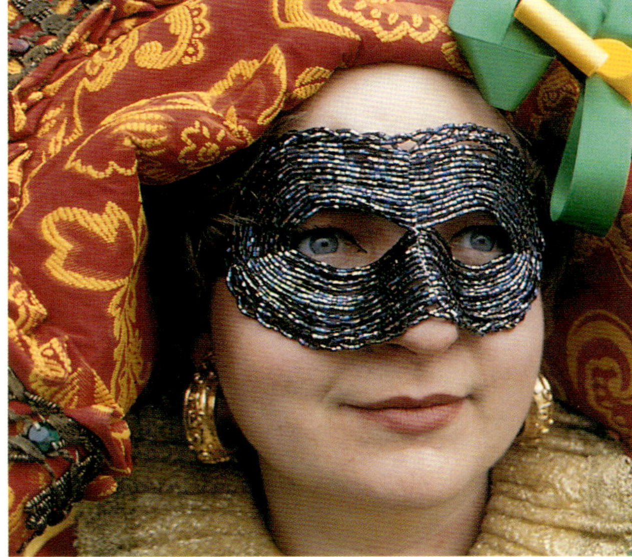

The two masks the models are wearing are original creations of Nella Sammartini Lopez y Royo and the author. Their design is adapted from traditional Venetian carnival masks.

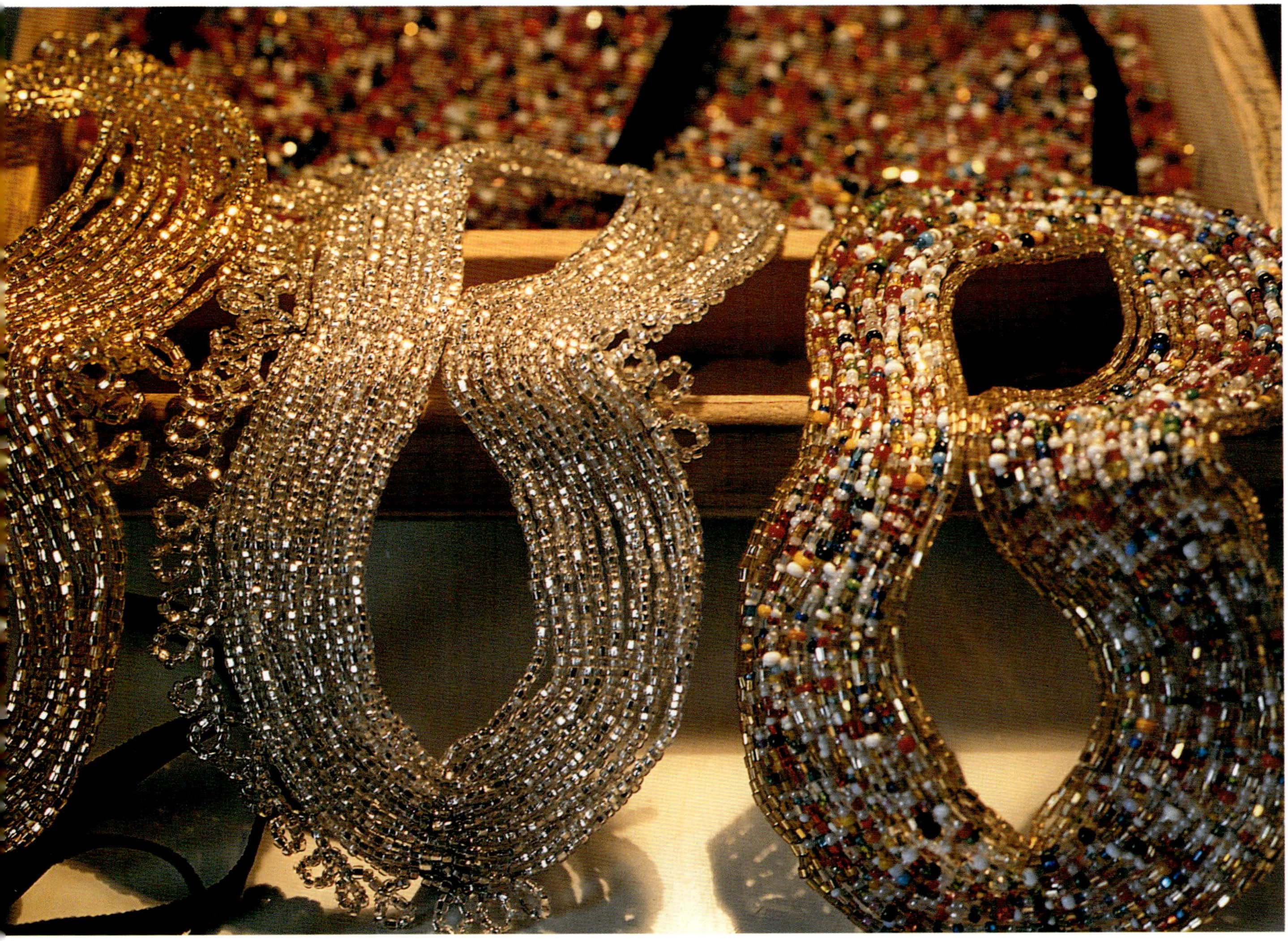

Glossary

Avventurina

Also called "goldstone." A clear or pale colored glass, with gold glints obtained by throwing into the molten glass microscopic metal flecks or chips, usually made of copper.

Cane

A thin glass tube obtained by stretching a mass of molten glass. Different colors can be incorporated into a cane.

Faïence

A direct ancestor of glass, faïence is a type of ceramic with a core of quartz lined with glass. It is made with partially fused quartz sand to which coloring minerals have been added. It was probably invented as a low cost replacement for precious materials such as lapislazuli and turquoise. Faïence was produced especially in Egypt and Asia minor.

Furnace

A heat producing structure in which glass is produced or fused at the desired temperature. Sometimes the furnace has an inner chamber used for tempering glass. The chamber is also used to glaze or to heat finished objects that are waiting to be decorated.

Bead stringer

Stringing glass beads was traditionally done by women and children on the islands and in the working-class districts of Venice. Until a few decades ago, the beads were strung on silk or cotton cords for display in shops, thus guaranteeing the customers that the beads were all perforated. The traditional Venetian term is impiraressa *from* impirar, *to string.*

Flame technique

A technique for heating glass in specific spots with the flame from a specially designed torch.

Margarede

This ancient term, from which the woman's name Margherita *is derived, is common to all ancient* Mediterranean *cultures. It referred to* conteria *glass beads. The etymology of the word is "born from the sea" and initially referred to deep-sea pearls. With the discovery of glass and its use to make beads, the term was also applied to the Venetian beads. The* margaritaio *is the artisan who makes them.*

Millefiori

This term, "a thousand flowers," refers to a technique of blowing glass objects incorporating them into thin cane sections, creating multi-colored effects with floral or other patterns.

Mosaic

In this technique, glass objects are created by fusing together small tiles (tesserae) or glass cane sections.

Paternostri

This term, from paternostro *which literally means "Our Father," refers to beads made by cutting glass pipes of at least ⅜ of an inch diameter, which are then smoothed and rounded by hand in kilns. They are used to make rosary beads, thus the term* paternostri. *In the Middle Ages, when strict Catholic custom allowed only the rosary as decoration, these beads were very popular because they were inexpensive imitations of semiprecious stones.*

Wound-glass beads

A very rare type of bead, they are no longer produced and only a few samples survive. They were made with the lume *(lamp) technique. The bead maker softened a thin glass cane until it was as thin as hair, and wove a small hollow bubble by rapidly rotating the cane, all the while heating it with flame from a specially made lamp. These beads were popular in the nineteenth century as hair ornaments. A contemporary American artist, Tootsie Zinsky, is currently using the same technique to create wonderful glass containers.*

Venetian beads

A generic term that denotes all glass beads made in Venice. They fall into two major classes: beads that are worked individually, hand shaped and decorated, usually large (at least ⅜ of an inch in diameter), and smaller beads that are produced in uniform batches. Lampwork beads, rosetta beads, paternostri, *and wound glass beads are hand made.*

The so-called conteria *beads, produced mechanically by cutting long, hollow glass pipes, belong to the second class.*

Eye beads

Beads made with any type of material, decorated with circular or point patterns, are called eye beads. The patterns can be fairly simple or as complex as those of granule beads, mosaic beads, and beads made with natural or processed stone.

Rosetta beads

Any type of bead made from a stretched glass cane bearing inside patterns created with successive processes. In particular, star beads *are* rosettas *with a cross-section star design,* chevron beads *are* rosettas *with cut or beveled edges.*

Pontello

A thin metal rod (the "mandrel") used in glass heat processing, that allows the glass maker to shape the molten glass mass (called "gather") into an object.

Bibliography

Italian publications

Morazzoni, G. and M. Pasquato, Le conterie veneziane *(Venetian* conteria *beads), Venice 1953.*

Zecchin, L. Sulla storia delle conterie veneziane *(On the history of Venetian* conteria *beads), Venice 1955.*

Sherr Dubin, L. La storia delle perline *(A history of beads), Milan 1988.*

Davanzo Poli, D. Le conterie nella moda e nell'arredo. Perle e impiraperle *(*Conteria *beads in fashion and interior decoration. Beads and bead stringers). Exhibition catalogue, Venice 1990.*

Marascutto-Stainer, P. Perle veneziane *(Venetian beads), Verona 1991.*

Lopez y Royo Sammartini, N. Fiori di Perle a Venezia *(Beaded flowers of Venice), Venice 1992.*

Wolters, N. Les perles au fil de textile *(Beads and textiles), Paris 1996.*

Other Publications

Beads & Button
P.O. Box 1612, Waukesha, WI 53187
Customer Service: 1-800 533-6644
www.beadandbutton.com *(bi-monthly)*

Beadwork
201 E. Fourth St., Loveland, CO 80537-5655
Subscription Inquiries: 1-800 340-7496
www.interweave.com

Jewelry Crafts
Subscription Inquiries: 1-800 528-1024
Email: JCM@printmail.com
www.JewelryCrafts.com

Lapidary Journal
60 Chestnut Ave., Suite 201, Devon, PA 19333-1312 (monthly)
Customer Service: 1-800 676- 4336
www.lapidaryjournal.com

Ornament
P.O. Box 2349, San Marcos, CA 92079-2349
Subscription Inquiries: 1-800 888-8950

Useful Addresses

Shops selling conteria *beads at retail in Venice and Murano are not easy to find; shops selling hand-made, lampwork or blown-glass pearls are more numerous. It is still possible to find both antique and contemporary beads that are authentic works of art, both for their workmanship and the quality of the glass. Contemporary imported beads are also available, easily recognizable because of the different production techniques and lower prices. Some antique shops have collections of pearls, beads and beaded objects—a kaleidoscope of shapes and colors that provide a glimpse into the history of Venetian women's labor.*

Conteria Beads

Costantini Cleto - *Via Cimitero 6, Murano (Province of Venice). Tel. (041) 736143.*

Mrs. Gianna offers a wide selection of glass beads and is the only store in Venice and Murano that sells exquisitely made fringes.

Costantini Dario - *Calle Zaguri, 26-27, Venice (near Campo San Maurizio). Tel. (041) 5210789.*
In this shop you can find conteria *and other beads, both old and new.*

Perle Veneziane - *Ponte della Canonica, Castello 4308, Venice (near Piazzetta dei Leoni, next to Saint Mark's Basilica). Tel. (041) 5289059.*

A shop specializing in conteria *and other types of beads; it also sells wonderful antique and modern necklaces.*

La perla veneziana - *Marco Polo Airport, Venice. Tel. (041) 5830128.*

This shop sells old and new beads, necklaces and costume jewelry items.

Antique Shops

Anticlea - *Sestiere Castello 4719, San Provolo, Venice. Tel. (041) 5286946.*
For over twenty years, this shop has been collecting and offering for a sale a large selection of Venetian glass beads and beaded objects such as necklaces, purses, and antique and new costume jewelry for a demanding and sophisticated clientele.

Antiquariato Fabris - *2606 Campo San Maurizio, Venice. Tel. (041) 5237074.*

Mrs. Giuliana has a collection of leaves, flowers, miniature boats, paintings, purses, and countless other objects manufactured with Murano conteria. *Antique Venetian beads are also on sale: they are wonderful mounted on custom-made necklaces.*

Antiquariato Trois - *Campo San Maurizio, 2666, San Marco, Venice. Tel. (041) 5222905.*

This shop is the exclusive retailer of exquisite Fortuny fabrics and flowers manufactured by Nella Sammartini Lopez y Royo and Giovanna Poggi Marchesi.

The antique dealer Rampazzo, in Saint Mark's Square, and Mrs. Zaggia's shop in Toletta are other shops that stock beaded flowers of their own production and lampwork pearls.

Museums and Associations

The Bead Museum
5754 West Glenn Drive, Glendale, AZ 85301
Phone: (623) 930-7395
www.TheBeadMuseum.com

Associazione Settemari - *4701 Cannaregio, Venice. Tel. (041) 5206708.*
An association of energetic ladies devoted to Venetian arts and crafts. The group organizes courses on Burano lace and on beaded flower making. Ms. Annabella Bortoluzzi coordinates and leads the group's activities.

Museo Vetrario, Murano
This museum dedicated to glass has currently only a few, though splendid, examples of beads and beadwork. An extension of this collection is being planned.

Museo Archeologico, Quarto d'Altino
On display in this museum is glass jewelry from the Roman era found in the Venetian Lagoon.

Other European Associations
The Hungarian Bead Society, *c/o Anna Feher, Harmat U. 65/b 3, 1104 Budapest, Hungary.*

The Bead Society of Great Britain,
c/o Carole Morris, 1 Casburn Lane,
Burwell, Cambridgeshire CB5 OED, U.K.

Beads and Supplies

Tools and supplies are readily available from your local bead shop or mail order companies. For a specific reference of a shop near you, contact:

The Beadsmith/ Helby Import Co., 37 Hayward Ave., Carteret, NJ 07008, Phone: (732) 969-5300, Fax: (732) 569-5310, Email: helby@idt.net

Photo Credits

Giovanna Dal Magro, Milan
Pages 9, 12, 15, 72, 92, 98, 99, 115, 116, 121, 124 (2 photos at bottom of page), 126 (bottom of page), 127.

Meri Gallo, Venice
Pages 7, 17 , 21, 46-47 (bottom center), 74, 80 (bottom), 92 (bottom), 104, 120 (bottom), 128-129 (bottom), 138 (bottom).

Editor's Notes

Craft wire

Craft wire made for this purpose is available in most local shops, craft departments, bead shops and bead and craft supply catalogs. Several recommended brands of craft wire are: "The Beadsmith,"® which comes in several sizes and gold, silver and copper colors. "Artistic Wire"® comes in a very large selection of colors and sizes from 18 gauge to 36 gauge. "Beadery"® wire comes in several good colors and several sizes.

Choose the size and color most compatible with your particular project. When making a red rose, red wire blends so well that it is not even noticed, likewise green wire for leaves and stems.

Craft wire is sized by "gauge". Just as with beads and bead sizes, the larger the number used for the gauge of the wire, the finer the diameter of the wire. The size wire to use will be determined by the size of the beads being used.

In general, most projects would be best constructed from size 11/o seed beads. The color palette in size 11/o beads is almost unlimited. Accordingly, 24 gauge or 26 gauge wire is most compatible with size 11/o beads and also has the widest range of colors available. Smaller wire can be used with smaller beads, but structurally may not afford the same degree of stiffness or support and the finished flower may droop. If too heavy a wire is used, it may not fit into the holes on ALL the beads or may be too stiff or inflexible for the flower construction.

The larger gauge wire, 18, 16, even 14 is used for stalks, branches and stems. Many craft suppliers have it in the floral section for use in flower arranging. Avoid using coated floral wire in any gauge as the color coating can peel off. With the array of wonderful craft wires before us, be advised to also avoid using hardware wire, pig iron or zinc wire. Use the best supplies available to you. The amount of work that you will be putting into these breathtaking bouquets warrants nothing but the very best. Experiment with the sizes and colors of wire and beads to achieve the best effect for your project.

Beads

Beads other than the Venetian conterie *that can be used for flower making are the Czech seed beads that come strung on fine thread and are usually sold in hanks. These are ideal for our purposes, as they can be strung directly onto the proper wire from the thread. Simply slip the end of the wire along the thread and feed the beads from the thread onto the wire; very easy, very efficient.*

Japanese seed beads can also be used for magnificent flowers and offer many colors and subtle gradings of colors. Since they are packaged "loose", it is necessary to string them one by one onto the wire. Or—use a "bead spinner". Follow the directions for the use of the spinner, substituting the end of the wire for the needle and thread to be filled with beads. This can save a huge amount of time and tedium!

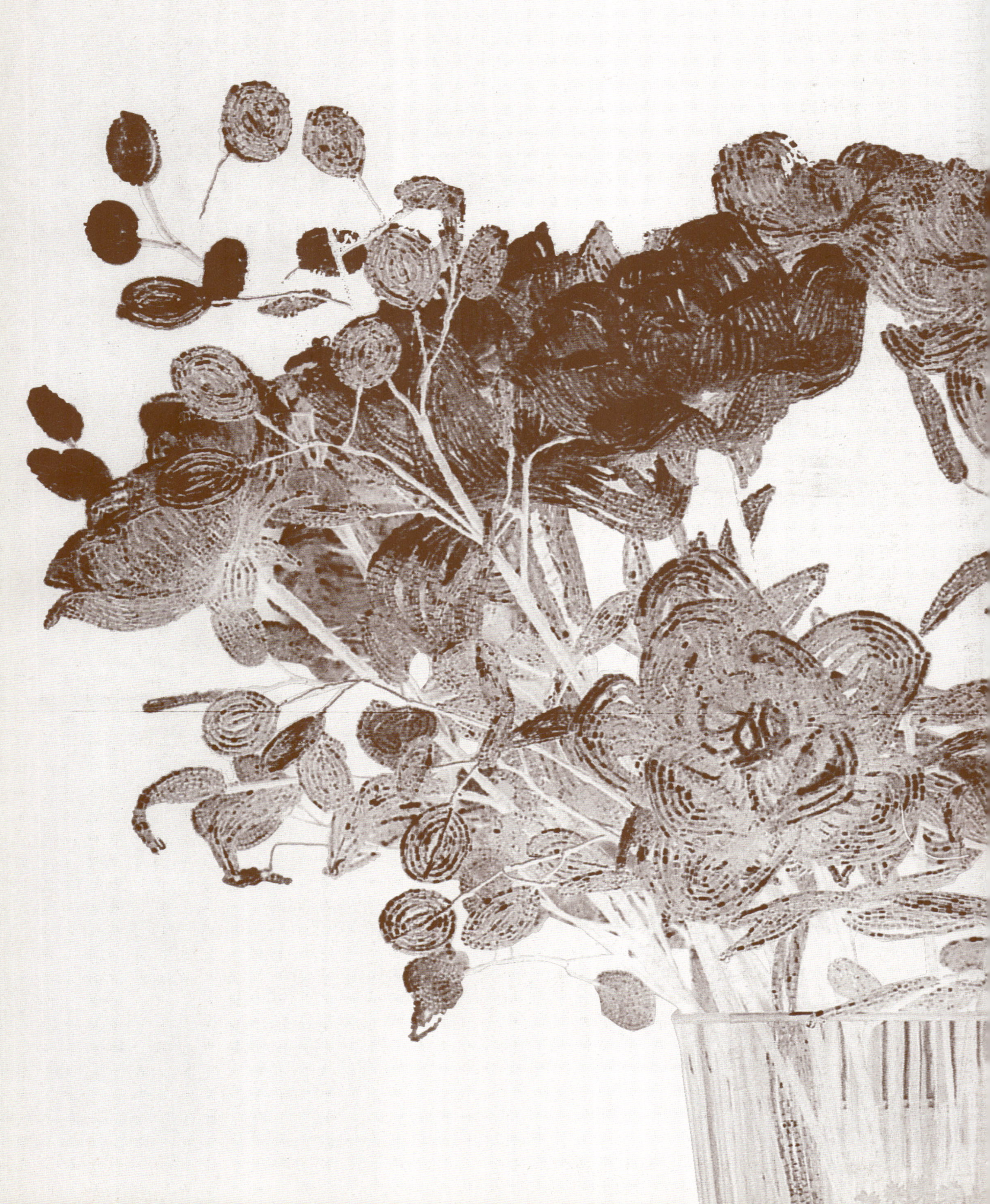